CorelDRAW X4

IN SIMPLE STEPS

CorelDRAW X4

IN SIMPLE STEPS

Authored by:

Kogent Solutions Inc.

Published by:

ISBN: 10-81-7722-859-5
13-978-81-7722-859-5

Edition: Revised Edition, 2009

Printed at: Printed and Bound at Anand Book Binding House, Delhi – 31

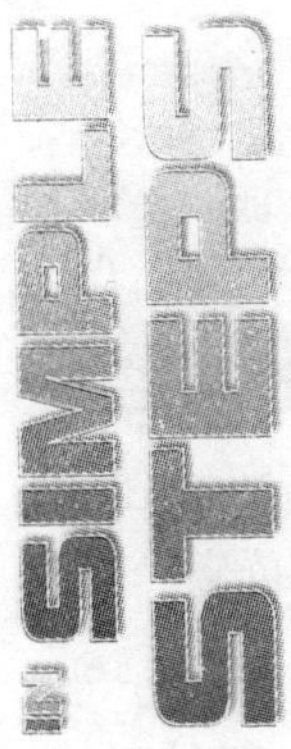

CONTENTS

Chapter 1 ■ Introduction to CorelDRAW Graphics Suits X4 1

IN SIMPLE STEPS

IN SIMPLE STEPS

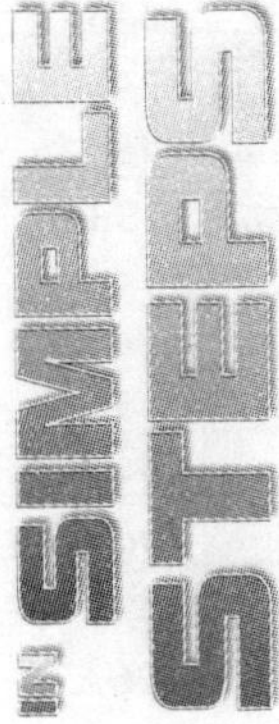

IN SIMPLE STEPS

Chapter 1

Introduction to CorelDRAW Graphics Suite X4

In this Section

- CorelDRAW Graphics Suite X4
- Getting Started with CorelDRAW X4
- Workspace of the CorelDRAW Application Window
- Drawing Basic Geometric Figure
- Undoing, Redoing, and Repeating Actions
- Saving the Drawing
- Opening an Existing Document
- Previewing a Drawing
- Viewing a Drawing in Different Views
- Working with Page Layout
- Help in CorelDRAW
- Closing the Drawing and Quitting CorelDRAW

CorelDRAW is a graphic design, page layout, and photo editing software. Through the years, CorelDRAW has built a reputation for delivering innovative and trusted products that are easier to learn and use, and helps people achieve new levels of productivity. CorelDRAW Graphics Suite X4, commonly known as CorelDRAW X4, is the latest version of CorelDRAW, which has been developed and commercialized by Corel Corporation of Ottawa, Canada. This new version of CorelDRAW is ideal for a novice as well as a professional designer. CorelDRAW X4 provides you high-quality content help and precision tools such as Pick tool, Sharp tool, Text tool, Table tool, and so on, which help you to create a wide range of drawings, such as distinctive logos, signs, and technical and industrial designs. CorelDRAW Graphics Suite X4 has introduced additional applications, such as Corel PHOTO-PAINT X4, and services to help meet your requirements. This new version of CorelDRAW is a great combination of superior design capabilities, speed, and ease of use.

In this chapter, you explore the user interface and features of CorelDRAW X4 to use CorelDRAW Graphics Suite X4. You also learn to draw basic geometric figures, save a drawing, and open an existing drawing in CorelDRAW. In addition, you learn to preview a drawing, view a drawing in different view modes, work with page layout, close a drawing, and quit CorelDRAW.

CorelDRAW Graphics Suite X4

CorelDRAW Graphics Suite X4 is a vector drawing program. This version of CorelDRAW is supported by Windows Vista and other Windows based operating system such as Windows 2000 and Windows XP. The older versions of CorelDRAW (up to version 12) are now upgraded with additional tools and easy to use interface. This upgraded version has now redesigned interface to present a clean and easy to use workspace and has new and enhanced features such as, creating independent page layers, creating tables, mirror Paragraph text and so on. This newly version of CorelDRAW have a substantial library of royalty-free artwork, including 100 high-resolution photos suitable for commercial projects.

Let's first discuss various applications included in the CorelDRAW Graphics Suite X4 applications.

CorelDRAW Graphics Suite X4 Applications

The major applications included in the CorelDRAW Graphics Suite application are CorelDRAW X4, and Corel PHOTO-PAINT X4.

CorelDRAW X4 is an application mainly used for graphics design and page layout. Corel PHOTO-PAINT X4 is an image-editing application. You can use this application to adjust the color and tone of a photo or retouching images or masking images.

Let's now discuss the new features in CorelDRAW X4.

New and Enhanced Features in CorelDRAW Graphics Suite X4

The CorelDRAW Graphics Suite X4 includes various new and enhanced features such as creating independent layers for each page, creating and editing tables, live preview of text before applying any formatting to the text, mirroring paragraph text, and supporting various file formats such as Adobe Illustrator CS3, Photoshop CS3 and so on. Let's discuss each feature in brief.

Creating Independent Layers

In CorelDRAW X4, you can create and edit layers independently for each page in the document. These layers help you to organize and arrange the objects in a layout where too many objects (created within the CorelDRAW or imported to the CorelDRAW) are used. CorelDRAW provides you two types of layers, Local layers and Master layers. Local layer consists of the contents specific to a particular page. While a Master layer consists of the contents that are applied to all pages in the document.

The Object Manager docker available on the right side of the CorelDRAW window shows various created layers in each page (Fig.CD-1.1).

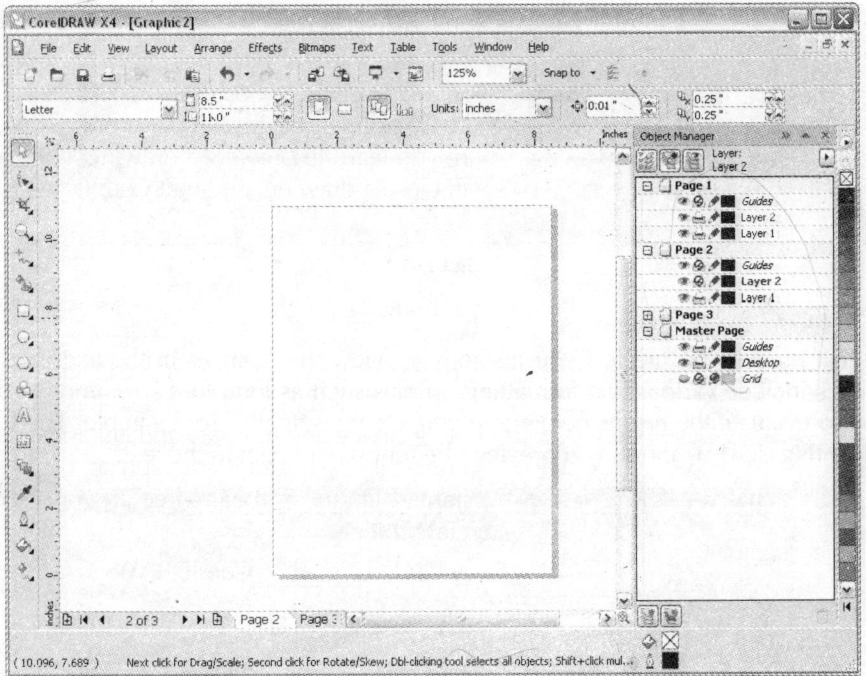

Fig.CD-1.1

Creating and Editing Tables

Tables let you type and view the information in easy to understand manner. In CorelDRAW X4, you can use table to type and display the information with the help of Table tool. With this tool, you can draw tables quickly and precisely. Once the table is drawn, you can make necessary changes to the table such as adding or deleting rows and columns, typing text in cells, place an image in the table. You can see a design page from the Fig.CD-1.2 in which we have used tables.

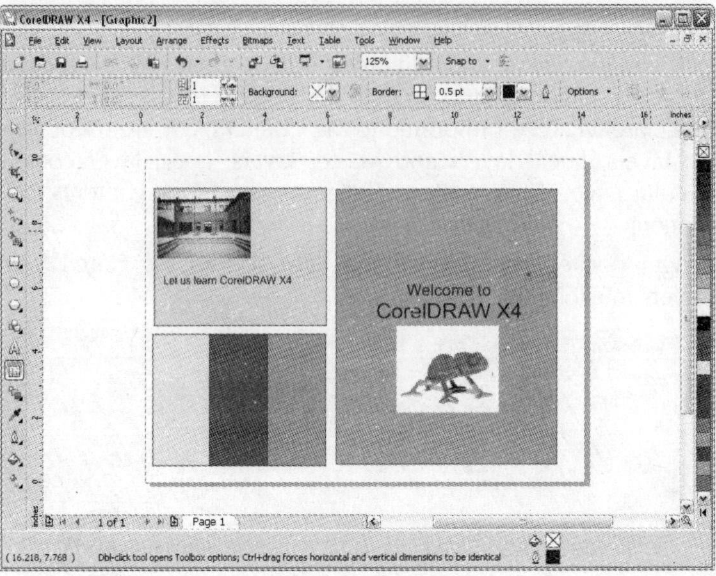

Fig.CD-1.2

Live Text Preview

The live text preview feature lets you instantly preview the changes in the text that you select. The changes include various text formatting options such as font, font size, and alignment. This helps you to evaluate the results before applying changes finally. For example, The CorelDRAW X4 window (Fig.CD-1.3) shows you preview the font size impact in the text.

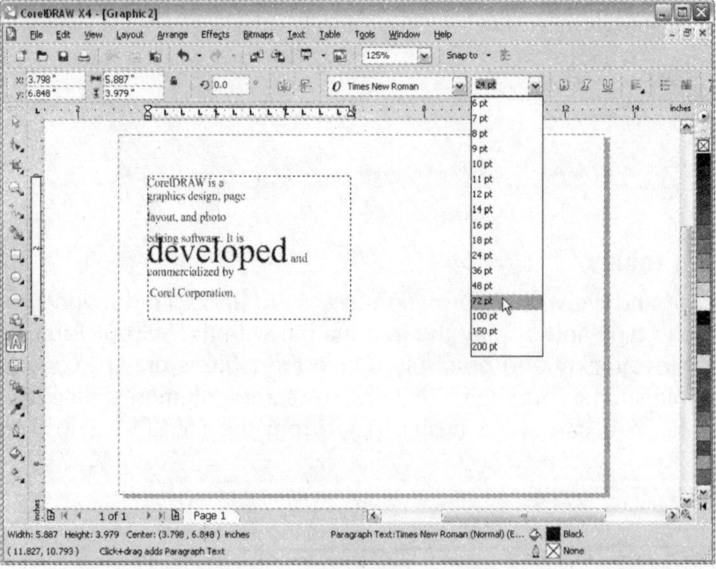

Fig.CD-1.3

Mirror Effect for Text

In CorelDRAW X4, you can apply the Mirror effect easily to the Paragraph text horizontally or vertically. After applying this effect, objects appear in reflected form as if they are viewed by looking at the mirror. Fig.CD-1.4 is showing horizontal and vertical Mirror effect.

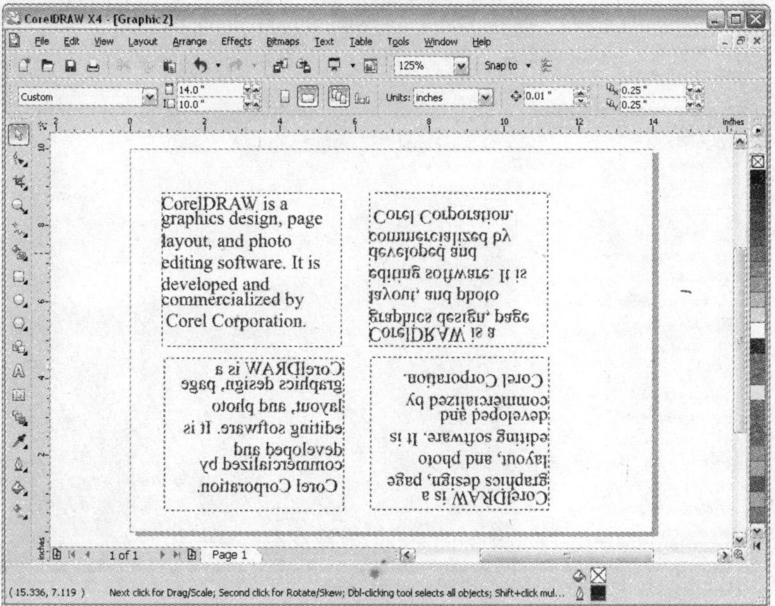

Fig.CD-1.4

New File Format Support

As new software emerges in the market, the issue related to file compatibility comes first in the mind of the user. Taking care of this issue, CorelDRAW X4 has expanded its capabilities in handling new file extension. User can now open the files of latest versions of applications in CorelDRAW X4. The CorelDRAW X4 supports now some more file formats such as Adobe Illustrator CS3, Photoshop CS3, AutoCAD (DXF and DWG), Microsoft Word 2007 (DOC or RTF, import only), Microsoft Publisher 2002, 2003, and 2007 (PUB, import only), Adobe Portable Document Format (PDF 1.7 and PDF/A, including PDF comments), and Corel Painter X.

Now, let's discuss how to get started with CorelDRAW X4.

Getting Started with CorelDRAW X4

When CorelDRAW Graphic Suite X4 has been installed in your computer and completed the registration process, you can open CorelDRAW X4 application and start working with a new blank page, creating a document based on a template or opening an existing drawing. Let's first open CorelDRAW X4 application.

To open CorelDRAW, undertake the following step:

1. *Select* **start→All Programs→CorelDRAW Graphics Suite X4→CorelDRAW X4** (Fig.CD-1.5).

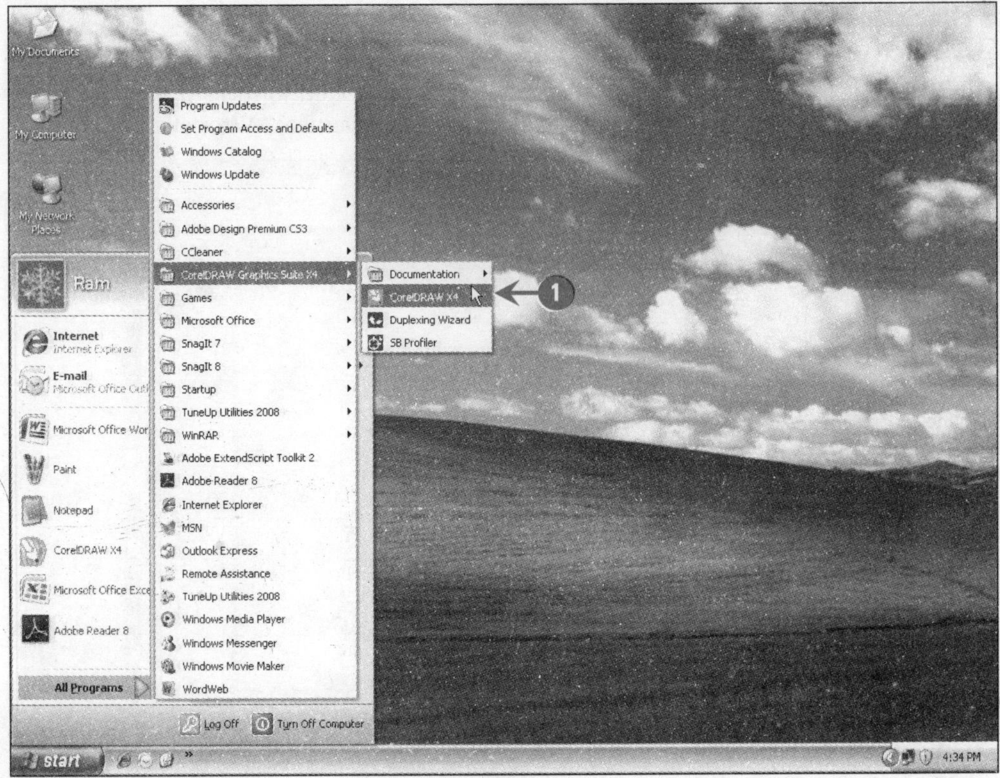

Fig.CD-1.5

A Welcome screen appears, as shown in Fig.CD-1.6.

From this Welcome screen, you can:

- Create a new blank document
- Create a document based on some template
- View the list of recently opened documents
- Preview a recently opened document from the list of recently opened document
- View the information related to the document such as document size, date of creation, and path of the document
- Browse and open documents other than recently opened documents
- Click tabs to view information of your interest on CorelDRAW
- Personalize the Welcome screen

Fig.CD-1.6 is showing important components listed earlier.

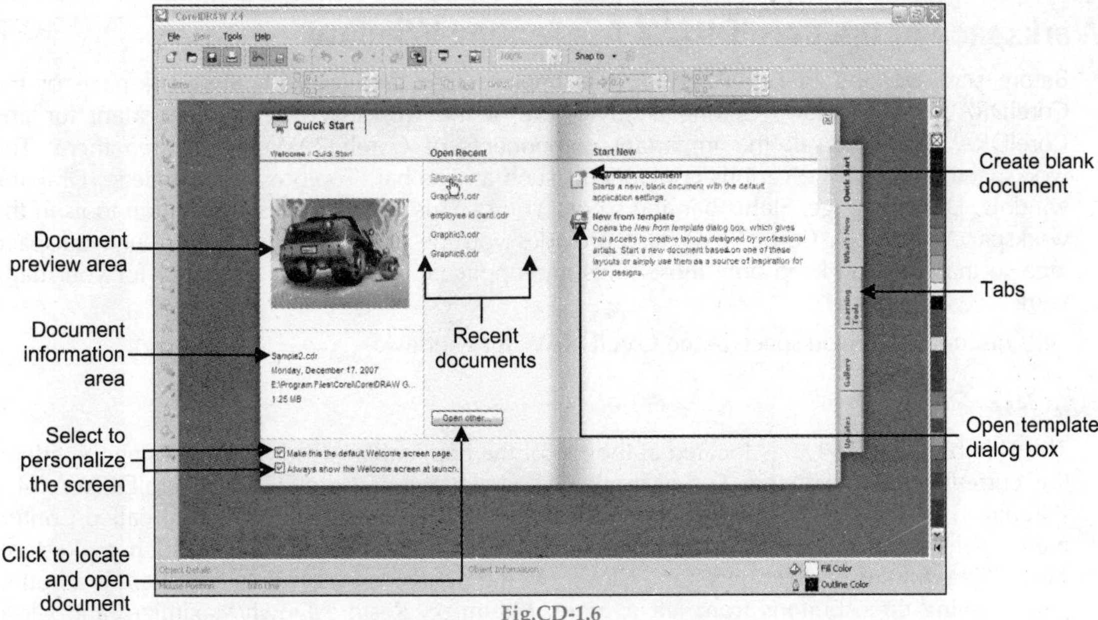

Fig.CD-1.6

Let's now learn to open a new blank document in CorelDRAW.

Opening a New Blank Document

To start drawing in a new blank document, click the **New blank document** option under **Start New** in the Welcome screen (Fig.CD-1.6). The CorelDRAW X4-[Graphics1] window appears with a blank document as shown in Fig.CD-1.7. Graphics 1 is the file name by default.

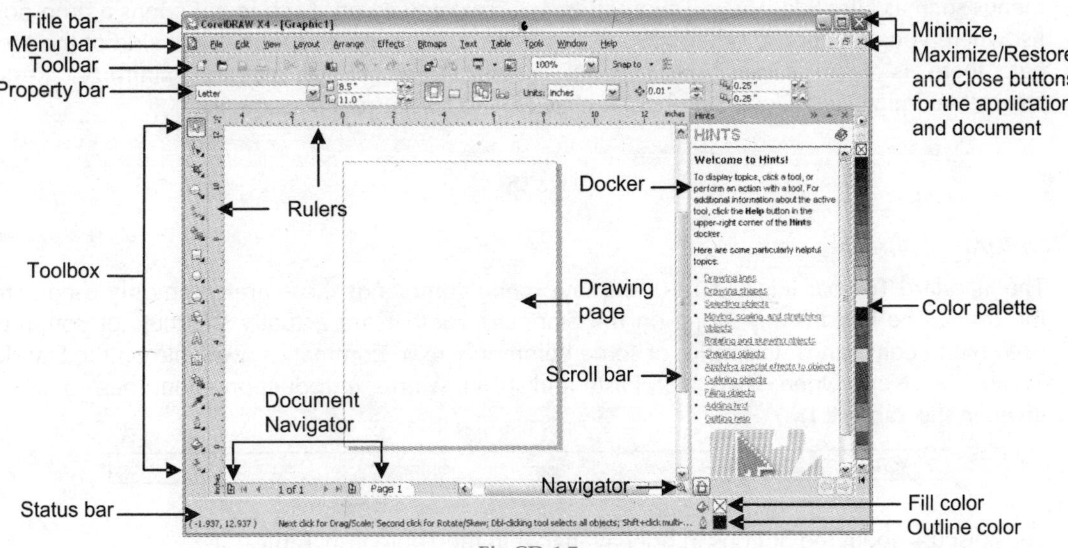

Fig.CD-1.7

Let's now learn about the workspace of CorelDRAW X4 window.

Workspace of the CorelDRAW Application Window

Before start working in CorelDRAW, it is important to familiar with the workspace of the CorelDRAW X4 window. Getting an overview of the workspace is very important for any CorelDRAW user, as all the important components of CorelDRAW are located there. The workspace included the various components such as Toolbar, Toolbox, Color palette, Drawing window, Drawing page, Status bar and so on. You can also find various application tools in the workspace area only. CorelDRAW also provides you the liberty to customize your workspace area so that you can keep only those tools and application which are necessary for your daily work.

Let's discuss about workspace of the CorelDRAW X4 window.

Title Bar

The Title bar (Fig.CD-1.8) is located at the top of the application window, containing the title of the currently open drawing. For example, when you open CorelDRAW, CorelDRAW X4 - [Graphics1] is the default title. On the left side of the Title bar, there is an icon, called Control menu. When you click this icon, a drop-down list appears having options such as Restore, Move, Size, Minimize, Maximize, and Close. On the right side of this Title bar, there is a button panel having three buttons from left to right, Minimize, Restore Down/Maximize, and Close button.

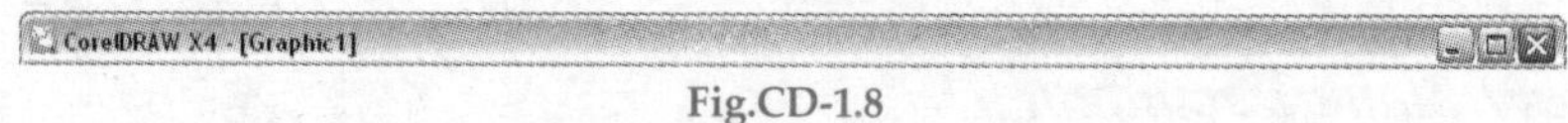

Fig.CD-1.8

Menu Bar

The Menu bar (Fig.CD-1.9) is located below the Title bar of the CorelDRAW window. It contains menus such as File, Edit, View, Layout, Bitmaps, Text and so on. Each menu opens a drop-down list where you can choose other options as per your requirement. On the right side of the Menu bar, there is again same button panel, having three button named Minimize, Restore Down/Maximize, and Close, but these are specific to the current document.

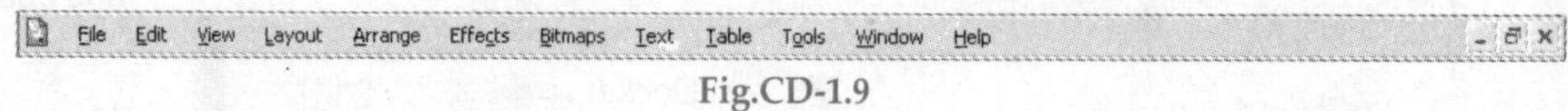

Fig.CD-1.9

Standard Toolbar

The Standard Toolbar (Fig.CD-1.10) displays menu commands those are commonly used across the users. The buttons appearing on the Standard Toolbar are actually shortcuts of commonly used menu commands. Examples of some commonly used commands available on the Standard Toolbar are New, Open, Save, Cut, Paste and so on. A brief introduction about these buttons is given in the Table-1.1.

Fig.CD-1.10

Let's discuss about the buttons in brief available in the Toolbar in Table-1.1.

Table-1.1: Toolbar Buttons

Button Icon	Button Name	Description
	New	Click this button to open a new document
	Open	Click this button to open an existing file in CorelDRAW
	Save	Click this button to save a new file or save the changes in an existing file
	Print	Click this button to take the print of the open document
	Cut	Click this button to move the item(s) from one location to another
	Copy	Click this button to make a duplicate copy of item(s), or object (s)
	Paste	Click this button to paste the item(s) that is being copied to the CorelDRAW or any other application
	Undo	Click this button to reverse the last action performed one by one
	Redo	Click this button to restore the actions reversed by the Undo command
	Import	Click this button to import a graphics file in a CorelDRAW document
	Export	Click this button to save the CorelDRAW drawing in different file format
	Application Launcher	Click this button to open CorelDRAW X4 Graphics Suite applications such as Corel PHOTO-PAINT X4 directly from the CorelDRAW X4 window
	Welcome Screen	Click this button to open the Welcome screen
100%	Zoom Levels	The Zoom Levels combo box is used to select a zoom level among the various available zoom levels of the CorelDRAW document.
Snap to	Snap To	Click this button to disable or enable the alignment for the grid, guidelines, objects, and dynamic guides automatically
	Options	Click this button to open the Options dialog box

Property Bar

The Property bar (Fig.CD-1.11) displays options and buttons related to the tool or object selected by the user. Thus, we can say property bar keeps on changing according to the user's action. For example, when we select the Pick tool on the Toolbox, the Property bar shows Paper Type/Size list box, Paper Width and Height spin box, portrait command and so on.

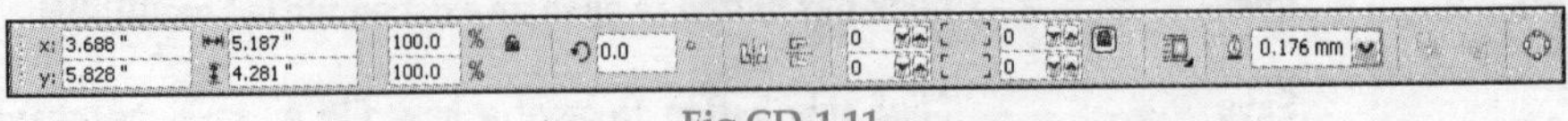

Fig.CD-1.11

Toolbox

The Toolbox (Fig.CD-1.12) is located on the left side of the application window in CorelDRAW. It contains tools for creating, filling, and modifying objects in the drawing. The Toolbox contains various tools such as Pick tool, Crop tool, Shape tool and so on. Each tool (Except the Pick tool, Text tool, and Table tool) contains a small arrow in right-lower corner of the button that indicates a flyout which is used to display a set of related CorelDRAW tools.

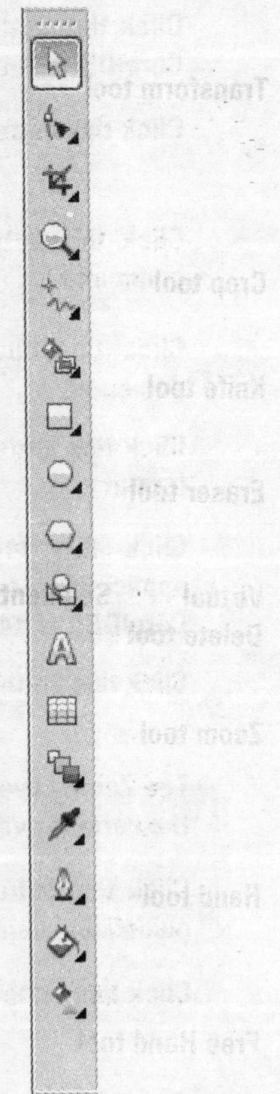

Fig.CD-1.12

Let's discuss in brief about the various tools available on the Toolbox in CorelDRAW in Table 1.2.

Table-1.2: Description about Tools on the Toolbox

Name of tools group/Flyout	Tools Icon Icons	Tool Name	Description
Selection tool		Pick tool	The Pick tool is used to select, resize, skew, and rotate the objects or images on the document page
Shape Edit tools		Shape tool	The Shape tool allows you to edit the shape of the object by manipulating their nodes and segments
		Smudge Brush tool	This tool allows you to distort a vector object by dragging along its outline
		Roughen Brush tool	This tool allows you to distort the outline of a vector object by dragging along the outline of the object
		Transform tool	This tool allows you to transform an object by rotating it around a fix point, mirroring it, scaling it, and skewing the object
Crop tools		Crop tool	This tool helps you to remove the undesirable area in the object
		Knife tool	This tool helps you to create two separate objects by cutting them
		Eraser tool	The Eraser tool allows you to remove or erase the areas of your drawing
		Virtual Segment Delete tool	This tool helps you to delete the portion of the objects that are between intersections
Zoom tools		Zoom tool	This tool allows you to change the magnification level in the drawing window
		Hand tool	Hand tool lets you view that area of a drawing that is not exhibited
Curve tools		Free Hand tool	This tool lets you draw the single line segments and the curves
		Bezier tool	This tool allows you to draw curved line segments

Table-1.2: Description about Tools on the Toolbox

Name of tools group/Flyout	Tools Icon Icons	Tool Name	Description
		Artistic Media tool	This tool provides access to Brush, Sprayer, Calligraphic, and Pressure tools
		Pen tool	This tool lets you draw straight as well as curved line segments
		Polyline tool	This tool allows you to draw lines and curves in preview mode
		Connector tool	This tool is used to join the two objects with a line
		Dimension tool	This tool is used to draw vertical, horizontal, slanted or angular dimension lines
Smart tools		Smart Fill tool	This tool helps to identify the enclosed area when one object overlaps the other one and fill the enclosed areas
		Smart Drawing tool	This tool is used to convert your freehand strokes to basic shapes and smoothed curves
Rectangle tools		Rectangle tool	This tool is used to draw a rectangle
		3 -Point Rectangle tool	This tool is used to draw rectangles at a rotation angle
Ellipse tools		Ellipse tool	This tool helps to draw an ellipse
		3-Point Ellipse tool	This tool is used to draw ellipse at a rotation angle
Object tools		Polygon tool	This tool is used to draw symmetrical polygons
		Star tool	This tool is used to draw perfect star
		Complex Star tool	This tool is used to draw complex stars that have intersecting sides
		Graph Paper tool	This tool is used to draw a grid of lines
		Spiral tool	This tool is used to draw symmetrical and logarithmic spirals

Table-1.2: Description about Tools on the Toolbox

Name of tools group/Flyout	Tools Icon Icons	Tool Name	Description
Perfect Shapes tools		Basics Shapes tool	This tool allows you to choose from a full set of shapes, including hexagram, a smiley face, and a right-angle triangle
		Arrow shapes tool	This tool allows you to draw arrows of different shape, direction, and add arrow-heads at the starting and ending points
		Flowchart Shapes tool	This tool is used to draw the flow chart symbols
		Banner Shapes tool	This tool allows you to draw the ribbon objects and explosion shapes
		Callout Shapes tool	This tool is used to draw the callouts and labels
Text tool		Text tool	This tool allows you to type words instantly on the Document page as Artistic or Paragraph text
Table tool		Table tool	This tool is used to draw and edit the table
Interactive tools		Interactive Blend tool	This tool lets you blend two objects
		Contour tool	This tool allows you to apply a contour to an object
		Distort tool	This tool allows you to apply a push or pull distortion, a zipper distortion, or a twister distortion
		Drop Shadow tool	This tool is used to apply a drop shadow to an object
		Envelop tool	This tool allows you to distort an object by dragging the nodes of envelop
		Extrude tool	Use this tool to apply an effect which gives impression to the viewer as if object is originating from a certain or specified point

Table-1.2: Description about Tools on the Toolbox

Name of tools group/Flyout	Tools Icon Icons	Tool Name	Description
		Transparency	This tool allows you to apply transparency to objects
Eyedropper tools		Eyedropper tool	This tool allows you to select and copy the object properties, such as fill, line thickness, size, and effects, from an object on the Drawing window
		Paintbucket tool	This tool allows you to apply object properties, such as fill, link thickness, size and effects, to other objects
Outline tools		Outline Pen tool	This tool allows you to change the appearances of outlines by using the controls present in the dialog box appeared after clicking this tool. For example, you can specify the color, width, and style of outlines
		Outline Color tool	This tool allows you to set the options to define the outline color of the object from the dialogue box appeared after clicking this tool
		None	The outline of the shape will be disappeared after clicking this tool
		Hairline tool	This tool allows you to create a thin line like a human hair
		½ pt tool	This tool allows you to create the ½ point thick outline
		1 pt tool	This tool allows you to create the 1 point thick outline
		2 pt tool	This tool allows you to create 2 point thick outline
		8 pt tool	This tool allows you to create 8 point thick outline
		16 pt tool	This tool allows you to create 16 point thick outline

Table-1.2: Description about Tools on the Toolbox

Name of tools group/Flyout	Tools Icon Icons	Tool Name	Description
		24 pt tool	This tool allows you to create 24 point outline
		Color tool	This tool allows you to set the color model and color values while filling the object or applying color to outline from the Color docker that appears after clicking this tool
Fill tools		Fill Tool	This tool allows you to fill the object or closed paths in different styles
		Uniform Fill tool	This tool allows you to apply solid color to the object
		Fountain Fill tool	This tool is smooth progression of two or more colors that adds depth to objects
		Pattern Fill tool	This tool is used to fill object with 2-color, Full color, or Bitmap color
		Texture Fill tool	This tool allows you to give your objects a natural appearance. CorelDRAW provides preset textures and each texture has a set of options that you can change as per your requirement
		PostScript Fill tool	This tool is used to apply PostScript texture fills to objects. A PostScript texture fill is created by using the PostScript language
	X	None	This tool is used to give no color to the object
		Color tool	This tool allows you to set the color model and color values while filling the object or applying color to outline from the Color docker that appears after clicking this tool
Interactive Fill tools		Interactive Fill tool	This tool allows you to fill the object with uniform fills, pattern fills, texture fills, and fountain fill
		Mesh Fill tool	This tool allows you to apply a mesh grid to an object

Drawing Page

The Drawing page (Fig.CD-1.13) is a rectangular area inside a Drawing window. It is the printable area of your work area. Whenever you open CorelDRAW, the Drawing appears with the default size but you can set the size and orientation of the Drawing page from the Property bar as per your requirement.

Fig.CD-1.13

Note

> The region outside the Drawing page is known as Drawing window and it can be used to place objects which are used frequently. For example, you can draw a rectangle and place outside the Drawing page and use it again and again by making its copies. Objects placed outside the Drawing page are not printed but they increase the size of the document. Thus, after finalizing the document, it is recommended to remove all objects outside the Drawing page in order to maintain the document size.

Docker

Dockers display the controls, such as command buttons, options, and list boxes. Dockers are same as the dialog box but the main difference between Dockers and dialogue box is that you can keep dockers open while working on a document but, you cannot work on the document keeping the dialog box open. An example of the docker is Object Properties docker as shown in Fig.CD-1.14. It displays the Fill Type list box, Color palette, and some buttons such as Advanced, Apply and so on.

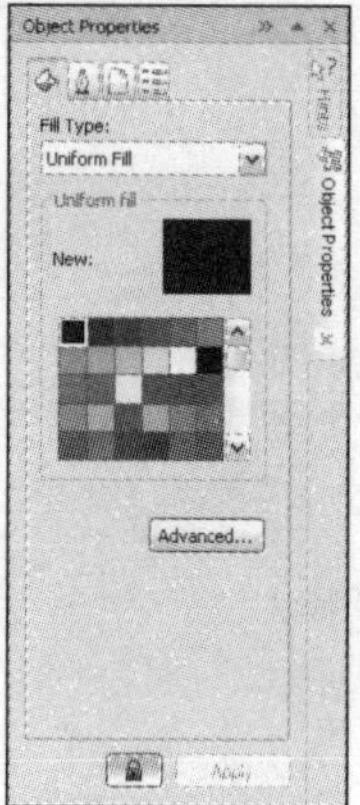

Fig.CD-1.14

Color Palette

A Color palette (Fig.CD-1.15) is a collection of the solid colors from which you can select colors for filling and outlining or for highlighting the text. The Color palette is displayed on the right side of the application window of the CorelDRAW. It consists number of colors and all cannot be visible in a single strip. You can scroll up and down arrow button on the Color palette to view more colors or click the left arrow button at the bottom of the Color palette to view more strips of colors (Fig.CD-1.16).

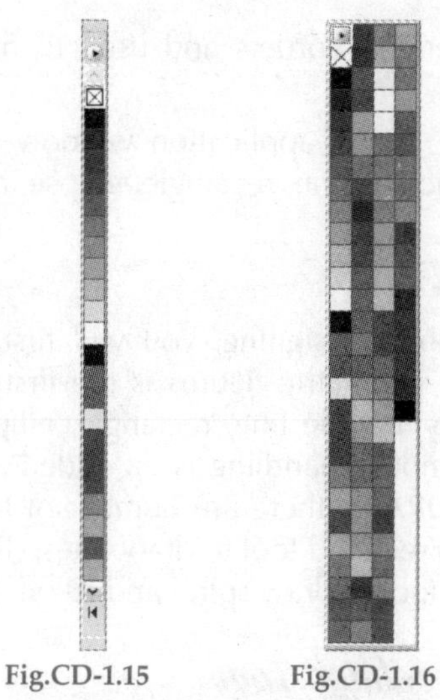

Fig.CD-1.15 Fig.CD-1.16

Document Navigator

Document navigator (Fig.CD-1.17) is an area at the bottom left of the application window and just above the Status bar. It has controls to add multiple pages and to move between pages. The controls are '+' sign that is used to add more pages and back and forward buttons to move between pages.

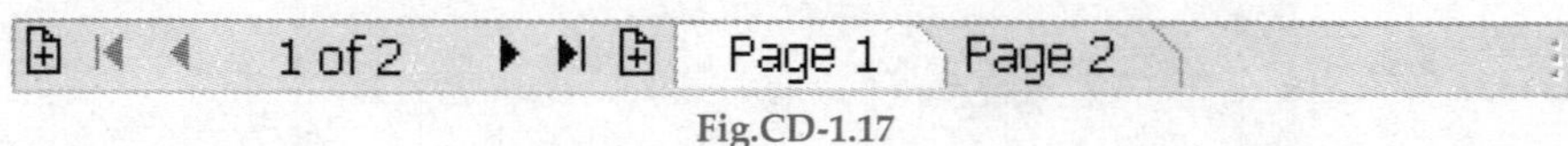

Fig.CD-1.17

Status Bar

The status bar (Fig.CD-1.18) is located at the bottom of the application window in CorelDRAW. It contains the information about object properties such as type, size, and color. The Status bar also shows the current mouse position.

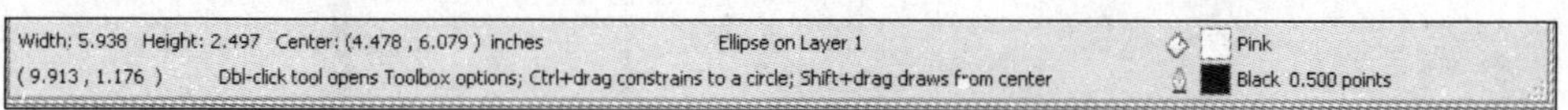

Fig.CD-1.18

Scroll Bars

The vertical and horizontal scroll bars are used to view the document (Fig.CD-1.7).

Navigator

By using the Navigator button (🔍), you can open a smaller display of the Drawing window that helps to move around a drawing (Fig.CD-1.7).

Ruler

Rulers are the horizontal and vertical borders and used to find out the size and position of objects in a drawing (Fig.CD-1.7).

After understanding the interface of the application window of CorelDRAW, let's now learn some basic geometric drawings such as line, rectangle, ellipse, and spiral.

Drawing Basic Geometric Figure

While you are learning the graphics designing, you will first need to work with some basic geometric figures. Drawing basic geometric figures is the first step towards creating advanced designing. Basic geometric figures include line, rectangle, ellipse, triangle and so on. To draw basic geometric shapes, a good mouse handling is an added advantage in application such as MS Paint, CorelDRAW. In CorelDRAW, there are number of tools which you can use to draw these basic shapes. For example, Freehand tool to draw lines, Rectangle tool to draw rectangles, Ellipse tool to draw ellipse, Spiral tool to draw spiral and so on. Let's first start by drawing lines.

Drawing a Line by using the Freehand Tool

By using the Freehand tool, you can draw the straight as well as a curve line. After drawing the line, the smoothness of the line can be set.

Undertake the following steps to draw a line by using the Freehand tool:

1. *Click* the **Freehand** tool on the Toolbox (Fig.CD-1.19).

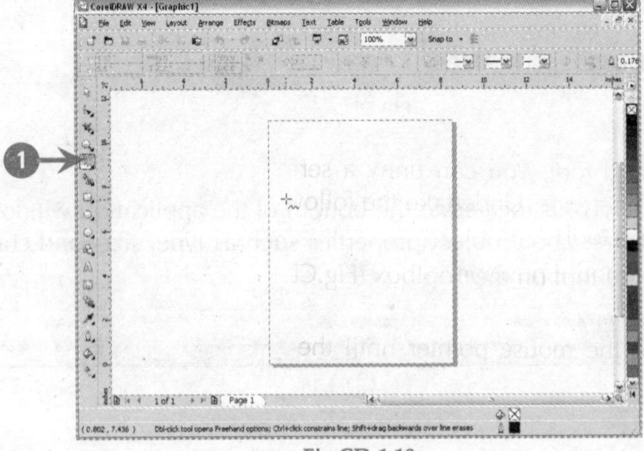

Fig.CD-1.19

2. In the Drawing page, *click* to specify the starting point of the line, as shown in Fig.CD-1.20.
3. Drag the mouse-pointer and *click* at a location in the Drawing page to specify the end point of the line, as shown in Fig.CD-1.20.

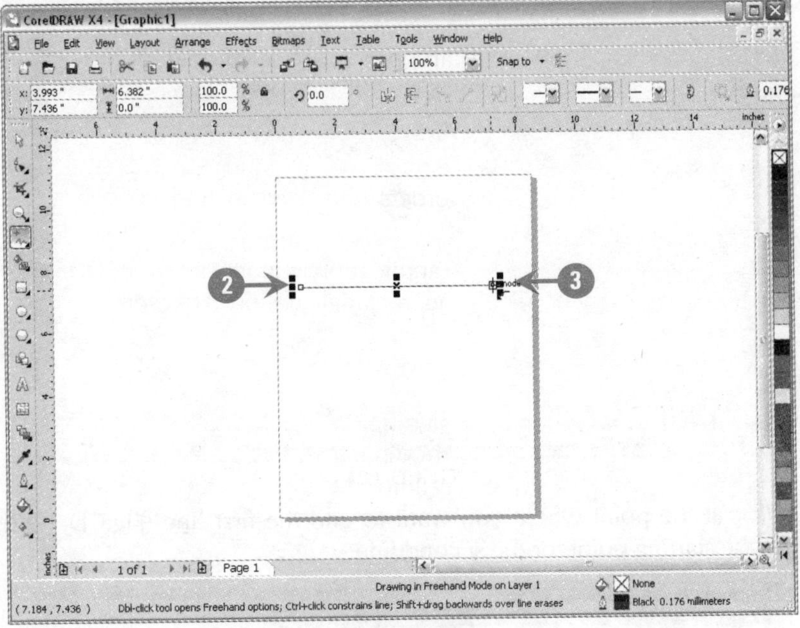

Fig.CD-1.20

Note

> To rotate a line at an angle, move the mouse-pointer at desired angle at the time of specifying the starting point of the line and then draw the line.
>
> You can also draw a curve line by using the Freehand tool. Select where you want to start the curve, and drag the mouse-pointer.

You have drawn a straight line by using the Freehand tool, let's now learn to draw a pattern of connected lines by using Freehand tool.

Joining Freehand Lines

By using the Freehand tool, you can draw a series of connected lines. Each line begins from where the previous line ends. Undertake the following steps to draw a pattern of connected lines by using the Freehand tool:

1. *Click* the **Freehand** tool on the Toolbox (Fig.CD-1.21) and then place the mouse pointer over the Drawing page.
2. *Click* and move the mouse pointer until the line reaches at the desired angle and length (Fig.CD-1.21).

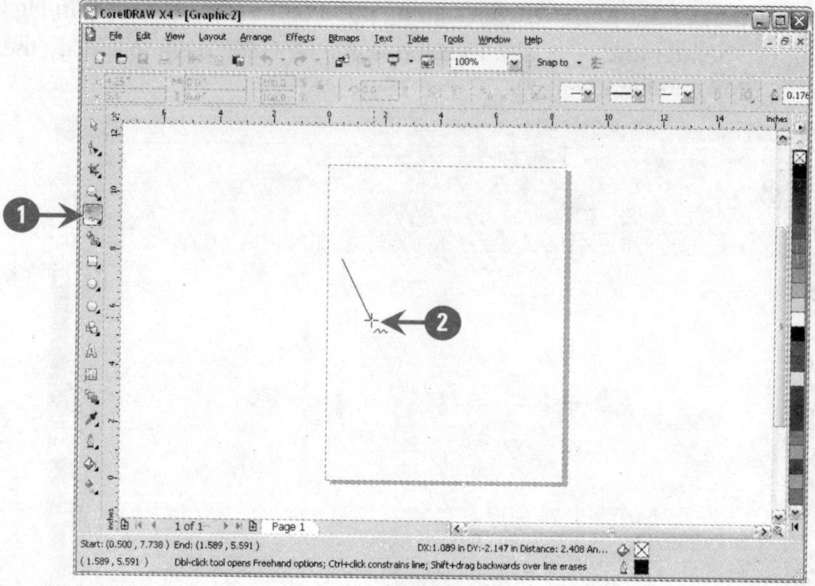

Fig.CD-1.21

3. *Double-click* at the point where you want to end the first line (Fig.CD-1.22). This point is also being the starting point for the second line.

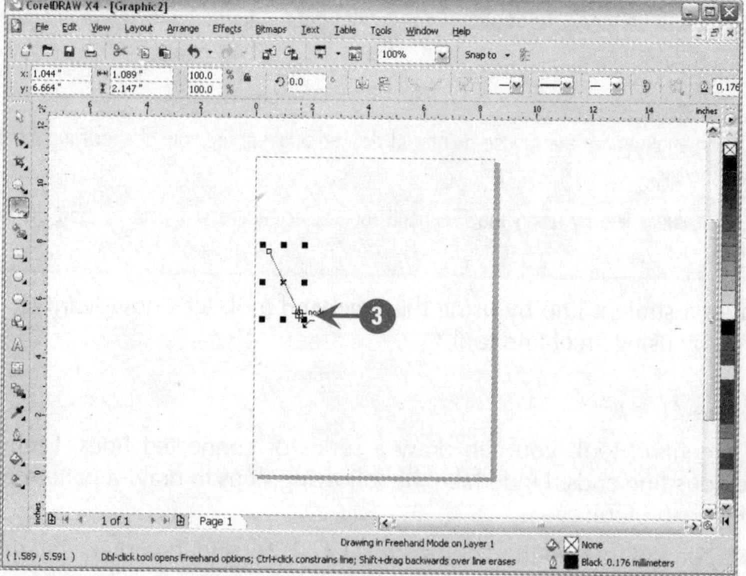

Fig.CD-1.22

4. Again move the mouse pointer until the line reaches at the desired angle and length as shown in Fig.CD-1.23.

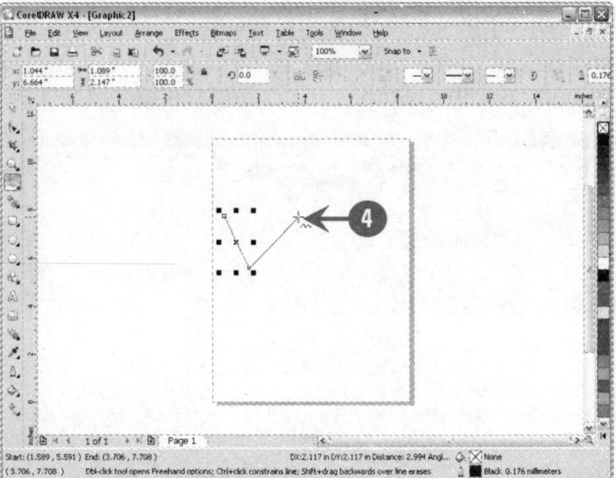

Fig.CD-1.23

5. *Double-click* where you want to end the second line. This point also will be the starting point for the third line (Fig.CD-1.24).

Repeat the same steps to draw the pattern as shown in Fig.CD-1.24.

6. *Click* at the final point of the last line to finish the line (Fig.CD-1.24).

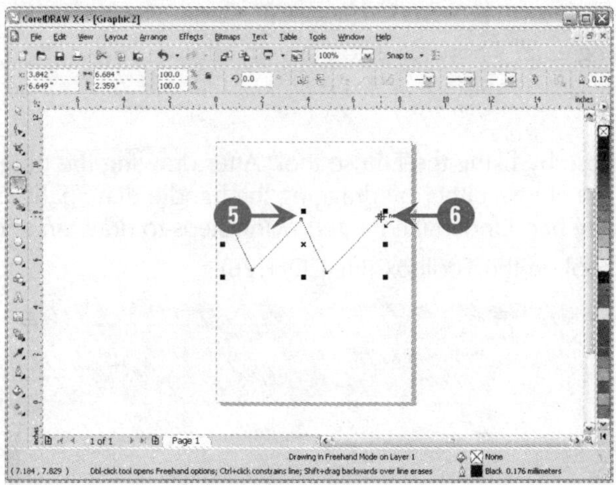

Fig.CD-1.24

After using the Freehand tool to draw a pattern of joint lines, let's now learn to draw a rectangle by using the Rectangle tool.

Drawing a Rectangle

You can draw a rectangle using the Rectangle tool. Once you draw a rectangle, you can re-size it by using the handles on its boundary or specify its height and width on the Property bar.

Undertake the following steps to draw a rectangle:

1. *Click* the **Rectangle** tool on the Toolbox as shown in Fig.CD-1.25.

2. *Click* and drag the mouse-pointer to draw the rectangle as shown in Fig.CD-1.25.
3. *Type* the width and height of the rectangle in the **Object (s) Size** text boxes on the Property bar to re-size it. In our case, the width is **7.289** and the height is **3.871**.

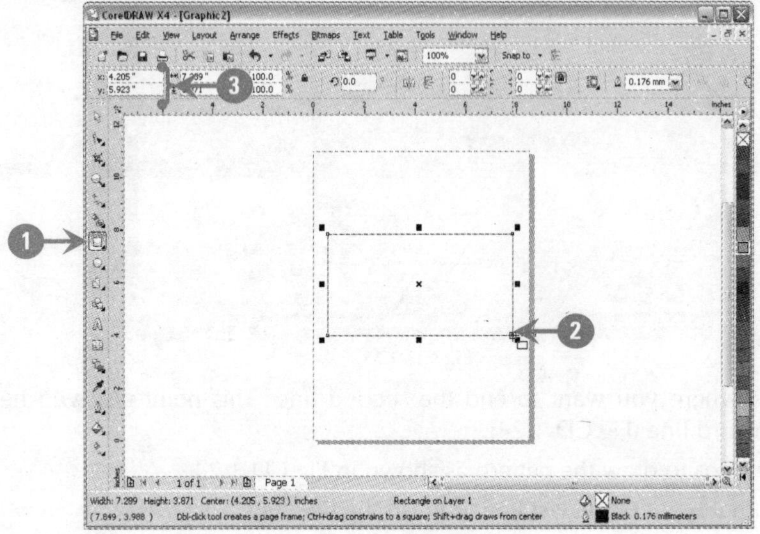

Fig.CD-1.25

After drawing a rectangle, let's now learn to draw an ellipse.

Drawing an Ellipse

You can draw an ellipse by using the Ellipse tool. After drawing the object, you can change the height and width of the ellipse either by dragging the handle diagonally or setting the height and width from the Property bar. Undertake the following steps to draw an ellipse:

1. *Click* the **Ellipse** tool on the Toolbox (Fig.CD-1.26).

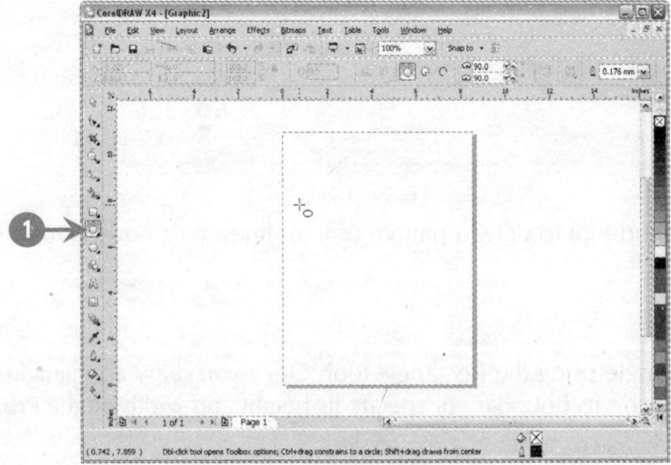

Fig.CD-1.26

2. *Click* and drag the mouse-pointer to draw the ellipse (Fig.CD-1.27).
3. *Type* the width and height of the ellipse in the **Object (s) Size** text boxes to re-size it. In our case, the width is **6.926** and the height is **4.022**.

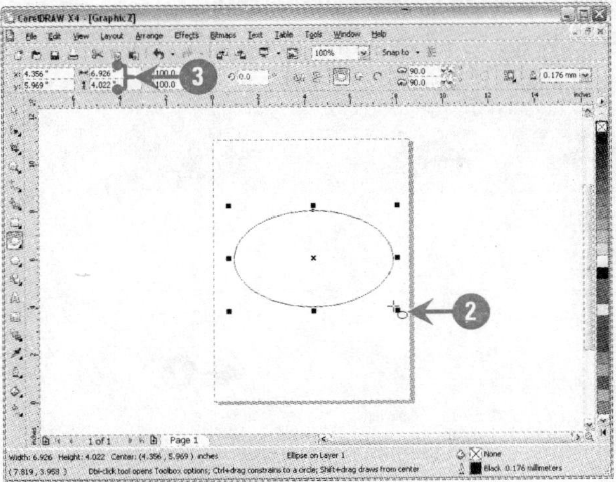

Fig.CD-1.27

After drawing the ellipse by using the Ellipse tool, let's now learn how to draw a spiral.

Drawing a Spiral

You can draw spiral by using the Spiral tool. There are two types of spiral shape, symmetrical and logarithmic. You can set the number of revolutions of the spiral from the Property bar. A greater value will lead to increase the number of spirals in the object whereas a low value will reduce the number of spirals in the object.

Undertake the following steps to draw a spiral:

1. *Open* the Object tools flyout and *select* the **Spiral** tool as shown in Fig.CD-1.28.

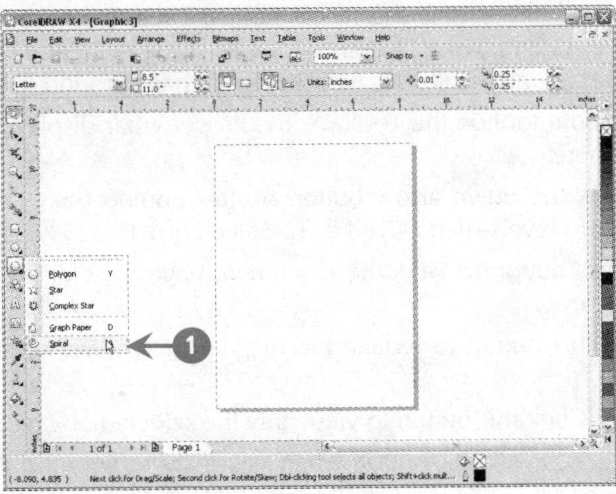

Fig.CD-1.28

2. Now, to change the number of revolution of the spiral, *type* a value in the **Spiral Revolutions** spin box on the Property bar (Fig.CD-1.29).
3. *Click* one of the button either symmetric or Logarithmic button as per your choice (Fig.CD-1.29). We have selected **Symmetrical Spiral** button.
4. *Click* and drag to draw the spiral as shown in Fig.CD-1.29.

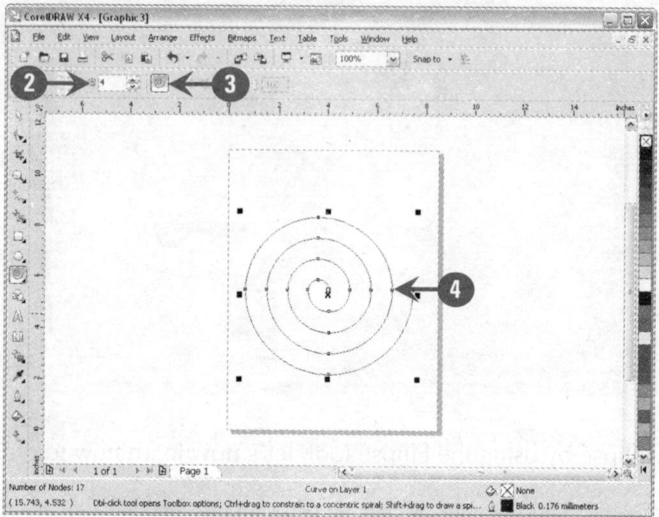

Fig.CD-1.29

Till now, you learned to draw the basic geometric figures such as line, rectangle, ellipse, and then spiral. Let's now learn how to zoom and pan the view of a drawing.

Zooming and Panning the View of a Drawing

The view of a drawing can be changed by zooming in or out to acquire a closer look or more distant look of a drawing. When you are viewing an object in a high magnification level, it might happen that you are not able to view the whole object. Then, Panning is the way to view those particular missing areas of a drawing. It is also done by using the Hand tool. Panning allows you to view those areas that are not exhibited, by moving the page around in the Drawing window.

When you click the Zoom tool on the Toolbox, the Property bar displays various buttons, which are discussed in brief here:

- **Zoom Levels:** Click the down arrow button on this combo box, a drop down list appears having various zoom levels such as To Fit, To Selected, 10%, 25%, 50% and so on.
- **Zoom In:** Click this button to view the Document page or selected area on the Document page in enlarged view.
- **Zoom Out:** Click this button to reduce the magnification level of an active image in your drawing.
- **Zoom to Selected:** Click this button to view only the selected objects in enlarged form.
- **Zoom to All Objects:** Click this button when you want to zoom in the entire objects in the drawing page.

- **Zoom to Page:** Click this button to fit the Drawing page in the Drawing window.
- **Zoom to Page Width:** Click this button to view the page widthwise.
- **Zoom to Page Height:** Click this button to view the page height wise.

Let's now learn how to zoom and pan the view of an object.

Zooming the View of a Drawing

You can magnify or reduce the view of your drawing whenever needed. CorelDRAW provides the Zoom tool to have a desired view of your drawing. Undertake the following steps to learn how to zoom a drawing:

1. *Click* the **Zoom** tool on the Toolbox (Fig.CD-1.30).
2. *Click* the **Zoom In** button on the Property bar (Fig.CD-1.30).

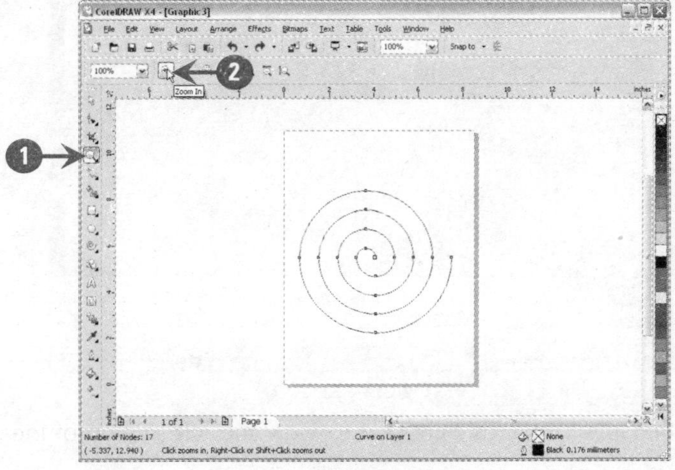

Fig.CD-1.30

The enlarged view of the spiral appears as shown in Fig.CD-1.31.

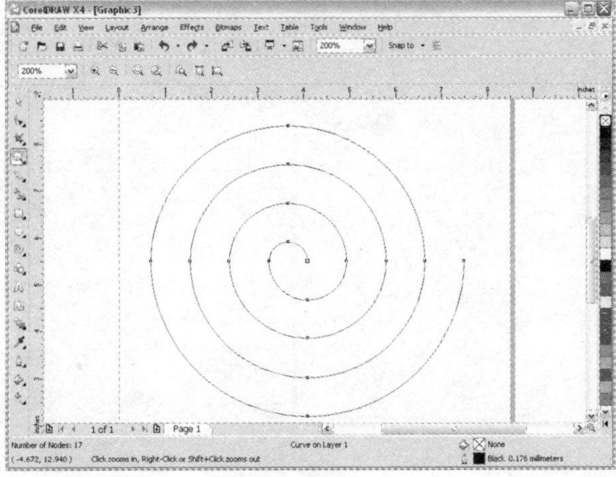

Fig.CD-1.31

After viewing how to use the Zoom tool, let's now learn about panning the view of a drawing.

Panning the View of a Drawing

If you are viewing an image at high magnification level, it might be that some part of the image is not visible. To view a part of the image that is not visible, you can use the Hand tool.

Undertake the following steps for panning a view of an object:

1. Open the Zoom tools flyout and *click* the **Hand** tool as shown in Fig.CD-1.32.

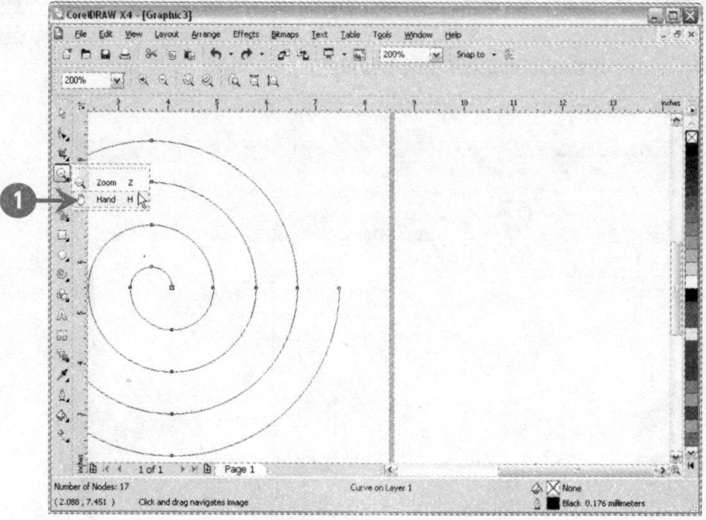

Fig.CD-1.32

2. *Click* and *drag* the spiral towards right-side to view the left section of the spiral that is not visible (Fig.CD-1.33).

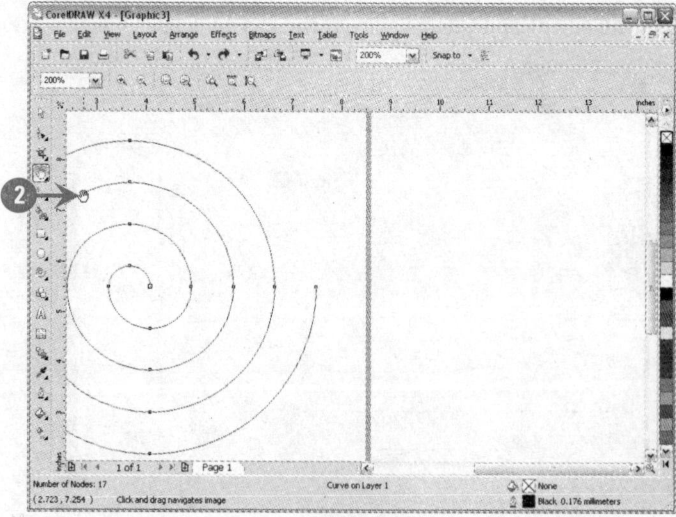

Fig.CD-1.33

Now, you can view the left section of the spiral as shown in Fig.CD-1.34.

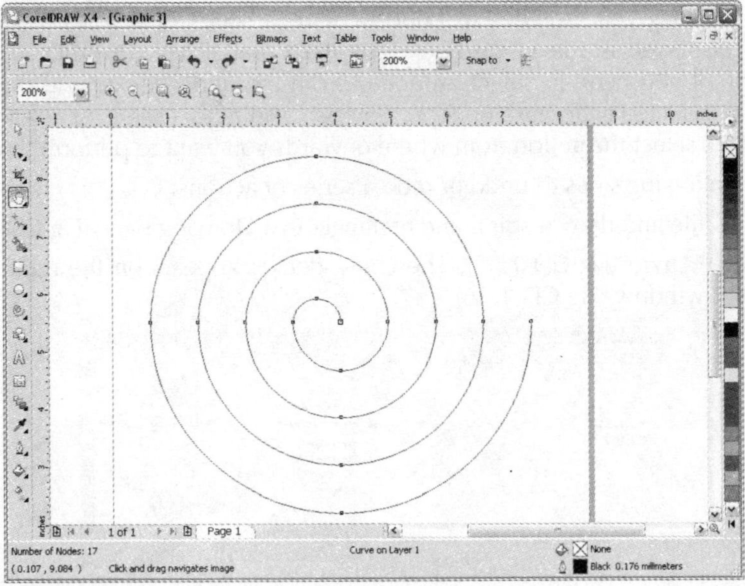

Fig.CD-1.34

Note

> You can scroll left and right the horizontal slider to view the spiral.

After learning zooming and panning the view of a drawing, let's now learn how to undo, redo and repeat the actions.

Undoing, Redoing, and Repeating Actions

Undo command lets you reverse any operation, such as deletion, insertion or modification. The undo process begins with the last action performed by the user. If you want to get back to the output of last action reversed by you, then use the Redo command.

Commands available under the Edit menu for undoing, redoing and repeating the actions are listed here:

- **Undoing an Action:** You can undo the actions that you perform on your drawing. To undo an action, select **Edit→Undo.**
- **Redoing an Action**: Once you have undone an action, you can redo it. To redo an action, select **Edit→Redo.**
- **Repeating an Action:** You can repeat an action on another object or a group of objects. Undertake the following steps to repeat an action:

1. *Select* the object in which you want to repeat the action.
2. *Select* **Edit→Repeat.** The action will be applied on the selected object.

Let's now learn to undo or redo a series of actions.

Undo or Redo a Series of Actions

CorelDRAW provides you facilities to undo or redo a series of actions. All your actions are recorded and displayed in the Undo docker by the CorelDRAW. In order to undo a series of actions, first of all you need to select an action from the undo docker. All the actions that are listed below the selected action are undone. You can also redo a series of actions from the Undo docker. To do so, select the action from where onwards you want to perform the redo.

Undertake the following steps to undo or redo a series of actions:

1. *Open* a new file and draw a spiral and rectangle in a Drawing page (Fig.CD-1.35).
2. *Select* **Tools→Undo** (Fig.CD-1.35). The **Undo** docker appears on the right hand side of the CorelDRAW window (Fig.CD-1.36).

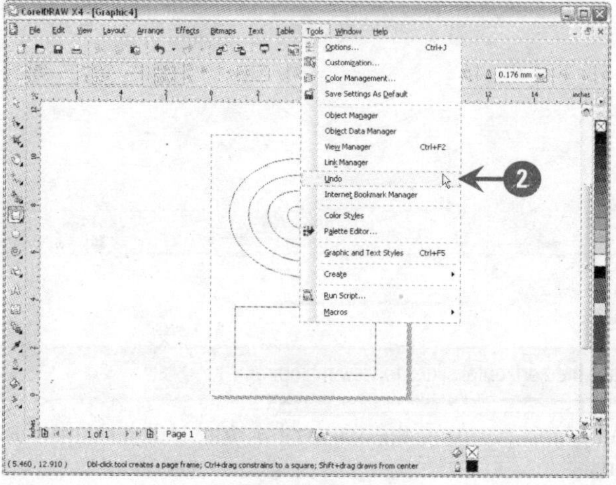

Fig.CD-1.35

3. *Select* the action from the Undo docker. For example, we have selected the **Create** option (second option from the top in the Undo docker) as shown in Fig.CD-1.36.

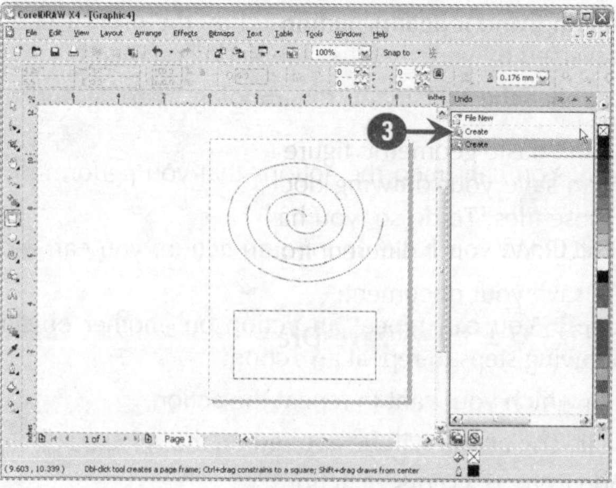

Fig.CD-1.36

The actions that listed below the Create (second action from the top on the Undo docker) are undone, as shown in Fig.CD-1.37. In our case, only one action, **Create** (Third action from the top) is undone. Means the rectangle is deleted from your Drawing page (Fig.CD-1.37).

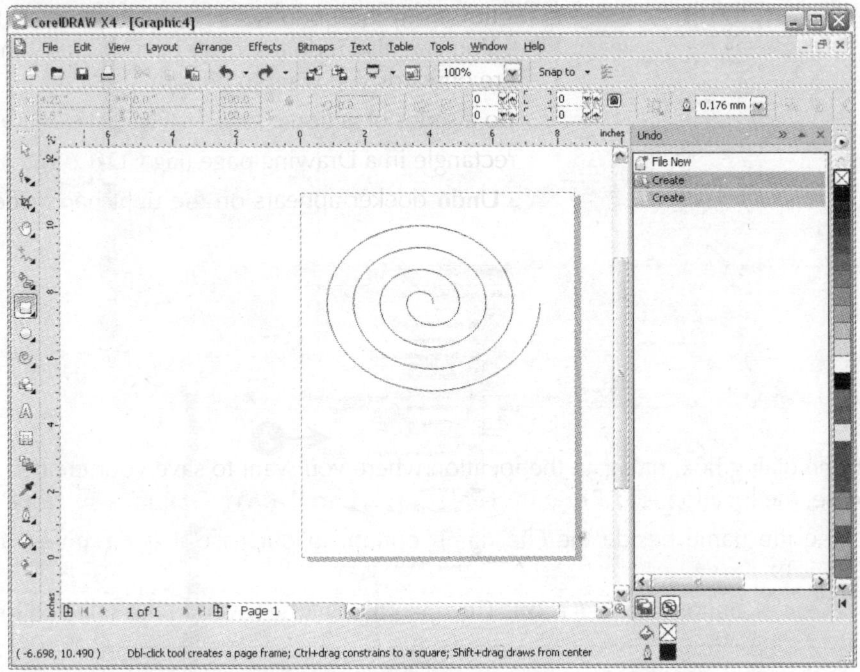

Fig.CD-1.37

Note

> After undo a series of actions when you select an action in Undo docker, all actions listed between the selected action and the last undone action are redone.

After learning undoing, redoing, and repeating action, let's now learn how to save the drawing.

Saving the Drawing

You have learned to draw the basic geometric figure such as a line, rectangle, ellipse, and spiral in CorelDRAW X4. You can save your drawing documents on the appropriate location so that you can further work on those files. To do so, you have to give the file name and the file format. Saving a document in CorelDRAW is not different from any other application.

Undertake the following to save your document:

1. *Select* **File→Save As** (Fig.CD-1.38). A **Save Drawing** dialog box appears as shown in the Fig.CD-1.39.

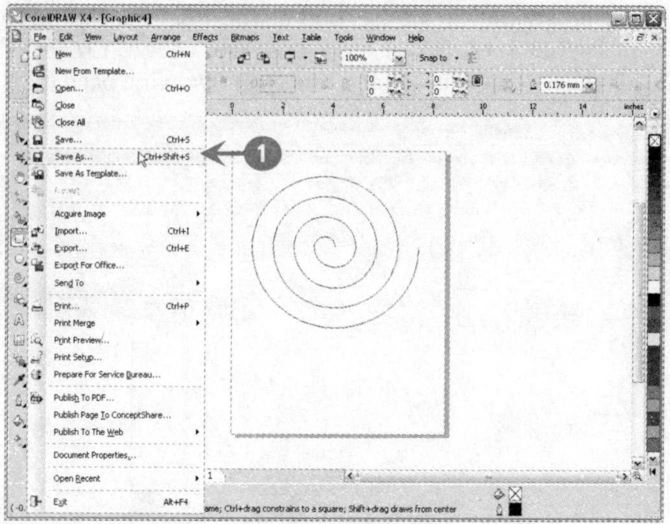

Fig.CD-1.38

2. From the dialog box, navigate the location where you want to save your created drawing. In our case, the location is **E:\Program Files\Corel\CorelDRAW Graphics Suite X4\Draw**.
3. *Type* the file name beside the **File name** option. In our case it is **Graphic4** as shown in Fig.CD-1.39.
4. *Click* the **Save** button (Fig.CD-1.39). The open file will be saved in the selected location.

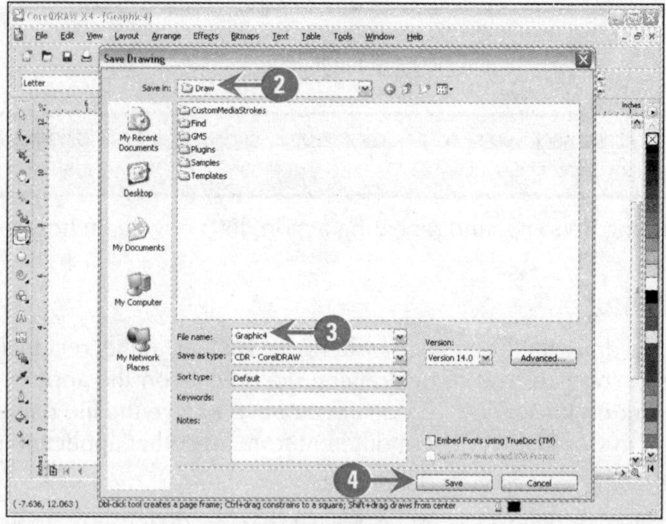

Fig.CD-1.39

As soon as, you click the Save button, the title name of the drawing in Title bar will be changed. It will add the location along with the name of the file. For example, now the file name of the drawing along with its location is **E:\Program Files\Corel\CorelDRAW Graphics Suite X4\Draw\Graphics4.cdr** as shown in Fig.CD-1.40.

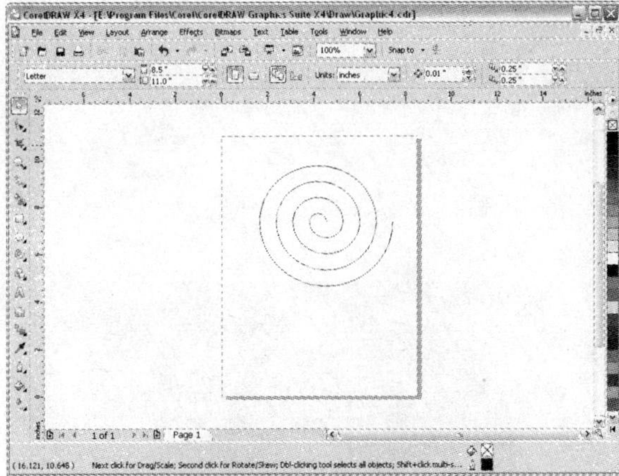

Fig.CD-1.40

After saving the drawing, let's now see how to open an existing file.

Opening an Existing Document

Till now, you have learned to create a document in the form of simple drawing such as some basic geometric figures and also learned how to save them on your computer. CorelDRAW consists of several inbuilt files (.cdr files) as well as the files which were created by the users. You can directly work on those files.

Undertake the following steps to open an existing file:

1. *Select* **File→Open**. An **Open Drawing** dialog box appears (Fig.CD-1.41).
2. From the **Look in** combo box, *select* the location from where the files are stored (Fig.CD-1.41). For example, in our case, the files are located under **Samples** folder of **E:** drive.
3. *Click* the file name to select it. For example, *select* **Sample2** file (Fig.CD-1.41).
4. *Click* **Open** button in the dialog box (Fig.CD-1.41).

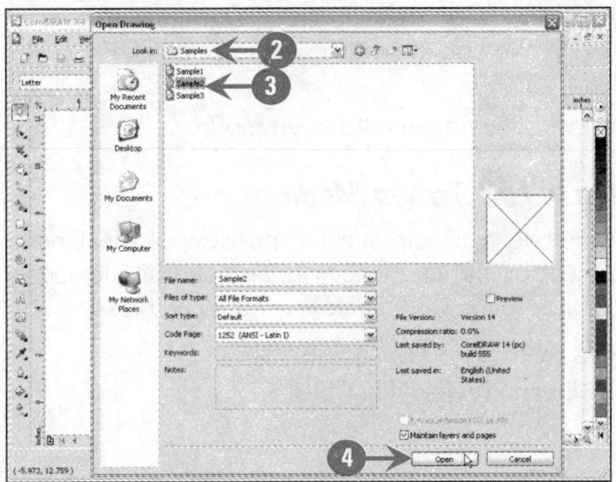

Fig.CD-1.41

The document will be opened as shown in Fig.CD-1.42

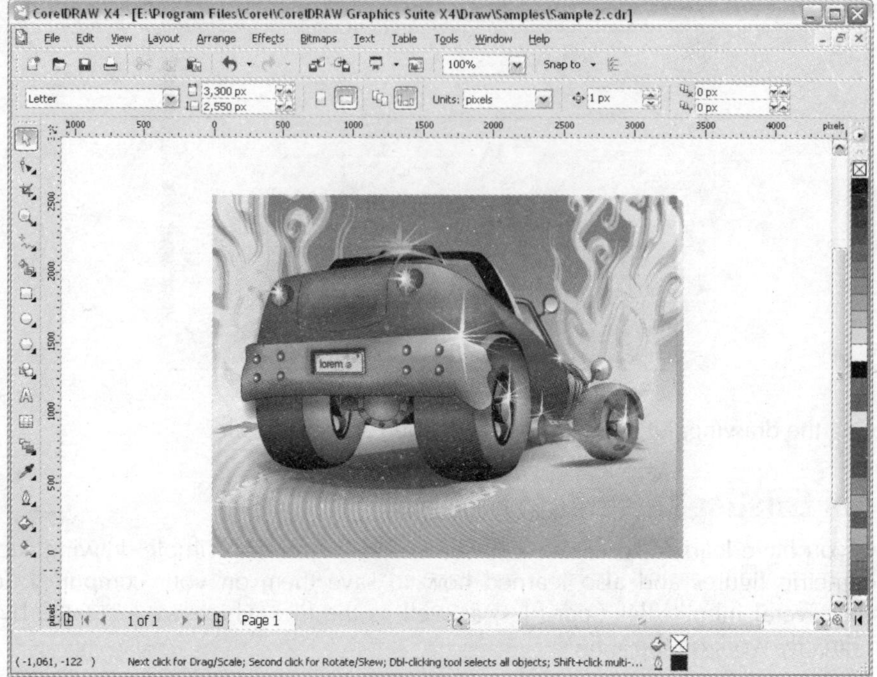

Fig.CD-1.42

Let's now learn to preview a drawing.

Previewing a Drawing

Before printing or exporting a drawing, you can preview your drawing to see how it will look. While you are previewing a drawing, the objects on the Drawing page and in the intermediate area of the Drawing window area are exhibited. You can preview all objects or a particular object of your drawing. While you are previewing a particular object, the remaining objects of the drawing are hidden.

Let's first learn to preview a drawing in full screen mode.

Previewing a Drawing in Full Screen Mode

In full screen preview mode, you can see the preview of the Document window in the full screen. All objects present on the Drawing window, can be viewed in the full screen preview mode and you will get back to the CorelDRAW window by pressing any key.

Undertake the following steps to preview a drawing:

1. *Select* **View→Full Screen Preview** (Fig.CD-1.43).

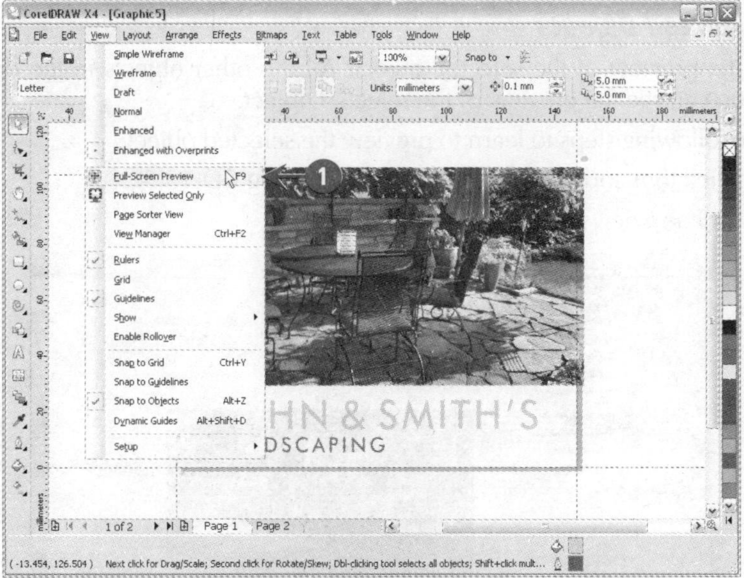

Fig.CD-1.43

The Full Screen preview of the drawing appears on the whole screen (Fig.CD-1.44). Click anywhere on the screen or press any key to return back to original window.

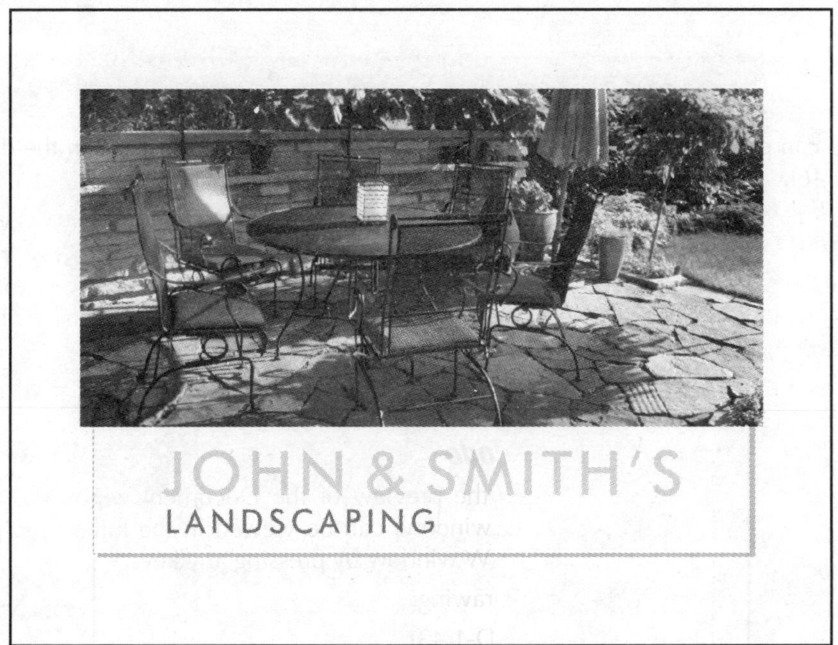

Fig.CD-1.44

After previewing a drawing, let's now preview a selected object in the drawing.

Previewing Selected Objects

You can see the preview of the selected object. All the other objects in the drawing would be hidden and you can see the preview of the selected object.

Undertake the following steps to learn to preview the selected object:

1. *Select* the **Pick** tool and *click* an object to *select* it (Fig.CD-1.45).
2. *Select* **View→ Preview Selected Only** (Fig.CD-1.45).

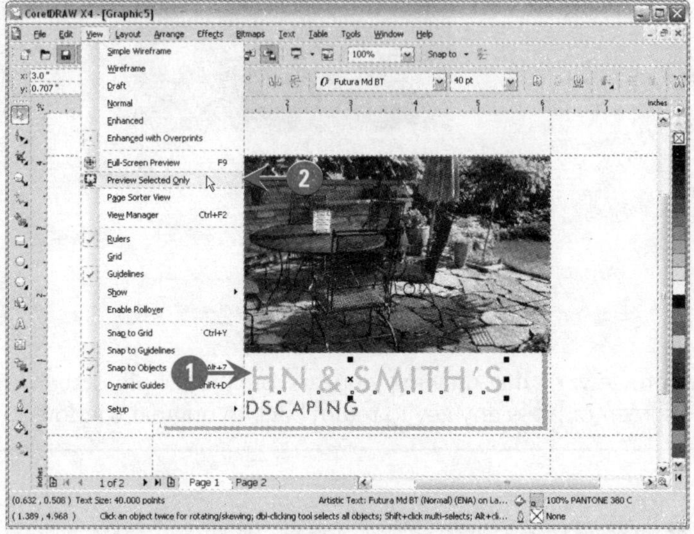

Fig.CD-1.45

Now, you can preview only the selected object that is rectangular drawing in the drawing page (Fig.CD-1.46).

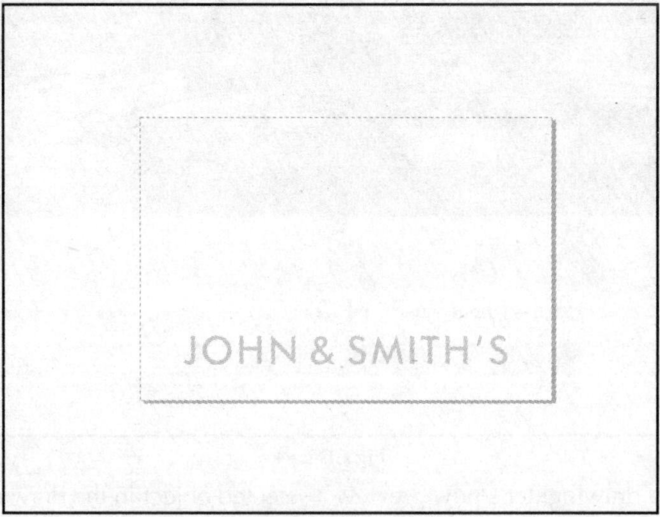

Fig.CD-1.46

Now you have learned to view the preview of the selected object in the drawing. Let's now learn to view the drawing in different view modes.

Viewing a Drawing in Different Views

Views refer to the mode of viewing documents. There are six types of Views modes in CorelDRAW. Let's discuss those CorelDRAW view modes in brief here:

- **Simple Wireframe:** This view mode shows the bitmaps in monochromes means in black and white. It shows the outline of the drawing and hides the complex properties such as fills, contours, drop shadows, intermediate blend shapes and so on. This mode allows you to quickly preview the introductory component of a drawing.
- **Wireframe:** This view mode is same as Simple Wireframe view mode. The main difference is that the Wireframe also shows the intermediate blend shapes.
- **Drafts:** This view shows a drawing's fills and bitmaps but with low resolution (Fig.CD-1.47).

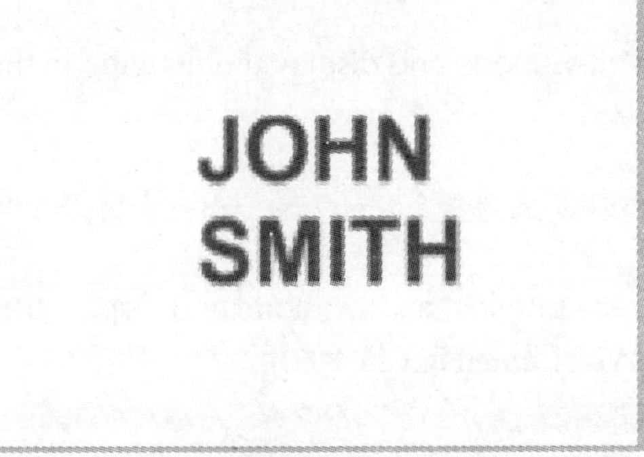

Fig.CD-1.47

- **Normal:** This view shows a drawing without PostScript fills or high resolution bitmaps (Fig.CD-1.48).

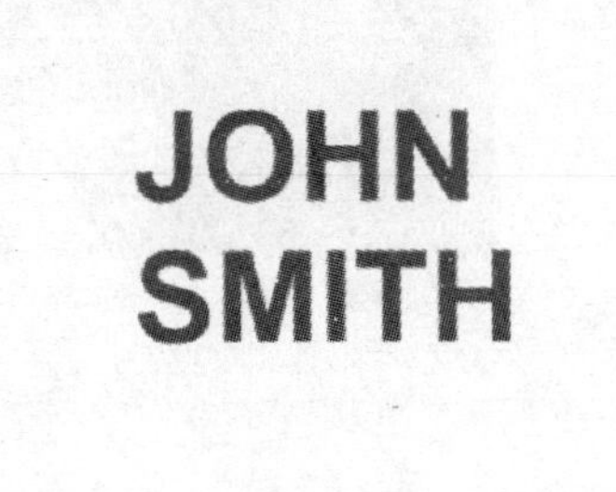

Fig.CD-1.48

- **Enhanced:** This view shows a drawing with PostScript fills, high-resolution bitmaps, and anti-aliased vector graphics (Fig.CD-1.49).

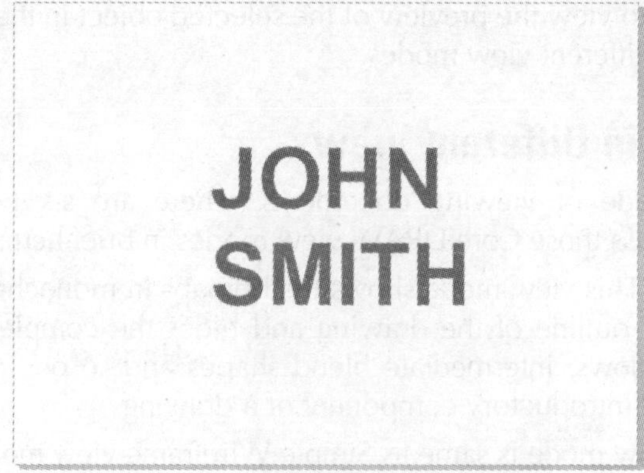

Fig.CD-1.49

- **Enhanced with Overprints:** This view simulates the color of areas where overlapping objects were set to overprint and shows PostScript fills, high resolution bitmaps, and anti-aliased vector graphics.

Let's now learn to select a view mode and display the drawing in the selected mode.

Using the View Modes

There are various types of view modes, which you can display all these modes in drawing as per your requirements.

Undertake the following steps to select a view mode and display the drawing in that view mode:

1. *Select* **View→Simple Wireframe**(Fig.CD-1.50).

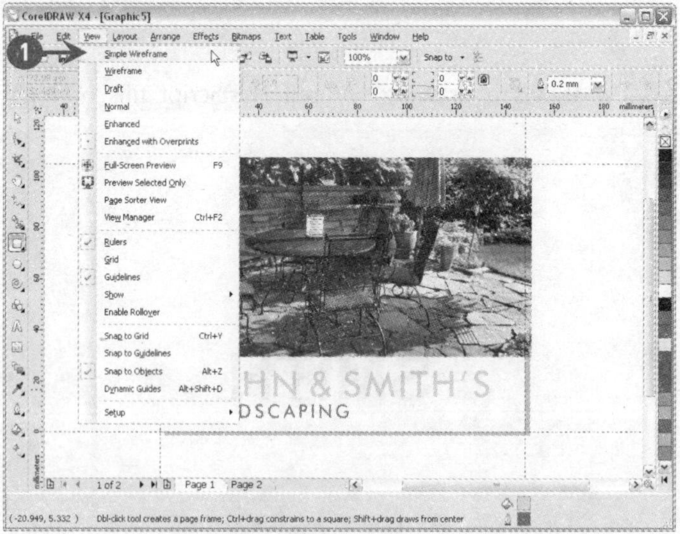

Fig.CD-1.50

The Simple Wireframe view of the drawing appears, as shown in Fig.CD-1.51. This view mode shows the drawing in black and white.

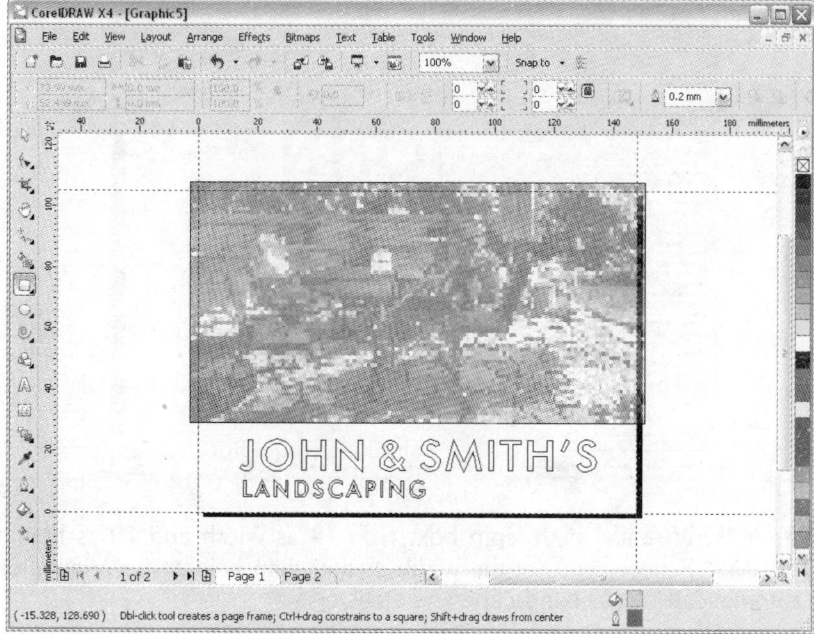

Fig.CD-1.51

By this way, you can use the other modes of viewing a drawing, let's now learn to work with page layout.

Working with Page Layout

When you open CorelDRAW, the Drawing page appears with the default size, orientation, and background and layout style. However, you can set the size, orientation, background, and layout of the page as per your requirement. You can also add guidelines in your drawing page that help in the placement of object. You can add any number of pages in your drawing, rename them and also can delete the pages whenever required.

Modifying Size and Orientation of a Page

For defining a page size, there are two options, choosing a preset page size, and creating the custom page size by specifying the page dimension. If the preset page size does not fulfill your requirements, you can make custom page size by defining the drawing dimensions (width and height).

There are also two types of page orientation, landscape and portrait. If the width of the Drawing page is greater than its height, the orientation of the page is landscape. If the height of the Drawing page is greater than its width, then the orientation of the page is portrait.

Undertake the following steps to modifying the size and orientation of a page:

1. From the **Paper Type/Size** drop-down list, *select* a paper type option. In our case, it is **Custom** (Fig.CD-1.52).

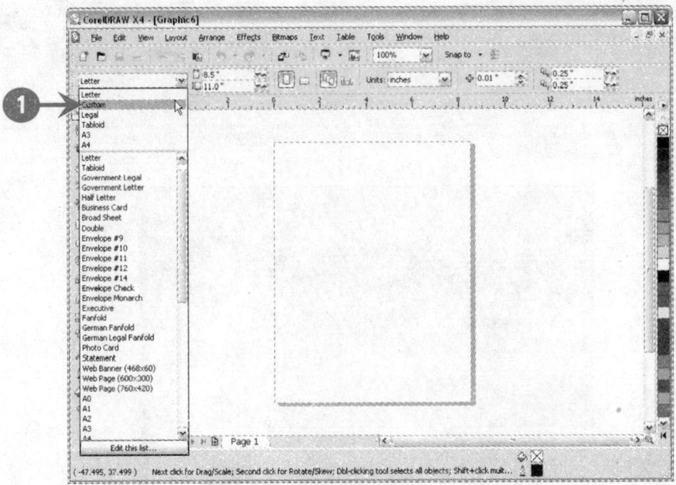

Fig.CD-1.52

2. In the **Paper Width and Height** spin box, *type* **14** as width and **10** as height of the page (Fig.CD-1.53). Whenever you set the width greater than height, the orientation of the page will be automatically set as Landscape and vice versa.
3. To set the zoom level as 125%, *type* **125** in the **Zoom Levels** combo box (Fig.CD-1.53) and *press* the **ENTER** key.

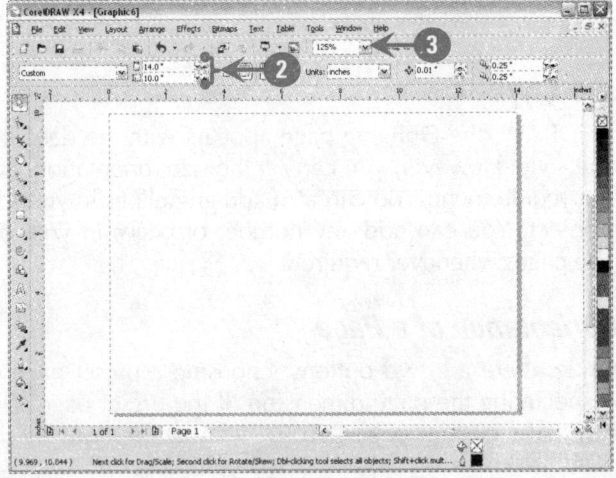

Fig.CD-1.53

Note

Click the Apply Page Layout to All Pages () button for applying page size and orientation settings to all pages in a drawing. If you are applying the settings only in the current page then click the Apply Page Layout to Current Page Only button() on the Property bar of the CorelDRAW window (Fig.CD-1.53).

Let's now learn to work with the guidelines.

Working with Guidelines

Guidelines are horizontal, vertical or slanted lines which can be added in the Drawing page of the CorelDRAW window. Guidelines help in the placement of objects in your drawing. Guidelines can be set for the individual page or can be set for the entire pages. Once the guidelines are set in your Drawing page, you can hide them at any time.

Undertake the following steps to add horizontal or vertical guidelines in your drawing:

1. To draw horizontal guideline, *click* on the horizontal Ruler, and drag the mouse-pointer from the horizontal Ruler to the Drawing Page where you want to add guideline (Fig.CD-1.54). As soon as, you start dragging the mouse-pointer, the guideline appears.
2. To draw the vertical guidelines, *click* on the vertical Ruler, drag the mouse-pointer from the vertical Ruler to Drawing page where you want to draw guidelines as shown in Fig.CD-1.54.

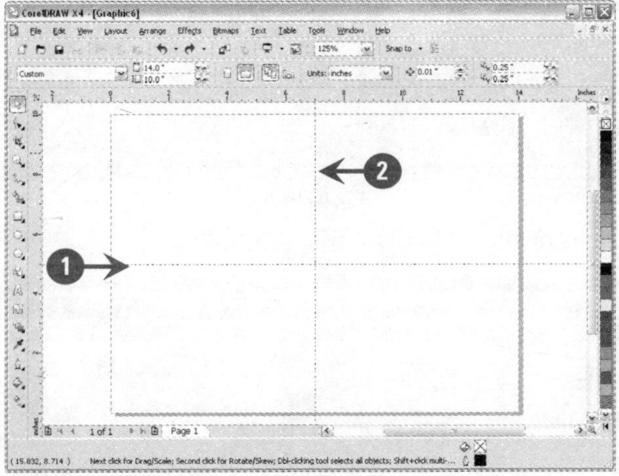

Fig.CD-1.54

You can add more guidelines (Fig.CD-1.55), by following the step no. 1 and 2.

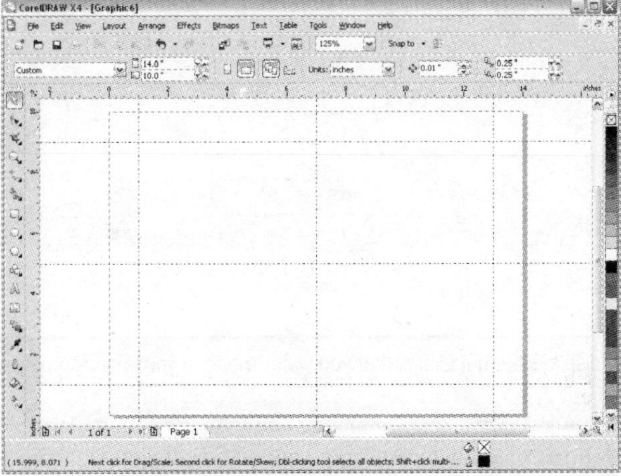

Fig.CD-1.55

3. To delete a guideline, *select* it and then *press* the **DELETE** key (Fig.CD-1.56).

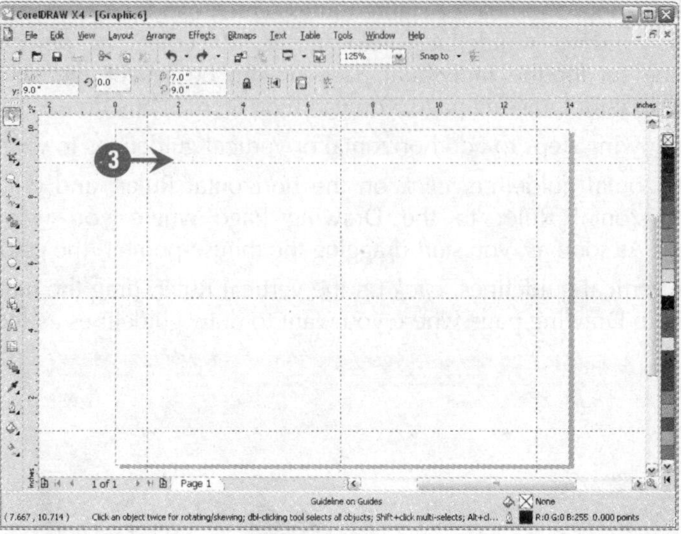

Fig.CD-1.56

The selected guideline is deleted (Fig.CD-1.57).

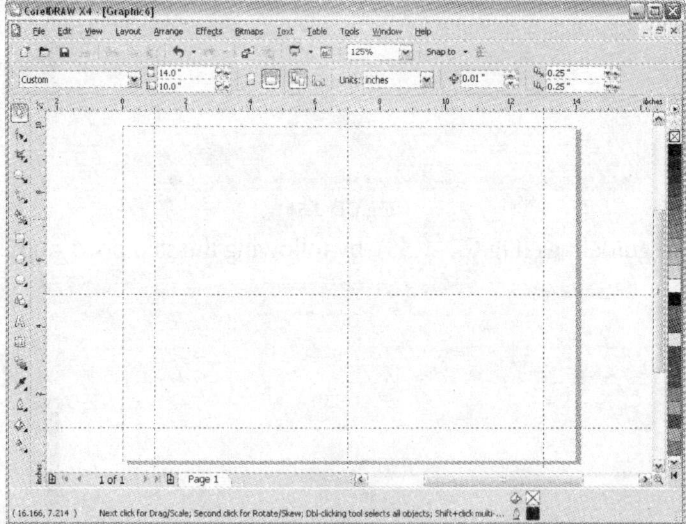

Fig.CD-1.57

Note

> By default, the application displays the guidelines that you want to add in your Drawing page. You can hide the guidelines by selecting View→Guidelines.

After adding the guidelines in your Drawing page, you will now learn how to select and remove the background of the Drawing page.

Setting Page Background

By default, the background of a page appears without any color. But you can change the background of the page by applying the color to it. A color in the background of the page enhances the look of your work. Usually, a color is set as a background of a document when user is preparing some broacher or cover page of some magazine. In CorelDRAW, you can apply solid color or image to the background of the Document page.

To change the background, you can select solid color or a bitmap. You can also remove the background, whenever you did not need it.

Undertake the following steps to select a background for a drawing:

1. *Select* **Layout→Page Background** (Fig.CD-1.58). An **Options** dialog box appears (Fig.CD-1.59).

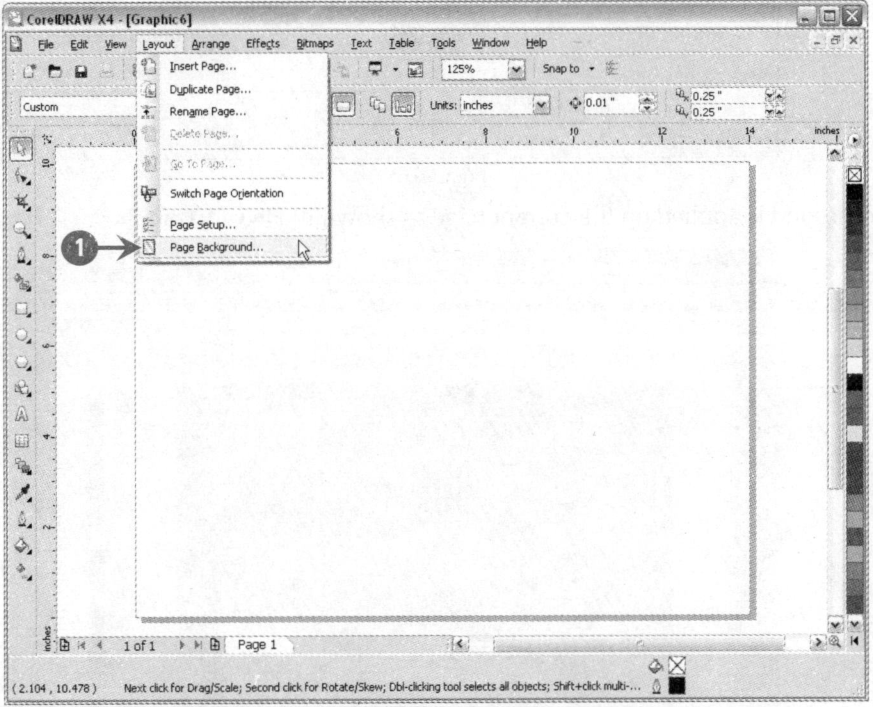

Fig.CD-1.58

2. *Click* the **Document** category and *select* **Background** option under **Page** sub-category. (Fig.CD-1.59). The background details settings options displayed.
3. *Select* the radio button beside the **Solid** option (Fig.CD-1.59).
4. *Select* a background color from the color flicker beside the **Solid** option as shown in Fig.CD-1.59.
5. *Click* **OK** button (Fig.CD-1.59).

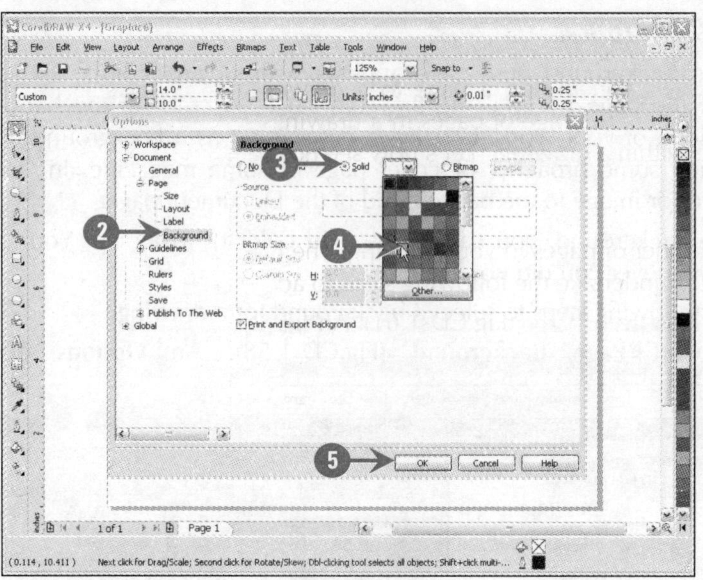

Fig.CD-1.59

The background is applied on the current page as shown in Fig.CD-1.60.

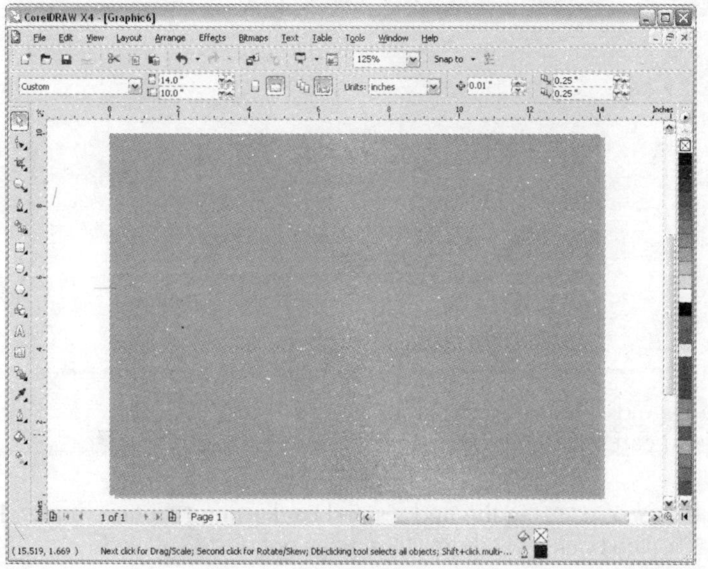

Fig.CD-1.60

Note

To remove the background, select the radio button beside the No Background option in the Options dialog box (Fig.CD-1.59).

Adding, Renaming, and Deleting Page to a Drawing

CorelDRAW allows you to add a page to a drawing. You can rename it and also delete an individual page or entire range of pages in a drawing. The objects can be moved from one page to another page within a drawing. Let's now see how to add, rename, and delete a page.

Adding a Page

You can add number of pages in your drawing. The inserted page(s) can be added before or after the current page. Undertake the following steps to add a page:

1. *Select* **Layout→Insert Page** (Fig.CD-1.61). An **Insert Page** dialog box appears (Fig.CD-1.62).

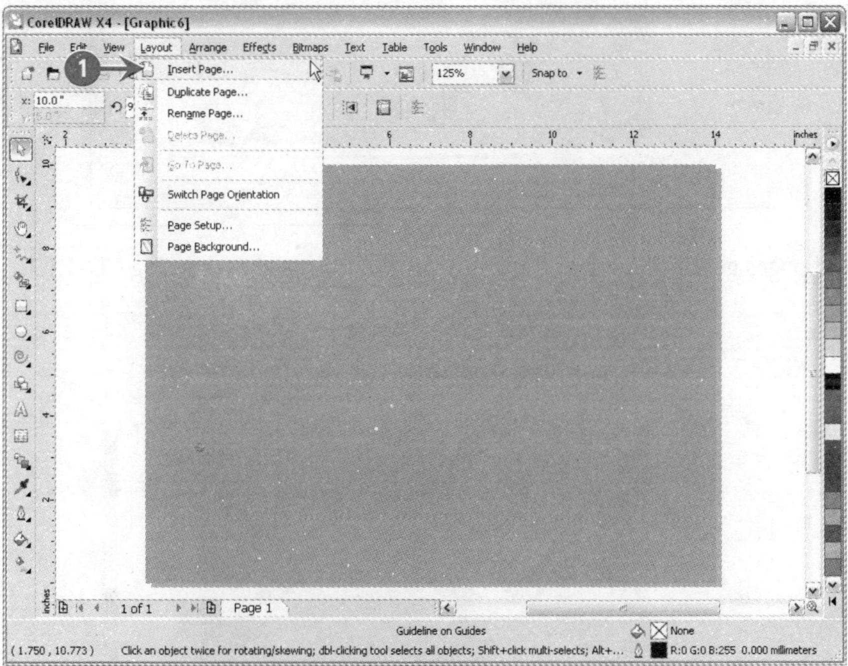

Fig.CD-1.61

From this Insert Page dialog box, you can set the number of pages that you want to insert in your drawing. Even you can insert the pages after or before any page either it is the current page, first page or last page.

2. *Type* the number of pages in the **Insert** spin box, in our case it is **2** (Fig.CD-1.62).
3. *Select* the radio button beside **Before** or **After** option. In our case, it is **After** (Fig.CD-1.62).
4. *Type* the page number in the **Page** spin box if you want to insert pages other than the current page. In our case, it is the **1** that is the current page (Fig.CD-1.62).
5. *Click* the **OK** button (Fig.CD-1.62).

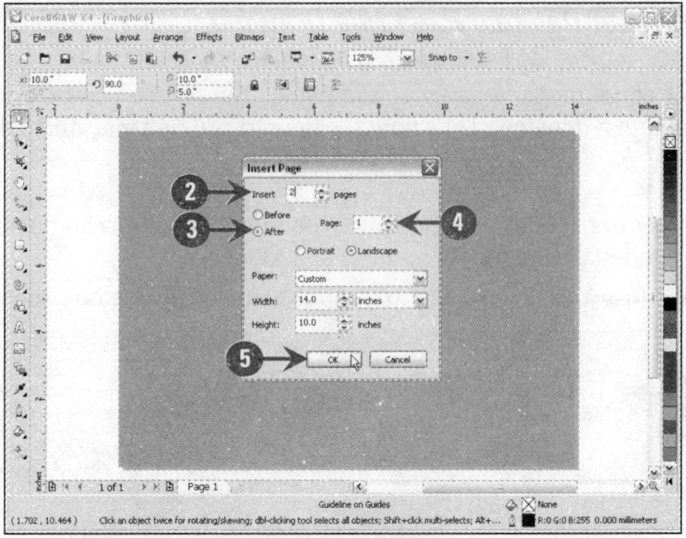

Fig.CD-1.62

The inserted pages get displayed on the Drawing window as shown in Fig.CD-1.63.

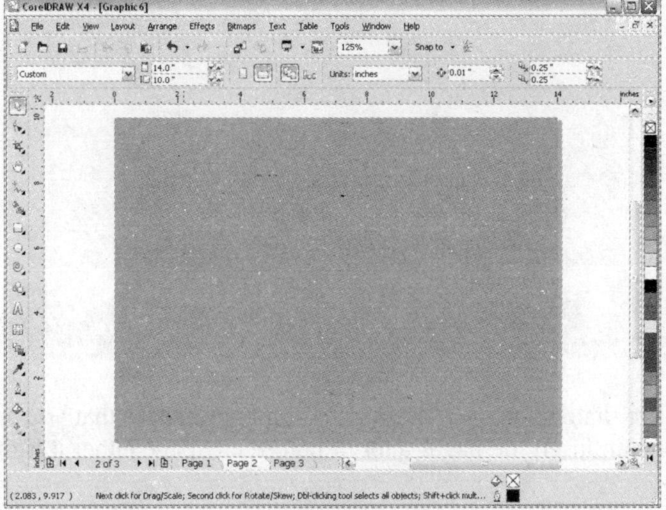

Fig.CD-1.63

Let's now see how to rename a drawing page.

Renaming a Page

When you add a page, it appears with the default name on the Document Navigator. However, you can rename the page as per your requirement. Undertake the following steps to rename a page:

1. *Select* **Layout→Rename Page** (Fig.CD-1.64). A **Rename Page** dialog box appears (Fig.CD-1.65).

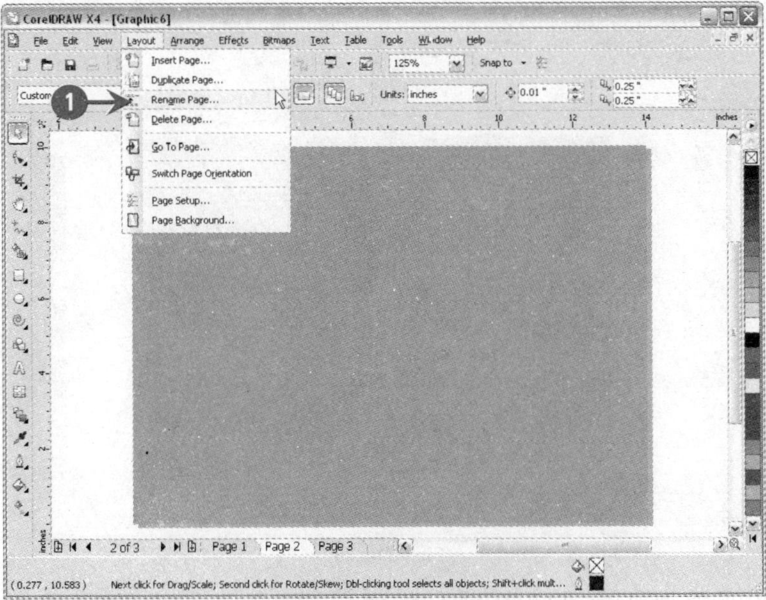

Fig.CD-1.64

2. *Type* the page name in the text box under **Page name** option. For example, we have given the page name as **Kogent-2** as shown in Fig.CD-1.65.
3. *Click* the **OK** button (Fig.CD-1.65).

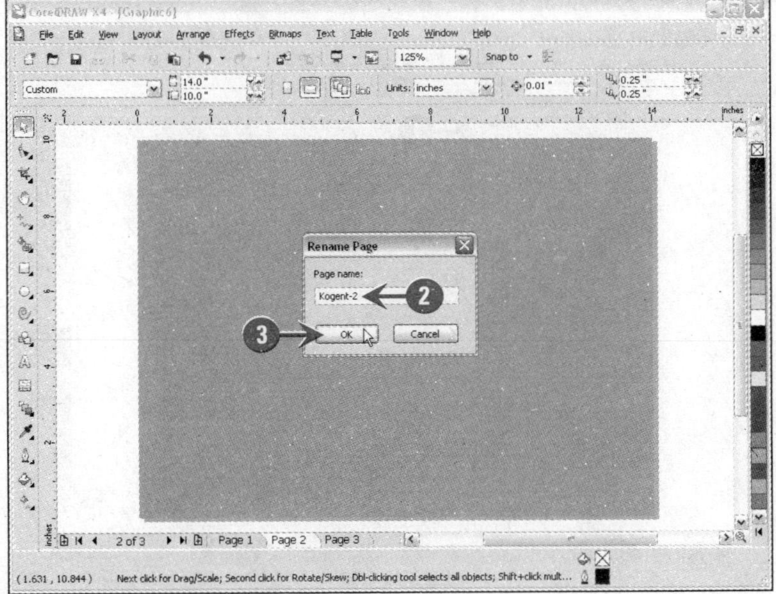

Fig.CD-1.65

The drawing page will be renamed. You can see it in the Document Navigator (Fig.CD-1.66).

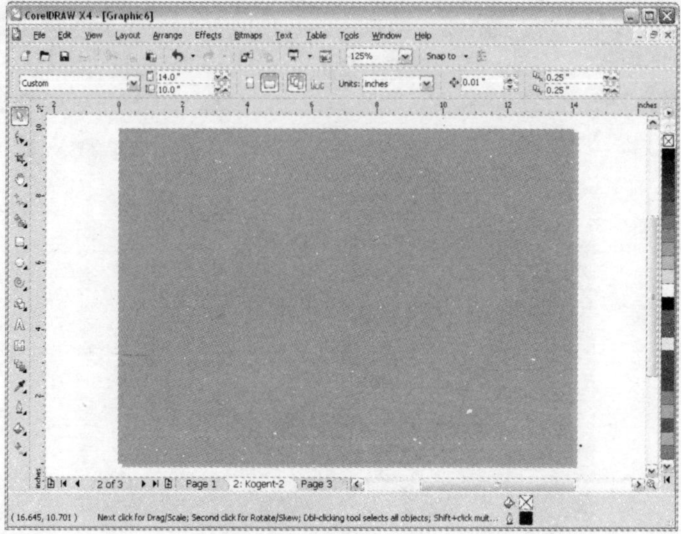

Fig.CD-1.66

Let's now learn how to delete a Drawing page.

Deleting a Page

You can delete an individual page or a range of pages from your drawing. Undertake the following steps to delete a page:

1. *Select* **Layout→Delete Page** (Fig.CD-1.67). A **Delete Page** dialog box appears (Fig.CD-1.68).

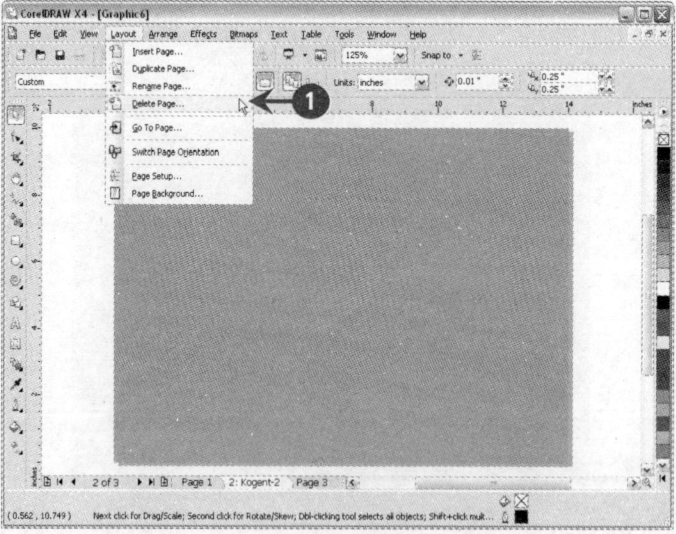

Fig.CD-1.67

2. *Type* the page number that you want to delete in the **Delete page** spin box (Fig.CD-1.68).
3. *Click* the **OK** button (Fig.CD-1.68). The selected page will be deleted.

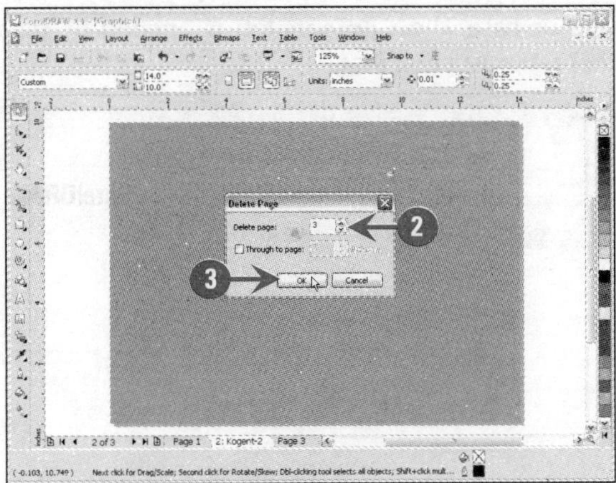

Fig.CD-1.68

After working with page layout, let's now learn about Help provided by CorelDRAW.

Help in CorelDRAW

CorelDRAW Help provides you the comprehensive information about product characteristics. You can open Help directly from the CorelDRAW window.

When you open the Help in CorelDRAW, The CorelDRAW Help window displays the information depending upon the selected options under a particular tab. The window contains four tabs as discussed here:

- **Contents:** Click this tab to view a list of topics in the help. You can select the topics by clicking it and view the corresponding information.
- **Index:** This tab allows you to use the index to find a topic.
- **Search:** Under this tab, you can search full text of the Help for a specific word or phrase.

Undertake the following steps to open help in CorelDRAW:

1. *Select* **Help→Help Topics** (Fig.CD-1.69). The **CorelDRAW Help** window appears (Fig.CD-1.70).

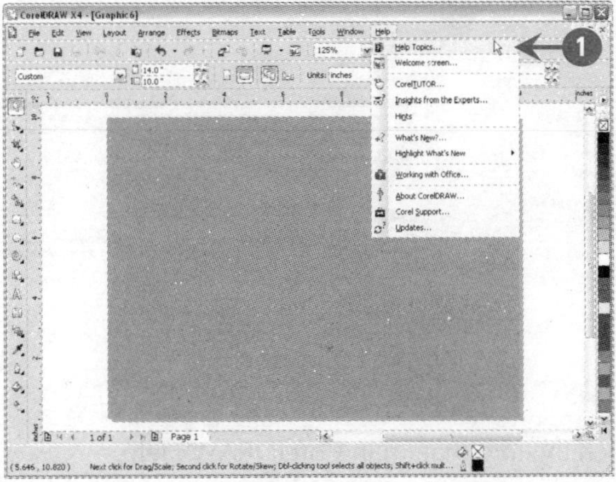

Fig.CD-1.69

2. Now, *click* a tab. In our case, the **Contents** tab is opened by default (Fig.CD-1.70). If you want to select another tab, just click that.

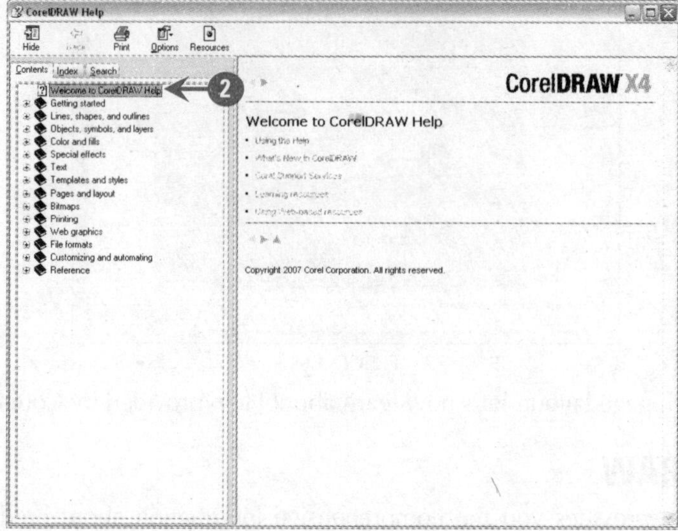

Fig.CD-1.70

3. Under **Contents** tab, *click* the **Getting started** option to expand it (Fig.CD-1.71).
4. *Click* the **CorelDRAW workspace tour** option, and then *select* **Workspace tools** option under **CorelDRAW workspace tools** option. The information about the selected option appears as shown in Fig.CD-1.71.

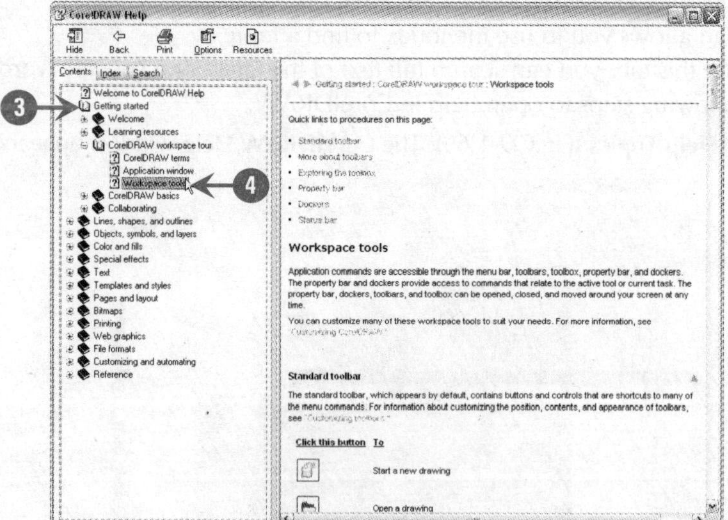

Fig.CD-1.71

Let's now learn to search the information in CorelDRAW Help.

Searching the Help

CorelDRAW provides facility to search your required topics that are related to CorelDRAW in CorelDRAW Help. The searched result will appear on the CorelDRAW Help window. Undertake the following steps to search the information in Help:

1. *Click* the **Search** tab (Fig.CD-1.72).
2. *Type* a word or phrase in the text box below **Type in word(s) to search for** option. For example, we have typed **Line**.
3. *Click* the **List Topics** button (Fig.CD-1.72). A list of topics gets displayed under the **Search topic.**
4. *Select* a topic from the list as shown in Fig.CD-1.72. For example, we have selected **Drawing line.**
5. After viewing information, you can close the CorelDRAW Help window by *clicking* the **Close** button on the Title bar of the window (Fig.CD-1.72.

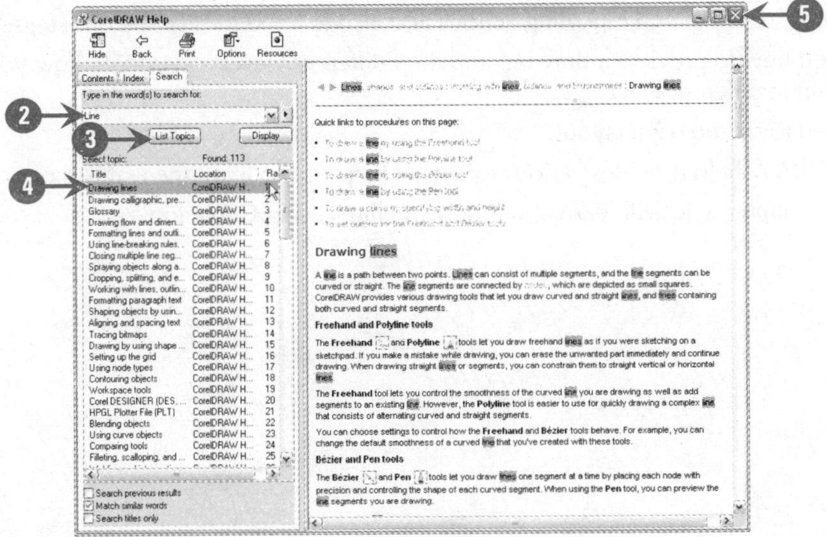

Fig.CD-1.72

Let's now learn to close the drawing and then quitting the CorelDRAW window.

Closing the Drawing and Quitting CorelDRAW

When we have finished working in CorelDRAW and want to close it. Then, firstly you have to save it and then you can close it. You can quit from the CorelDRAW window, whenever you want but before it, save your files. Suppose you forget to save your files and you quit the CorelDRAW window then a message box appears, asking whether you want to save the file or not. You can save the file at that time and quit from CorelDRAW window.

Undertake the following steps to close a drawing:

1. *Select* **File→Close**, The file will be closed.

2. After closing the document, if you want to quit from the CorelDRAW window, *select* **File→Exit**. You will now quit from the CorelDRAW window.

Note

You can also quit CorelDRAW window, by clicking the Close button on the Tile bar.

With this, we come to the end of the chapter. Before proceeding ahead towards the next chapter, let's summarize the main points of this chapter.

Summary

In this chapter, we have learned about:

- CorelDRAW Graphics Suite X4 is the newly version of the CorelDRAW. It lets you create graphics designs, page layout and edit photo.
- Drawing the basic geometric figures such as lines, rectangle, ellipse, and spiral.
- Undoing, redoing, and repeating actions and also learned to save the drawings.
- Learned how to preview a drawing and then different view modes that allow you to see your drawing in different views.
- Learned to set the page layout.
- CorelDRAW help provides various tools that help you to learn the features of CorelDRAW.

In the next chapter, you will learn about drawing lines using Curve tools.

Chapter 2

Working with Lines

In this Section

- About Lines in CorelDRAW
- Drawing Calligraphic, Pressure-Sensitive, and Preset Lines
- About Outline Tool
- Using Brush Strokes

After getting an overview of CorelDRAW X4 in the previous chapter, let us now learn about lines. A line can be defined as a path between two points on the Drawing page. A line may not always be straight; it may be a curve as well. In CorelDRAW, you can draw a line using different tools, such as the **Freehand tool**, **Bezier tool**, **Artistic Media tool**, **Pen tool**, **Polyline tool**, and **3 Point Curve tool**.

Apart from drawing lines, you can also format the outlines that surround various drawing objects. In CorelDRAW, you can add effects to the lines by applying brush strokes to them. These brush strokes can be preset brush strokes or custom brush strokes, and you can also format these brush strokes if required.

In this chapter, you learn about drawing lines using various tools, drawing Calligraphic, Pressure-sensitive, and Preset lines, changing the appearance of line and outlines, and using brush strokes.

About Lines in CorelDRAW

CorelDRAW provides you with different tools to draw lines; these are Freehand tool, Polyline tool, Bezier tool, and Pen tool. These tools offer various styles to draw a line. A line tool can be selected depending upon your requirements. You can access these tools by clicking the bottom right corner arrow of a Curve tool from the Toolbox. While working with Freehand or Polyline tool its like creating a sketch in a drawing book. With these tools you can easily erase the irrelevant part of the drawing and continue with the rest of the drawing. Pen tool lets you draw a line but it shows a preview of the line before drawing. When you do not want to manipulate the nodes, you need to draw a curve by specifying the width and height. For this purpose you can use 3 Point Curve tool.

Drawing a Curve by Fixing Width and Height

A line that deviates from straightness in a smooth, continuous manner is known as curve. CorelDRAW lets you to draw a curve using various tools available, such as Freehand, Bezier, Artistic Media, Pen, Polyline, 3 Point Curve, Connector, and Dimension tools. Freehand tool is the default tool selected on the Curve tool flyout in the Toolbox. Let us draw a curve using 3 Point Curve tool.

Undertake the following steps to draw a curve by fixing width and height using 3 Point Curve tool:

1. *Open* the **Curve** tools flyout by *clicking* the arrow on the bottom-right corner of the **Freehand** tool ( ) from the Toolbox of CorelDRAW window, as shown in Fig.CD-2.1.

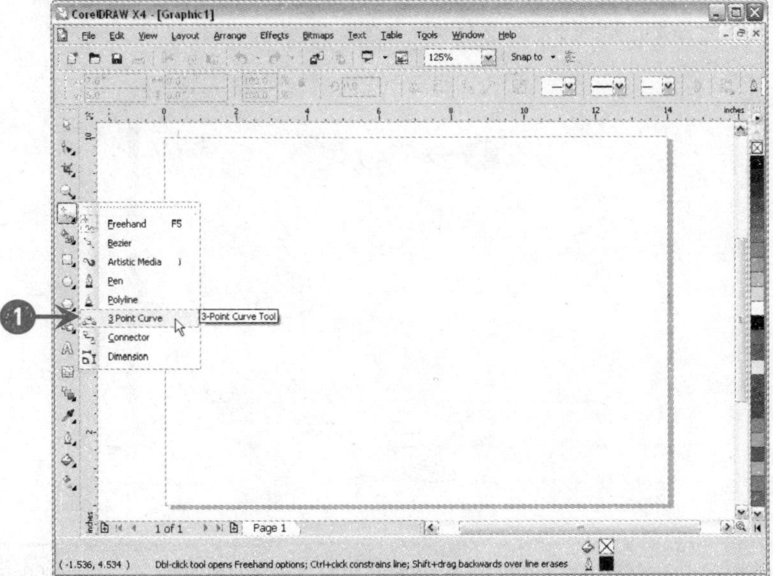

Fig.CD-2.1

2. *Click* the **3 Point Curve** tool and *drag* the mouse-pointer to draw a straight line (Fig.CD-2.2). While drawing the straight line do not move the mouse-pointer back or forth.

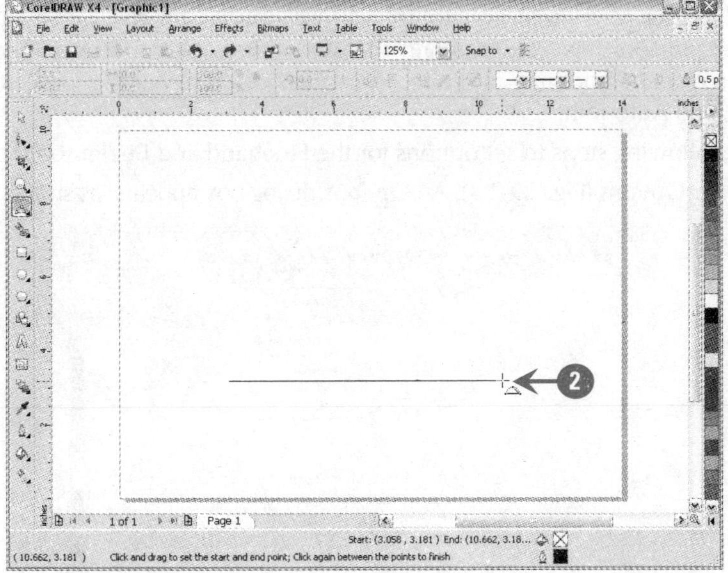

Fig.CD-2.2

3. After drawing the straight line, move the mouse-pointer upward and *click* the mouse-button. A curve will appear (Fig.CD-2.3). *Click* anywhere in the Drawing page to remove highlight from the curve.

A curve drawn by specifying width and height is shown in Fig.CD-2.3.

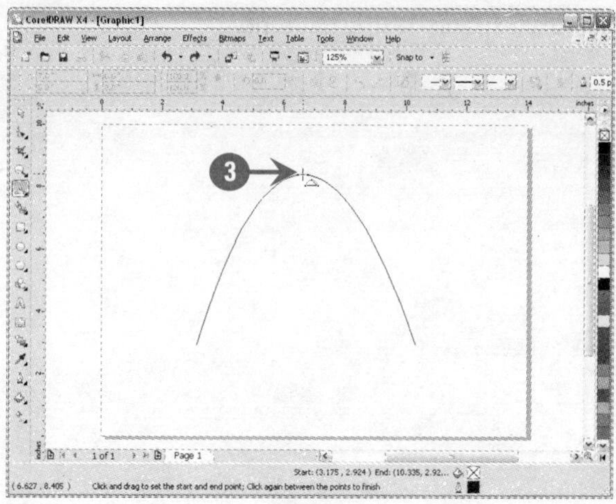

Fig.CD-2.3

Note

You can also customize the width and height of the curve from the Property bar and selecting Object size text box (8.116" 3.0").

Setting Option for Freehand and Bezier Tools

Freehand and Bezier tools help you to set various options for the curves and enhance their usability. Freehand tool lets you maintain the smoothness of the curved line. It helps you to manage the Freehand smoothing and alter the values of these fields: Corner threshold, Straight line threshold, and Auto-join.

Undertake the following steps to set options for the Freehand and Bezier tools:

1. *Select* **Tools→Options** (Fig.CD-2.4). An **Options** dialog box appears, as shown in Fig.CD-2.5.

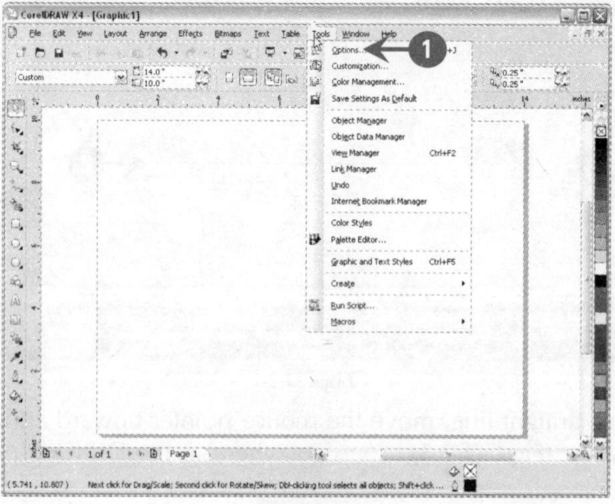

Fig.CD-2.4

2. In **Options** dialog box, expand **Workspace** node by *clicking* the plus (+) sign beside it, as shown in Fig.CD-2.5.

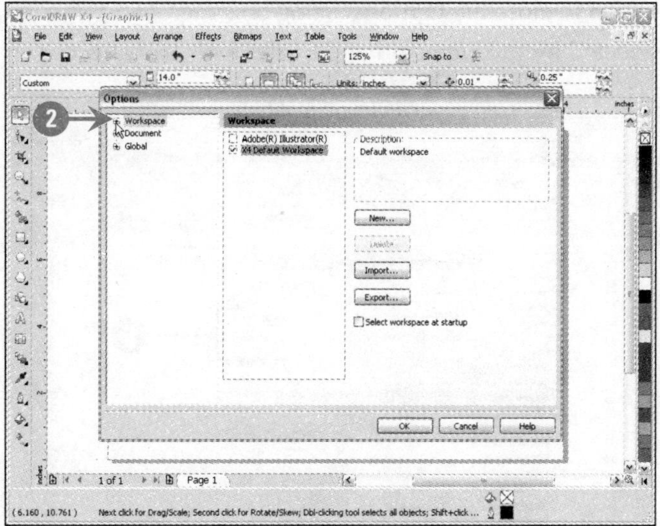

Fig.CD-2.5

3. Again under **Workplace** node, expand **Toolbox** category by *clicking* plus (+) sign beside it. Various options available under **Toolbox** appear, as shown in Fig.CD-2.6.
4. Under **Toolbox** category, *select* **Freehand/Bezier** tool and the properties of **Freehand/Bezier** tool appears (Fig.CD-2.6).
5. *Type* a value beside the **Freehand smoothing** option. You can also set the value by moving the **slider** appearing beside **Freehand smoothing** option (Fig.CD-2.6).

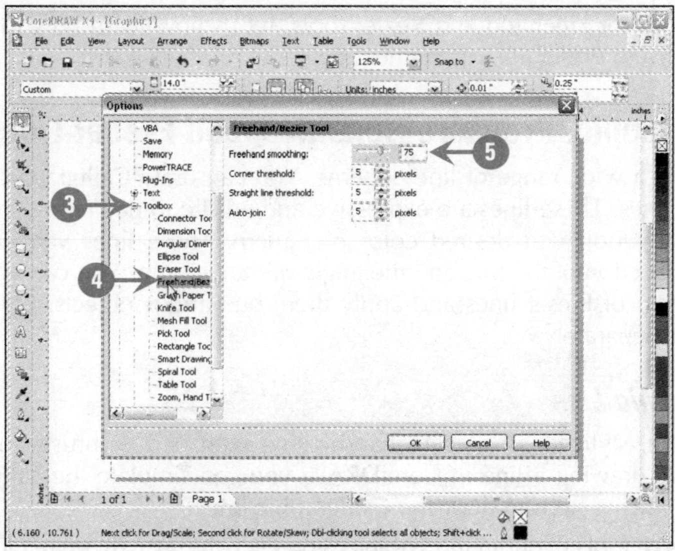

Fig.CD-2.6

6. *Similarly*, repeat step 5 and set values for **Corner threshold**, **Straight line threshold**, and **Auto-join** options (Fig.CD-2.7).
7. *Click* the **OK** button to close the **Options** dialog box (Fig.CD-2.7).

Different options selected for the Freehand and Bezier tools have been selected, as shown in the Fig.CD-2.7.

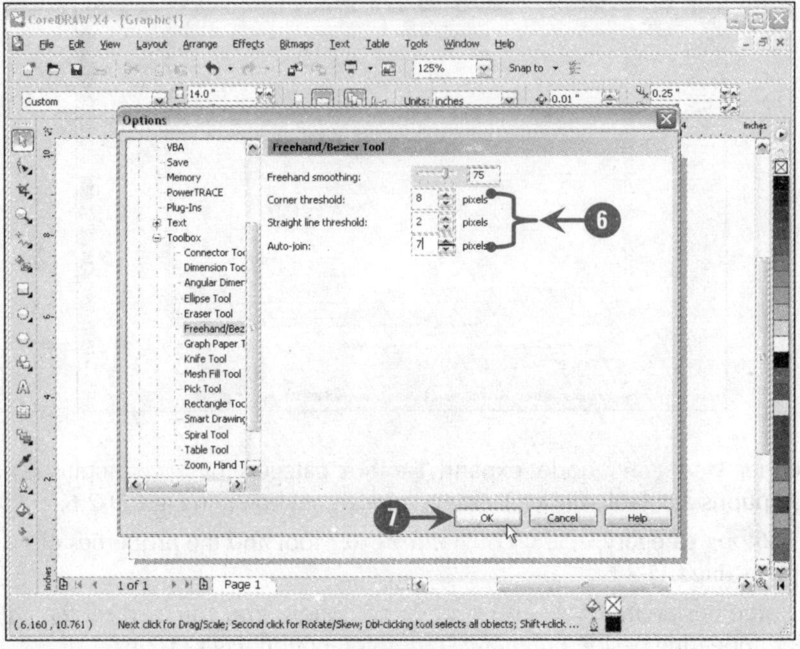

Fig.CD-2.7

After setting options for Freehand and Bezier tools, let us now learn how to draw Calligraphic, Pressure-sensitive, and Preset lines in the next section.

Drawing Calligraphic, Pressure-Sensitive, and Preset Lines

CorelDRAW offers a wide range of line patterns. You can draw Calligraphic, Pressure-sensitive as well as Preset lines. These lines are expressive and artistic in nature and you can create them by using the brush tool with desired color or pattern. These lines vary in thickness, which depends on the direction of the line and the angle of the pen nib. You can apply thick strokes to a line with the help of Preset lines and apply them on various objects. Let us discuss each of these line patterns separately.

Drawing Calligraphic Line

An art of beautiful, stylized, or elegant handwriting with pen or brush and ink is known as calligraphy. While drawing a line in CorelDRAW you can simulate the calligraphic pen effect. Undertake the following steps to draw the Calligraphic line:

1. *Open* the **Curve** tools flyout in the Toolbox and *click* the **Artistic Media** tool (Fig.CD-2.8).

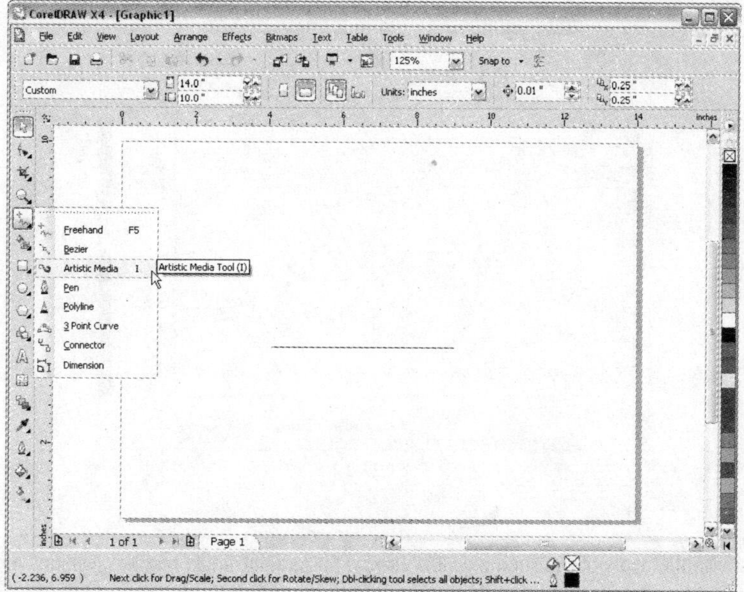

Fig.CD-2.8

2. In the Property bar, *click* the **Calligraphic** button (), as shown in Fig.CD-2.9.

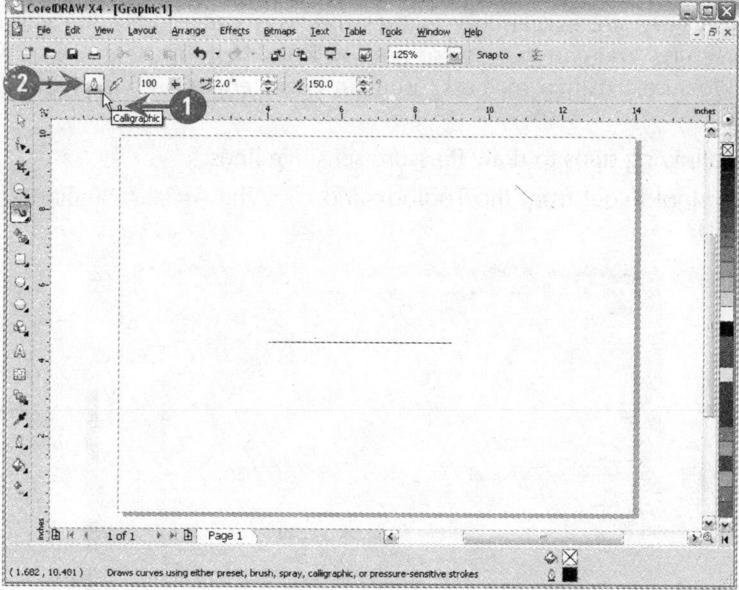

Fig.CD-2.9

3. In the Property bar, type a value in the **Artistic Media Tool Width** text box to change width of the line (Fig.CD-2.10). In our case, we have typed 1.95 units in the **Artistic Media Tool Width** text box.

A Calligraphic line appears on the Drawing page, as shown in the Fig.CD-2.10.

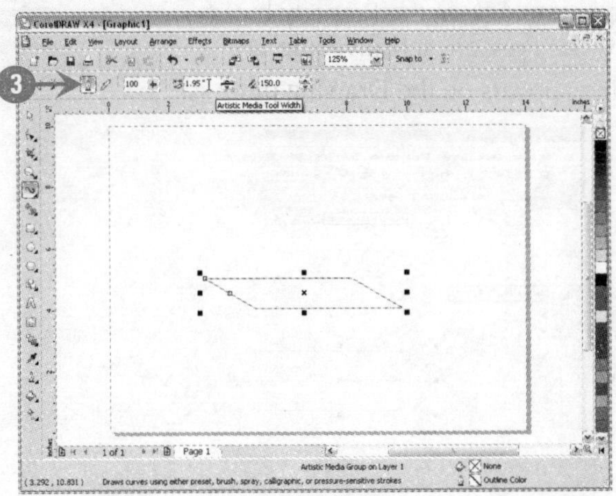

Fig.CD-2.10

Note

> You can also increase the angle of the line by double clicking Calligraphic angle text box. Options related to Calligraphic lines can be accessed by selecting the Artistic Media option under the Effects menu.

Drawing Pressure-Sensitive Line

Pressure-sensitive lines are susceptible to pressure, you can modify the width of the line by applying the pressure. You can draw these lines with the help of using Artistic Media tool. Lines created using Pressure-sensitive method results in curve edges and varying width lines along a path.

Undertake the following steps to draw Pressure-sensitive lines:

1. *Open* **Curve** tool flyout from the Toolbox and *click* the **Artistic Media** tool from the flyout (Fig.CD-2.11).

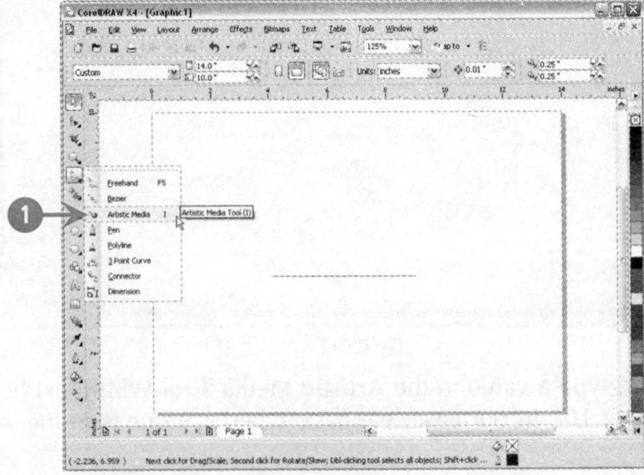

Fig.CD-2.11

2. *Click* the **Pressure** button on the Property bar and type a value in the **Artistic Media Tool Width** box to draw the Pressure-sensitive line, as shown in Fig.CD-2.12.

A Pressure-sensitive line appears on the Drawing page, as shown in Fig.2.12.

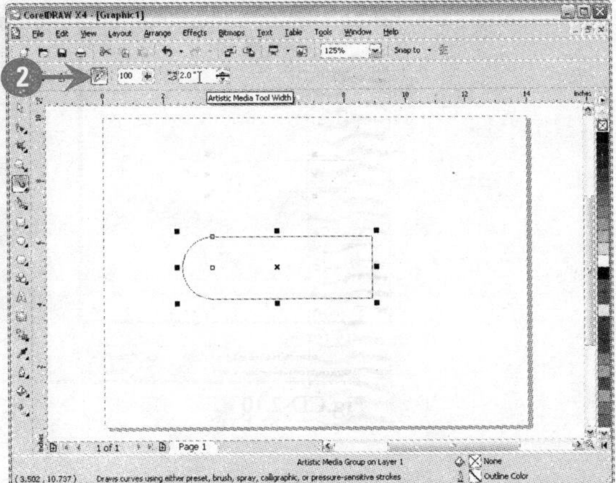

Fig.CD-2.12

Note

Pressure-sensitive line can be access by clicking Effects->Artistic Media.

Drawing Preset Line

CorelDRAW offers a broad range of Preset line patterns. You can select a pattern from a drop down list of the available design patterns in the CorelDRAW window. These Preset lines allow you to create the thick line strokes.

Undertake the following steps to draw a Preset line:

1. *Open* **Curve** tools flyout from the Toolbox and *click* the **Artistic Media** tool from the flyout (Fig.CD-2.13).

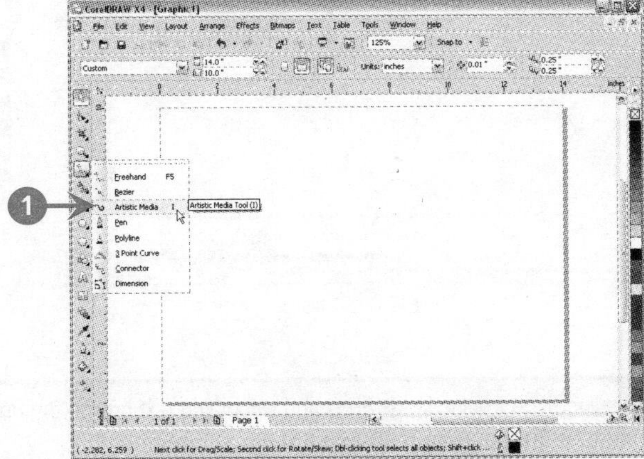

Fig.CD-2.13

2. On the Property bar, *click* the **Preset** button (), as shown in Fig.CD-2.14.
3. *Select* a **Preset** line shape from the Preset stroke drop down list (Fig.CD-2.14).

Fig.CD-2.14

4. *Draw* the stroke on the Drawing page selected in the Step 3, as shown in Fig.CD-2.15.

A Preset line appears on the Drawing page, as shown in Fig.CD-2.15.

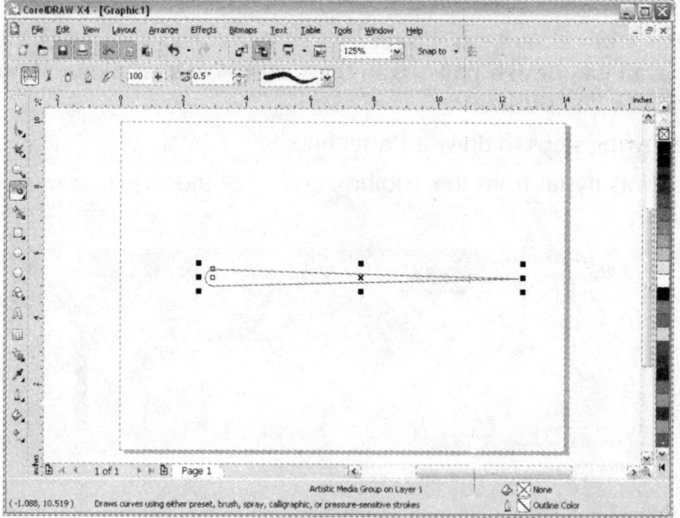

Fig.CD-2.15

Note

To smooth the edges of a Preset line, type a value in the Freehand smoothing text box on the Property bar. You can also increase width by typing a value in the Artistic Media Tool Width text box.

After drawing Preset line, let us now learn how to change the appearances of lines and outlines in the following section.

About Outline Tool

Using the Outline tool in CorelDRAW, you can change the color and thickness of outlines surrounding any object. For changing thickness of line, open the flyout menu of Outline tool and choose the desired thickness. If you wish to change the color of outline then right click the desired color swatch in the Color palette appearing on the right side of the Drawing page. If you want to explore and use advance options related to outline thickness and color then you have to opt for Outline Pen and Outline Color tools.

- **Outline Pen**: The Outline Pen tool lets you work with the outline of an object as well as lines. Besides changing the thickness of objects and lines, you can use the Outline Pen tool to change the shape of the object in different ways. Besides changing outline color, you can use the Outline Color tool to create your own custom colors, add them to color palette and apply them on outlines of objects as well as to lines.

Defining Lines and Outlines Settings

An outline marks the outer boundaries of an object. CorelDRAW lets you perform the various settings regarding the outlines. Using the Outline Pen dialog box you can change the appearance of the outlines, you can change the color, width, and, style of the outlines. You can also set Miter limits for the lines and outlines.

Undertake the following steps to define lines and outlines settings:

1. *Select* an object using **Pick** tool (![]) on the Drawing page, as shown in Fig.CD-2.16.
2. *Open* the **Outline** tools flyout in the Toolbox and *click* the **Outline Pen** tool (Fig.CD-2.16). An **Outline Pen** dialog box appears, as shown in Fig.CD-2.17.

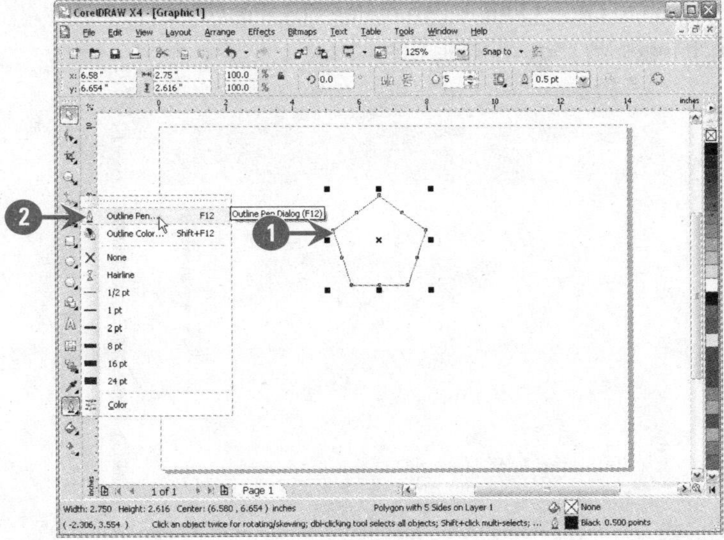

Fig.CD-2.16

3. *Click* the **Color** drop down list in the **Outline Pen** dialog box and *select* a color for the outline (Fig.CD-2.17).

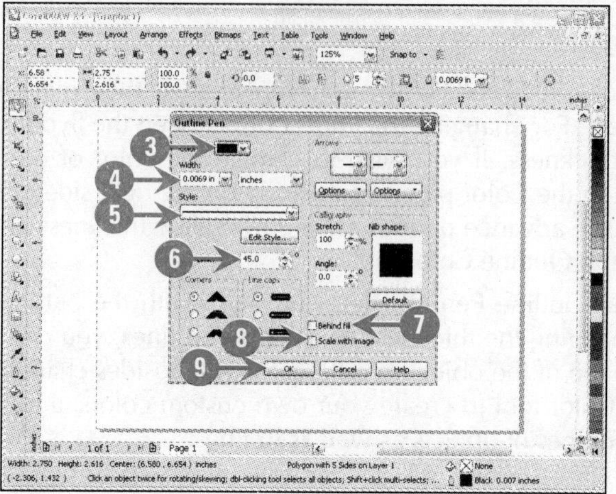

Fig.CD-2.17

4. *Type* a value in the **Width** text box to adjust the thickness and unit of the outline (Fig.CD-2.17). In our case, the value is 0.0069 units.
5. To change the outline style, *click* the **Style** option in the **Outline Pen** dialog box and *select* an outline style from the style drop down list (Fig.CD-2.17).
6. *Type* a value in the **Miter Limit** text box to enter the miter limit (Fig.CD-2.17). In our case, the value is 45.0.
7. *Select* **Behind** fill check box to apply an outline behind an object's fills (Fig.CD-2.17).
8. *Select* **Scale** with image check box to link the outline thickness to an object's size (Fig.CD-2.17).
9. *Click* the **OK** button to close Outline Pen dialog box (Fig.CD-2.17).

Outline of object changes, as shown in Fig.CD-2.18.

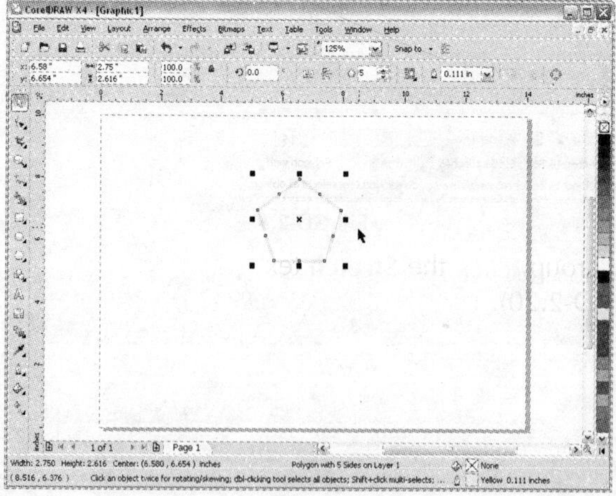

Fig.CD-2.18

Note

> You can access the Outline Pen dialog box by clicking the outline icon on the Status bar. You can also change the outline width of a selected object by typing a value in the Outline width box on the Property bar.
>
> You can also edit the outline style by clicking the Edit Style... button (Edit Style...) and moving the slider.

Creating a Calligraphic Outline

Calligraphic outlines add a hand-made drawing look to the objects. These outlines are similar to the handmade sketch which you draw on the paper and have varied thickness.

Undertake the following steps to create a Calligraphic outline:

1. *Select* an object using **Pick** tool. In our case, we have selected a polygon (Fig.CD-2.19).
2. *Open* the **Outline** tools flyout and *click* the **Outline Pen** tool (Fig.CD-2.19). An **Outline Pen** dialog box appears, as shown in Fig.CD-2.20.

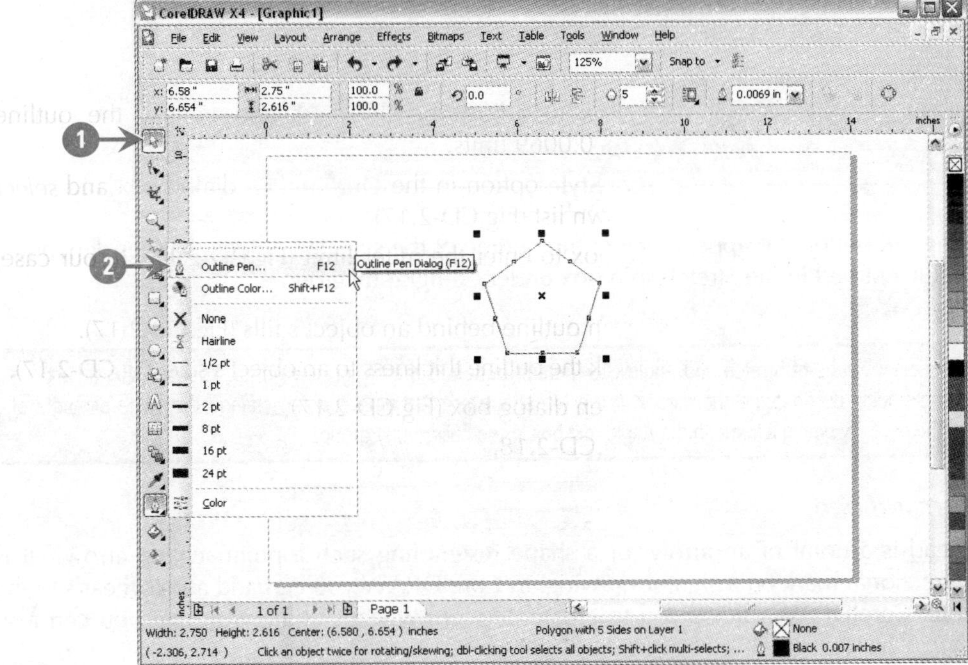

Fig.CD-2.19

3. In the **Calligraphy** group, *click* the **Stretch** text box and *type* a value to change the width of the pen's nib (Fig.CD-2.20).

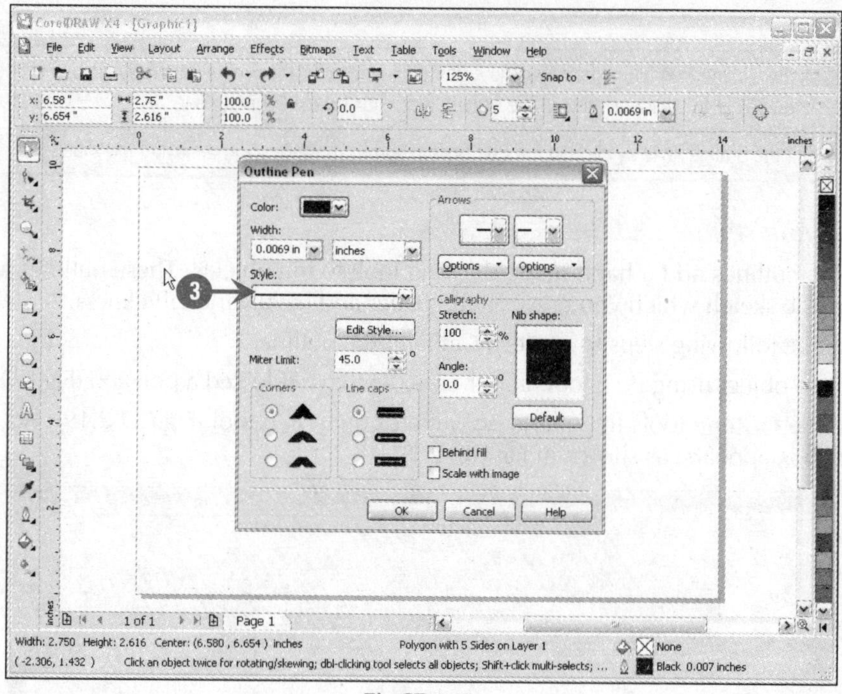

Fig.CD-2.20

After clicking OK button the appearance of the outline of the selected object changes depending upon the value entered in the Stretch spin box under Calligraphy group.

Note

> To reset the original values of Stretch and Angle click Default button in the Calligraphy group. You can also adjust the Stretch and Angle fields by dragging the cursor in the Nib shape preview box. You can change the value of Angle of orientation of the pen, by typing a value in the Angle text box in the Calligraphy group.

Adding an Arrowhead

An Arrowhead is a point of an arrow, or a shape resembling such a point called arrow. It is used as a directional mark on a sign or drawing. In CorelDRAW you can add anrrowheads to the line or curve. CorelDRAW allows you to create new arrowheads along with that you can also edit those arrowheads.

Undertake the following steps to add an Arrowhead:

1. *Select* a line using **Pick** tool (Fig.CD-2.21).
2. *Open* the **Outline** tools flyout and *click* **Outline Pen** tool (Fig.CD-2.21). An **Outline Pen** dialog box appears, as shown in Fig.CD-2.22.

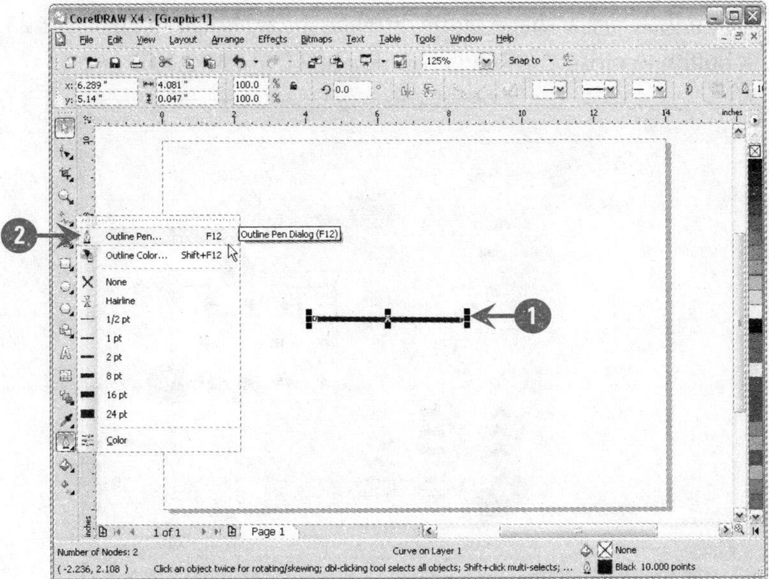

Fig.CD-2.21

3. Under **Arrows** group, *open* the drop down list to define the shape at the starting point of the line (Fig.CD-2.22).
4. In the drop down list, *click* a shape of the arrowhead, as shown in Fig.CD-2.22.

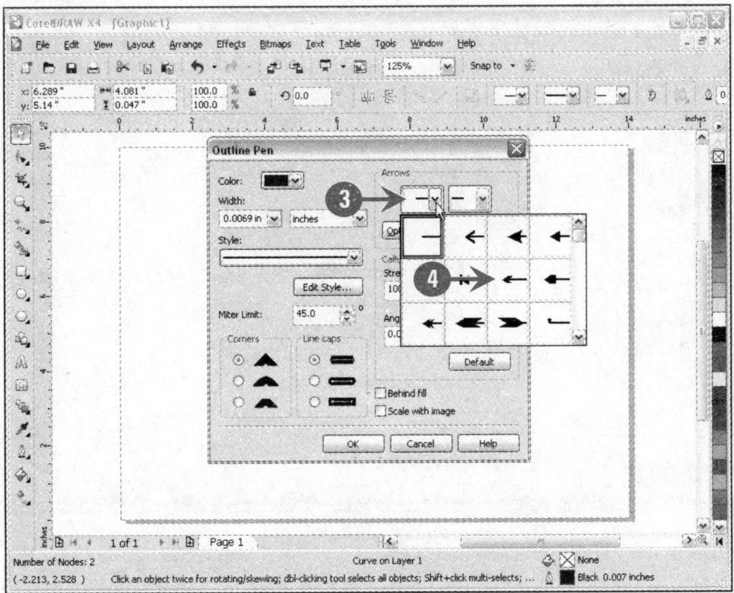

Fig.CD-2.22

5. Under **Arrows** group, *open* the adjacent drop down list to define the shape at the ending point of the line (Fig.CD-2.23).

6. In the drop down list, *click* a shape of the arrowhead, as shown in Fig.CD-2.23.
7. *Click* the **OK** button to close **Outline Pen** dialog box (Fig.CD-2.23).

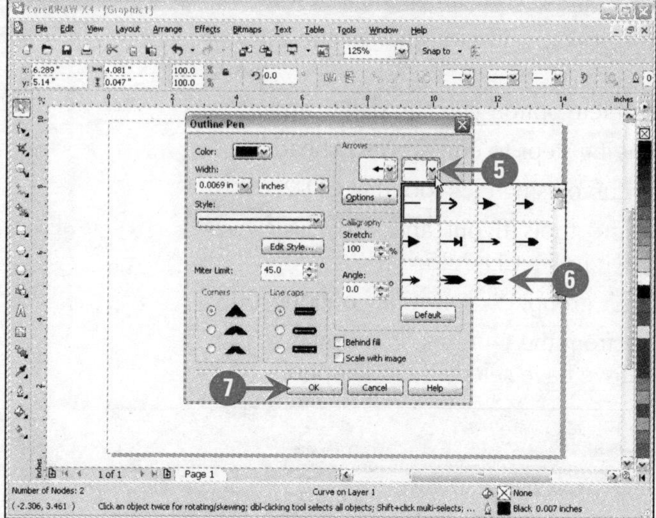

Fig.CD-2.23

The line appears with specified start and end arrowheads, as shown in Fig.CD-2.24.

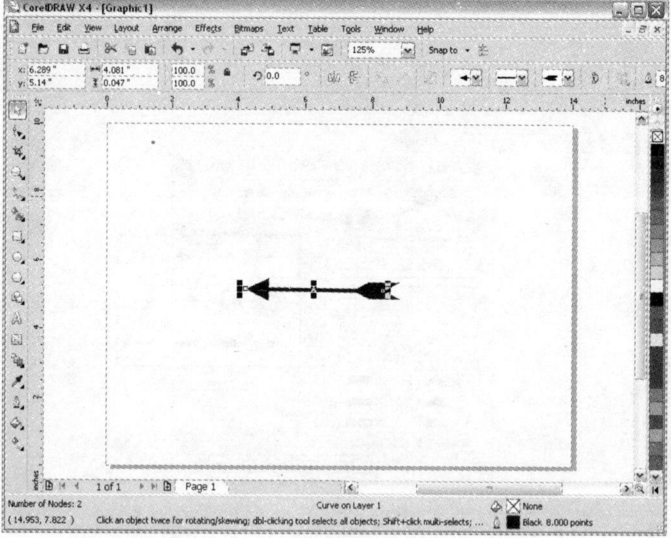

Fig.CD-2.24

Editing an Arrowhead

You can create a new Arrowhead as well as edit its shape by using Options drop down list in the Arrows group. You can also delete and swap an Arrowhead. In CorelDRAW there are four options under the Options button. These are:

- **None**: Using None option you can remove the arrowhead from the line.
- **Swap**: Using Swap option you can swap the head and tail arrow of the line.
- **New**: Using New option you can create a new arrowhead shape.
- **Edit**: Using Edit option you can change the appearance of the applied arrowhead on the line.
- **Delete**: Using Delete option you can delete an applied arrowhead.

Undertake the following steps to edit an Arrowhead:

1. *Select* a line or curve using **Pick** tool (Fig.CD-2.24).
2. *Open* the **Outline** tools flyout and *click* **Outline Pen** tool. An **Outline Pen** dialog box appears, as shown in Fig.CD-2.25.
3. Under the **Arrows** group, *click* **Options** button. A drop down list appears (Fig.CD-2.25).
4. *Select* an option from the **Options** drop down list and select an option to perform the desired task. In our case we have selected **None** option (Fig.CD-2.25).

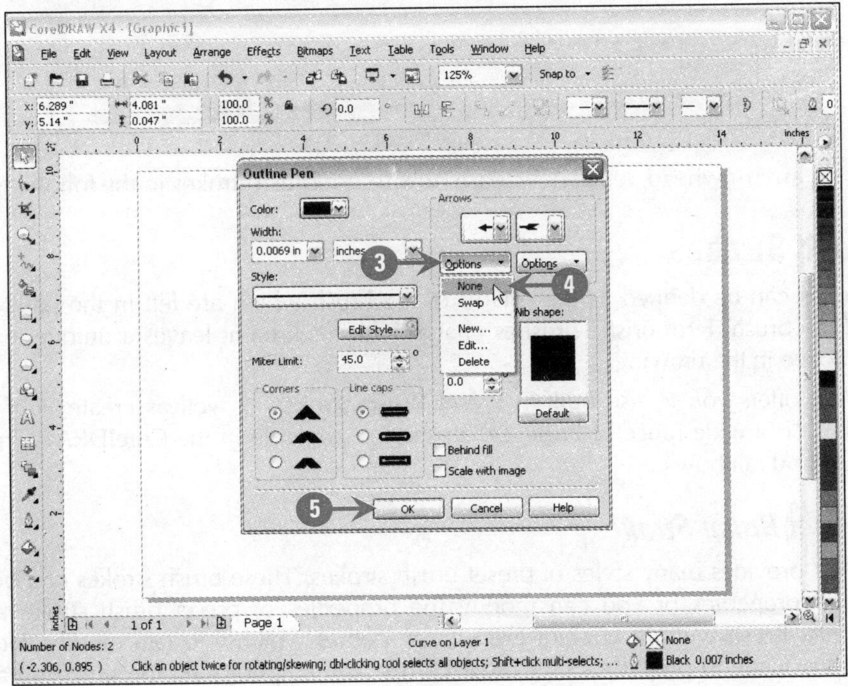

Fig.CD-2.25

5. *Click* **OK** button (Fig.CD-2.25). The Outline Pen dialog box disappears, as shown in Fig.CD-2.26.

As soon as, you *click* the **OK** button, the Arrowhead will be removed from the Drawing page, as shown in Fig.CD-2.26.

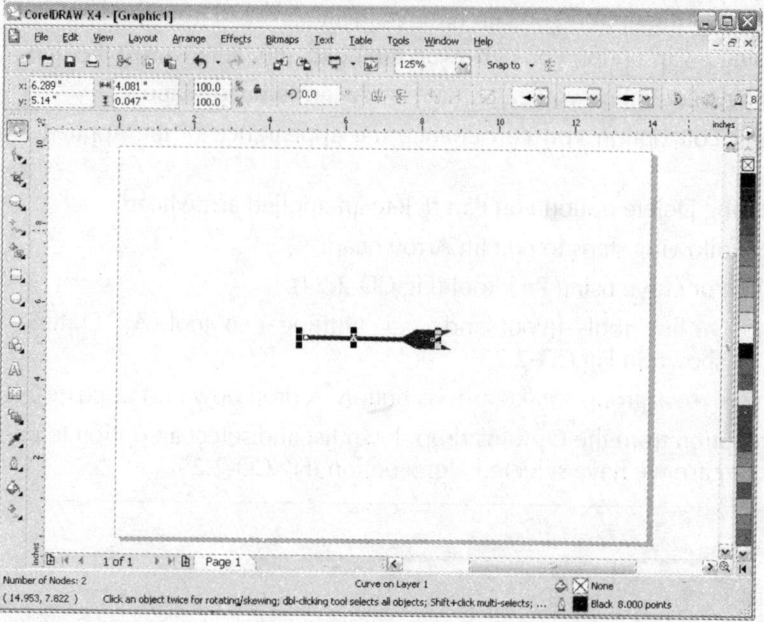

Fig.CD-2.26

After editing an Arrowhead, let us now learn how to use brush strokes in the following section.

Using Brush Strokes

Brush strokes can be defined as the marks of the brush which are left in the paint passage by sliding of the brush. Firm bristle brushes charge with thick paint leaves a unique texture which looks attractive in the drawing.

CorelDRAW offers you to use built-in Preset Brush Strokes as well as create your own Brush Stroke. There is a wide range of Preset brush strokes available in the CorelDRAW including the arrowheads and rainbows.

Using a Preset Brush Stroke

CorelDRAW provides many styles of preset brush strokes. These brush strokes can be used with their default properties or you can modify the properties of preset brush stroke as per your requirements. Brush width and color are two properties which you can modify. However, the modifications made to properties of a Brush Stroke are temporary till the time you are using it. No sooner you switch to another Brush Stroke; all modifications made are restored to their default state. Preset brush strokes are the Pre-build brush strokes which you can use in CorelDRAW.

Undertake the following steps to use the Preset brush strokes:

1. *Open* the **Curve** tools flyout and *select* **Artistic Media** tool (Fig.CD-2.27).
2. *Click* the **Brush** button on the Property bar and *select* a brush stroke from the **Brush Stroke** drop down list (Fig.CD-2.27).

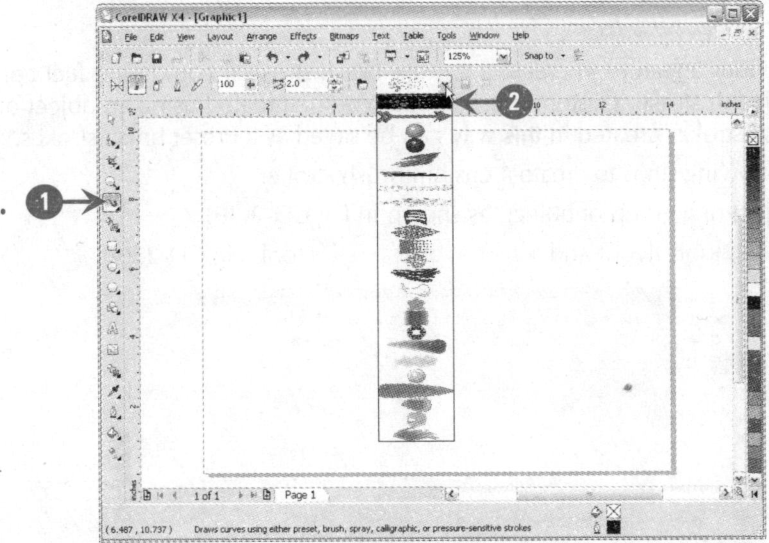

Fig.CD-2.27

3. On the Property bar, *type* a value in the **Freehand Smoothing** text box to smooth the edges of the brush stroke
4. *Drag* the cursor for obtaining the desired shape on the Drawing page (Fig.CD-2.28).

The modified brush stroke now appears on the Drawing page, as shown in the Fig.2.28.

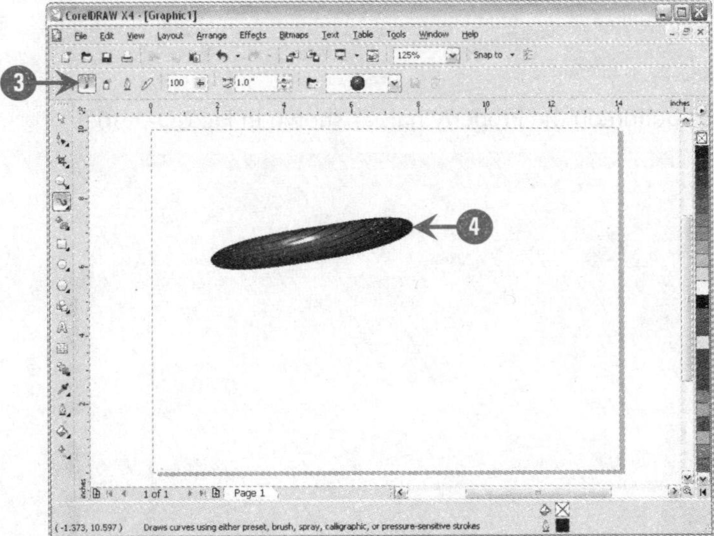

Fig.CD-2.28

Note

You can also change the width of the stroke by typing a value in the Artistic Media Tool Width box on the Property bar and drag the mouse cursor on the Drawing page until you get the desired shape of the stroke.

Creating a Custom Brush Stroke

CorelDRAW provides a feature to create a custom brush stroke if you do not feel comfortable in using the Preset brush stroke. Custom brush strokes can be created using an object or a group of objects. The brush strokes created in this way can be saved as a Preset brush strokes.

Undertake the following steps to create a custom brush stroke:

1. *Select* an object or a group of object, as shown in Fig.CD-2.29.
2. Open the **Curve** tools flyout and select **Artistic Media** tool (Fig.CD-2.29).

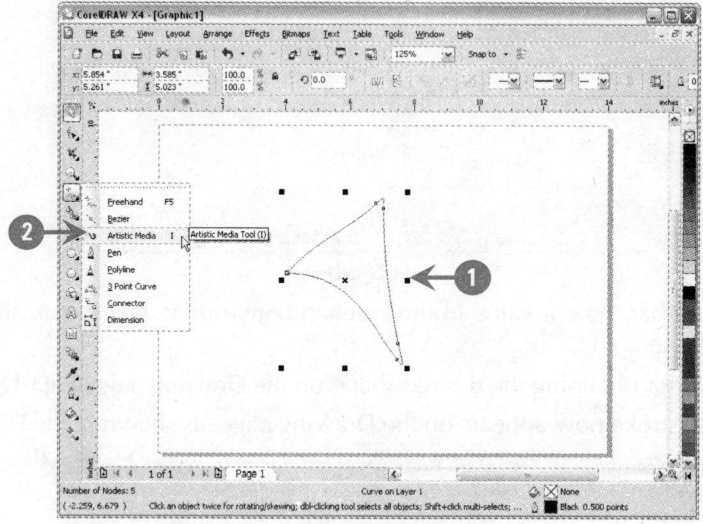

Fig.CD-2.29

3. *Click* the **Brush** button on the Property bar, as shown in Fig.CD-2.30.

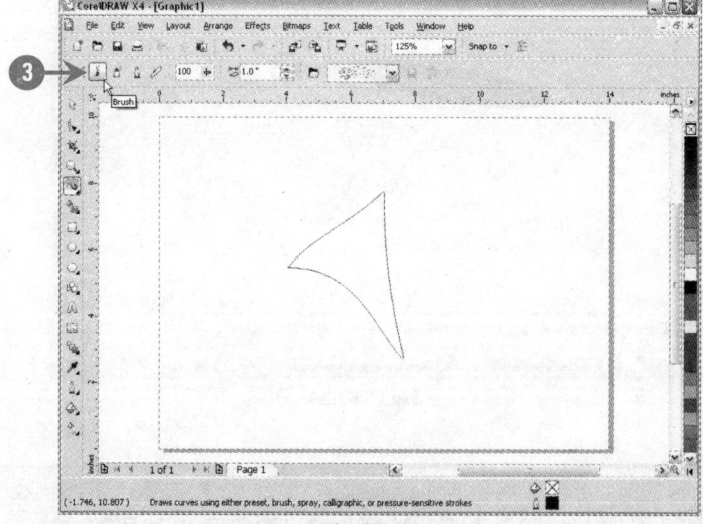

Fig.CD-2.30

4. *Select* the object and *click* the **Save Artistic Media Stroke** button (▣) on the Property bar. A **Save As** dialog box appears, as shown in Fig.CD-2.31.
5. *Type* a **File name** for the brush stroke and *click* **Save** button to close **Save As** dialog box (Fig.CD-2.31).

Note

By default, CorelDRAW saves newly created brush stroke in the CustomMediaStrokes folder.

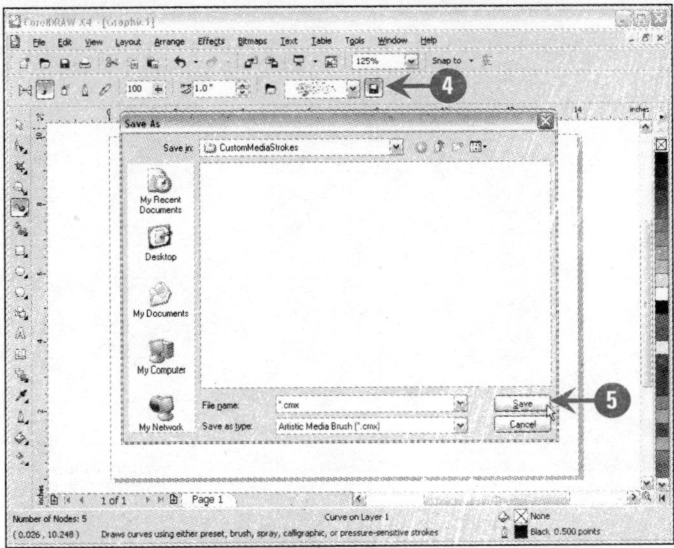

Fig.CD-2.31

With this we come to the end of the chapter. Before proceeding ahead towards the next chapter, let us refresh the learning by summarizing main points.

Summary

In this chapter, you learned about:

- Drawing Lines in CorelDRAW
- Drawing Calligraphic, Pressure-sensitive, and Preset lines
- Drawing outlines using Outline Tool
- Using Brush Strokes

In the next chapter, you will learn how to work with shapes and how to apply different types of alterations in the shapes.

Chapter 3

Working with Objects

In this Section

- Selecting and Deselecting Objects
- Selecting Objects
- Copying, Duplicating, and Deleting Objects
- Selecting Color for an Object
- Boundaries in CorelDRAW
- Copying Object Properties, Transformations and Effects
- Positioning Objects
- Aligning and Distributing Objects
- Sizing and Scaling Objects
- Rotating and Mirroring Objects
- Order of Objects
- Combining and Breaking Objects
- Grouping in CorelDRAW

An object is a physical body with unique characteristics, such as shape and size, which help to define it. An object can also be defined as a thing or entity, which you can detect with your sense organs. An object can be determined by its external boundary and other aspects the object may have, such as its color, content (for example, text), or substance (whether it is a solid or liquid) which the object is composed of, its size, and from the object's position and orientation in space.

In this chapter, you learn how to perform various tasks on objects in CorelDRAW, such as selecting or deselecting objects to perform certain actions on them; editing objects, which includes cutting or removing an object from its original location, copying the properties of the object, and pasting the object to a new location. In addition, the chapter tells you how to select the color for objects, create a boundary of an object, and apply effects such as sizing, scaling, rotating and mirroring of objects. Finally, you learn how to position, align, and order objects so that they are properly placed in a document.

We begin with selecting and deselecting objects.

Selecting and Deselecting Objects

In CorelDRAW, you can perform various actions on objects by selecting them. For example, you can add the fill color to a selected object. After you have performed the desired actions on the selected object, you can deselect it. Therefore, selecting and deselecting objects play an important role whenever you want to make any changes in the objects. In this section, you learn more about this fundamental but central feature of CorelDraw.

Selecting Objects

In CorelDRAW, we use the Pick tool to select or deselect an object. To perform any modification in an object, you need to first select the object. You can select a single or multiple objects.

Undertake the following steps to select an object:

1. *Open* the CorelDRAW X4 window with a new blank document.
2. *Select* the **Polygon** tool and draw a polygon on the Drawing page, as shown in Fig.CD-3.1.
3. *Select* the **Pick** tool (⬚) (Fig.CD-3.1).
4. *Select* the polygon from the Drawing page by *clicking* it (Fig.CD-3.1).

Small black squares appear around the polygon. These squares are known as selection handles, and indicate that the object is selected (Fig.CD-3.1).

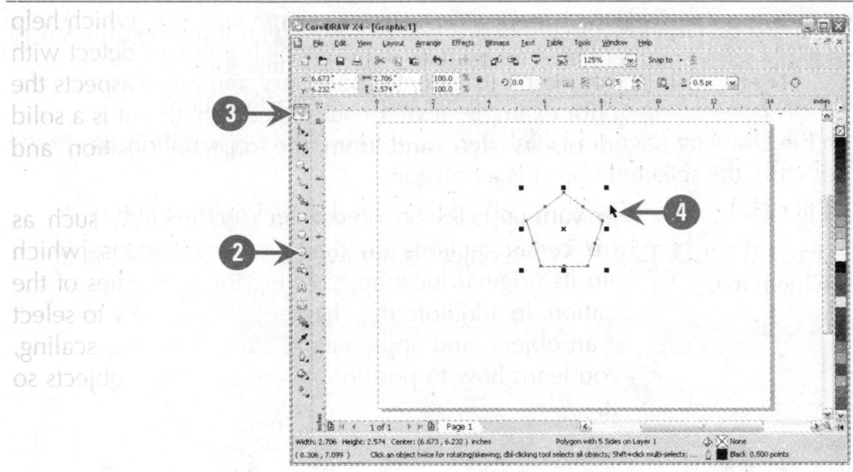

Fig.CD-3.1

Note

You can also use the marquee selecting method to select an object on the Drawing page. For this, first select the Pick tool and then drag around the object, which you want to select, on the Drawing page. To select multiple objects, hold down the SHIFT key on the keyboard and click each object you want to select or alternatively, select Edit→Select All→Objects.

To deselect objects, click a blank area on the Drawing page. If you want to deselect a single object from a group, hold down the SHIFT key on the keyboard and *click* the object by using the Pick tool.

Next, let's learn how to copy, duplicate, and delete objects in CorelDRAW.

Copying, Duplicating, and Deleting Objects

CorelDRAW allows you to perform various editing tasks, including copying an object, creating a duplicate of the object, and deleting the object. You can easily perform these tasks with the help of various edit options located in the CorelDRAW window. When an object is cut or copied, it is moved to the clipboard. The object is retrieved from the clipboard when you paste it on the desired location on the Drawing page.

Note

The clipboard is a software program that allows cut or copied data to be temporarily stored and retrieved later by the application in which we are working.

In the following sections, you learn about the **Copy**, **Cut**, **Paste**, **Duplicate** and **Delete** options related to objects in CorelDraw.

Copying, Cutting and Pasting an Object

CorelDRAW offers you the basic **Copy**, **Cut**, and **Paste** options to edit objects. While copying an object, the source object is kept intact at its original location and a copy of the object is created, but if you are performing the cutting operation, the source object is removed from its original location. When you use these commands, the clipboard comes into effect. It temporarily stores the objects that you are copying or cutting until the completion of the operation.

Undertake the following steps to edit an object by using the Copy and Paste options:

1. *Select* the object on the Drawing page on which you want to use the Copy option, as shown in Fig.CD-3.2. In our case, the selected object is a polygon.
2. *Select* **Edit→Copy** (Fig.CD-3.2). These actions copy the selected object on the clipboard.
3. Again, *select* **Edit→Paste** (Fig.CD-3.2). Now the object is retrieved from the clipboard and it appears on the Drawing page.

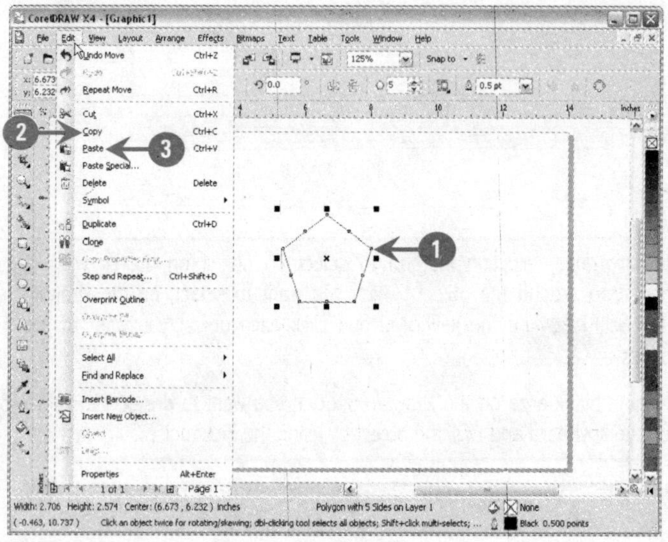

Fig.CD-3.2

Note

> You can also perform the cut, copy and paste operations by clicking the Cut (), Copy (), and Paste () buttons, respectively on the Toolbar located on the left side of the CorelDRAW X4 window.

Duplicating an Object

Duplication is very important when working with complex object forms, where you need to have multiple copies of the same object, and you do not want to reflect any changes in the original object. Instead of creating a new object from scratch, you can create its duplicate. Duplication, unlike copying, where the copied object is first placed on the clipboard and then pasted on the Drawing page, does not use the clipboard but places a copy of the object directly on the Drawing page. Duplicating is much faster than copying.

Undertake the following steps to duplicate an object:

1. *Select* the object you want to duplicate by using the **Pick** tool (), as shown in Fig.CD-3.3.
2. *Select* **Edit→Duplicate** (Fig.CD-3.3).

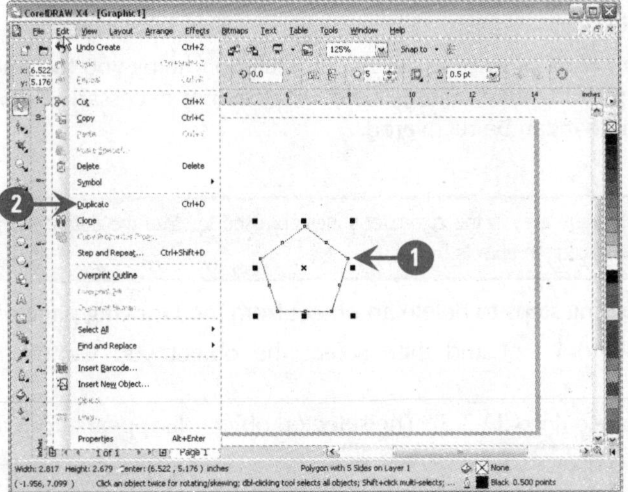

Fig.CD-3.3

A duplicate of the object appears on the Drawing page, as shown in Fig.CD-3.4.

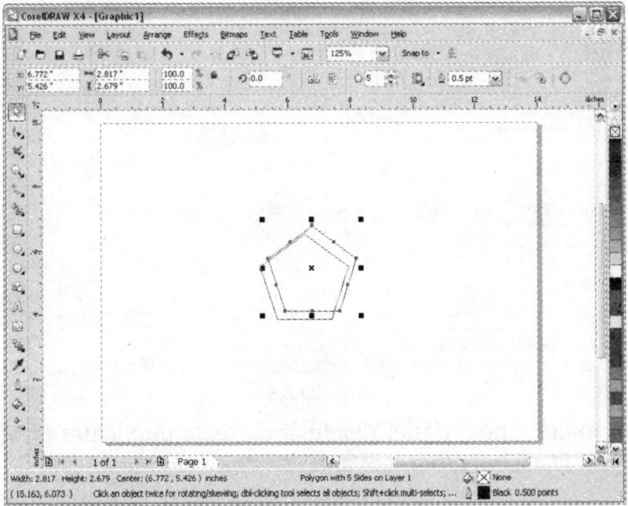

Fig.CD-3.4

Note

If you are duplicating an object for the first time, a Duplicate Offset dialog box appears on your screen. Type a value in the Horizontal Offset and Vertical Offset boxes in this dialog box to specify the distance between the duplicate and original objects along the X and Y axes.

* To place the duplicate object on top of the original object, type the offset value 0.

* To place the duplicate object up and to the right of the original object, type any positive offset value.

* To place the duplicate object down and to the left of the original object, type any negative offset value.

Deleting an Object

Deleting means removing or erasing an object. Deletion helps you to remove unwanted objects from the Drawing page. Unlike cutting, deletion does not necessarily leave the removed object in a buffer from where it can be recovered.

Note

> Buffer is a temporary storage area in the computer's memory used to store the output or input data, where data can mean anything from text to code to objects.

Undertake the following steps to delete an object from the Drawing page of CorelDRAW:

1. *Select* the **Pick** tool ( ) and then select the object you want to delete, as shown in Fig.CD-3.5.
2. *Select* **Edit→Delete** (Fig.CD-3.5). The selected object disappears from the Drawing page.

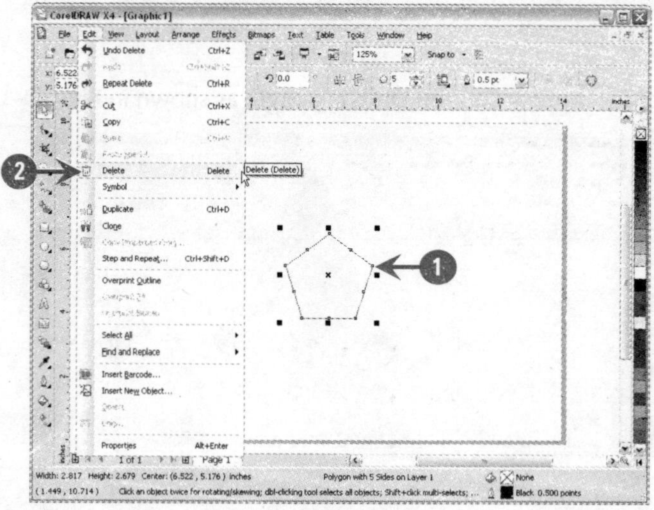

Fig.CD-3.5

You now know how to cut, copy, paste, delete and create duplicates of objects in CorelDRAW. In the next section, you learn how to select and use colors in an object.

Selecting Color for an Object

Colors are an integral part of any drawing. They add charm and luster to a drawing besides making it attractive and pleasing to the eye. CorelDRAW provides you a feature that you can use to fill color in an object. Filling colors in objects is really quite easy. All you have to do is select a color for the object from the Color palette with the help of the Pick tool and the color is applied on the selected object. CorelDRAW offers you many options to fill color in your object. For example, you can select the fill and outline colors by using fixed or custom color palettes, color harmonies, color blends, or the color viewer. The Color palette offers a selection of a wide range of colors from which you can select your choice.

Let's now learn how to select a color from the default Color palette.

Selecting a Color Using the Default Color Palette

CorelDRAW offers color palettes, also known as swatch palettes, to select colors for different objects in your drawing. A Color palette is a collection of color swatches. The default Color palette contains 99 colors from the CMYK color model. CMYK represents the Cyan, Magenta, Yellow, and Black colors.

Undertake the following steps to select a color from the default Color palette:

1. *Select* an object that you want to fill with color by using the **Pick** tool, as shown in Fig.CD-3.6.
2. *Select* a color swatch from the default Color palette as a fill color for the selected object. In our case, we have selected the red color from the default Color palette (Fig.CD-3.6).

The object is filled with the selected color (Fig.CD-3.6).

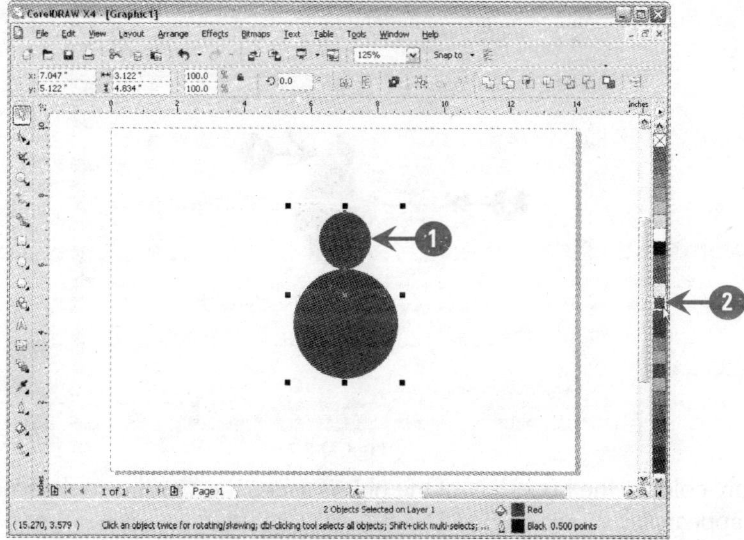

Fig.CD-3.6

Note

> To select an outline color for an object, right-click a color swatch on the default Color palette and select the desired outline color from the Color palette. The outline color will be applied to the object.

Now that you know how to select a color from the default Color palette, we move on to the next topic, where we learn to create a boundary around an object.

Boundaries in CorelDRAW

In CorelDraw, every object has a boundary, which describes the area occupied by the object on the Drawing page. Boundary can be stated as a closed path around a selected object. A boundary defines the extent and layout of the object. In CorelDRAW, you can use different colors for the boundary of an object.

Creating a Boundary around an Object

In CorelDRAW, you can create a boundary around one or more objects by selecting them. We often use the Create Boundary option so that a number of objects can have a single common boundary. Creating a boundary around multiple objects removes any intersecting portions of the boundary. In this way, you can change the color and size of all the objects in the boundary in one go.

Undertake the following steps to create a boundary around an object and apply color to the boundary:

1. *Select* the object that you want to surround with a boundary, as shown in Fig.CD-3.7.
2. *Select* **Effects→Create Boundary** (Fig.CD-3.7). A boundary appears around the object depending on the shape of object, as shown in Fig.CD-3.8.

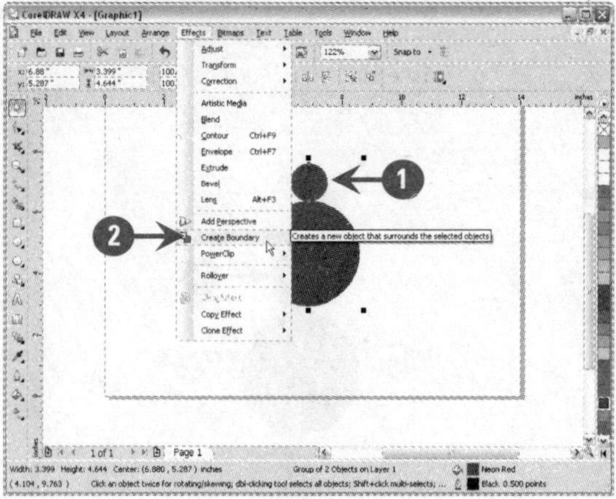

Fig.CD-3.7

3. To apply color to the boundary of the object, *open* the **Outline** tools flyout in the Toolbox. A flyout appears, as shown in Fig.CD-3.8.

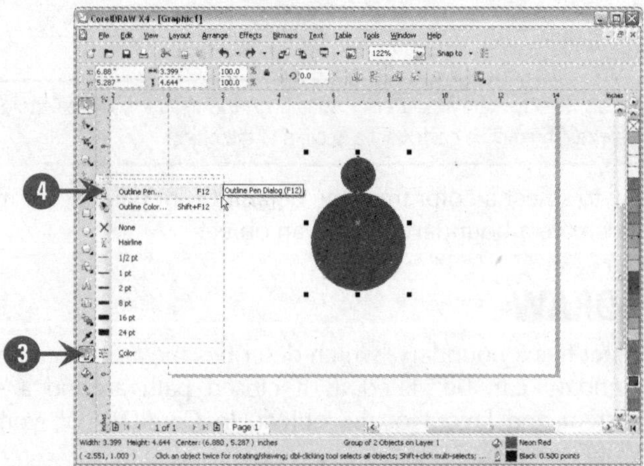

Fig.CD-3.8

4. *Select* **Outline Pen** from the **Outline tool** flyout. An **Outline Pen** dialog box appears, as shown in Fig.CD-3.9.
5. *Click* the down arrow button beside the **Color** option and select a color from the Color palette for the boundary (Fig.CD-3.9).

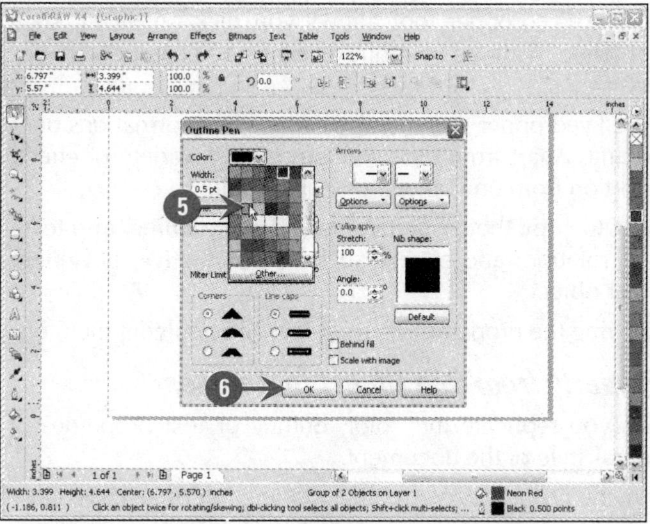

Fig.CD-3.9

6. After *selecting* the color, *click* the **OK** button to close the **Outline Pen** dialog box (Fig.CD-3.9).

The boundary color of the object changes according to the selected color, as shown in Fig.CD-3.10.

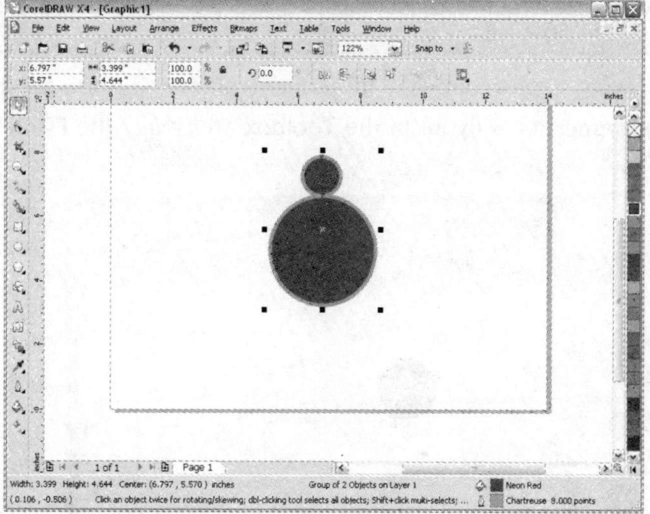

Fig.CD-3.10

After creating a boundary around an object, let's learn how we can copy the properties, transformations, and effects from one object to another object.

Copying Object Properties, Transformations and Effects

Every object has some individual properties and attributes. CorelDRAW provides you with a feature to copy the attributes and effects from one object to another. For example, you can copy an object's properties such as fill, outline and text. This is done by using the Eyedropper and Paintbucket tools. The Eyedropper tool allows you pick an effect, such as color, pattern, or texture of an object. Then, with the Paintbucket tool, you can apply that color, pattern, or texture to a different object.

You can also use the Eyedropper tool to copy various transformations of objects such as rotating, positioning, and sizing. Apart from this, you can copy a variety of effects, such as Perspective, Envelope, and Distortion from one object to another object.

Here, you learn how to copy the properties (such as fill, outline, and text), transformations (such as size, position, or rotation) and effects (such as **Perspective**, **Envelope**, and **Distortion**) from one object to another object.

Let's begin with copying the properties of an object and applying them on another object.

Copying the Fill Property from One Object to Another

CorelDRAW allows you replicate the color, outline or text properties of objects, so that they blend with the general style of the document.

Before we can copy the properties of an object to another object, we have to create two objects. We therefore create a polygon and a star and then fill colors in these objects, as shown in Fig.CD-3.11.

Note

> To draw and color a polygon and star, refer to the "Selecting Objects" and "Selecting a Color Using Default Color Palette" sections, respectively of this chapter.

Undertake the following steps to copy the fill property of one object to another:

1. *Open* the **Eyedropper** tools flyout in the Toolbox and *select* the **Eyedropper** tool, as shown in Fig.CD-3.11.

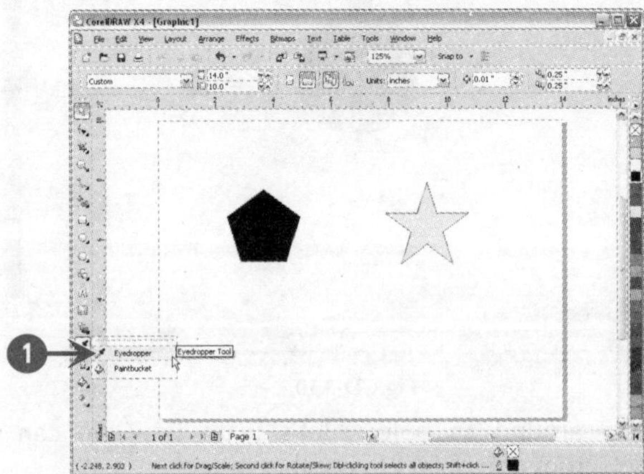

Fig.CD-3.11

2. *Select* the **Object Attributes** option from the drop down list on the Property bar, as shown in Fig.CD-3.12.

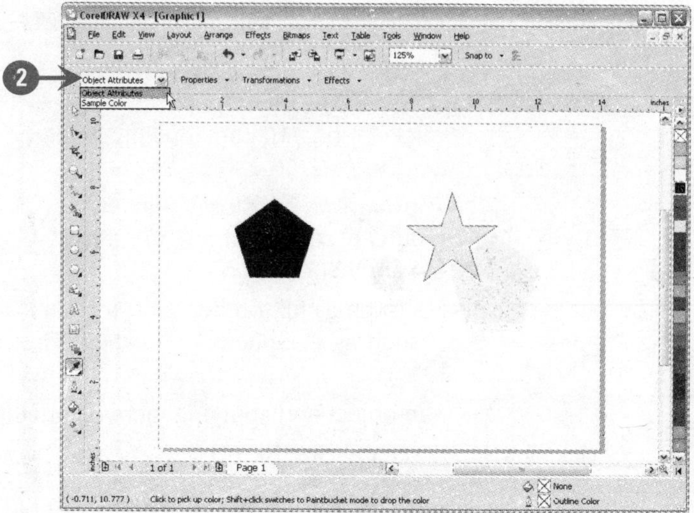

Fig.CD-3.12

3. *Click* the **Properties** button on the Property bar and *select* any of the check boxes beside the **Outline**, **Fill**, and **Text** options from the drop down list (Fig.CD-3.13). In our case, we have selected the **Fill** check box.
4. *Click* the **OK** button, as shown in Fig.CD-3.13.

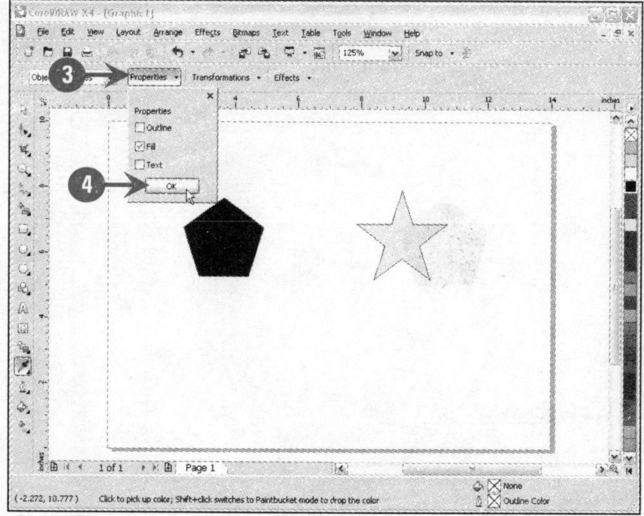

Fig.CD-3.13

Note

You can also copy the Outline or Text properties from one object to another or copy all the properties simultaneously.

5. *Click* the object (in our case the object is polygon) whose fill property you want to copy by using the **Eyedropper** tool. The fill color of the polygon is copied, as shown in Fig.CD-3.14.

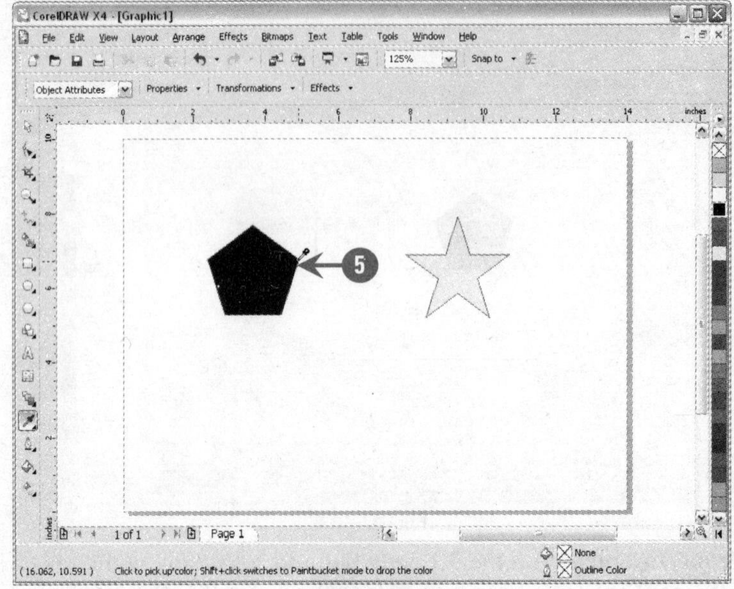

Fig.CD-3.14

6. *Open* the **Eyedropper** tools flyout and *select* the **Paintbucket** tool, as shown in Fig.CD-3.15.

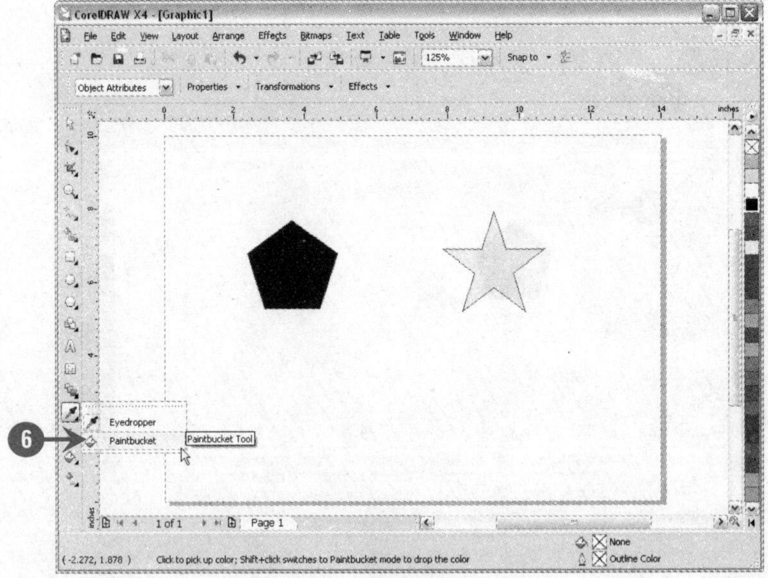

Fig.CD-3.15

7. Now, *click* the object on which you want to apply the copied fill property. The fill property of the object changes from yellow to purple, as shown in Fig.CD-3.16.

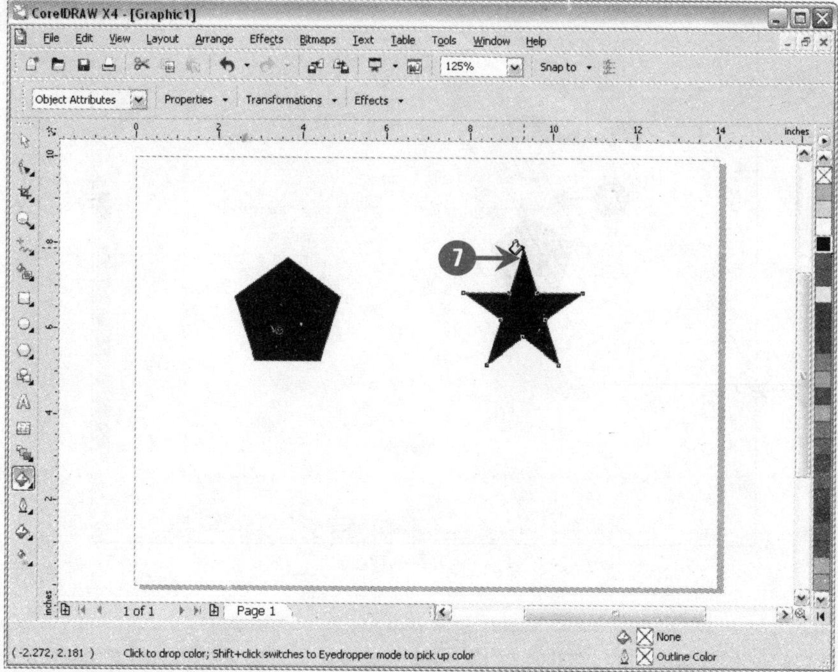

Fig.CD-3.16

Note

> Alternatively, you can right-click the mouse button on the object whose properties you want to copy and drag over to the object, on which you want to copy the properties. A shortcut menu appears. From the shortcut menu, select the Copy fill here, Copy outline here, or Copy all properties option to copy the fill, outline, or text properties.

Copying the Size of one Object to Another

With the help of CorelDRAW, you can copy the physical attributes of an object and apply them to another object. By using the Transformations button on the Property bar, you can modify the size of an object with respect to another object. You can also copy the position as well as rotation properties of the object and later apply these properties to another object.

Undertake the following steps to copy the size of one object to another:

1. *Open* the **Eyedropper** tools flyout in the Toolbox and *select* the **Eyedropper** tool to copy the size of an object, as shown in Fig.CD-3.17.
2. *Select* the Object Attributes option from the drop down list on the Property bar (Fig.CD-3.17).
3. *Click* the **Transformations** button on the Property bar and *select* any of the check boxes beside the **Size**, **Rotations**, and **Position** options (Fig.CD-3.17). In our case, we have selected the **Size** check box.
4. *Click* the **OK** button (Fig.CD-3.17).

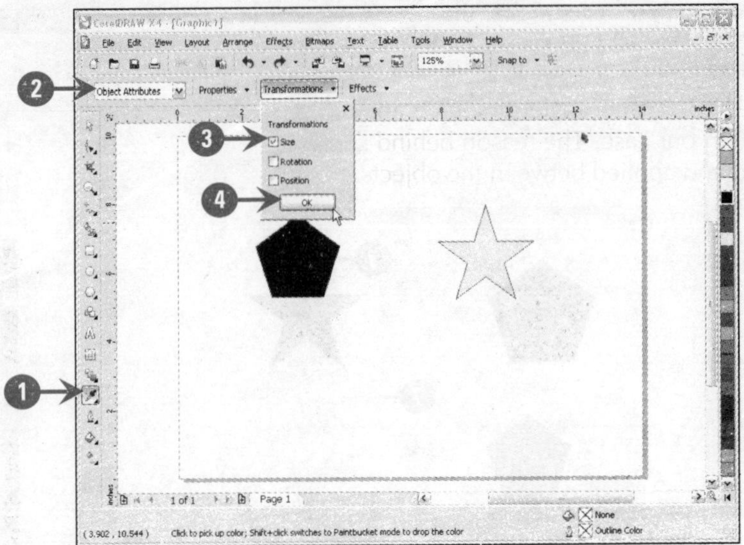

Fig.CD-3.17

Note

In the same way, you can select the Rotation or Position check box to copy the rotation or position of an object to another object. You can also copy all the three transformations simultaneously.

5. *Click* the object whose size you want to copy by using the **Eyedropper** tool. The size of the selected object is copied, as shown in Fig.CD-3.18.

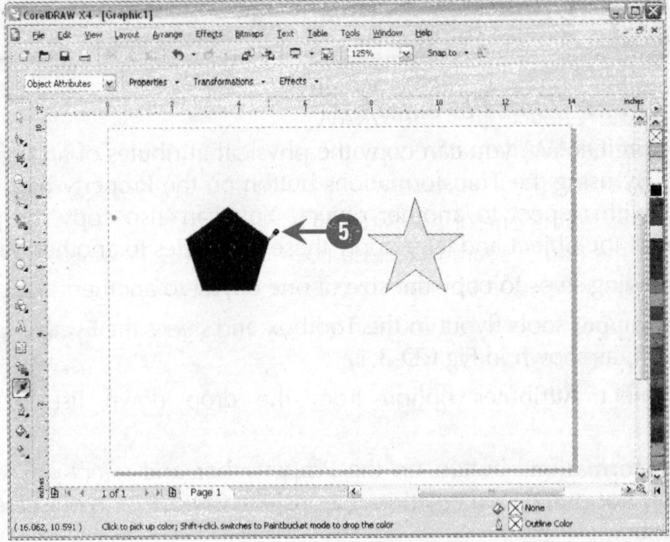

Fig.CD-3.18

6. *Open* the **Eyedropper** tool flyout and *select* the **Paintbucket** tool, as shown in Fig.CD-3.19.

7. *Click* the object to which you want to apply the copied size property. The size of the object changes, as shown in Fig.3.19.

Depending upon the size and angle of source and destination objects, the size could increase randomly, just like in our case. The reason behind random increment in size is angles as well as dimensions copied and applied between the objects.

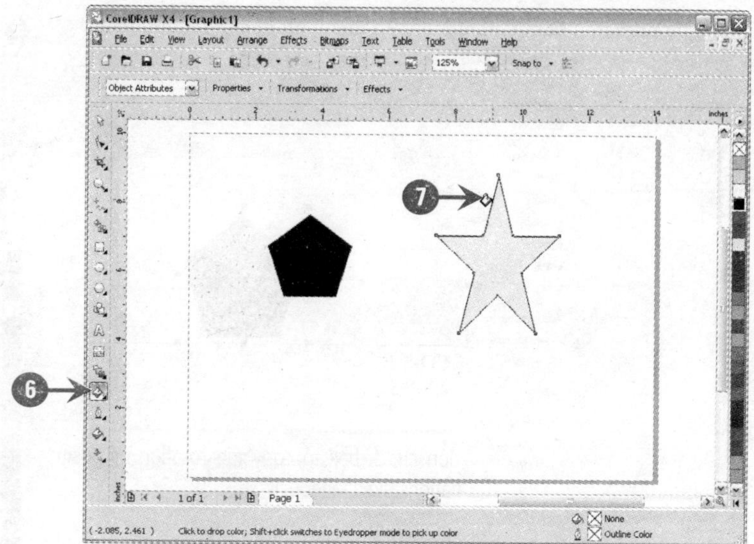

Fig.CD-3.19

Copying Effects from One Object to Another

An effect is an outward appearance of an object. Sometimes you want to copy the various effects of one object to another object. CorelDRAW allows you perform this action by providing the option for copying the effects. In CorelDRAW, you can find various effects tools in the Interactive tools flyout menu. Alternatively, you can click the Effects button on the Property bar. Some commonly used effects are:

- **Perspective:** By shortening one or two sides of an object, you can create a perspective effect. This effect makes the object seem to recede in one or two directions, thereby creating a one-point perspective or a two-point perspective.
- **Envelope:** By applying envelopes, you can change the shape of objects. You can shape the envelopes by moving the nodes present in the envelopes; moving the nodes results in the change in the shape of the object.
- **Drop Shadow:** This effect simulates light falling on an object from one of five perspectives: right, left, bottom, top, and flat.
- **Distortion:** This effect allows you to twist a regular shape of an object into a new shape.

Undertaking the following steps to copy these effects in CorelDRAW:

1. *Suppose* we want to add the Perspective effect on an object, a polygon in our case. To do so, *select* the object first, as shown in Fig.CD-3.20.

Note

To copy an effect from an object, you need to first add that effect to an object in case that effect is not already applied in that object. We therefore add the Perspective effect in the Step 1 before copying the effect to another object.

2. *Select* **Effects→Add Perspective** (Fig.CD-3.20).

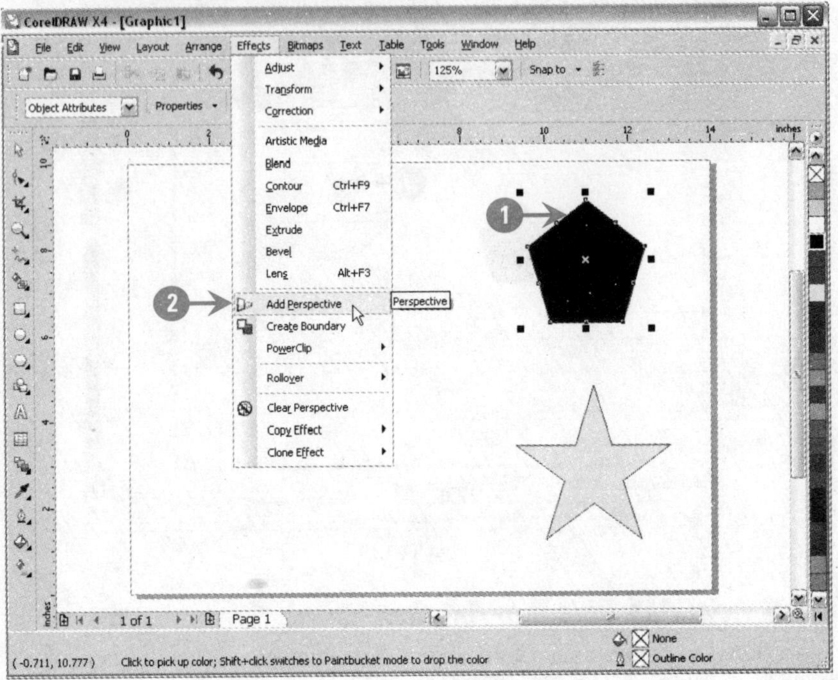

Fig.CD-3.20

3. *Drag* the corner handles of the object to change the perspective (or view) of the object, as shown in Fig.CD-3.21.
4. *Open* the **Eyedropper** tools flyout in the Toolbox and *select* the **Eyedropper** tool (Fig.CD-3.21).
5. *Select* the Object Attributes option from the drop down list on the Property bar (Fig.CD-3.21).
6. *Click* the **Transformations** button on the Property bar and *select* the check box beside the **Perspective** option from the drop down list (Fig.CD-3.21).
7. Then, *click* the **OK** button (Fig.CD-3.21).
8. Now, *click* the object whose effect you want to copy by using the **Eyedropper** tool. In our case, we have selected the Perspective effect from the polygon (Fig.CD-3.21).

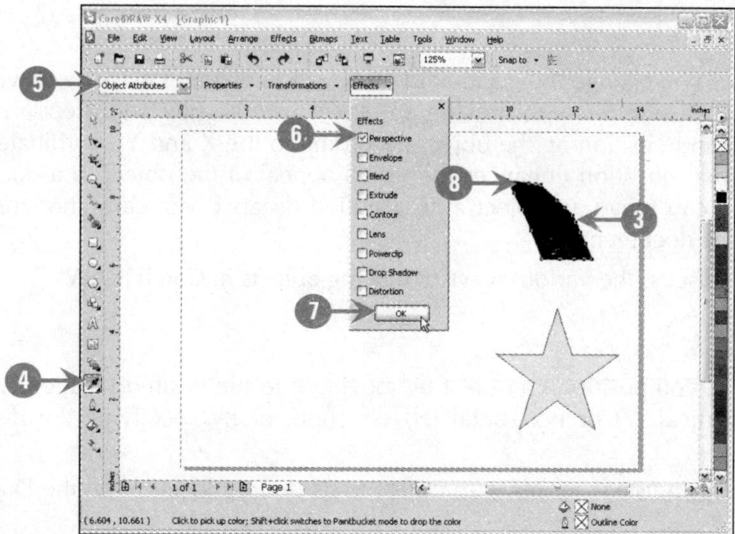

Fig.CD-3.21

Note

You can also select more than one effect simultaneously from the Effects button on the Property bar.

9. *Open* the **Eyedropper** tools flyout and *select* the **Paintbucket** tool (Fig.CD-3.22).
10. *Click* the object to which you want to apply the Perspective effect (a star in our case).The appearance of the star changes, as shown in Fig.CD-3.22.

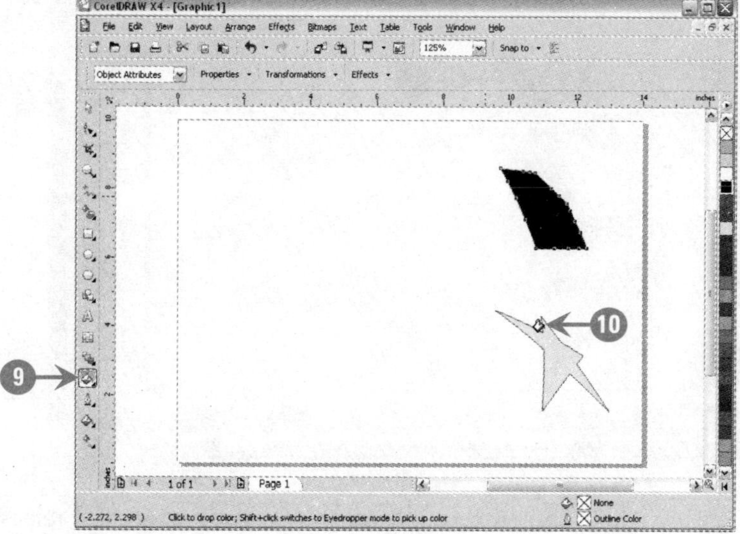

Fig.CD-3.22

Now that you know how to copy the effects of one object to another object, let's now learn how to position objects in CorelDRAW.

Positioning Objects

CorelDRAW allows you change the position of an object in different ways by moving the object, nudging the object (which refers to moving an object very slightly and precisely according to your requirement) and positioning the object according to the X and Y coordinates. Positioning the object at a proper location enhances the visual appeal of the object in a document. Using these options, you can move an object at a specified distance vertically, horizontally, or to a specific point on the document.

In this section, we discuss the various ways of moving objects in CorelDRAW.

Moving an Object

CorelDRAW allows you position an object by moving it to the desired location. You can move the object in a vertical (**V**) or horizontal (**H**) direction, or by specifying the distance on the Drawing page.

Undertake the following steps to move an object to its desired location on the Drawing page of CorelDRAW:

1. *Select* the object whose position you want to change, with the help of the **Pick** tool, as shown in Fig.CD-3.23.
2. *Keeping* the mouse button pressed, *drag* the object from its center point. Observe that the shape of mouse-pointer changes to a position cursor (Fig.CD-3.23).

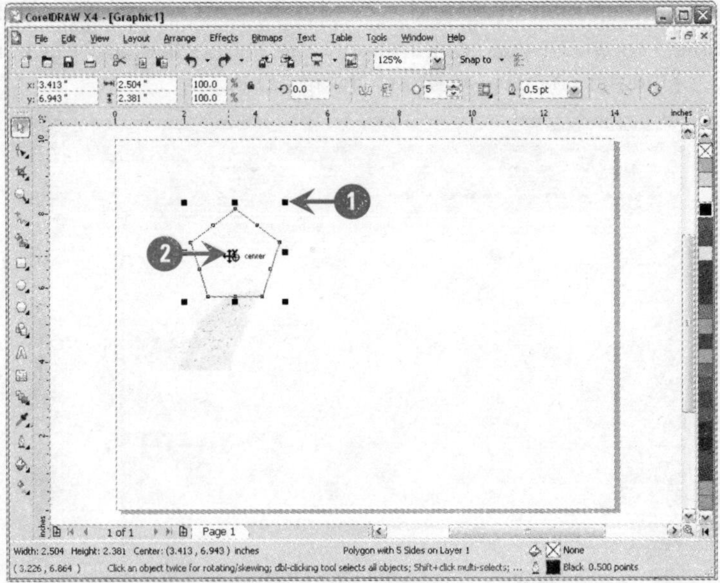

Fig.CD-3.23

3. Position the object at the desired location on the Drawing page and release the mouse-button, as shown in Fig.CD-3.24.

The object is now placed at a new position on the Drawing page (Fig.CD-3.24).

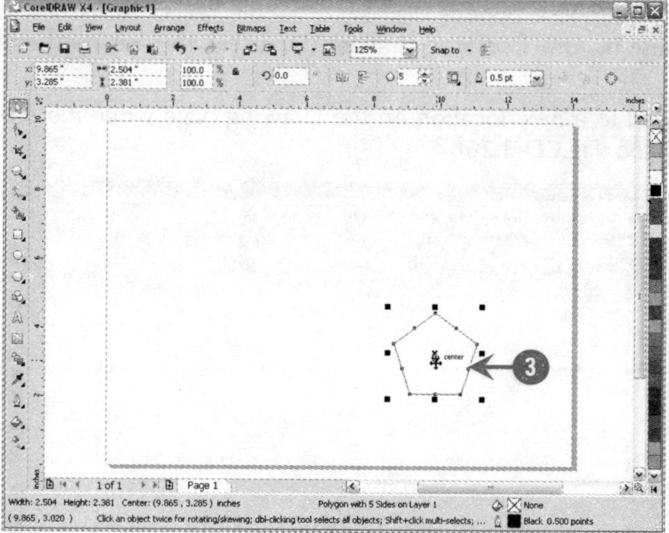

Fig.CD-3.24

Moving an Object while Drawing

CorelDRAW allows you to move an object while you are still drawing it. That is, you are still drawing the object but you can move the incomplete object from one place to another. Undertake the following steps to learn how to move an object that you still haven't finished drawing:

1. *Draw* a shape of your choice, say a polygon, while keeping both the mouse buttons (that is, the left and right) pressed, as shown in Fig.CD-3.25.

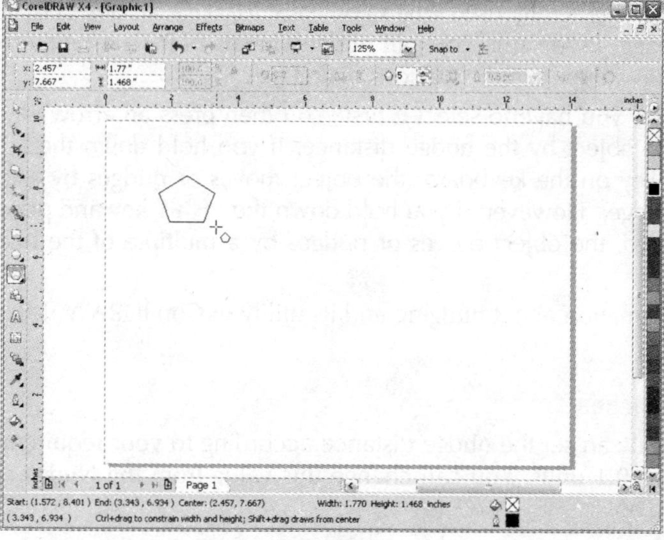

Fig.CD-3.25

2. *Keeping* both the mouse buttons *pressed*, *drag* the object to its new position and release the right mouse-button. Continue drawing by using the left mouse-button, as shown in Fig.CD-3.26.

The object is moved to a new location on the Drawing page while the process of drawing the object is still going on (Fig.CD-3.26).

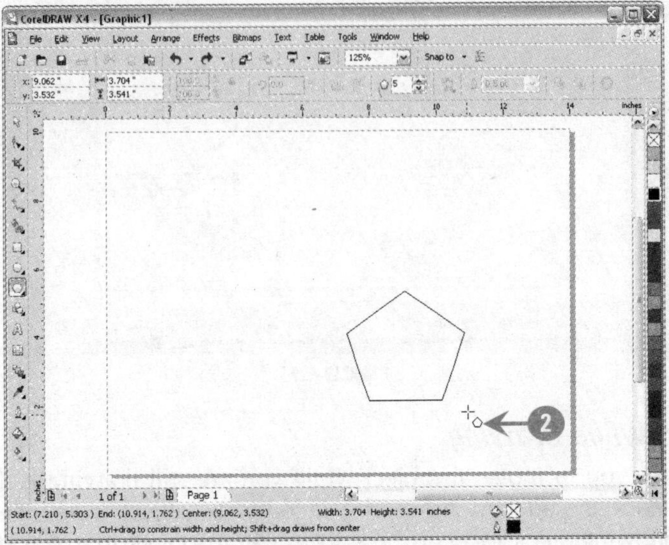

Fig.CD-3.26

Nudging an Object

Nudging refers to moving an object in increments by using the navigation arrow keys on the keyboard. Nudging is generally used when you want to move an object by a very small distance on the Drawing page. By default, you can nudge objects in 0.1 unit increments. However, you can also change this value from the Options dialog box.

To nudge an object, you have to select it first. You then press an arrow key on the keyboard to nudge the selected object by the nudge distance. If you hold down the **CTRL** key and press a navigation arrow key on the keyboard, the object moves or nudges by a fraction of the nudge distance (Micro-nudge). However, if you hold down the **SHIFT** key and press a navigation arrow key on the keyboard, the object moves or nudges by a multiple of the nudge distance (Super-nudge).

After this brief information about nudging and its utility in CorelDRAW, let's learn how to set the nudge distance.

Setting Nudging Distances

In CorelDRAW, you can set the nudge distance according to your requirements. By default, the nudging distance is 0.1 units. You can change this value from the Nudge spin box provided in the Options dialog box.

Undertake the following steps to set the nudging distance:

1. *Select* an object to nudge. In our case, we have selected a polygon (Fig.CD-3.27).
2. *Select* **Tools→Options** (Fig.CD-3.27). An **Options** dialog box appears, as shown in Fig.CD-3.28.

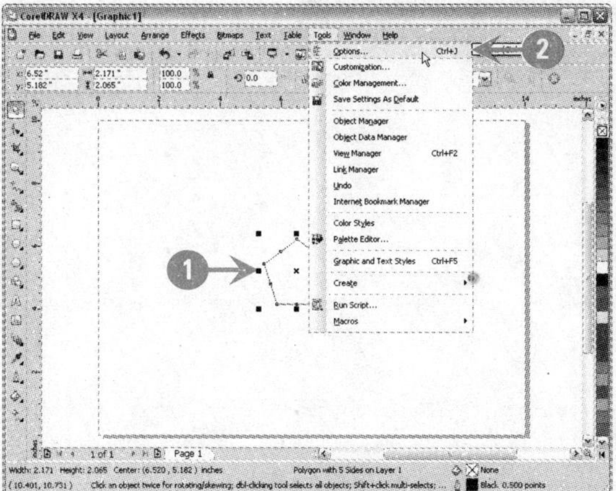

Fig.CD-3.27

3. In the **Options** dialog box, *expand* the **Document** node and *click* the **Rulers** category. The **Rulers** property page appears (Fig.CD-3.28).
4. *Type* a value in the **Nudge** spin box, the **Super nudge** spin box, or the **Micro nudge** spin box (Fig.CD-3.28). In our case, we have typed 0.2 in the **Nudge** spin box and for **Super nudge** and **Micro nudge**, we have taken the default values.

Note

> Super nudge: Moves an object by a multiple of the nudge distance.
>
> Micro nudge: Moves an object by a fraction of the nudge distance.

5. After typing the value, *click* the **OK** button to close the **Options** dialog box (Fig.CD-3.28).

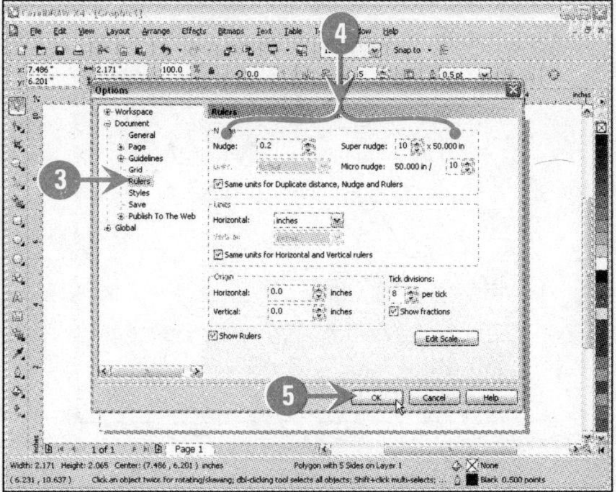

Fig.CD-3.28

6. Now, *press* the right navigation arrow key to move the selected object according to the specified nudge distance, as shown in Fig.CD-3.29.

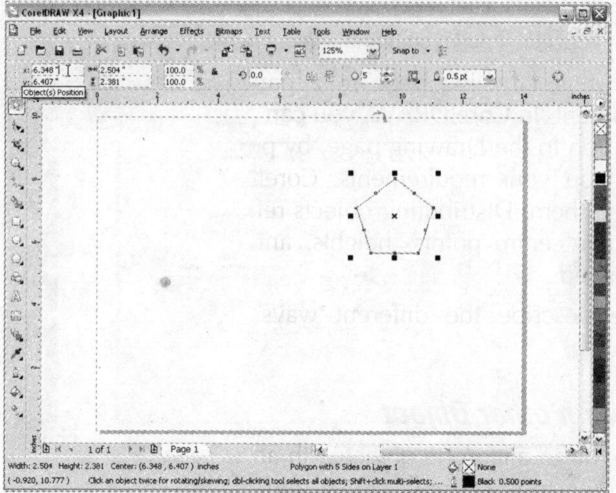

Fig.CD-3.29

Positioning an Object by the X and Y Coordinates

CorelDRAW allows you change the position of an object along the X and Y coordinates or axes. To do so, undertake the following steps:

1. Begin with the object in Fig.CD-3.29. *Type* a value for the **X** and **Y** coordinates in the **Object(s) Position** text box beside X and Y options on the Property bar, as shown in Fig.CD- 3.30.
2. *Press* the **ENTER** key on the keyboard. The position of the object changes as per the values typed in the **Object(s) Position** text box (Fig.CD-3.30).

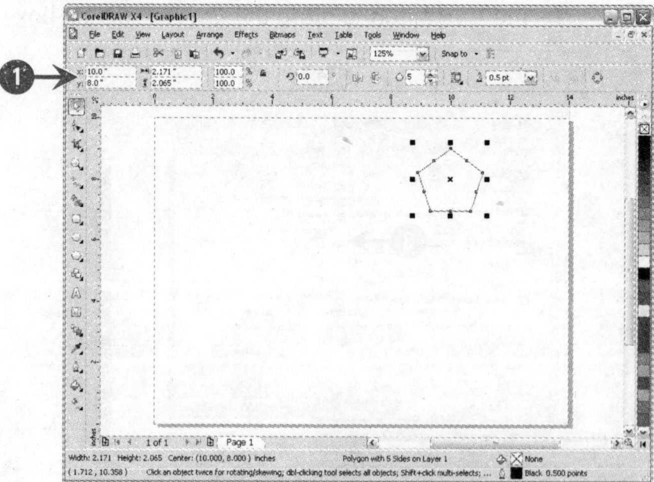

Fig.CD-3.30

You now know how to position objects in different ways in CorelDRAW. In the next section, you learn how to align and distribute objects on the Drawing page of CorelDRAW.

Aligning and Distributing Objects

Positioning objects on a Drawing page in a particular pattern is important for the proper structuring of a document. In CorelDRAW, you can position objects by aligning them either with each other or in relation to the Drawing page, by positioning them to the left, center, or right of the page depending on your requirements. CorelDRAW considers the center and edges of objects while aligning them. Distributing objects refers to the dispersion of spacing between the objects based on their centre points, heights, and widths. In a distributed drawing, objects appear evenly distributed.

In this section, we describe the different ways you can align and distribute objects in CorelDRAW.

Aligning an Object with other Object

CorelDRAW allows you to align one object with another. You can align objects with respect to each other or according to the center, edges, and grid of a Drawing page. If you are aligning objects with other objects, then you can align them by their centers or by their edges.

Note

> Grids are intersecting lines that are used to precisely align and position objects on a Drawing page.

Undertake the following steps to align an object with another object:

1. *Select* the **Polygon** tool from the Toolbox and draw three polygons on the Drawing page.
2. In the Toolbox, *select* the **Pick** tool, as shown in Fig.CD-3.31.
3. *Select* the objects and then *select* **Arrange→Align and Distribute→Align and Distribute** (Fig.CD-3.31). An **Align and Distribute** dialog box appears, as shown in Fig.CD-3.32.

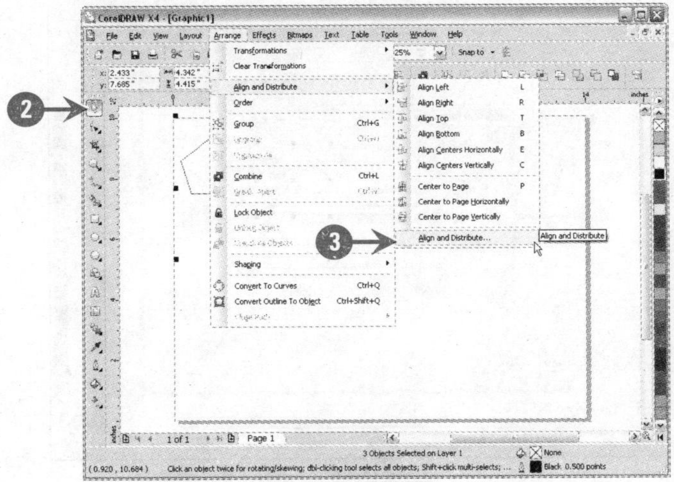

Fig.CD-3.31

4. *Select* the **Align** tab and then *select* the **Left**, **Centre**, or **Right** check box to align the objects along the vertical axis (Fig.CD-3.32). In our case, we have selected the **Center** check box.

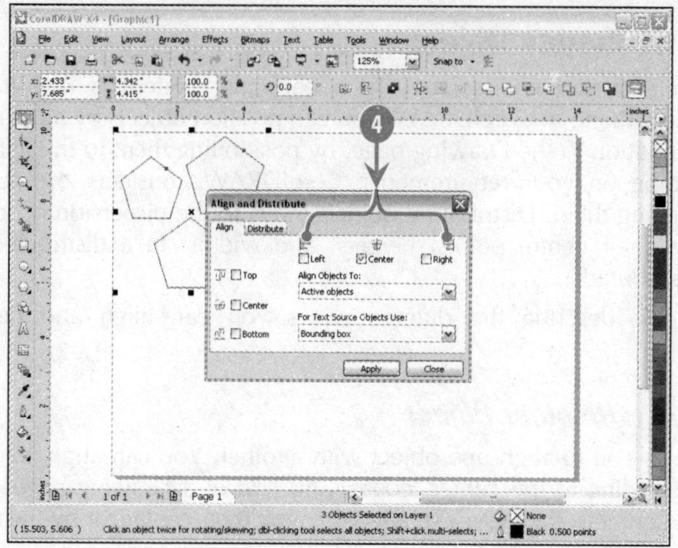

Fig.CD-3.32

5. *Select* the **Top**, **Centre**, or **Bottom** check box to align the objects along horizontal axis (Fig.CD-3.33). In our case, we have selected the **Top** check box.
6. *Select* an option from the **Align Objects To** drop down list with reference to which you want to align the object. In our case, we have selected the **Active objects** option (Fig.CD-3.33).

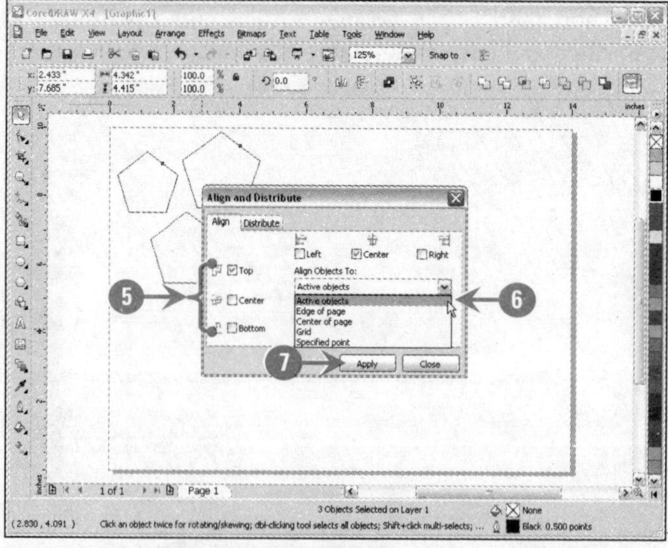

Fig.CD-3.33

7. *Click* the **Apply** button and then the **Close** button (Fig.CD-3.33). The selected objects after alignment are shown in Fig.CD-3.34.

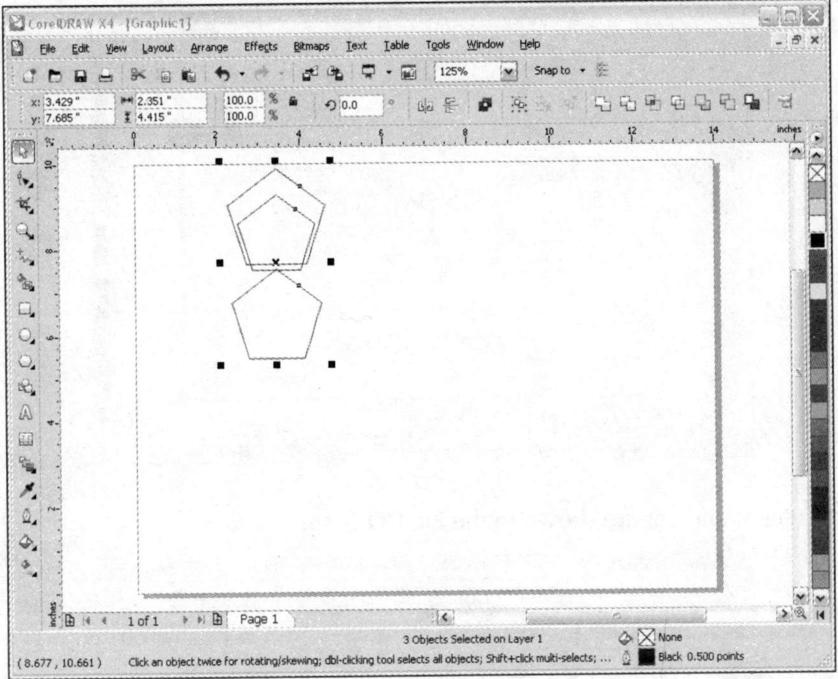

Fig.CD-3.34

Note

> Alternatively, you can align an object by selecting Arrange->Align and Distribute and then selecting any of the first six alignment commands (Fig.CD-3.31). You can also align objects by first selecting them and then clicking the Align and Distribute button ( ) on the Property bar.

Aligning an Object with the Center of the Drawing Page

In CorelDRAW, you can align an object or a group of objects with the center of the Drawing page by using the Center to Page, Center to Page Vertically, or Center to Page Horizontally options.

Undertake the following steps to align an object with the center of the Drawing Page:

1. *Select* the **Pick** tool and then *select* the object that you want to align with the center of the Drawing page. In our case, we have selected all the three polygons on the Drawing page we created in the previous section.

Note

> If you want to align multiple objects, you can marquee select the objects.

2. *Select* **Arrange→Align** and **Distribute→Center** to Page, as shown in Fig.CD-3.35.

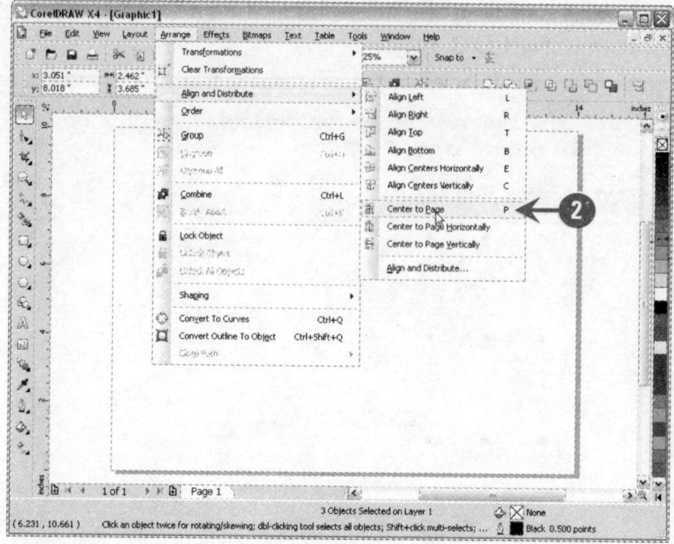

Fig.CD-3.35

The objects after alignment are shown in the Fig.CD-3.36.

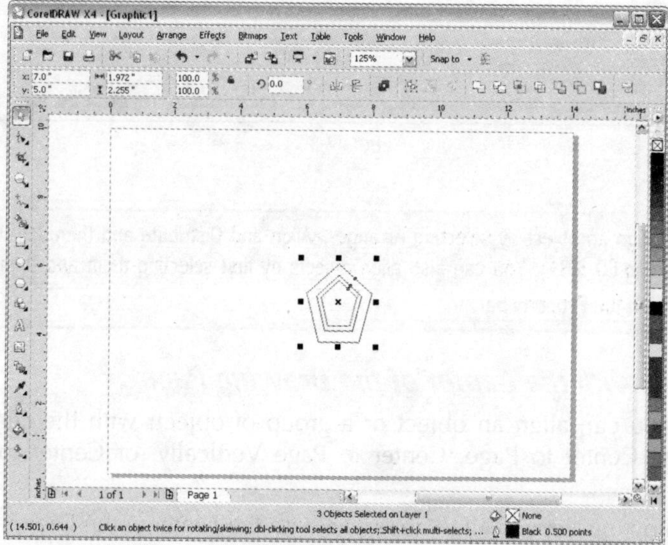

Fig.CD-3.36

You can see in Fig.CD-3.36 that the objects are aligned to the center of the Drawing page.

Distributing Objects

CorelDRAW allows you distribute objects horizontally or vertically at an equal spacing with respect to their center points, widths, and heights. To do so, undertake the following steps:

1. *Select* the **Pick** tool in the Toolbox, as shown in Fig.CD-3.37.

2. *Select* the objects that you want to distribute on the Drawing page and then *select* **Arrange→Align and Distribute→Align and Distribute** (Fig.CD-3.37). An **Align and Distribute** dialog box appears, as shown in Fig.CD-3.38.

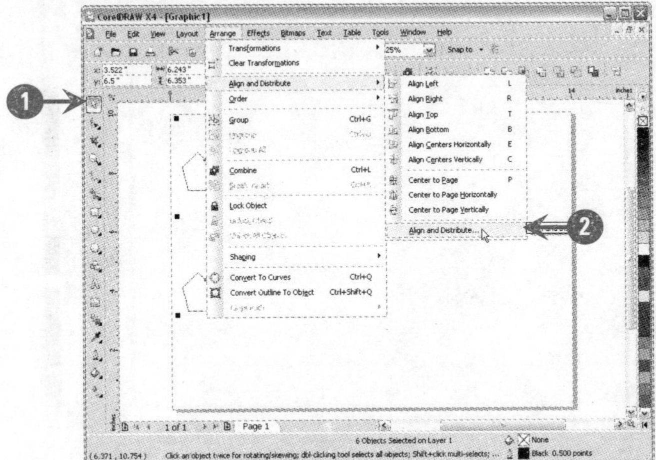

Fig.CD-3.37

3. *Select* the **Distribute** tab and then *select* the **Left, Center**, **Spacing**, or **Right** check box to distribute the objects horizontally (Fig.CD-3.38). In our case, we have selected the **Left** check box.
4. To distribute objects vertically, *select* the **Top**, **Center**, **Spacing,** or **Bottom** check box (Fig.CD-3.38). In our case, we have selected the **Top** check box.
5. *Select* the radio button beside the **Extent of selection** or **Extent of page** option under the **Distribute to** group to indicate the area over which the objects are to be distributed (Fig.CD-3.38). In our case, we have selected the **Extent of selection** option.
6. *Click* the **Apply** button and then the **Close** button (Fig.CD-3.38).

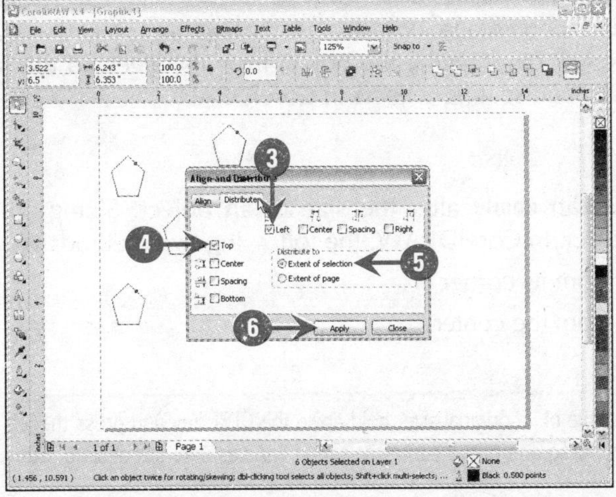

Fig.CD-3.38

The objects after distribution are shown in the Fig.CD-3.39.

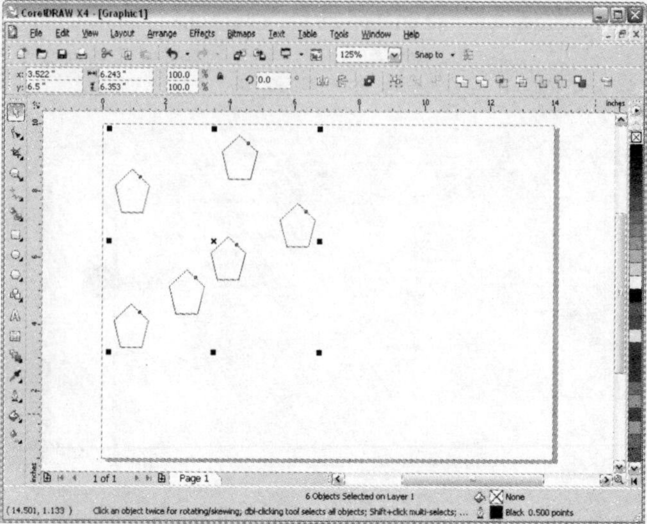

Fig.CD-3.39

Now that you know how to distribute objects on the Drawing page in CorelDRAW, let's learn how to size and scale objects in order to make them fit properly on the Drawing page.

Sizing and Scaling Objects

While working with a drawing you may need to change the size of objects in it according to your requirements. CorelDRAW allows you to change the dimensions of an object proportionally by preserving its aspect ratio, where aspect ratio is the ratio of an object's width to its height. This task is performed by sizing and scaling of the object. Sizing can be done by specifying values in the Property bar. You can also change the size of an object directly by dragging the control handles around the object. If you want to change the dimensions of an object by a specified percentage (known as scaling an object), you can do so from the Transformation docker or by dragging the object from its edges. In this section, we describe the different ways of sizing and scaling objects in CorelDRAW.

Sizing an Object

In CorelDRAW, you can easily alter the size of an object. Sizing an object is changing the dimensions of the object. In CorelDRAW, the following two methods are used to size an object:

- Sizing an object from its corner
- Sizing an object from the center

Note

To size an object to a multiple of its original size, hold down the CTRL key and press the left mouse-button. Keeping the left mouse-button pressed, drag one of the corner selection handles until the desired size is reach and then release the mouse-button.

Undertake the following steps to size an object from its corner:

1. *Select* the **Pick** tool and then *select* the object you want to size, as shown in Fig.CD-3.40.
2. *Drag* any corner selection handle of the object. The size of the object changes as you drag the corner handle (Fig.CD-3.40).

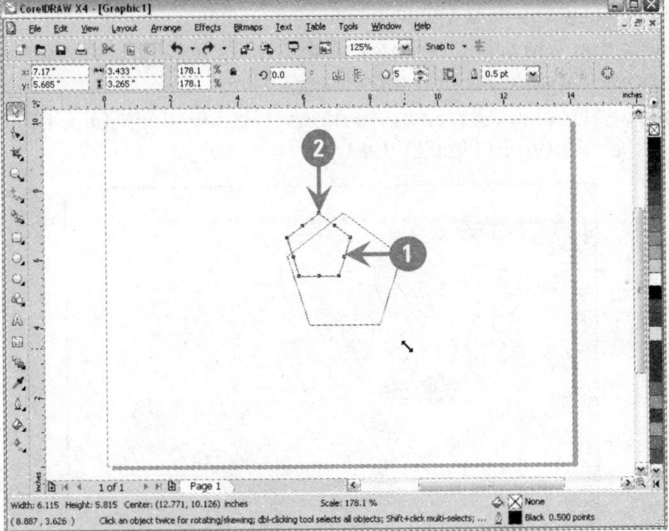

Fig.CD-3.40

3. To size a selected object (a polygon) from its center, hold down the **SHIFT** key on the keyboard. The cursor changes to cross bar. Now, *drag* a corner handle by using cross bar to size the polygon, as shown in Fig.CD-3.41.

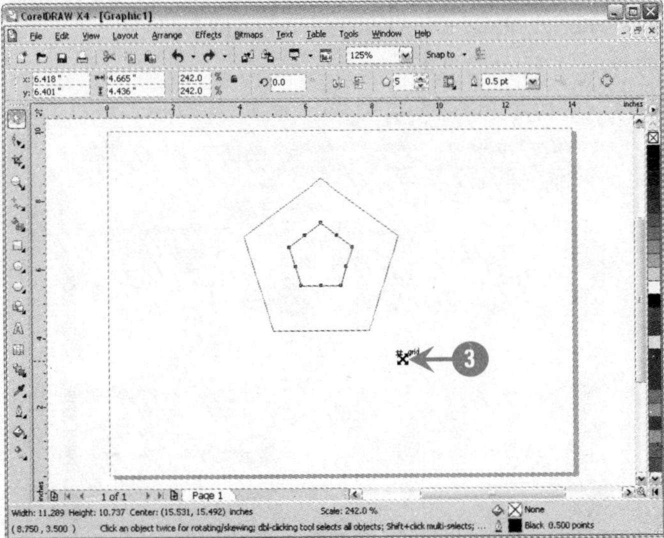

Fig.CD-3.41

The object appears with its new size on the Drawing page (Fig.CD-3.41).

Scaling an Object

Scaling refers to changing the dimensions of an object by a specified percentage. In scaling, the changes made in the object's dimensions are done proportionally so that its aspect ratio is preserved.

Undertake the following steps to scale an object:

1. *Select* the object that you want to scale, as shown in Fig.CD-3.42. Anchor points (in shape of black square boxes) appear around the object.
2. *Select* **Window→Dockers→Transformations→Scale** (Fig.CD-3.42). A **Transformation** docker appears, as shown in Fig.CD-3.43.

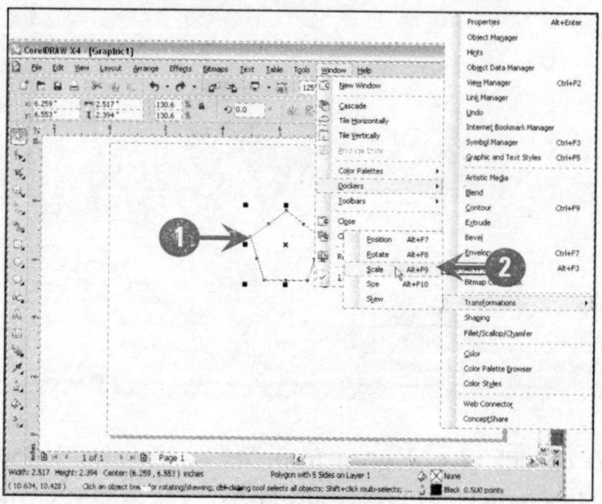

Fig.CD-3.42

3. In the **Transformation** docker, *type* the values in the text boxes beside the **H** and **V** options to scale the object horizontally and vertically (Fig.CD-3.43).
4. *Click* the **Apply** button (Fig.CD-3.43).

The scale of the object changes according to the specified values (Fig.CD-3.43).

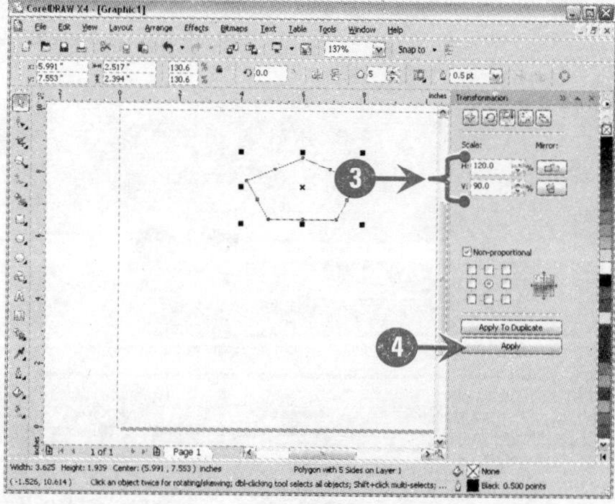

Fig.CD-3.43

Note

> Under the Non-proportional check box, select a check box that corresponds to the anchor point that you want to change and deselect the Non-proportional check box to maintain the aspect ratio of the object.
>
> An anchor point is a point that remains stationary when you stretch, scale, or mirror an object. Anchor points correspond to the eight handles that are displayed when an object is selected.
>
> You can also scale an object by dragging a corner selection handle. Alternatively, you can type a value in the Scale factor boxes (the boxes with the % signs) on the Property bar to do the same.

We now come to two important features that are commonly used in CorelDRAW—rotating and mirroring objects. Let's learn about them in the next section.

Rotating and Mirroring Objects

CorelDRAW allows you to rotate objects or create mirror images of them. The rotating and mirroring features allow you to make changes to the orientation of the object. To rotate an object you need to specify its horizontal and vertical coordinates. A negative value for the angle of rotation causes the object to rotate clockwise, while a positive value causes an anti-clockwise rotation. Mirroring, on the other hand, refers to the flipping of the object from left to right or top to bottom.

Let's learn how to rotate and mirror objects in the following sections.

Rotating an Object

Rotation refers to the motion of a rigid body around a fixed point. In CorelDRAW, you can rotate an object along the horizontal and vertical coordinates.

Undertake the following steps to rotate an object:

1. *Select* the object you want to rotate, as shown in Fig.CD-3.44.
2. *Select* **Window→Dockers→Transformations→Rotate** (Fig.CD-3.44). A **Transformation** docker appears, as shown in Fig.CD-3.45.

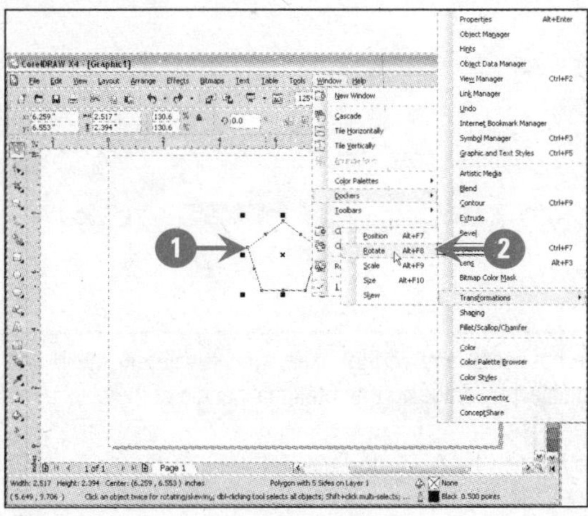

Fig.CD-3.44

3. *Clear* the **Relative Center** check box in the **Transformations** docker (Fig.CD-3.45).
4. *Type* a value in the text box beside the **Angle** option. In our case, we have typed **60.0** (Fig.CD-3.45).

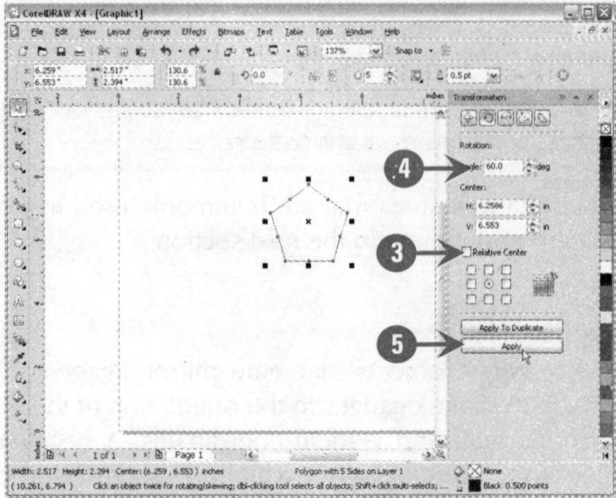

Fig.CD-3.45

5. *Click* the **Apply** button, as shown in Fig.CD-3.45.

The object rotates at the specified angle (Fig.CD-3.46).

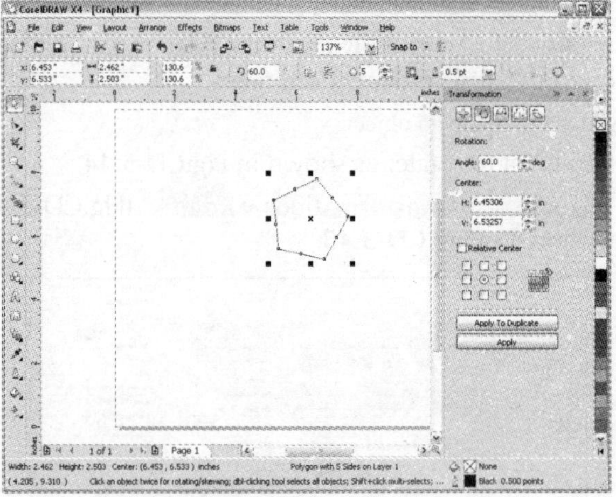

Fig.CD-3.46

Note

To rotate an object along the horizontal and vertical axes, type a value in the H and V boxes in the Transformation docker. You can also rotate an object by dragging the rotational handle of the object.

You can change the angle of rotation by typing the desired value in the Angle of Rotation box (0.0 °) on the Property bar.

Rotating an Object Around a Ruler Coordinate

CorelDRAW allows you rotate an object around a ruler coordinate. Ruler is a reference scale that helps you to draw, size, and align objects precisely.

You can make use of the ruler coordinates to rotate an object along the horizontal and vertical axes.

Undertake the following steps to rotate an object around ruler coordinates:

1. *Select* the object you want to rotate, as shown in Fig.CD-3.47.
2. *Select* **Window→Dockers→Transformations→Rotate** (Fig.CD-3.47). A **Transformation** docker appears, as shown in Fig.CD-3.48.

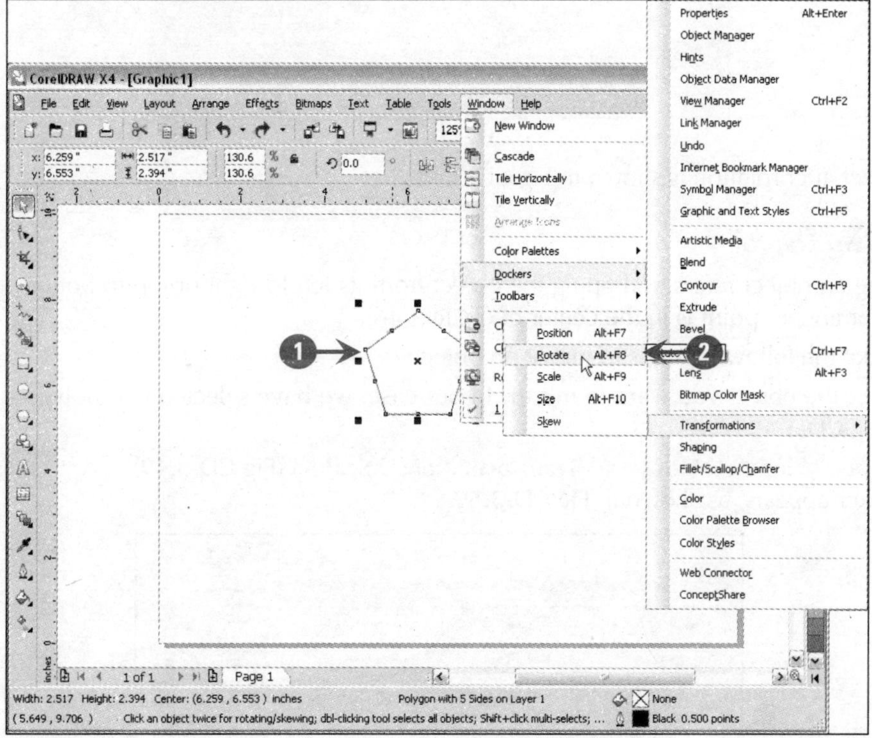

Fig.CD-3.47

3. *Clear* the **Relative Center** check box in the **Transformations** docker (Fig.CD-3.48).
4. *Type* a value in the spin box beside the **Angle** option. In our case, we have typed **45.0** (Fig.CD-3.48).
5. To specify the point at which the rotation takes place on the horizontal or vertical ruler, *type* a value in **H** and **V Center** spin boxes, respectively (Fig.CD-3.48).
6. After typing the values, *click* the **Apply** button (Fig.CD-3.48).

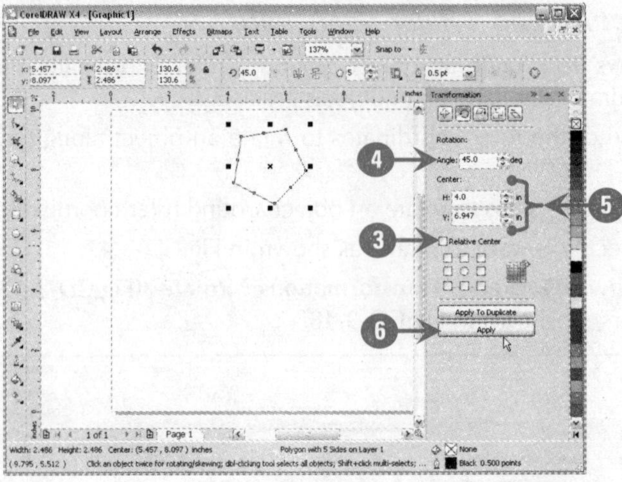

Fig.CD-3.48

The object after rotation is shown in Fig.CD-3.48.

Mirroring an Object

Mirroring an object refers to flipping the object from its left to right or top to bottom. By default, the mirror anchor point is in the center of object.

Undertake the following steps to mirror an object:

1. *Select* the object you want to mirror. In our case, we have selected two polygons, as shown in Fig.CD-3.49.
2. *Select* **Window→Dockers→Transformations→Scale** (Fig.CD-3.49). A **Transformation** docker appears, as shown in Fig.CD-3.50.

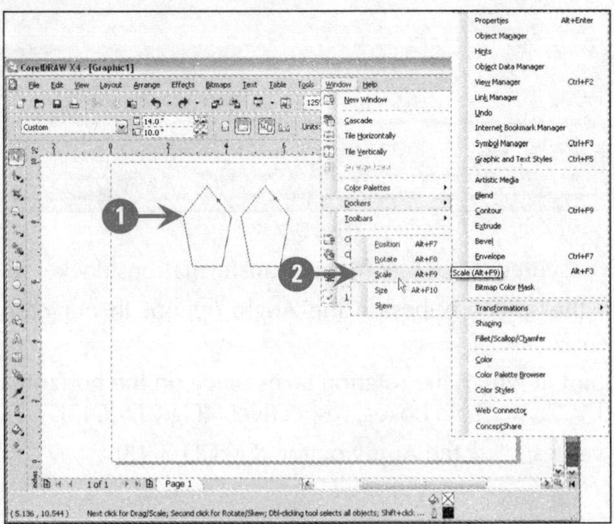

Fig.CD-3.49

3. To flip the objects from left to right, *click* the **Horizontal** mirror () button; or, if you want to flip the objects from top to bottom, *click* the **Vertical** mirror () button, as shown in Fig.CD-3.50. In our case, we have clicked the **Vertical** mirror button.
4. Next, *click* the **Apply** button (Fig.CD-3.50).

The objects after mirroring appear on the Drawing page, as shown in Fig.CD-3.50.

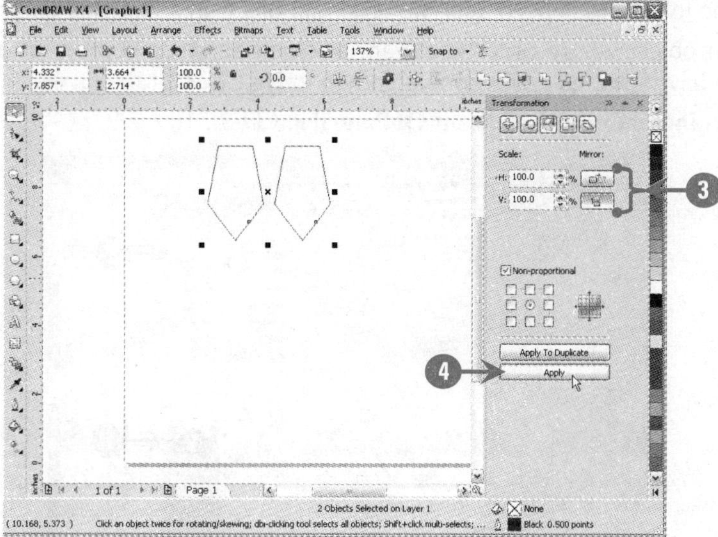

Fig.CD-3.50

Note

You can mirror a selected object by clicking the mirror buttons on the Property bar. You can also mirror a selected object by holding down the CTRL key and dragging a selection handler in a direction opposite to that of the object. Depending on the shape of the object, you can drag the handler in the top, bottom, left, right, and even diagonal directions to apply the mirror effect.

After mirroring an object, let's now learn how to arrange the order of objects on a Drawing page. By changing the order of objects, you can send an object to the back of another object or bring an object from the back to the front of the object. The order of objects is important when your Drawing page contains many objects.

Order of Objects

In CorelDRAW, by default, a newly created object is arranged over the previously created object. However, you can change this default arrangement and thereby determine which object appears in front and which object remains at the back. An object is sent back or brought forward in relation to a selected object. For example, you can change the arrangement order of an Oval shape and put it behind the Rectangle shape. In this way, the Rectangle shape appears in front and the Oval shape appears behind the Rectangle shape. In general practice, designers always arrange important objects in the front, while the other objects are placed at the back. In this section, you learn how to change the arrangement order of objects in CorelDRAW.

Changing the Arrangement Order of Objects

You can change the way objects are stacked in a Drawing page. By changing the stacking order of objects, you bring objects ahead of other objects while partially hiding the remaining objects. The technique of changing order is used when you want to display important objects ahead of other objects but without deleting remaining objects.

Undertake the following steps to alter the order of objects in a Drawing page:

1. *Select* an object whose order you want to change from a number of other objects. In our case, we have selected a polygon, as shown in Fig.CD-3.51.
2. *Select* **Arrange→Order→To Front Of Page** (Fig.CD-3.51).

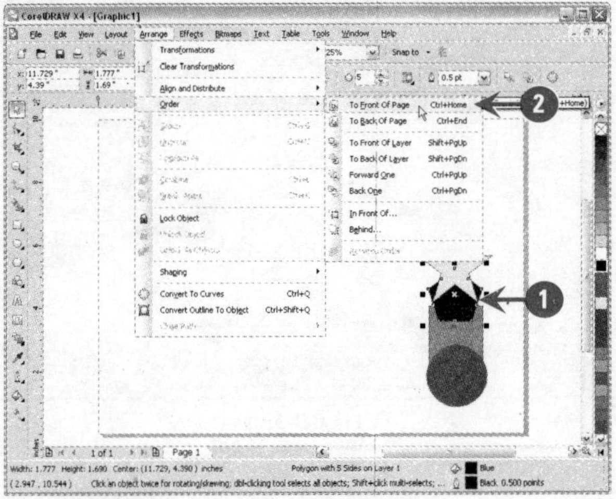

Fig.CD-3.51

3. On applying the **To front of Page** option, the polygon comes in front of all other objects, as shown in Fig.CD-3.52.

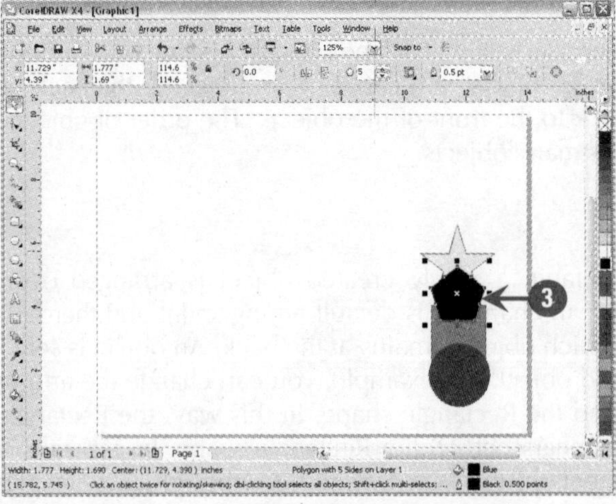

Fig.CD-3.52

Note

The Order option will have no effect if the selected object is already placed at the desired stacking order.

Now that you know how to altering the order of objects, let's learn how to combine objects in the following section.

Combining and Breaking Objects

In CorelDRAW, you can combine two or more objects. Combining objects transforms the objects that are combined in that the action results in a common fill and outline attributes for the objects. In CorelDRAW, you can break a combination to change the attributes of the individual objects in the combination. You can combine different shapes such as Rectangle, Ellipses, Polygons, Stars, Spirals, or even text.

In the following sections, you learn how to combine objects as well as break a combination.

Combining two or More Objects

As already mentioned, in CorelDRAW you can combine two or more objects so that they have common fill and outline attributes. While combining objects, the attributes of the initial object are reflected on the rest of the objects.

Undertake the following steps to combine two or more objects:

1. *Select* the objects you want to combine, as shown in Fig.CD-3.53.
2. *Select* **Arrange→Combine** (Fig.CD-3.53).

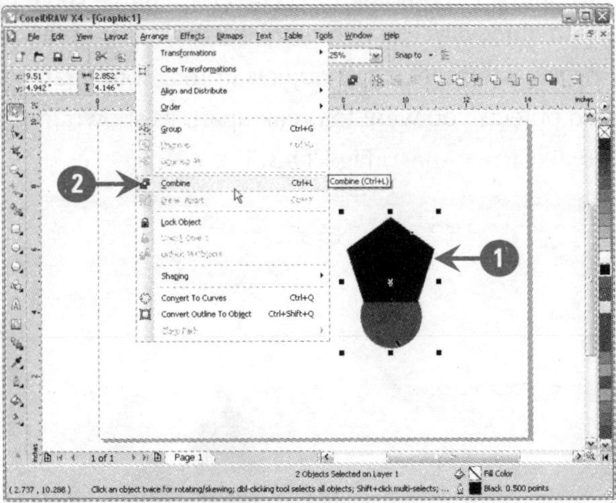

Fig.CD-3.53

The selected objects combine so that they have common fill color and outline attributes, as shown in Fig.CD-3.54.

Note that the objects, after combination, inherit the attributes of the initial object (Fig.CD-3.54). Because of this fact that polygon has inherited the fill color and outline attributes of the circle, some portion of the circle is appearing white.

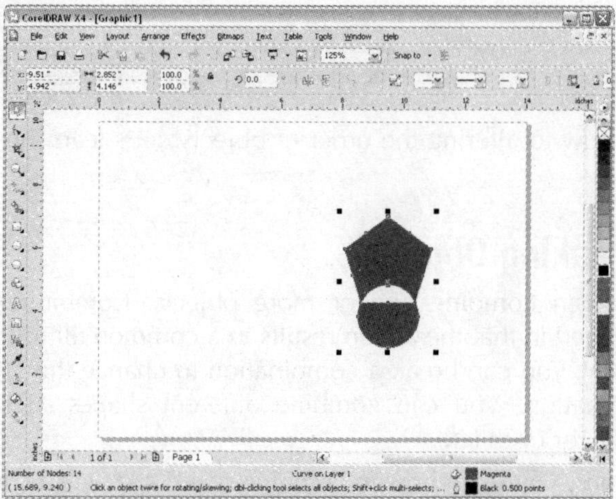

Fig.CD-3.54

Note

You can also combine objects by using the Combine button ( ) on the Property bar.

Breaking Apart Combined Objects

CorelDRAW allows you to separate an object from a combination. However, breaking apart objects form a combination results in the objects retaining the color and outline of the object with which they were initially combined. When you have separated the objects from a combination into separate objects, you can modify the attributes of the individual objects.

Undertake the following steps to break apart objects from a combination:

1. *Select* the combined objects you want to break apart, as shown in Fig.CD-3.55.
2. *Select* **Arrange→Break Curve Apart** (Fig.CD-3.55).

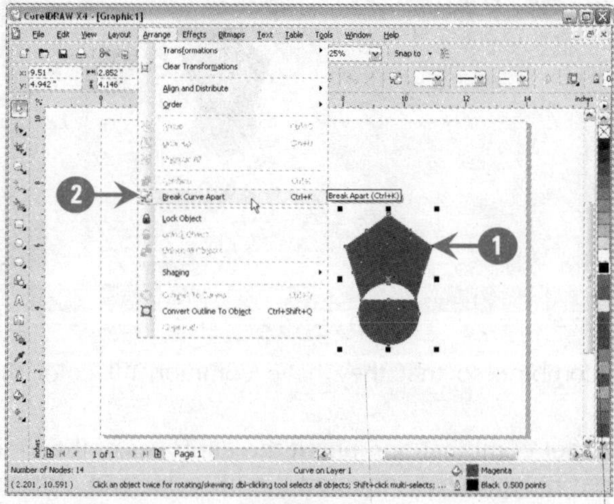

Fig.CD-3.55

The combined object breaks apart into individual objects, each having its own attributes. However, the color and outline properties of the combined objects have been changed, as all the objects inherit the color and outline properties of the object with which they were initially combined, as shown in Fig.CD-3.56.

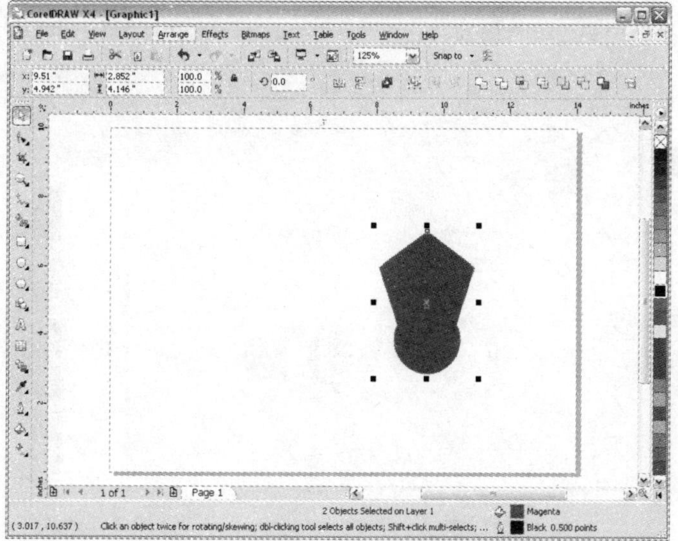

Fig.CD-3.56

Another feature similar to combining objects in CorelDRAW is grouping objects. Let's learn more about this feature next.

Grouping in CorelDRAW

In CorelDRAW you can group two or more objects. In a group, all the objects are treated as a single unit, but each object retains its default attributes such as outline, fill color, outline style and text properties until these attributes are changed by the user. If you apply a property, formatting effect or any other changes on the group, the changes will be reflected on all the objects simultaneously in the group.

Note

> The major difference between combining and grouping objects is that while combining results in a common fill color and outline attributes for the objects, in grouping, the objects retain their default attributes.

In this section, we discuss how to group objects, add an object to a group, edit individual objects of a group without affecting the other objects in the group, remove an object from the group, and break the group.

Grouping Objects

Grouping prevents you from accidentally changing the position of an object in relation to other objects. Not only this, once the objects are grouped, they can be located easily since you do not have to search for the objects individually on the Drawing page. As safe practice, you can pick commonly used or important objects, group them and keep them aside on the Drawing page. Doing so will help you in picking objects easily from a single location.

Undertake the following steps to group two or more objects:

1. *Select* the **Pick** tool, as shown in Fig.CD-3.57.
2. *Select the* objects you want to group and then *select* **Arrange→Group** (Fig.CD-3.57).

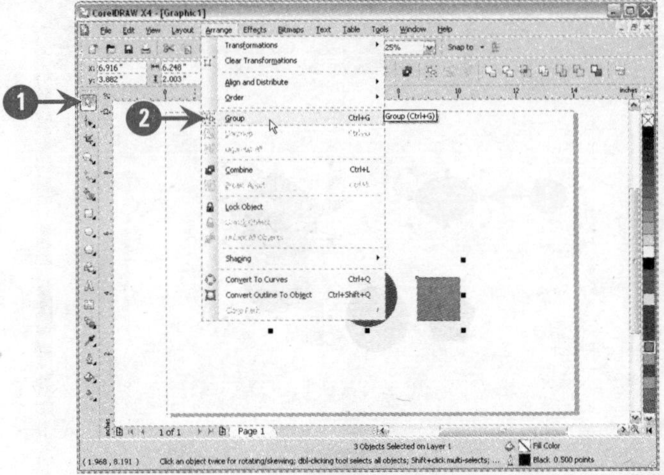

Fig.CD-3.57

The selected objects form a group. This is confirmed by the Status bar, which displays **Group of 3 Objects on Layer 1**, as shown in Fig.CD-3.58.

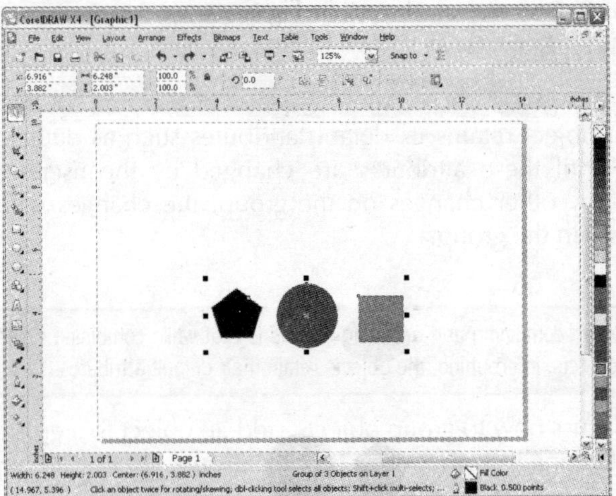

Fig.CD-3.58

Adding an Object to a Group

In CorelDRAW, after you have created a group you can add new objects, thereby increasing the number of objects in the group. To do this, undertake the following steps:

1. *Select* the object that you want to add in the group, as shown in Fig.CD-3.59.
2. *Select* **Window→Dockers→Object Manager** (Fig.CD-3.59). An **Object Manager** docker appears, as shown in Fig.CD-3.60.

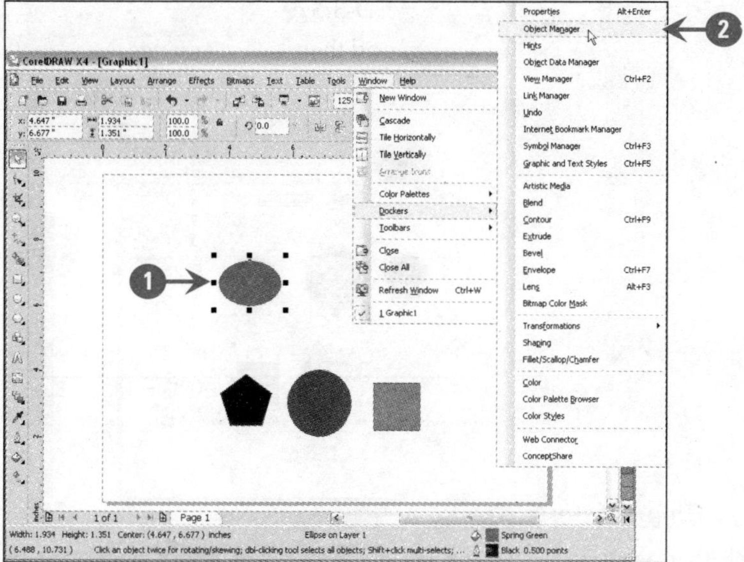

Fig.CD-3.59

3. In the **Object Manager** docker, *drag* the name of the object to be added to the name of the group. In our case, we have selected an ellipse, and dragged it to the name of our group, that is **Group of 3 Objects**, as shown in Fig.CD-3.60. Adding the new object changes this name to **Group of 4 Objects**, as shown in Fig.CD-3.61.

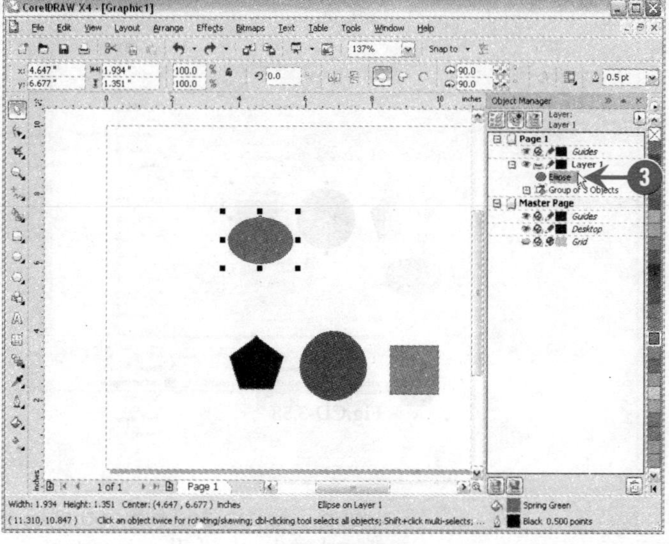

Fig.CD-3.60

In the same way, you can also add other objects or even more than one object to a group.

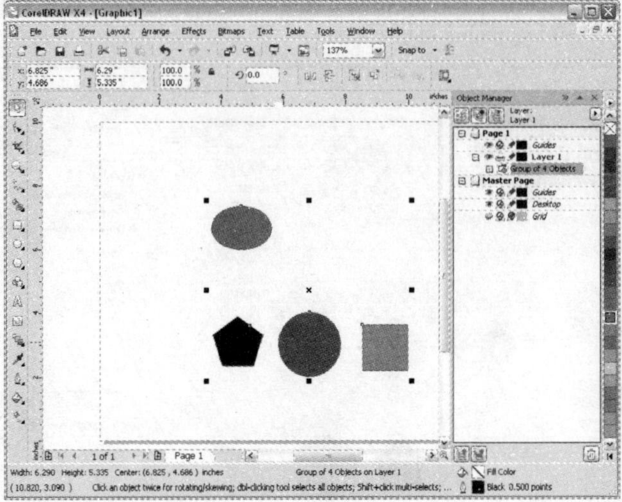

Fig.CD-3.61

Removing an Object from a Group

If you think that an object does not match a group or is not necessary in the group, you can easily remove the object with the help of the tools available in CorelDRAW.

Undertake the following steps to remove an object from a group:

1. *Select* the group from which you want to remove an object, as shown in Fig.CD-3.62.
2. *Select* **Window→Dockers→Object Manager** (Fig.CD-3.62). An **Object Manager** docker appears, as shown in Fig.CD-3.63.

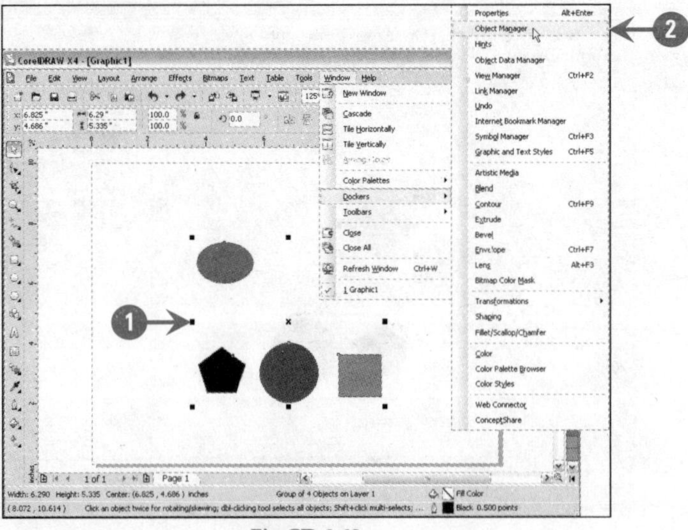

Fig.CD-3.62

3. *Expand* the category of **Group of 4 Objects**. A list of the four objects appears under the category, as shown in Fig.CD-3.63.

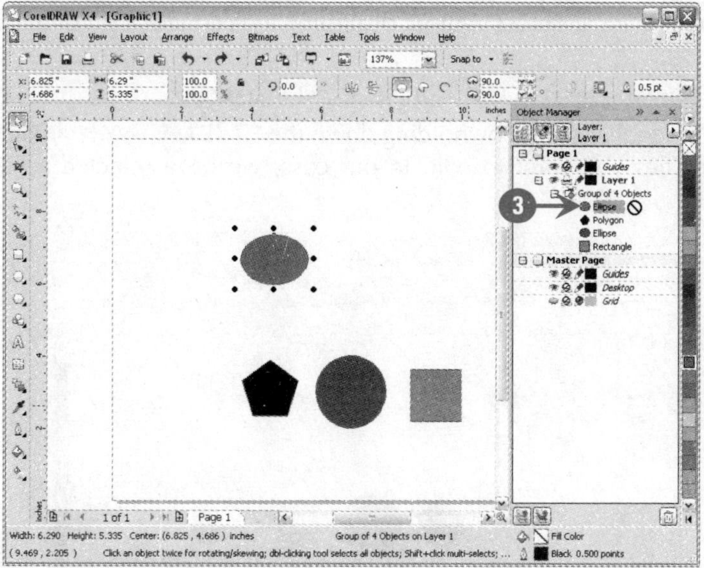

Fig.CD-3.63

4. In the **Object Manager** docker, *drag* the object outside of the group, which you want to remove, as shown in Fig.CD-3.64. In our case, we want to remove the ellipse from the group.

The ellipse is removed from the group (Fig.CD-3.64).

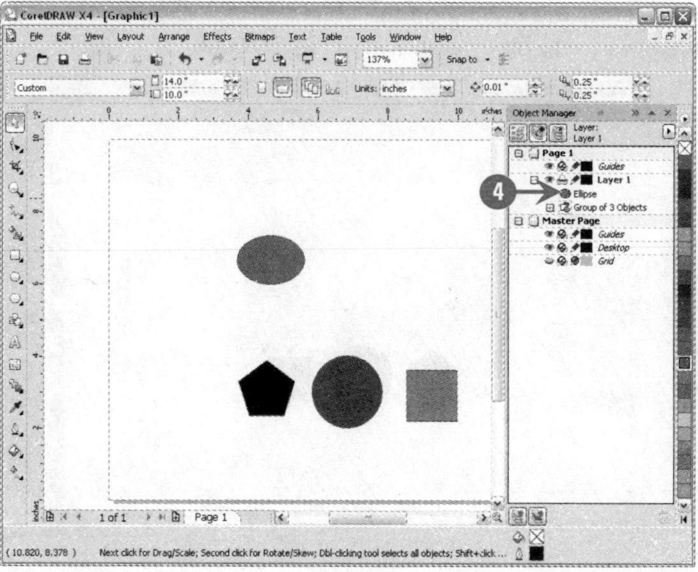

Fig.CD-3.64

Editing a Single Object in a Group

CorelDRAW provides you with a feature to edit a single object in a group of objects. This helps in modifying the individual object without disturbing the configuration of the other objects in the group.

Undertake the following steps to edit a single object in a group:

1. *Select* the **Pick** tool and then by holding down the **CTRL** key, *select* an object from the group whose properties you want to edit. In our case, we have selected a square, as shown in Fig.CD-3.65.

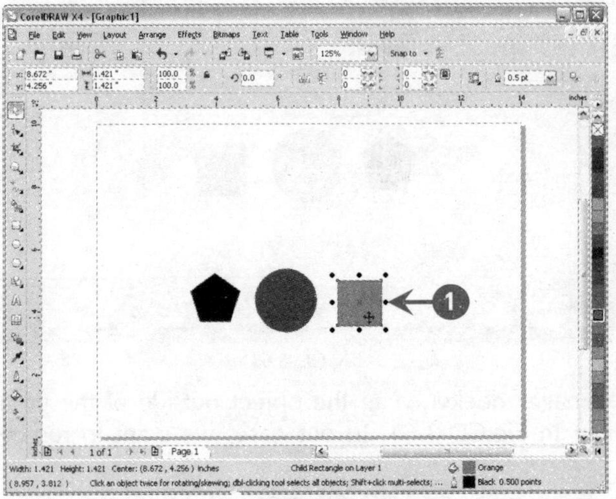

Fig.CD-3.65

2. Now, *perform* the desired editing on the object. In our case, we have changed the color of the square from orange to blue, as shown in Fig.CD-3.66.

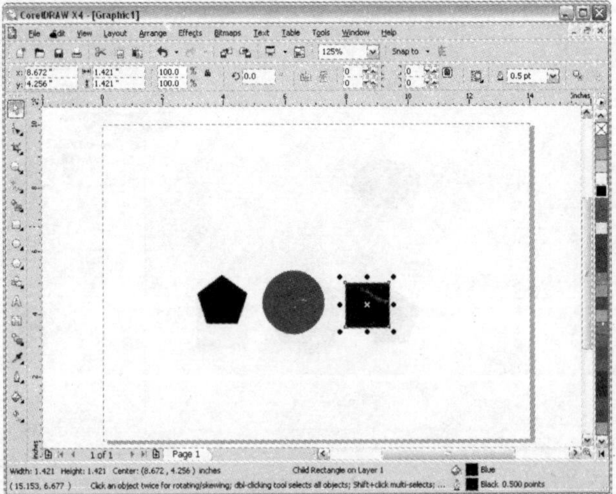

Fig.CD-3.66

Ungrouping Objects

Ungrouping objects refers to the removal of objects from a group. It may involve breaking a group into individual objects or a nested group into multiple groups. You can ungroup a single group and multiple groups into individual objects.

Undertake the following steps to ungroup objects:

1. *Select* one or more groups of objects, which you want to ungroup, as shown in Fig.CD-3.67.
2. *Select* **Arrange→Ungroup** (Fig.CD-3.67).

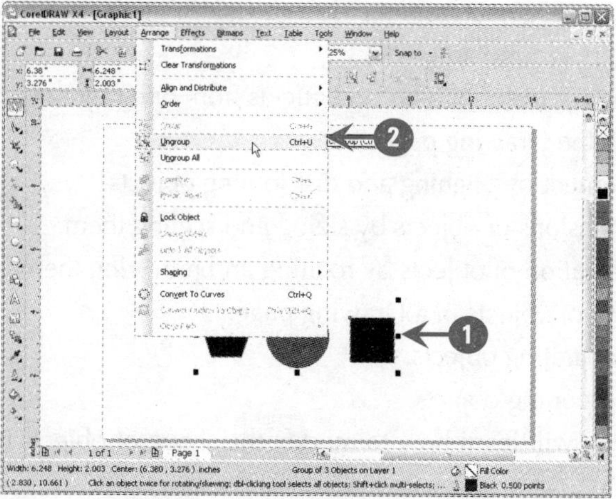

Fig.CD-3.67

The group's objects break apart into individual objects, as shown in Fig.CD-3.68. Compare the Status bar at the bottom of Fig.CD-3.67 and Fig.CD-3.68. In Fig.CD-3.67, the Status bar displays the message **Group of 3 Objects on Layer 1** whereas after ungrouping objects, the Status bar in Fig.CD-3.68 displays the message **3 Objects Selected on Layer 1**. This shows that all the objects in the group have now separated into individual objects.

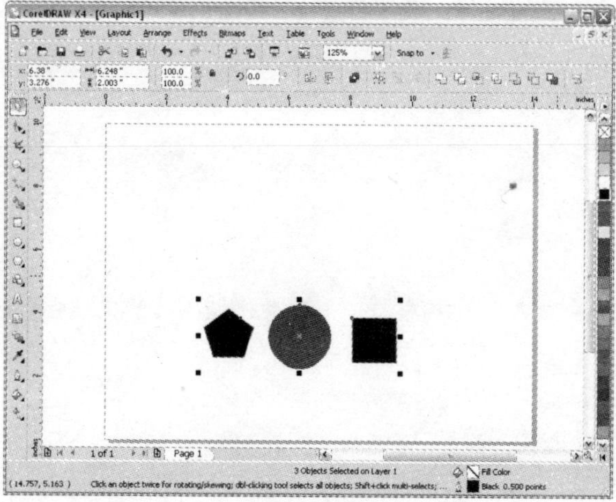

Fig.CD-3.68

With this, we come to the end of the section. This also concludes the chapter. However, before we proceed to the next chapter, let's recap the main points by going through a short summary.

Summary

In this chapter, you learned about:

- Selecting and deselecting objects from the Drawing page.
- Creating a copy of an object as well as its duplicate, and deleting an object.
- Applying a color on an object from the default Color palette.
- Creating a boundary around an object.
- Copying properties, transformations and effects from one object to another.
- Placing objects on the Drawing page.
- Structuring a document by aligning and distributing objects.
- Changing the dimensions of objects by sizing and scaling them.
- Changing the orientation of objects by rotating and mirroring them.
- Changing the order of objects in a Drawing page.
- Combining and separating objects.
- Grouping and ungrouping objects.

In the next chapter, you will learn how to modify the shape of objects by using the various tools available in CorelDRAW X4.

Chapter 4

Working with Shapes

In this Section

- Modifying Basic Objects
- Working with Grids and Guidelines
- Applying Convert to Curve Command on Objects
- Modifying the Shape of an Object by Applying Distortions
- Modifying the Shape of an Object by Cropping, Splitting, and Erasing it
- Modifying the Shape of an Object using the Fillet, Scallop and Chamfer Tools

In CorelDRAW X4, you can modify the shape, content, layout, and view of an object. It has various tools that help you perform modifications in an object according to the settings specified. CorelDRAW X4 lets you remove any unwanted or unnecessary portion of an object, add a portion in an existing object, and apply various effects to the object. Changes in the shape of an object can be made using various distortion effects and tools such as **Envelope**, **Crop**, **Split**, **Erase**, **Fillet**, **Scallop**, **Chamfer**, and so on.

In this chapter, you learn how to modify some basic objects such as rectangle, square, ellipse using the tools and techniques provided in CorelDRAW X4.

Modifying Basic Objects

In CorelDRAW X4, you can draw some basic objects such as rectangle, ellipse, polygon, star, and so on. You can also modify appearances of these objects with the help of the tools available in CorelDRAW X4.Let's learn how to apply different settings on an object to make changes in its shape.

Rounding the Corners of a Rectangle or a Square

As you know that in CorelDRAW X4, you can make changes in the shape of basic objects. For example, you can edit the shape of the corners of a rectangle or square to convert them into round shape or vice versa. Let's understand how to change the corners of a rectangle or square to round shape.

Perform the following steps to change the corners of a rectangle or square into round shape:

1. *Select* the **Rectangle** tool from the Toolbox (Fig. CD.4.1). As you *select* the **Rectangle** tool, the cursor changes to a cross-hair.
2. Keep the mouse button pressed and *drag* the mouse pointer on the Drawing page until you get a rectangle of the desired size (Fig.CD-4.1.).

A rectangle of the desired size appears on the Drawing page, as shown in Fig.CD-4.1.

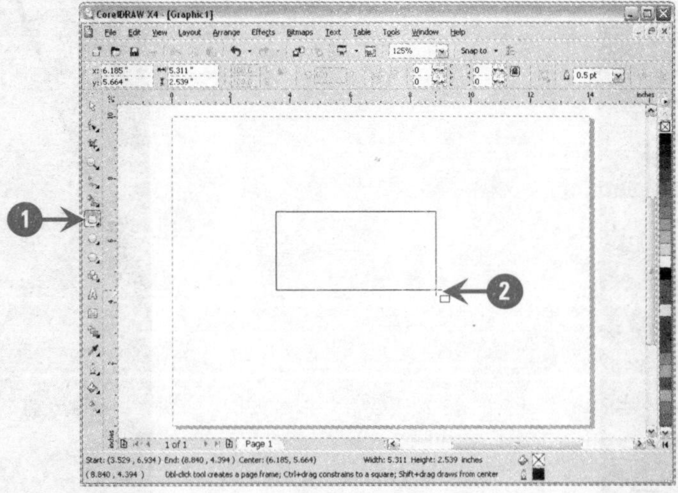

Fig.CD-4.1

Note

> To draw a square, click the Rectangle tool in the Toolbox. Hold down the CTRL key and drag the mouse pointer on the Drawing page until you get a square of the desired size.

3. In the Property bar, *click* the up arrow of any Corner roundness spin box to round the corners of the object. You can choose a value between 0-100 from the Corner roundness spin box (Fig.CD-4.2).

The shape of the corners of the rectangle changes, as shown in Fig.CD-4.2.

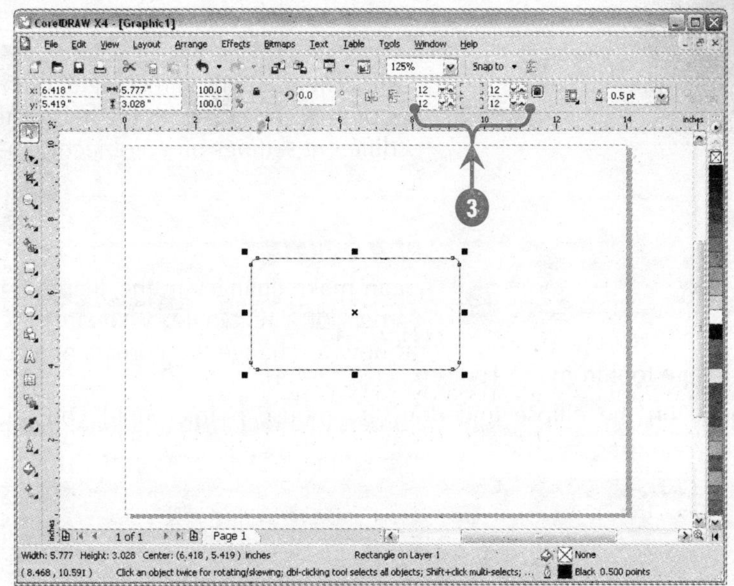

Fig.CD-4.2

Note

> To draw a rectangle by specifying the height and width, use 3 Point Rectangle tool ( ) present in the flyout menu of the Rectangle tool. For the same roundness of all corners, click the Round Corners Together ( ) button on the Property bar.

After learning how to round the corners of a rectangle or square, let us now learn how to convert an ellipse into a pie.

Converting an Ellipse into a Pie

In CorelDRAW X4, you can change the shape of an ellipse into a pie or an arc. Let's learn how to change an ellipse to a pie.

Perform the following steps to convert an ellipse to a pie:

1. *Select* the **Ellipse** tool from the Toolbox and *drag* the mouse pointer in the Drawing page until you get the desired shape/ size of the ellipse (Fig.CD-4.3).

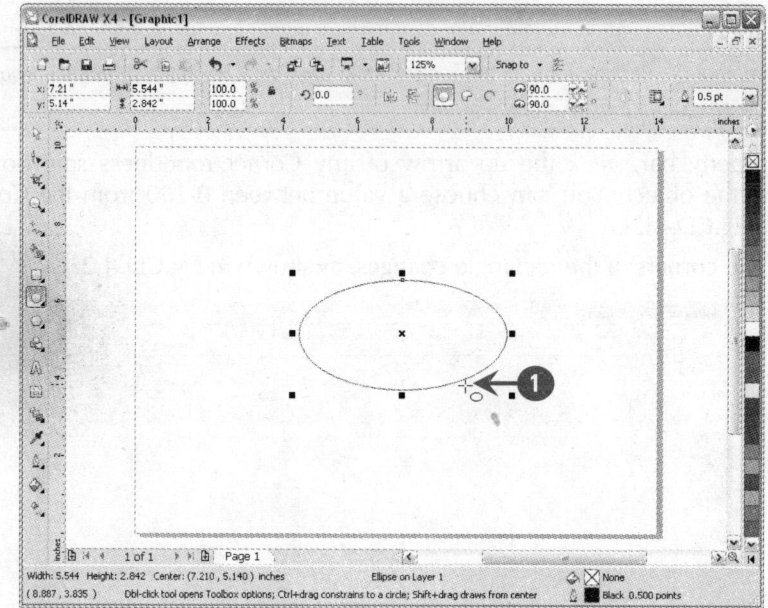

Fig.CD-4.3

2. *Select* the **Shape** tool from the Toolbox (Fig.CD-4.4).
3. *Click* a node on the ellipse and drag the mouse pointer until you get the desired pie (Fig.CD-4.4).

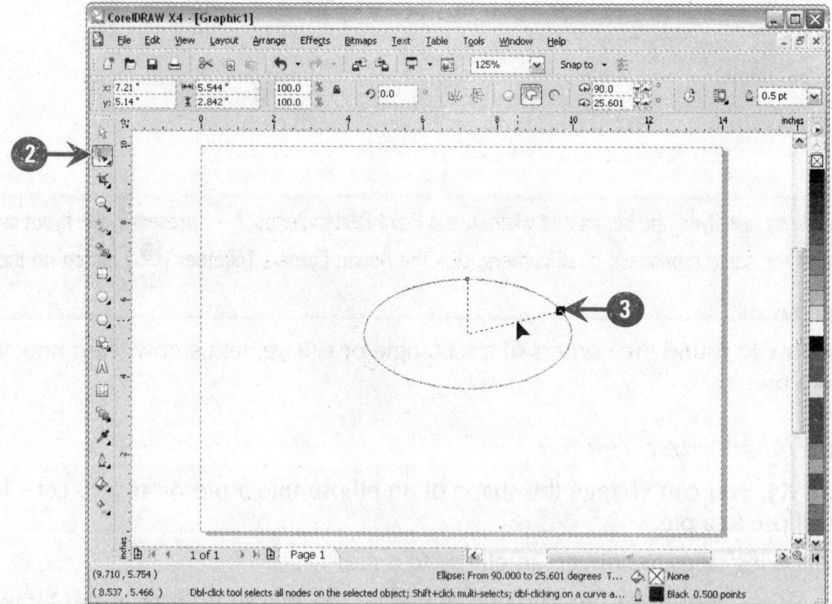

Fig.CD-4.4

The ellipse changes to a pie, as shown in Fig.CD-4.5.

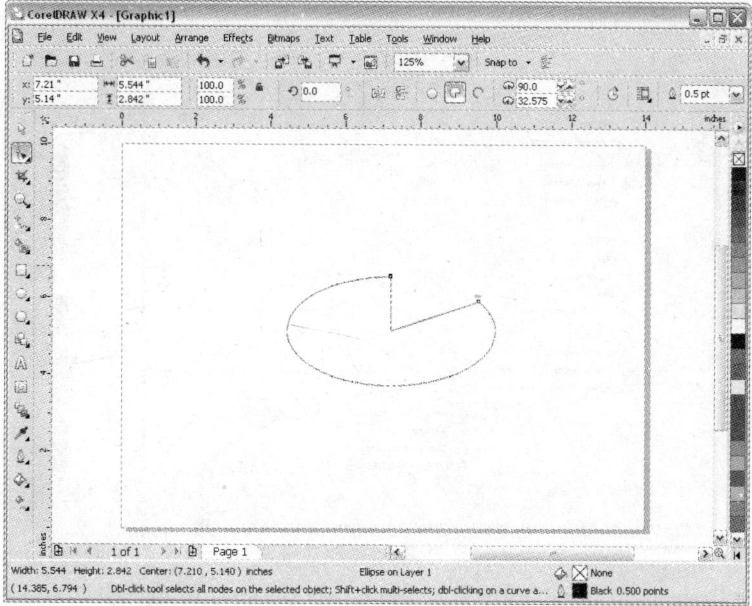

Fig.CD-4.5

After converting an ellipse into a pie, let us now learn how to work with grid and guidelines.

Working with Grids and Guidelines

CorelDRAW X4 provides you with the facility to align and position objects on the Drawing page with the help of grids. Grids are patterns of lines on a plane and represent the longitude and latitude distances. These distances help determine the absolute location of an object on the Drawing page. A grid can be represented in the form of intersecting lines. In CorelDRAW, you can set the distance between grid lines.

Guidelines help you place an object at a precise location on the Drawing page. There are three types of guidelines: Horizontal, Vertical, and Slanted.

Let's now learn to work with grids and guidelines.

Setting the Distance between Grid Lines

In CorelDRAW X4, you can modify the arrangement of the grid lines, such as altering the number of grids and changing the space between adjacent grids. This helps determine the object more accurately.

Perform the following steps to set the distance between the grid lines:

1. *Select* **View→Setup→Grid and Ruler Setup** (Fig.CD-4.6). The **Options** dialog box appears, as shown in Fig.CD-4.7.

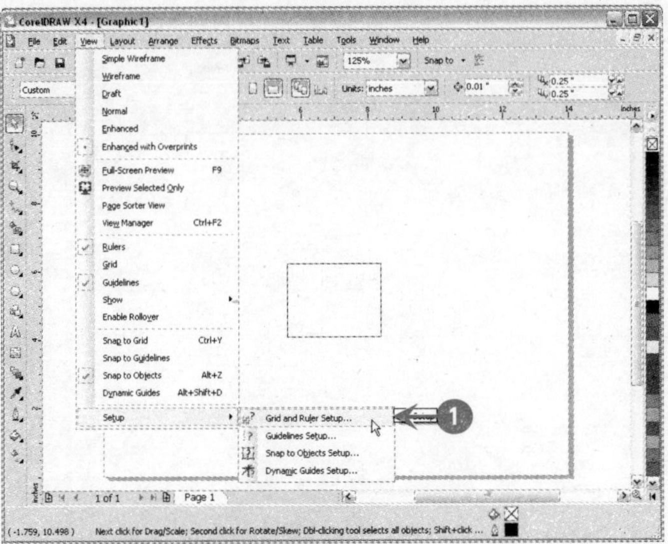

Fig.CD-4.6

2. *Expand* the **Document** node and *select* the **Grid** option from the list. Various options appear under the **Grid** title (Fig.CD-4.7).
3. *Select* the **Show grid** check box, as shown in Fig.CD-4.7.
4. *Select* the radio button beside the **Spacing** option and *type* values for the **Horizontal** and **Vertical** spin boxes under the **Spacing** group (Fig.CD-4.7).
5. *Click* the **OK** button (Fig.CD-4.7).

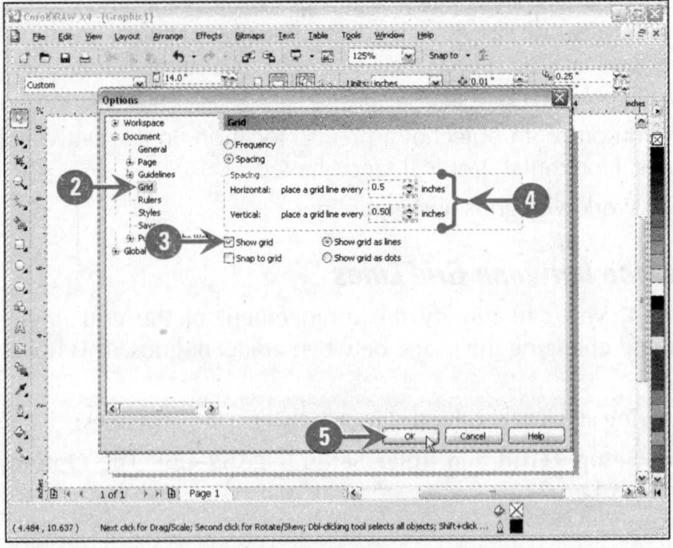

Fig.CD-4.7

As you click the **OK** button in the **Options** dialog box, the grid appears, as shown in Fig.CD-4.8

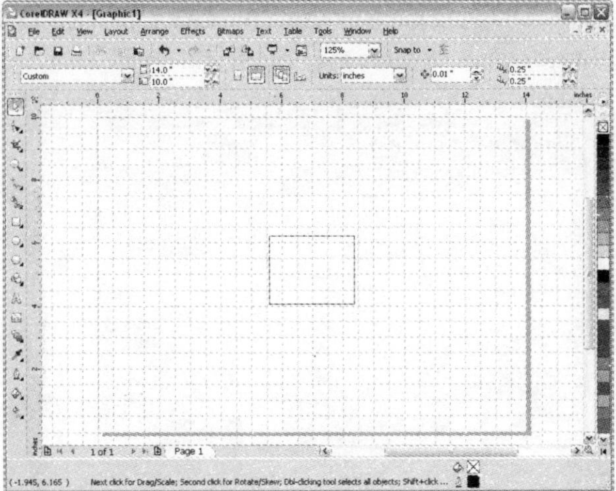

Fig.CD-4.8

Note

You can also select the Snap to grid check box to position the object to the closest intersection of the grid.

After setting the distance between grid lines, let us now learn how to snap objects to a grid.

Snapping Objects to Grid

In CorelDRAW X4, whenever you bring an object near the grid, the nearest grid suddenly holds the object. This sudden capturing of the object by the nearest grid, in CorelDRAW X4, is called snapping. Hence, snapping helps you to align objects.

Perform the following steps to snap an object to grid:

1. *Select* **View→Snap to Grid** (Fig.CD-4.9).

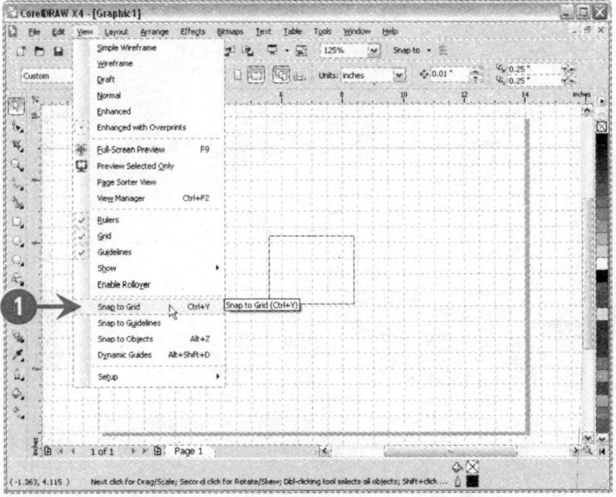

Fig.CD-4.9

2. *Move* the object on the Drawing page by using the **Pick** tool (Fig.CD-4.10).

The object moves but always comes closer to the nearest grid on the Drawing page (Fig.CD-4.10).

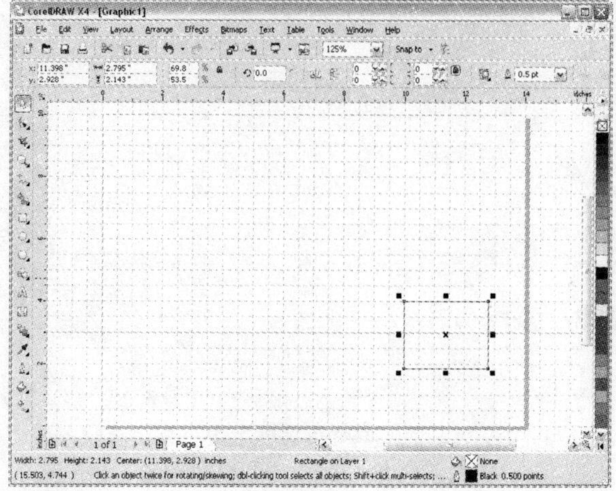

Fig.CD-4.10

After learning about snapping an object to grid, let us now learn how to snap the distance between guidelines.

Snapping the Distance between Guidelines

CorelDRAW X4 lets you add guidelines to properly align and place objects you have on your Drawing page. These guidelines can be placed anywhere on the Drawing page. There are three types of guidelines depending on their placement: Horizontal, Vertical, and Slanted. You can also use objects as guides.

Perform the following steps to snap the distance between guidelines:

1. *Select* **View→Snap to Guidelines** (Fig.CD-4.11).

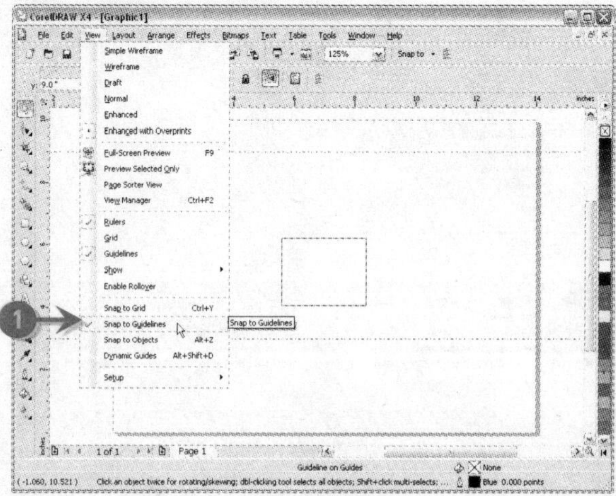

Fig.CD-4.11

2. *Drag* the object near the guideline with the help of the **Pick** tool (Fig.CD-4.12).

As soon as the object reaches to the guideline, the edge of the object aligns to the guideline, as shown in Fig.CD-4.12.

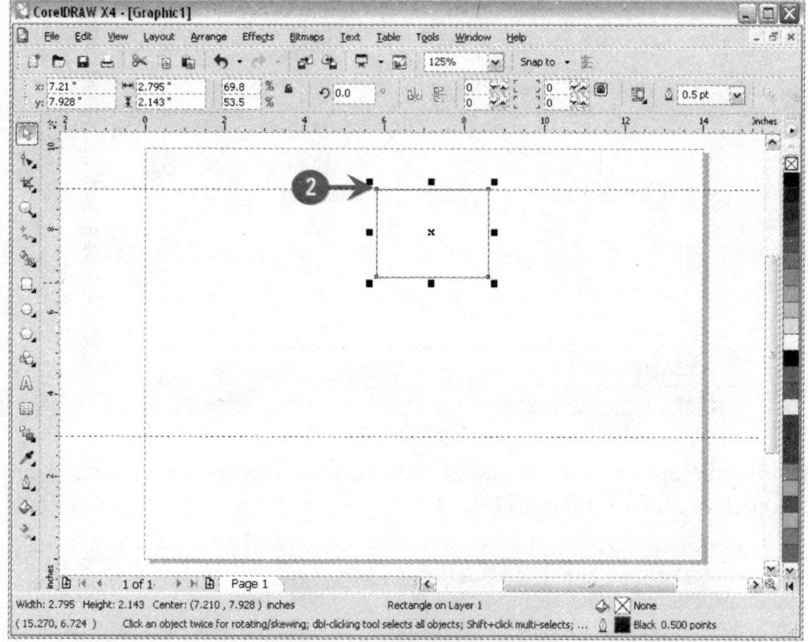

Fig.CD-4.12

After understanding about snapping the distance between guidelines, let us now learn about the Convert to Curve command.

Applying Convert to Curve Command on Objects

In CorelDRAW X4, you can change the shape of an object by converting it into a curve object. It is one of the ways to shape an object. A curve object contains nodes and control handles that can be used to change the shape of an object. These nodes appear along the outline of the object. The shape of a curve object can be like a straight line or curved line.

Converting an Object into a Curve Object

In CorelDRAW X4, most objects you add to the Drawing page are not curve objects. Therefore, if you want to modify the shape of an object, it is recommended to convert the object into a curve object.

Perform the following steps to convert an object into a curved object:

1. *Select* an object using the **Pick** tool (Fig.CD-4.13).
2. *Select* **Arrange→Convert To Curves** (Fig.CD-4.13).

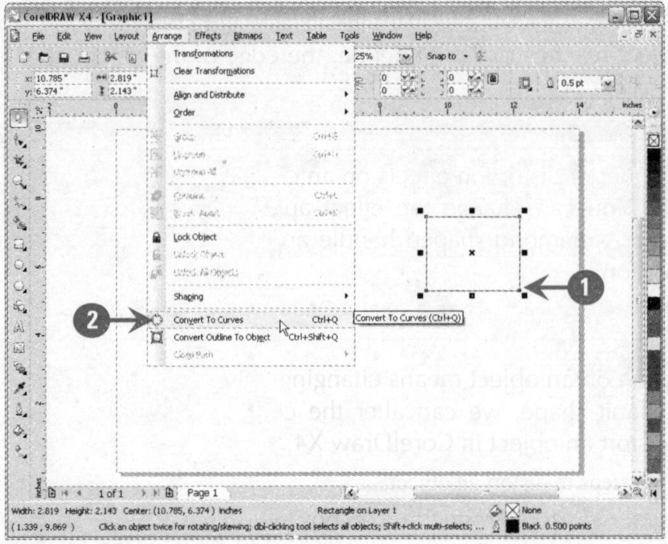

Fig.CD-4.13

A new control handle appears in the object. You can use the control handle to adjust the shape of the curve object, as shown in Fig.CD-4.14.

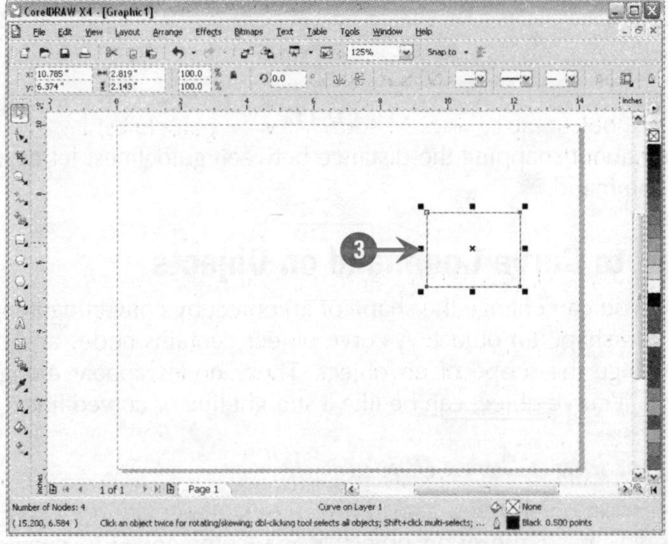

Fig.CD-4.14

Note

> You can also convert an object to curve object by clicking the Convert to curves button ( ) on the Property bar.

After converting an object into a curve object, let us change the shape of an object by applying distortion on it. The next section describes it.

Modifying the Shape of an Object by Applying Distortions

When you twist a regular shape of an object, it takes a new shape. This new shape is known as distorted shape. CorelDRAW X4 offers you three types of distortions: Push and Pull, Zipper, and Twister.

You can apply number of distortion effects on an object. You can also remove, copy and change a distortion effect. You can change the effect applied on a distorted object by changing the center of distortion. A diamond shaped handle around which the distortion appears represents the center of distortion.

Distorting an Object

Performing distortion on an object means changing the default look of the object and reshape it. To change the default shape, we can alter the center of distortion of an object. Let's learn through steps to distort an object in CorelDraw X4.

Perform the following steps to distort an object:

1. *Select* the **Rectangle** tool from the Toolbox and draw a rectangle on the Drawing page (Fig.CD-4.15).
2. *Open* the **Interactive** tools flyout and *select* the **Distort** tool (Fig.CD-4.15).

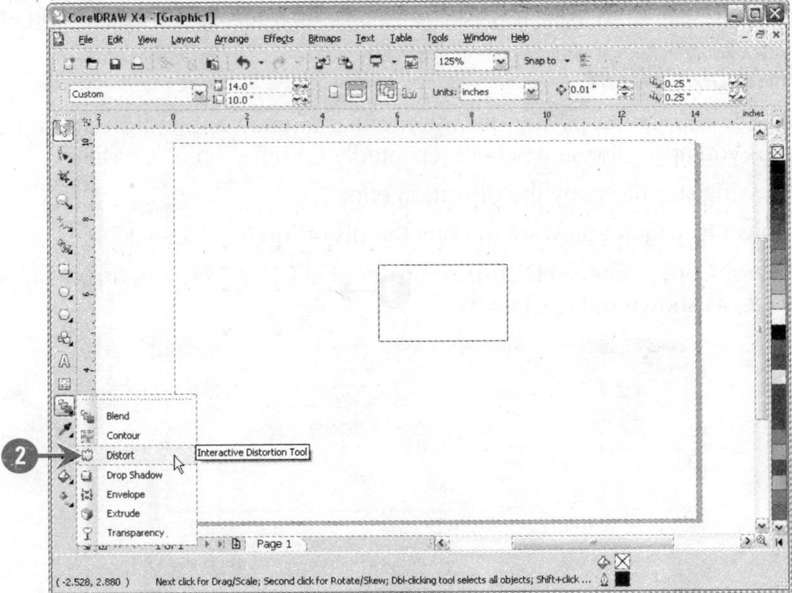

Fig.CD-4.15

3. To apply distortion effect on the object, *select* a distortion type from the Property bar. We select the **Twister Distortion** button (Fig.CD-4.16).
4. *Place* the mouse cursor on the object at the point where you want to place the center of distortion and drag it until you draw the desired shape of the object (Fig.CD-4.16).

The shape of the rectangle gets distorted, as shown in Fig.CD-4.16.

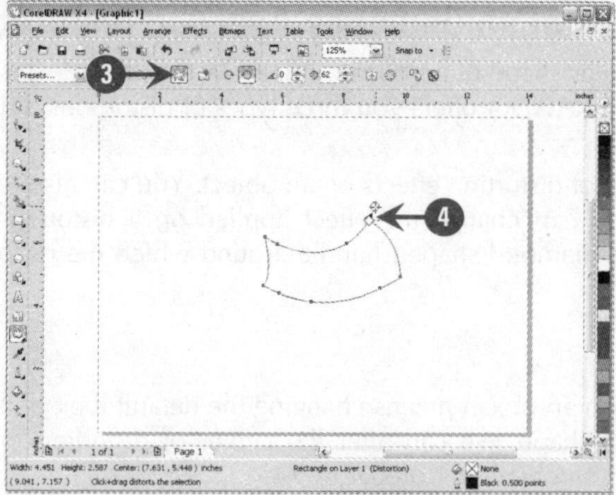

Fig.CD-4.16

Note

Click the Center Distortion button ( ) from the Property bar if you want to apply distortion at the center of the object.

After learning how to distort an object, let us now learn how to copy the distortion effect.

Copying the Distortion Effect

In CorelDRAW X4, you can copy the distortion effect already applied on an object to another object. This helps you apply the same effect repeatedly on other objects easily.

Perform the following steps to copy the distortion effect:

1. *Select* an object to which you want to copy the distortion (Fig.CD-4.17).
2. *Select* **Effects→Copy Effects→Distortion from** (Fig.CD-4.17). An arrow appears on the Drawing page, as shown in Fig.CD-4.18.

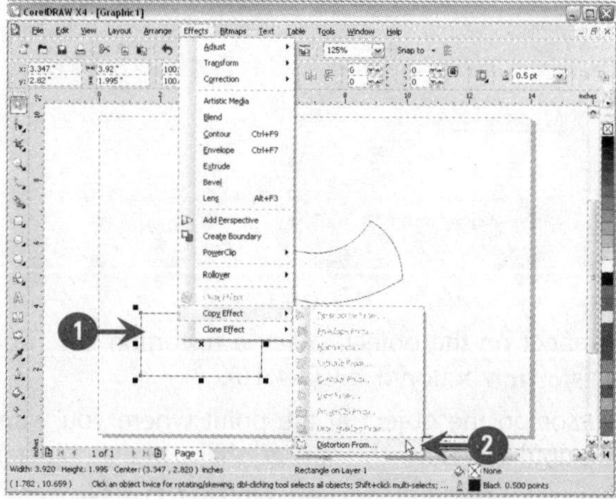

Fig.CD-4.17

3. *Click* the distorted object from which you want to copy the distortion effect (Fig.CD-4.18).

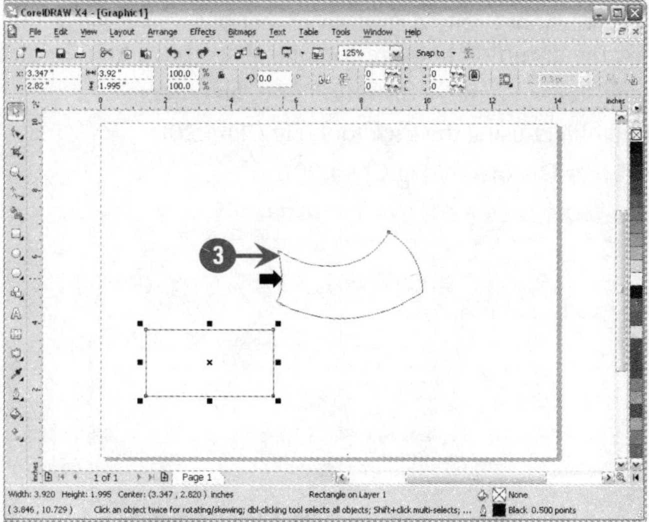

Fig.CD-4.18

As you click the distorted object, the distortion applies to the selected object, as shown in Fig.CD-4.19.

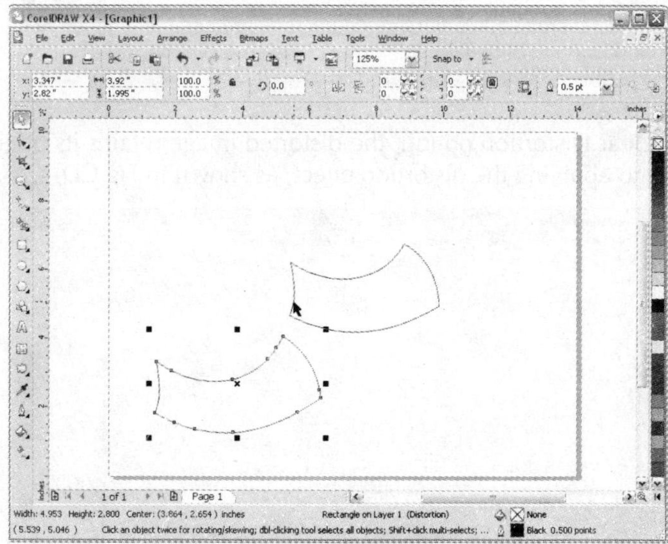

Fig.CD-4.19

Note

You can also use the Eyedropper tool from the Toolbox to copy an effect applied on an object.

After copying the distortion effect, let us now learn how to remove distortion effect from an object.

Removing a Distortion Effect

In CorelDRAW X4, you cannot only distort an object but also remove the distortion effect from an object. Removing the distortion helps restore the shape back to its original state.

Perform the following steps to remove distortion from an object:

1. *Select* a distorted object using the **Pick** tool (Fig.CD-4.20).
2. *Select* **Effects→Clear Distortion** (Fig.CD-4.20).

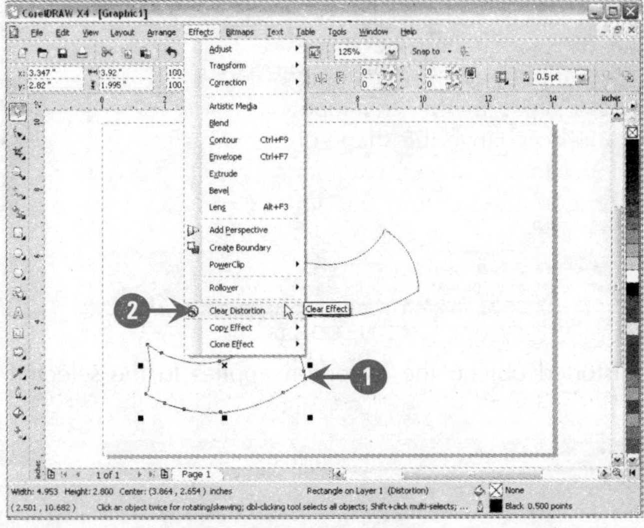

Fig.CD-4.20

As you select the Clear Distortion option, the distorted image retains its original state, that is the state it was in prior to applying the distortion effect, as shown in Fig.CD-4.21.

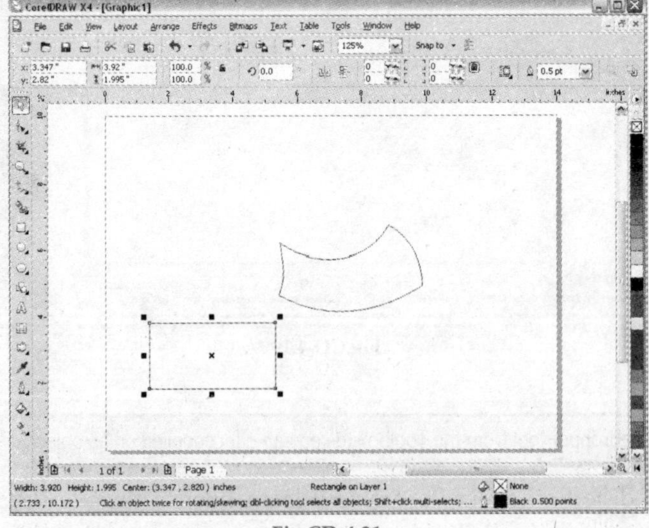

Fig.CD-4.21

Note

> The Clear Distortion removes the most recent distortion applied on the object. Use this option repeatedly to remove further distortions, if any.

After understanding how to remove distortion effect from an object, let us now learn to change the shape of objects using envelopes.

Modifying the Shape of an Object by using Envelopes

In CorelDRAW X4, you can change the shape of an object by using the Envelope tool. An envelope consists of multiple nodes. By moving these nodes, you can change the shape of the envelope. The changes done in the envelope bring changes in the shape of the object it envelopes to. You can also change the shape of the paragraph text with the help of envelopes. You can apply envelopes to any object by either choosing an envelope preset or clicking on an envelope mode button from the Property bar. On selecting an envelope preset, the shape of the object changes according to the selected preset. However, if you want to change the shape of the object manually, use an envelope mode. The list of available envelope modes is as follows:

- **Envelope Straight line Mode:** This mode helps you create envelopes based on straight lines. It also adds perspective to the object.
- **Envelope Single Arc Mode:** This mode helps you create envelopes with an arc shape on one side. Applying this mode on objects changes their appearances to concave or convex objects.
- **Envelope Double Arc Mode:** This mode helps you create envelopes with an S shape on one or more sides.
- **Envelope Unconstrained Mode:** This mode helps you create freeform envelopes that let you change the properties of the node. You can also add or delete a node with this mode.

CorelDRAW X4 allows you to copy and remove envelopes. You can also edit an envelope, which you have applied on an object.

Using an Envelope

You can apply an envelope to an object to bring it to a particular shape with the help of the nodes available with the envelope. Envelope contains the selected object and therefore, moving the nodes on the envelope reflects in simultaneous changes in the shape of the object it envelopes to.

Perform the following steps to use an envelope:

1. *Select* an object using the **Pick** tool (Fig.CD-4.22).
2. *Open* the **Interactive** tools flyout and *select* the **Envelope** tool, as shown in Fig.CD-4.22.

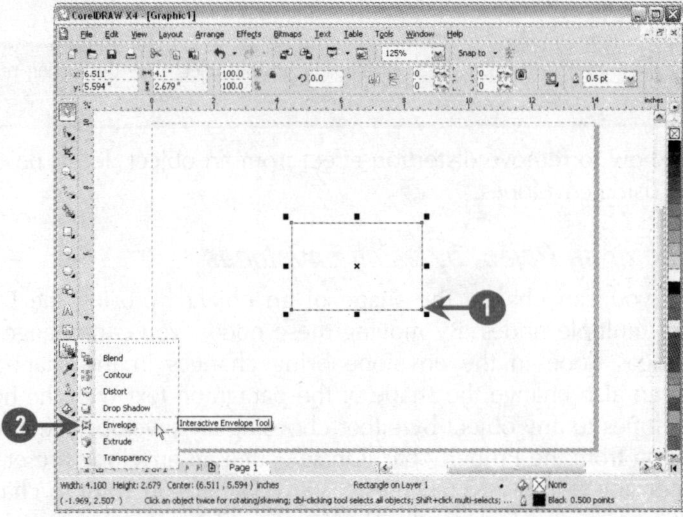

Fig.CD-4.22

3. *Select* an envelope mode button from the Property bar (Fig.CD-4.23). In our case, we select the **Envelope Unconstrained Mode** button.
4. *Click* the object and drag the nodes to give desired shape to the object (Fig.CD-4.23).

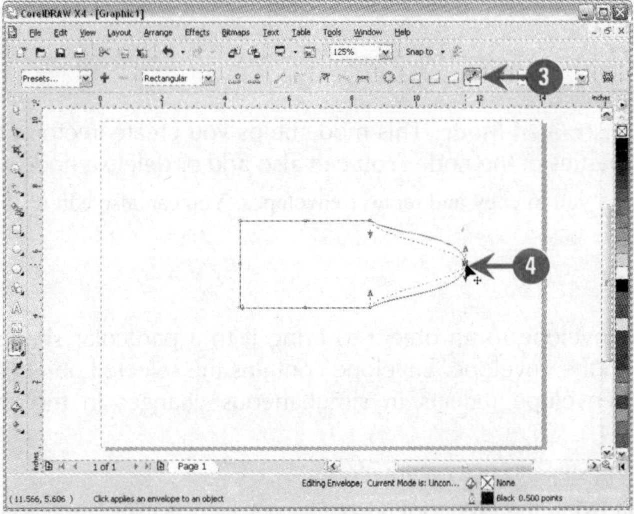

Fig.CD-4.23

After using an envelope on an object, let us now learn how to copy an envelope.

Copying an Envelope

You can copy an envelope from one object to another object. To learn how to copy an envelope, consider Fig.CD-4.23 in which we have applied envelope effect on a rectangle. Now, we draw a circle on which the envelope effect will be copied, as shown in Fig CD-4.24.

Perform the following steps to copy an envelope:

1. *Select* an object on which you want to copy the envelope (Fig.CD-4.24). In our case, we have selected the circle.
2. *Select* **Effects→Copy Effects→Envelope from** (Fig.CD-4.24). An arrow appears on the Drawing page, as shown in Fig.CD-4.25.

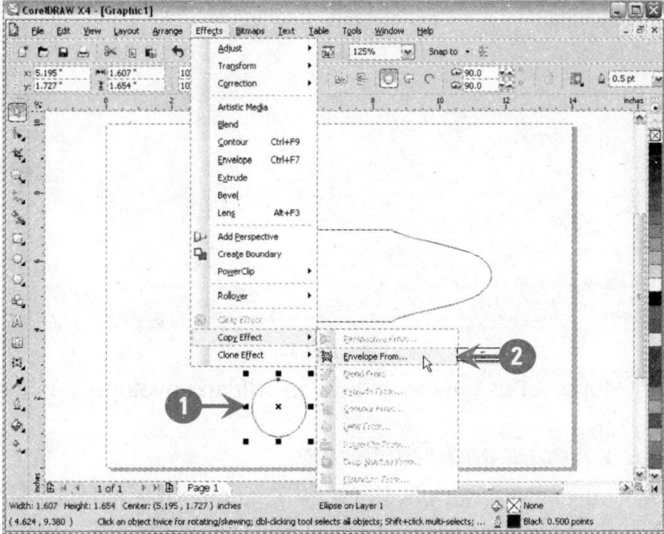

Fig.CD-4.24

3. *Select* the object from which you want to copy the envelope (Fig.CD-4.25).

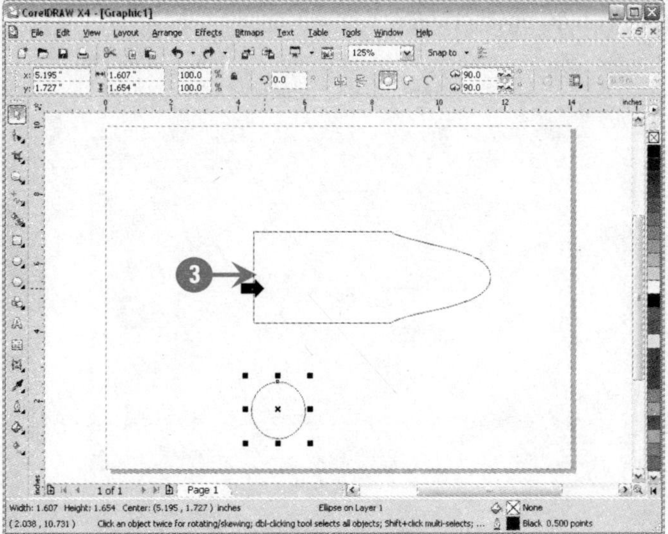

Fig.CD-4.25

The envelope effect applies to the selected object, as shown in Fig.CD-4.26.

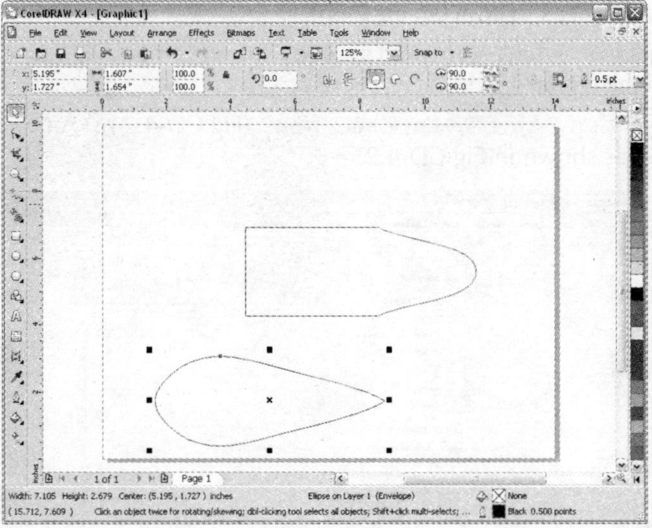

Fig.CD-4.26

After copying an envelope, let us now learn how to edit an envelope's nodes and segments.

Editing an Envelope's Nodes and Segments

In CorelDRAW X4, you can edit an envelope by changing the number of nodes. These nodes have square shape and can be increased or decreased depending on your requirements.

Perform the following steps to edit an envelope's nodes and segments:

1. *Open* the **Interactive** tools flyout and *select* the **Envelope** tool from the Toolbox (Fig.CD-4.27).
2. *Select* an object with an envelope (Fig.CD-4.27).

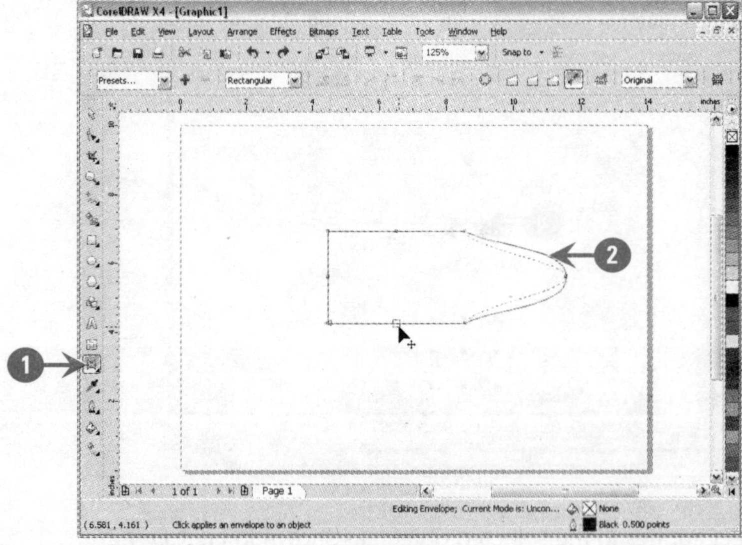

Fig.CD-4.27

3. *Double-click* a node to delete it from the object (Fig.CD-4.28).

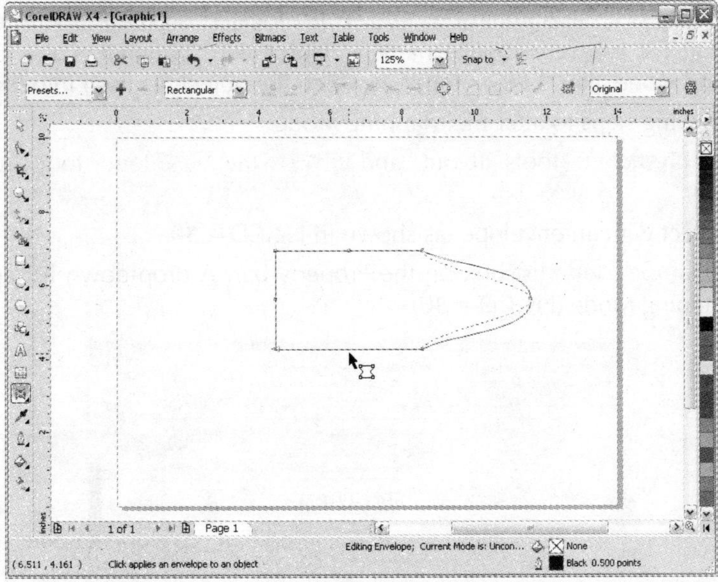

Fig.CD-4.28

4. *Double-click* another point on the envelope to add a node (Fig.CD-4.29).

A new node appears on the envelope, as shown in the Fig.CD-4.29.

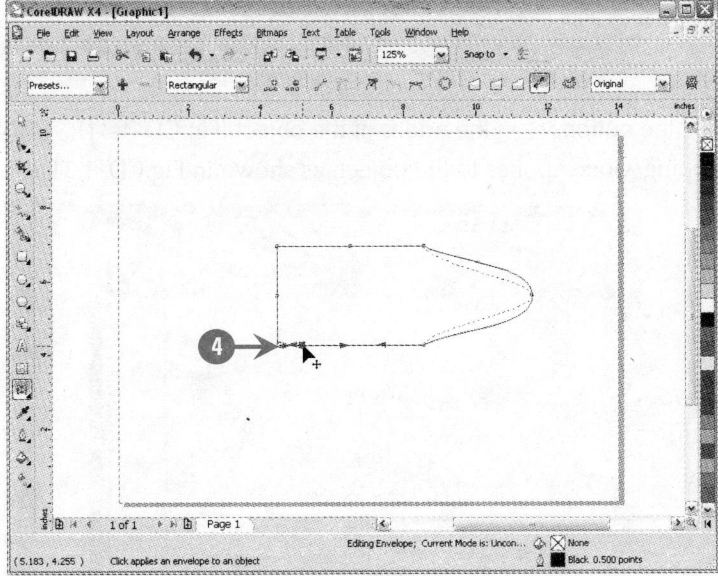

Fig.CD-4.29

After learning to edit an envelope's nodes and segments, let us now learn how to alter the Mapping Mode.

Altering the Mapping Mode

The Mapping Mode is an additional drop-down list located on the Property bar. The Mapping Mode drop-down list has four modes namely, Horizontal, Original, Putty, and Vertical. The selected Mapping Mode affects the manner in which the object fits itself into the envelope.

Perform the following steps to alter the Mapping Mode:

1. *Open* the **Interactive** tools flyout and *select* the **Envelope** tool from the Toolbox (Fig.CD-4.30).
2. *Select* an object with an envelope, as shown in Fig.CD-4.30.
3. *Click* the **Mapping Mode** list box on the Property bar. A drop-down list appears. *Select* the **Vertical** Mapping Mode (Fig.CD-4.30).

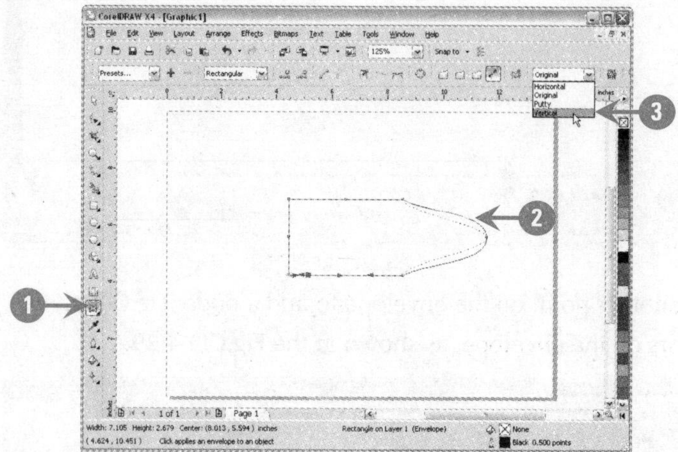

Fig.CD-4.30

4. After *selecting* the option, *drag* the nodes of the object (Fig.CD-4.31).

The Vertical Mapping Mode applies to the object, as shown in Fig.CD-4.31.

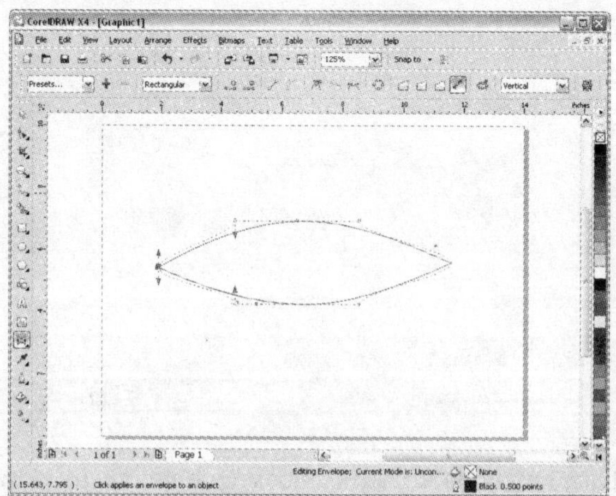

Fig.CD-4.31

After altering the Mapping Mode, let us now change the shape of an object by cropping, splitting, and erasing it.

Modifying the Shape of an Object by Cropping, Splitting, and Erasing it

CorelDRAW X4 allows you to crop, split, or erase any specified part of an object. Cropping is a method used to pick the desired portion of an object or trim an object to fit a certain size.

Splitting refers to partitioning an image. You can split a bitmap or vector object in two parts. While splitting an image, you can specify whether you want to close paths of the object automatically or keep them open. When you use the Eraser tool to erase a part of an object, the erased object changes into a curve according to the path taken by the Eraser tool.

Let's now learn how to crop, split and erase an object.

Cropping an Object

In CorelDRAW X4, you can crop an object. Cropping helps remove unwanted areas from the selected object. While cropping an object, you should define the cropping area. Cropping area is a rectangular area, which contains that part of the original object to which you want to retain, that is the area outside the cropping area will not appear in the final cropped object. You can also remove the cropping area if you do not want to crop an object.

Perform the following steps to crop an object:

1. *Select* an object that you want to crop (Fig.CD-4.32). In our case, we have selected a rectangle that surrounds a circle.

Note

> If you do not select any object and apply the Crop tool then all objects on the Drawing page will be cropped.

2. *Select* the **Crop** tool from the **Crop** tools flyout (Fig.CD-4.32).

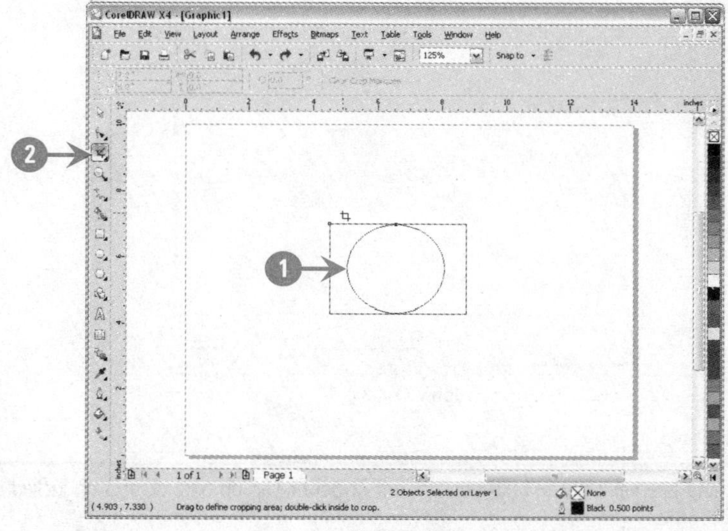

Fig.CD-4.32

3. *Drag* the mouse cursor to define the cropping area. The Drawing page except the cropping area, turns grey (Fig.CD-4.33).
4. *Double-click* inside the cropping area (Fig.CD-4.33).

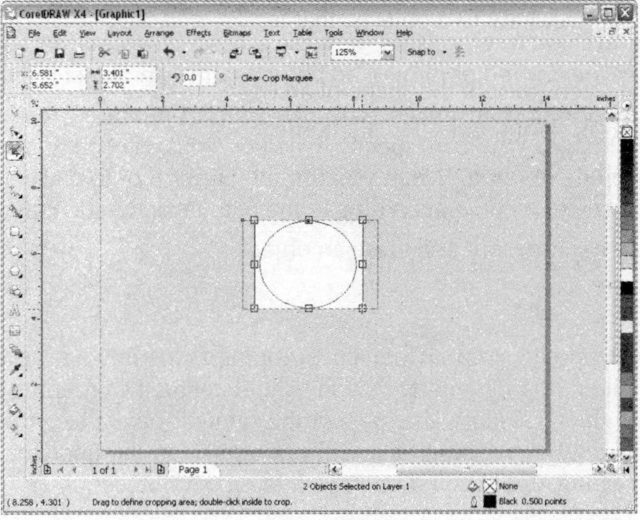

Fig.CD-4.33

The cropped object appears on the Drawing page and the grey highlight disappears, as shown in Fig.CD-4.34.

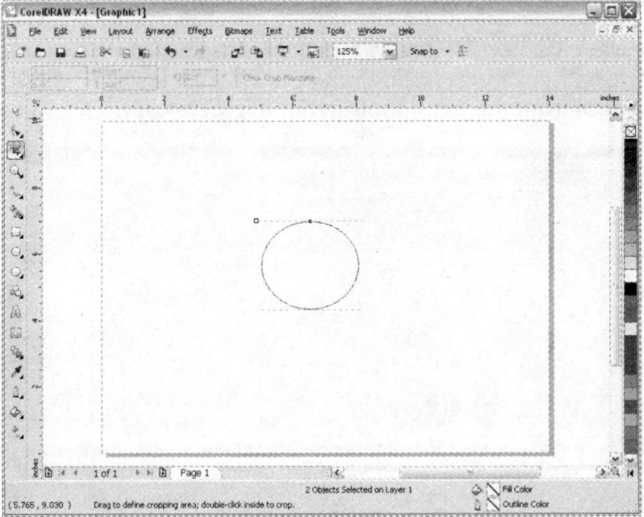

Fig.CD-4.34

Note

You cannot crop OLE and Internet objects, rollovers, content of power Clip objects, objects on locked, hidden, grid or guides layers.

After cropping an object, let us now learn to split it.

Splitting an Object

CorelDRAW X4 allows you to split an object into two parts. You can split an object by using the Knife tool. In our case, we draw two objects, that is, a circle within a rectangle. For splitting, we select the rectangle.

Perform the following steps to split the shape of an object:

1. *Open* the **Crop** tools flyout and *select* the **Knife** tool from the Toolbox (Fig.CD-4.35).

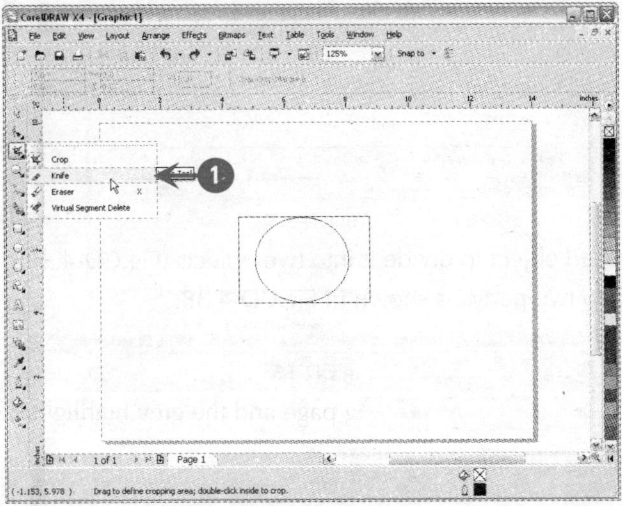

Fig.CD-4.35

2. *Place* the **Knife** tool over the outline of the object (rectangle) from where you want to split the object (Fig.CD-4.36).

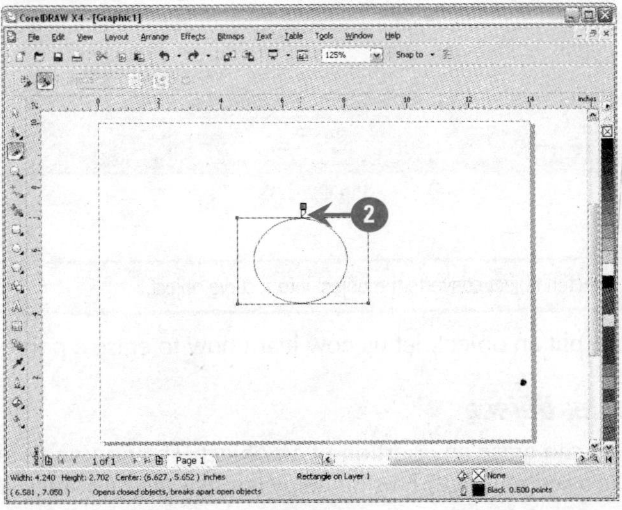

Fig.CD-4.36

3. Now *place* the **Knife** tool over the outline where you want to stop splitting the object (Fig.CD-4.37).

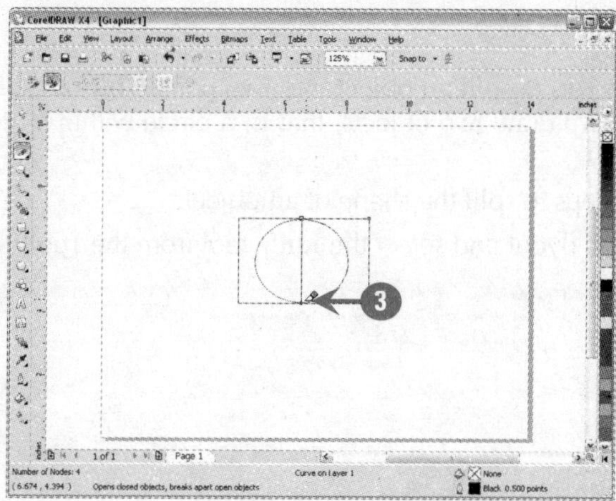

Fig.CD-4.37

4. *Drag* the partitioned object to divide it into two objects (Fig.CD-4.38).

The object divides into two parts, as shown in Fig.CD-4.38.

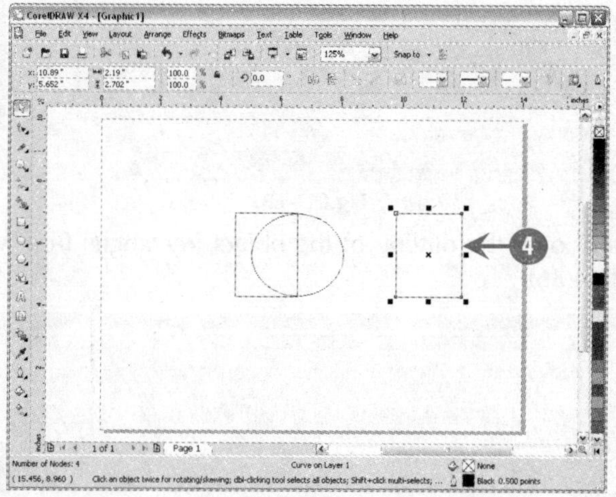

Fig.CD-4.38

Note

> Use of the Knife tool on selected object converts the object into a curve object.

After learning how to split an object, let us now learn how to erase a portion of an object.

Erasing a Portion of an Object

In CorelDraw X4, you can erase any portion of an object. The portion to be erased can be a part of the object or the text written on it. Erasing helps remove the unwanted areas from the selected object.

Perform the following steps to erase a portion of an object:

1. *Select* an object to be erased (Fig.CD-4.39).
2. *Open* the **Crop** tools flyout and *select* the **Eraser** tool from the Toolbox (Fig.CD-4.39). The mouse cursor converts into a rectangular shape.

Note

You can also change the shape of the eraser nib by clicking the Circle/Square button on the Property bar.

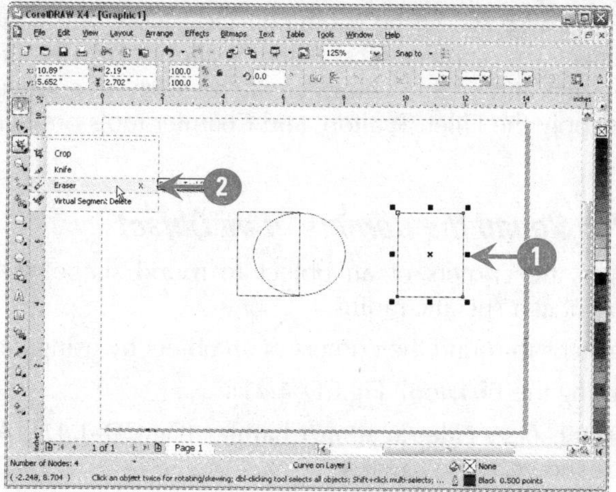

Fig.CD-4.39

3. *Move* the eraser tool over that part of the object to which you want to erase (Fig.CD-4.40).

Fig.CD-4.40 shows the object with erased portion.

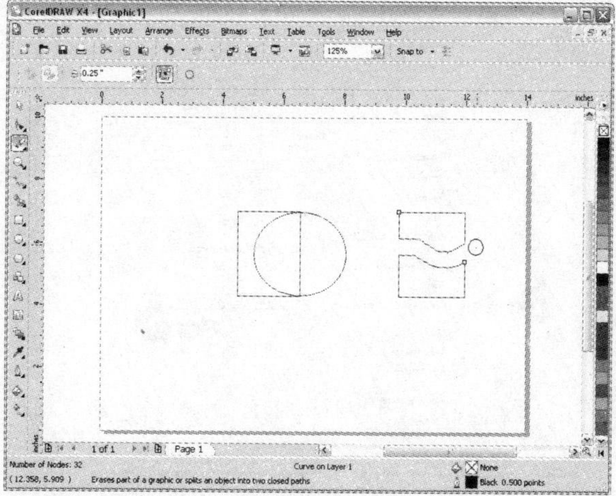

Fig.CD-4.40

Note

You can change the size of the eraser by typing a value in the Eraser thickness box located on the Property bar.

This is how you can erase a portion of an object. Let us learn to modify the shape of an object by filleting, scalloping, and chamfering the corners of the object.

Modifying the Shape of an Object using the Fillet, Scallop and Chamfer Tools

CorelDRAW X4 allows you to change the shape of an object by using the Fillet, Scallop, and Chamfer tools on the corners of an object. These methods enable you to apply corner effects to vector paths, which otherwise would be a difficult task. Now you can create curved, reverse-curved, or beveled effects by applying the Fillet, Scallop, and Chamfer shaping tools. These shortcuts save a lot of time and enable you to create a variety of complex effects on the corners of an object. You can apply the Fillet, Scallop, and Chamfer tools only on the undistorted curved objects.

Using the Fillet Tool to Round the Corners of an Object

The Fillet tool changes the corners of an object to round shape. It helps maintain uniform roundness around a point at a specific radius.

Perform the following steps to round the corners of an object by using the Fillet tool:

1. *Select* an object using the **Pick** tool (Fig.CD-4.41).
2. *Select* **Window→Dockers→Fillet/Scallop/Chamfer** (Fig.CD-4.41). A **Fillet/Scallop/Chamfer** docker appears, as shown in Fig.CD-4.42.

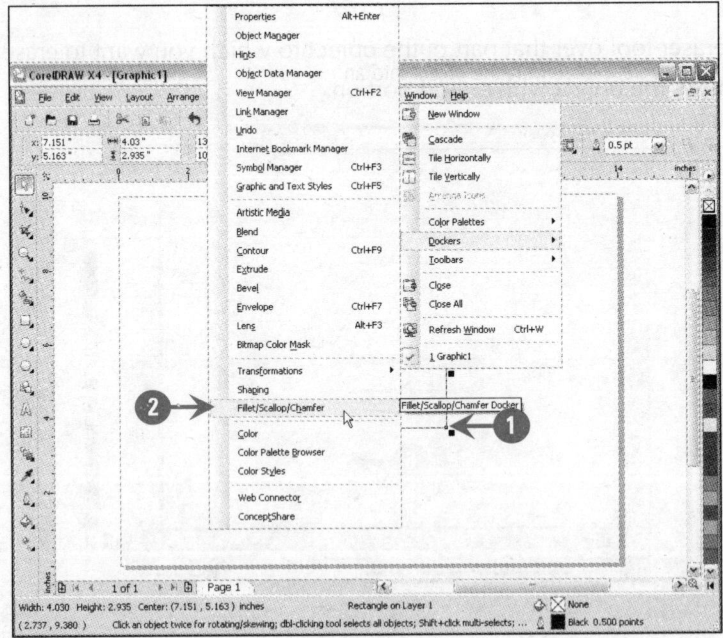

Fig.CD-4.41

3. *Click* the **Operations** drop-down list and *select* the **Fillet** option, as shown in Fig.CD-4.42.

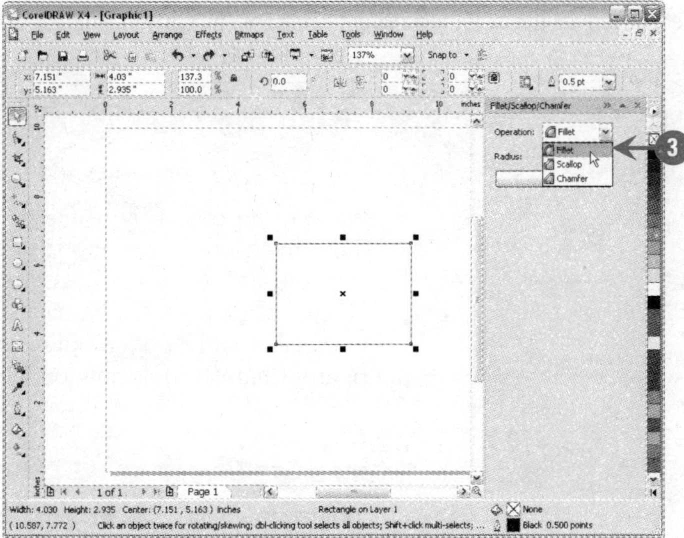

Fig.CD-4.42

4. *Type* a value in the **Radius** box and *click* the **Apply** button (Fig.CD-4.43).
5. If the object is not a curve object, a warning message box asking you to convert the object to an undistorted curve, appears (Fig.CD-4.43).
6. *Click* the **OK** button in the warning message, as shown in Fig.CD-4.43.

Note

Click the OK button if you want to convert the object into an undistorted curve; else click Cancel, if you do not want to make changes.

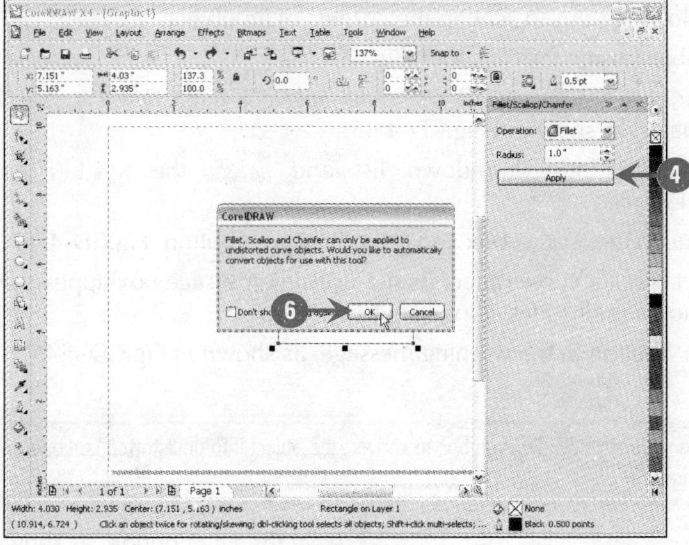

Fig.CD-4.43

The shape of the corners of the selected object changes, as shown in Fig.CD-4.44.

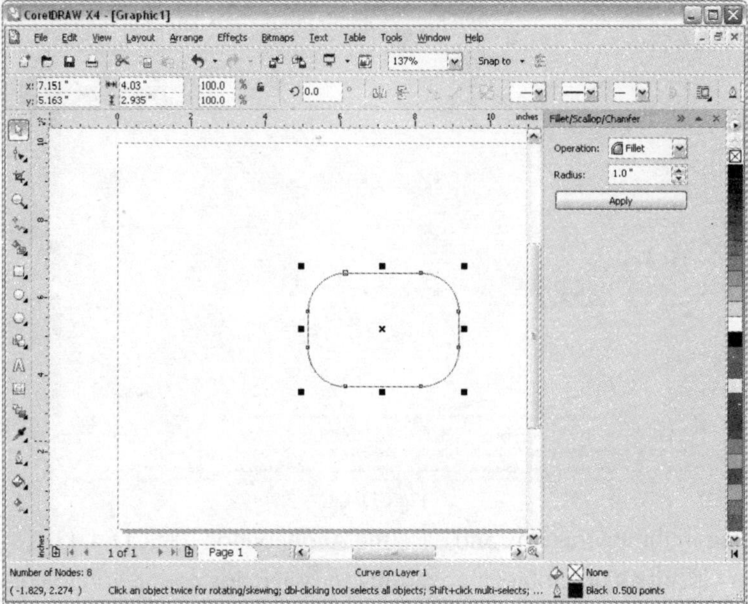

Fig.CD-4.44

After rounding the corners by the Fillet tool, let us now learn how to use Scallop tool.

Using the Scallop Tool on the Corners of an Object

CorelDRAW X4 allows you to create a notch by using the Scallop tool. Scallop tool helps create a notch by rounding the corners and then inverting them.

Perform the following steps to scallop the corners of an object:

1. *Select* an object using the **Pick** tool (Fig.CD-4.45).
2. *Select* **Window→Dockers→Fillet/Scallop/Chamfer** (Fig.CD-4.45). A **Fillet/Scallop/Chamfer** docker appears, as shown in Fig.CD-4.45.
3. *Click* the **Operations** drop-down list and *select* the **Scallop** option from the list (Fig.CD-4.45).
4. *Type* a value in the **Radius** box and *click* the **Apply** button (Fig.CD-4.45).
5. If the object is not a curve object then a warning message box appears asking you to convert the object to an undistorted curve (Fig.CD-4.45).
6. *Click* the **OK** button in the warning message, as shown in Fig.CD-4.45.

Note

Click the OK button in CorelDRAW message box to convert the object into undistorted curve, or click Cancel, if you do not want to make changes.

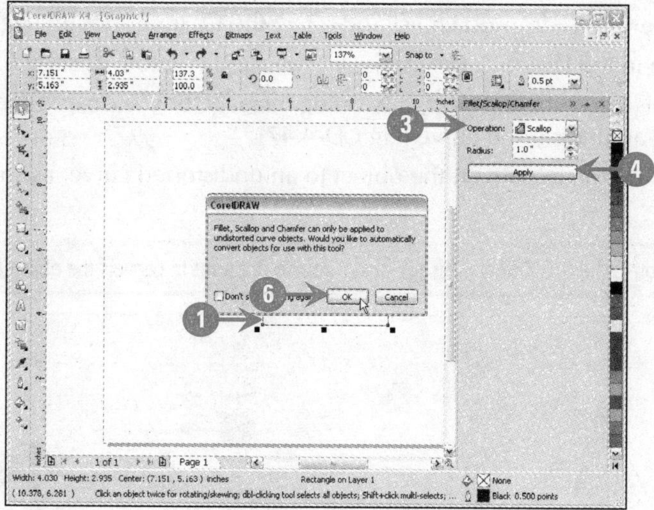

Fig.CD- 4.45

The shape of the corners of the object changes, as shown in Fig.CD-4.46.

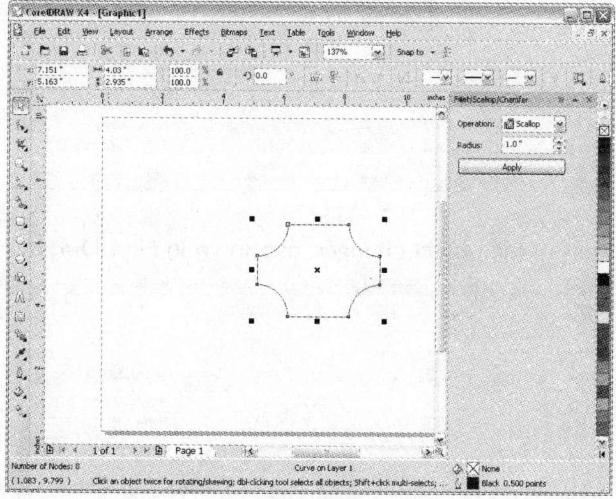

Fig.CD-4.46

Let us now learn how to bevel object corners by using the Chamfer tool.

Using the Chamfer Tool on the Corners of an Object

CorelDRAW X4 allows you to create flat corners by using the Chamfer tool. These chamfered corners help you convert the sharp corners of an object to uniform angled corners.

Perform the following steps to bevel object corners by using the chamfer tool:

1. *Select* an object using the **Pick** tool (Fig.CD-4.47).
2. *Select* **Windows→Dockers→Fillet/Scallop/Chamfer** (Fig.CD-4.47). A **Fillet/Scallop/Chamfer** docker appears, as shown in Fig.CD-4.47.

3. *Click* the **Operations** drop-down list and *select* the **Chamfer** option (Fig.CD-4.47).
4. *Type* a value in the **Distance** box and *click* the **Apply** button, as shown in Fig.CD-4.47.
5. If the object is not a curve object, a warning message box appears which asks you to convert the object to an undistorted curve (Fig.CD-4.47).
6. *Click* the **OK** button to convert the object to an undistorted curve, as shown in Fig.CD-4.48.

Note

Click the Cancel button in the CorelDRAW message box, if you do not want to convert the object to an undistorted curve.

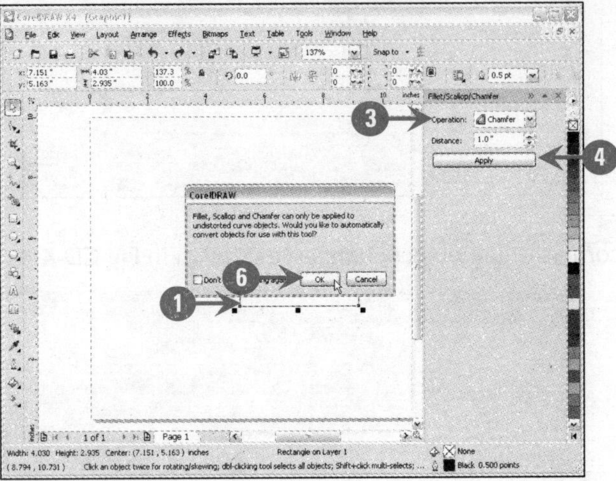

Fig.CD-4.47

The shape of the corners of the object changes, as shown in Fig.CD-4.48.

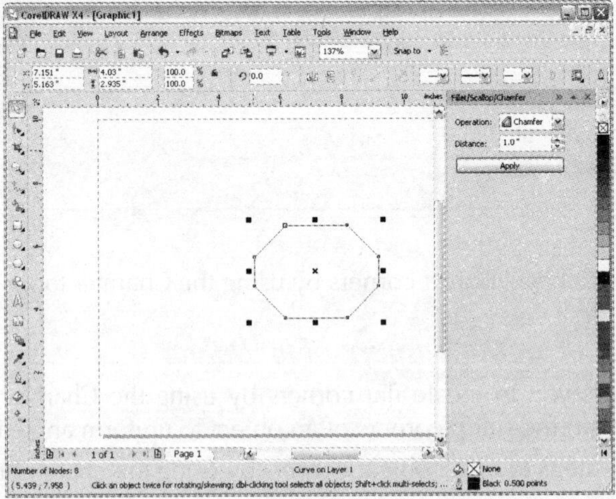

Fig.CD-4.48

With this, we conclude this chapter. Before proceeding further to the next chapter, here is the summary of the chapter.

Summary

In this chapter, you learned about:

- Modifying basic shapes such as rectangle and ellipse
- Setting grid lines and snapping objects to grids and guidelines
- Converting objects to curve objects
- Applying distortion to customize the shape of an object
- Using envelopes on objects
- Cropping, splitting, and erasing the shape of an object
- Applying Fillet, Scallop, and Chamfer tools on the corners

In the next chapter, you will learn how to fill an object by using colors and different effects.

Chapter 5

Filling Objects

In this Section

- Using Uniform Fills
- Using Fountain Fills
- Using Pattern Fills
- Using Texture Fills
- Using Mesh Fills
- Using Fills to Areas
- Selecting Colors by Using Color Palette
- Creating Custom Color Palette
- Editing Custom Color Palette

In any graphic and designing application colors play an important role in adding emphasis and vibrant look to your work. In CorelDRAW, there are number of ways to add colors to images, objects and text. The most common and easy to access method for adding color is by using the Color palette. However, if you are thinking beyond the Color palette and like to experiment on filling colors then CorelDRAW will not disappoint you. In CorelDRAW there are other tools which you can use to fill objects, images or text with complex color combination such as gradient and textured patterns. On the Toolbox, you can find such tools in the fly-out menu of Uniform Fill tool.

A brief introduction about these fill tools are:

- **Uniform Fill tool:** Use to apply solid color to the objects.
- **Fountain Fill tool:** Use fill an objects with a combination of two or more colors.
- **Pattern Fill tool:** Use to apply a pattern of two or more colors to an object.
- **Texture Fill tool:** Use to fill an object with a texture.
- **Interactive Fill tool:** Use to fill the objects with different types of fills such as uniform, fountain, pattern, and texture.
- **Mesh Fill tool:** Use to apply a mesh grid to an object.
- **Smart Fill tool:** Use to indentify the enclosed area when one object overlaps the other one and fill that enclosed are

In this chapter, you will learn to apply various fill types, such as, uniform fills, fountain fills, pattern fills, texture fills and mesh fills. You will also learn to fill the enclosed area by using the Smart Fill tool. Later, we will discuss about selecting the colors from the Color palette and creating as well as editing the custom Color palette. We will begin by discussing about using uniform Fills.

Using Uniform Fills

Uniform fills are solid colors in the Color palette. Besides using colors of Color palette, you can create your desired color by specifying color values in the chosen color model. Whenever Uniform fill is applied to an object, the object is filled with a solid color. To apply a uniform fill to an object you can use Interactive Fill tool, Uniform Fill tool on the Toolbox or select a color from the Color palette.

Let us undertake the following steps to apply uniform fills to objects:

1. *Select the* **Pick** tool. *Click* the object to select it in the Drawing page (Fig.CD-5.1).
2. *Select* the **Interactive Fill** tool on the Toolbox (Fig.CD-5.1).

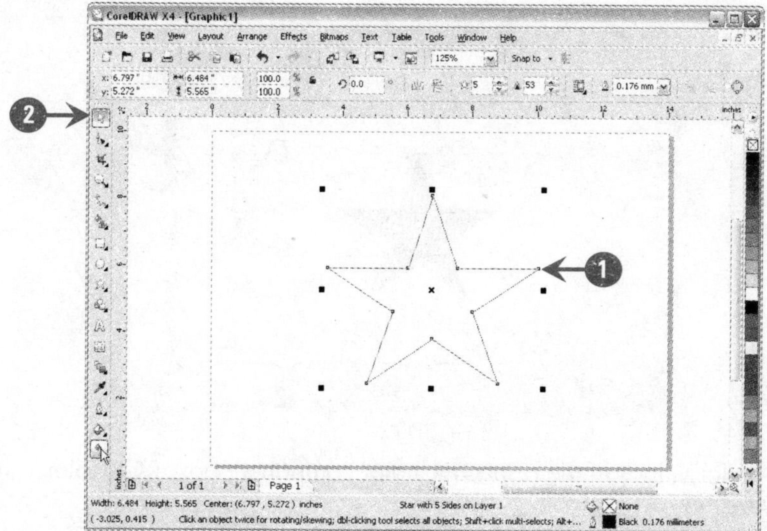

Fig.CD-5.1

Note

You can also use the Uniform Fill tool to apply the uniform fill to an object.

3. Next, *select* a fill type from the **Fill Type** drop-down list on the Property bar (Fig.CD-5.2). We have selected **Uniform Fill**.

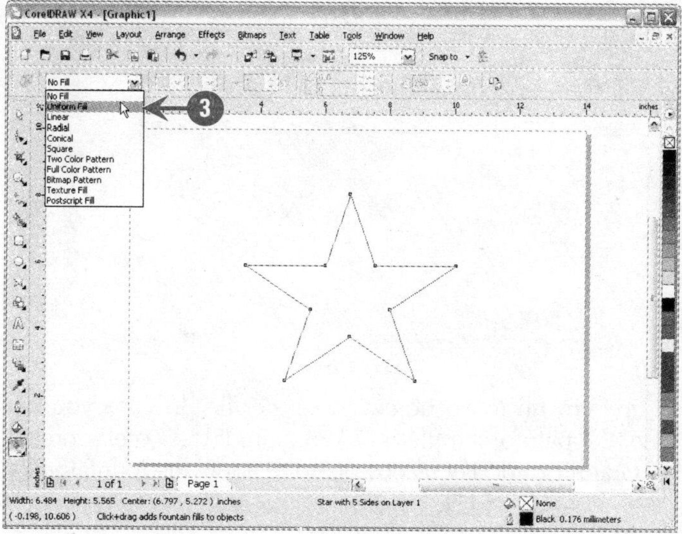

Fig.CD-5.2

4. *Select* a color model from the **Uniform Fill Type** drop-down list. We have *selected* the **RGB** (Red, Blue, and Green) color model, as shown in Fig.CD-5.3.

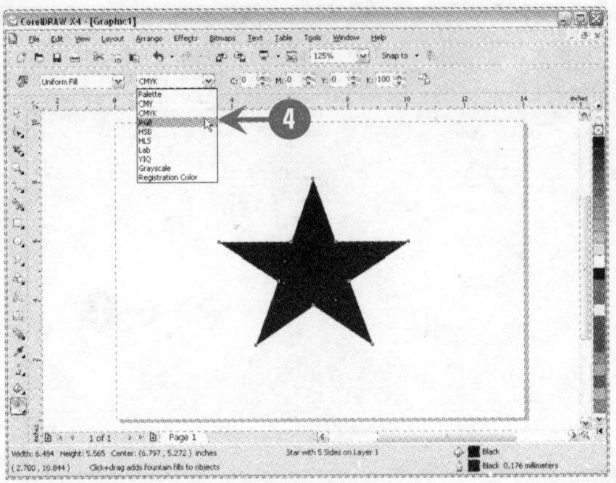

Fig.CD-5.3

Specify the RGB color values in the respective color component box, RGB color values includes the range from 0 to 255.

5. To set RGB color value, *type* **150** in the **First Color Component** spin box, **150** in the **Second Color Component** spin box and **100** in the **Third Color Component** spin box, as shown in Fig.CD-5.4 and *press* the **Enter** key.

The object is filled with the uniform colors, as shown in Fig.CD-5.4.

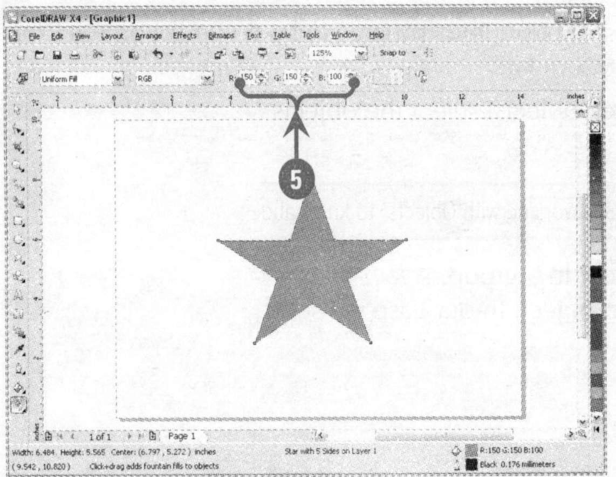

Fig.CD-5.4

After applying the uniform fill to an object, save the file, in case you need to reuse it when required. In our case, the path of the file is 'E:\Program Files\Corel\CorelDRAW Graphics Suite X4\Draw\Samples\Graphic1.cdr' Let us now learn to apply the fountain fills.

Using Fountain Fills

A fountain fill gives you the option to fill an object with a combination of two or more colors where one color gradually fades into another in different styles. Fountain fills are also known as gradient fills.

There are four categories of fill type to be applied in the fountain fills:

- **Linear:** In this type of fountain fill, one color is fades into another color in a straight line.
- **Radial:** In this type of the fountain fill, one color fades into another in the form of circle.
- **Conical:** In this type of fountain fill, one color fades into another color in a circular path that radiates from the center of the objects.
- **Square:** In this type of fountain fill, one color fades into another in the form of a square.

Let us now learn how to apply fountain fills using the default fountain fills and the custom fountain fills.

You can apply the fountain fill in three ways, preset fountain fill, two-color fountain fill or custom fountain fills.

Using a Preset Fountain Fill

Preset fountain fills come in-built with CorelDRAW. The large ranges of preset fountain fills help you to quickly apply the fountain fills to the object. After selecting a preset fountain fill, you can specify a fill type, fill's angle, center point, and edge pad.

Undertake the following steps to apply a preset fountain fill:

1. *Open* the drawing in which we applied Uniform fills from the location **(E:\Program Files\Corel\CorelDRAW Graphics Suite X4\Draw\Samples\Graphic1.cdr)** where you have save it.
2. *Draw* the shapes of a circle, a square and a triangle as shown in the Drawing page beside the star (Fig.CD-5.5).
3. For grouping three objects, *select* the objects and *select* **Arrange→Group** option.

Note

> You can refer to chapter 3: 'Working with Objects' to know about grouping objects in details under 'Grouping Objects'.

4. To select an object in a group, *select* the **Pick** tool in the Toolbox, hold down the **CTRL** key, and then *click* an object. In our case we select the rectangle (Fig.CD-5.5).

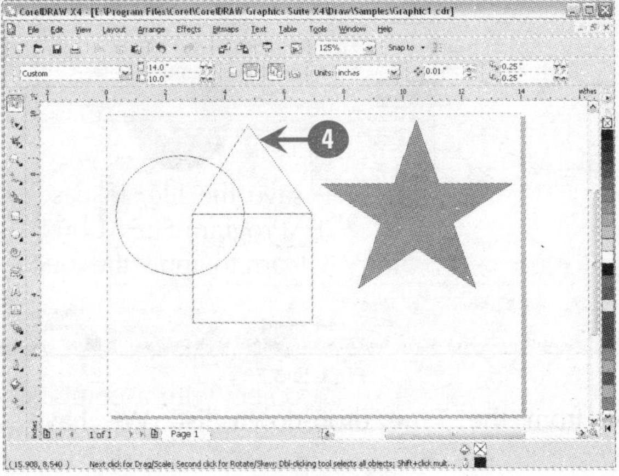

Fig.CD-5.5

5. *Click* the arrow on the lower-right corner of the **Fill** tool, and *select* the **Fountain Fill** tool from the flyout (Fig.CD-5.6). A **Fountain Fill** dialog box appears (Fig.CD-5.7).

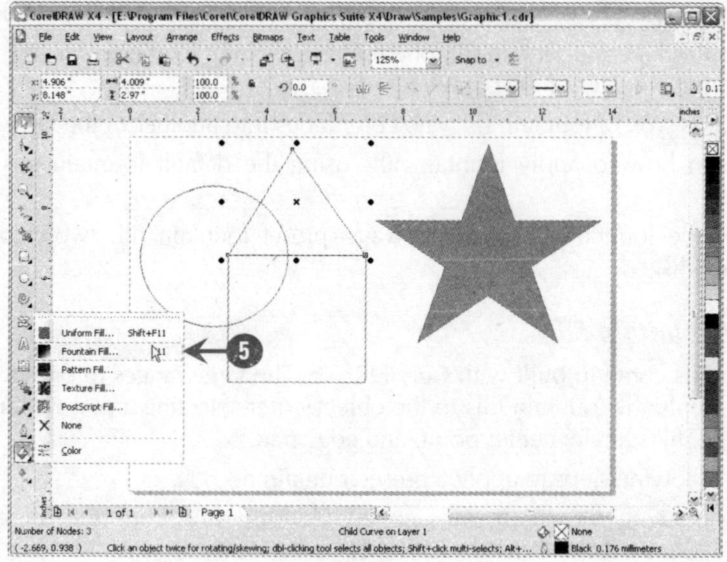

Fig.CD-5.6

6. *Select* a preset fountain fill from the **Presets** list (Fig.CD-5.7). In our case, it is **Forest Light** option.

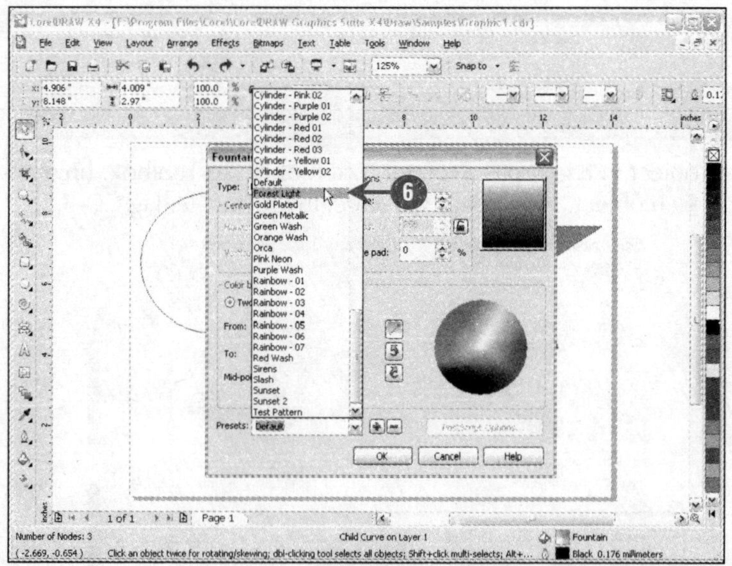

Fig.CD-5.7

7. *Select* a fill type from the **Type** drop-down list. We have selected **Conical** option (Fig.CD-5.8).

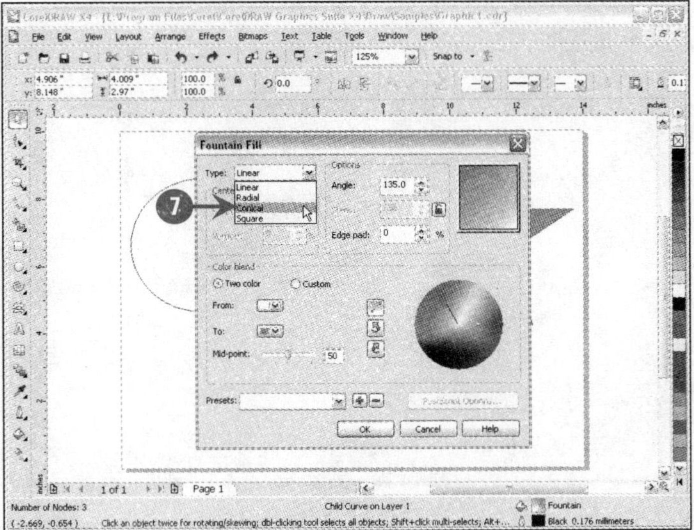

Fig.CD-5.8

8. Set the fill's angle in the **Angle** spin box. In our case it is **45** degree (Fig.CD-5.9). Fill's angle decides the direction of the fountain fills.
9. Set the center point of the Fountain fill by providing value in the **Horizontal** and **Vertical** spin boxes. In our case center is at (**0**, **0**), as shown in Fig.CD-5.9.
10. *Click* the **OK** button to apply the fill to the object (Fig.CD-5.9).

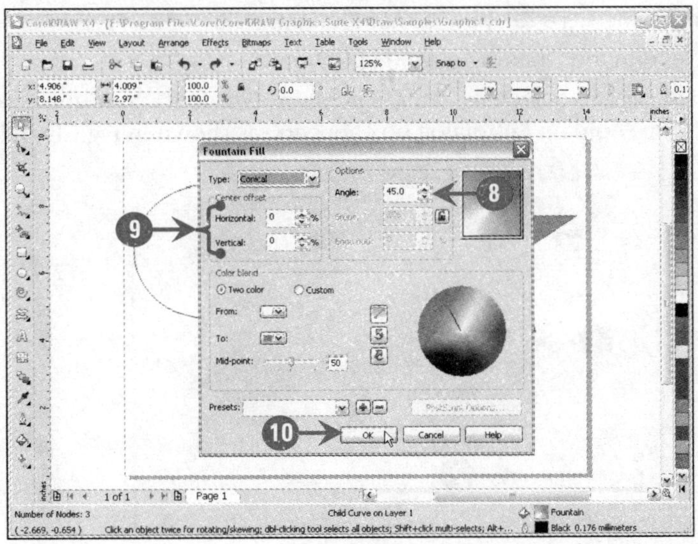

Fig.CD-5.9

You can see the preset fountain fill to an object, in our case it is a triangle, as shown in Fig.CD-5.10.

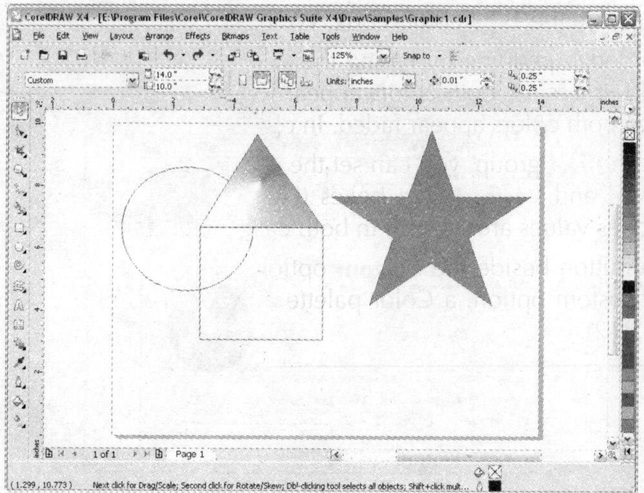

Fig.CD-5.10

Using a Custom Fountain Fill

Custom fountain fill can include two or more colors. In this fountain fill, user selects the colors manually and can also set the center point and the edge pad for the color fill. The center point adjustment allows you to set the center offset of a fill. The edge pad setting allows you to adjust the size of the outer edge fill color inwards. After applying a custom fountain fill, you can save it as a preset.

Undertake the following steps to apply custom fountain fill:

1. *Select* a circle from the Drawing page (Fig.CD-5.11).
2. *Open* the **Fill** flyout and *select* the **Fountain Fill** tool from the flyout, as shown in Fig.CD-5.11.The **Fountain Fill** dialog box appears, as shown in Fig.CD-5.12.

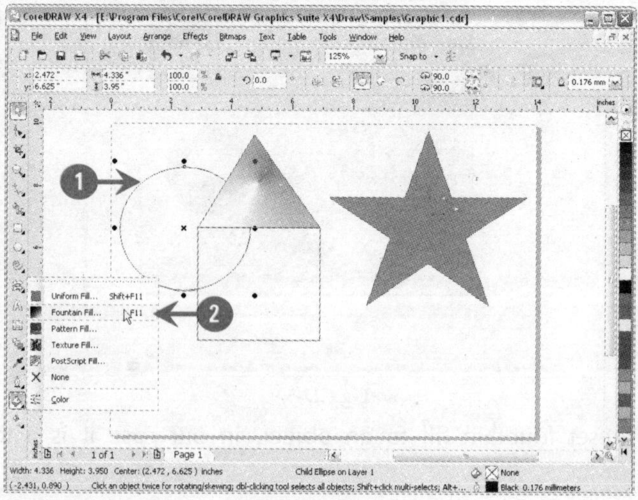

Fig.CD-5.11

3. *Select* a fill type from the **Type** combo box. We have selected **Radial** option (Fig.CD-5.12).
4. You can set the edge padding by typing the value in the **Edge pad** spin box. Its values lie between 0 to 49. If it is 49, both colors appear individually in the object. On the other hand if value is 0 then both colors appear faded. In our case edge pad value is **0** (Fig.CD-5.12).
5. From the **Center Offset** group, you can set the position of the center point of the fountain fill in the **Horizontal** and **Vertical** spin boxes (Fig.CD-5.12), in our case, the Horizontal and Vertical spin boxes values are **0** (zero) in both case, as shown in Fig.CD-5.12.
6. *Click* the radio button beside the **Custom** option under the **Color Blend** group. As soon as you select the Custom option, a Color palette appears on the right end of the **Color Blend** group (Fig.CD-5.12).

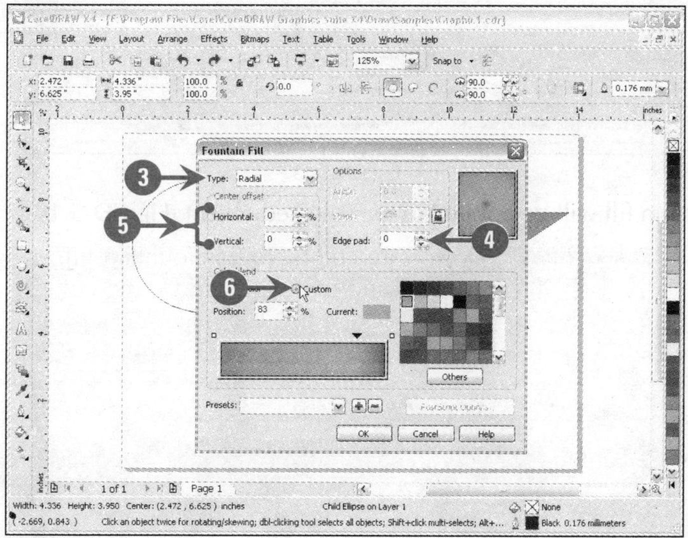

Fig.CD-5.12

7. *Click* the small square box present on the left side of the color band to activate the use of first fill color (Fig.CD-5.13).
8. Next, *click* on a color swatch in the Color palette (Fig.CD-5.13). This will specify the first fill color.
9. Now *click* the small square box present on the right side of the color band to activate use of second fill color (Fig.CD-5.13).
10. Next *click* on a color swatch in the Color palette to select a different second color (Fig.CD-5.13). This will specify the second fill color.
11. *Double-click* anywhere on the color band and drag the marker just above the color band (Fig.CD-5.13).

The marker lets you set the fading effect of selected colors in the object and decides the amount of both colors in filling the object. For example, dragging the marker towards the right side will fill the object more with the first color and vice-versa.

12. *Click* the **OK** button to apply the custom fountain fill to the object (Fig.CD-5.13).

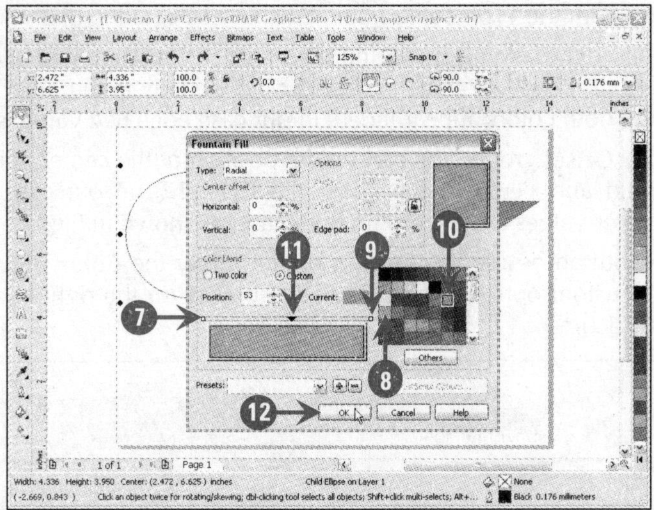

Fig.CD-5.13

The custom fountain fill will be applied to the selected object (Fig.CD-5.14).

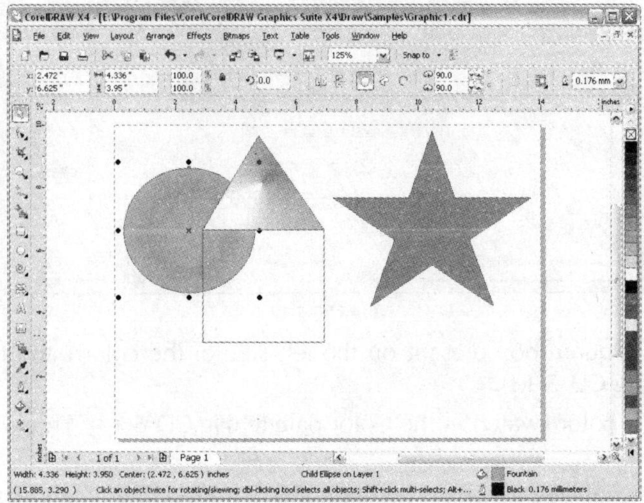

Fig.CD-5.14

After applying the fountain fills to an object, let us now learn to apply pattern fills.

Using Pattern Fills

In the pattern fills, you can apply a pattern of two or more colors to an object. You can fill the objects using the two-color, full color or bitmap pattern fills. A two-color pattern fills is made of two colors selected by you. The full color pattern fills are made of a complex vector graphics that can be composed of lines and fills. In the bitmap pattern fill, you select a bitmap image. In this section, you will learn how we apply a two-color, full color or bitmap color fills to an object.

CorelDRAW have preset pattern fills that you can directly apply to the objects. You can also create your own pattern fills from objects that you draw or images that you import.

Using Two-Color Pattern Fill

In the two-color pattern fill, we choose two colors, here you select a pattern, the front color, and the back color. You can also change the tile size of the pattern fills.

Undertake the following steps to apply the two-color pattern fill:

1. *Select* an object on the Drawing page, for example the square (Fig.CD-5.15).
2. *Click* the **Interactive Fill** tool (Fig.CD-5.15). As soon as you select the Interactive tool on the Toolbox, the various options on the Property bar changes.
3. Next, on the Property bar, *select* a fill type from the **Fill Type** drop-down list (Fig.CD-5.15). We have selected **Two Color Pattern** option (Fig.CD-5.15).

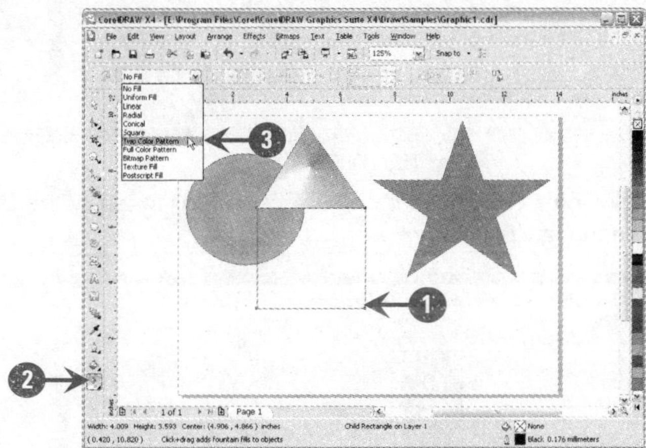

Fig.CD-5.15

4. *Select* a pattern on the **Fill Dropdown** drop-down list, as shown in Fig.CD-5.16.

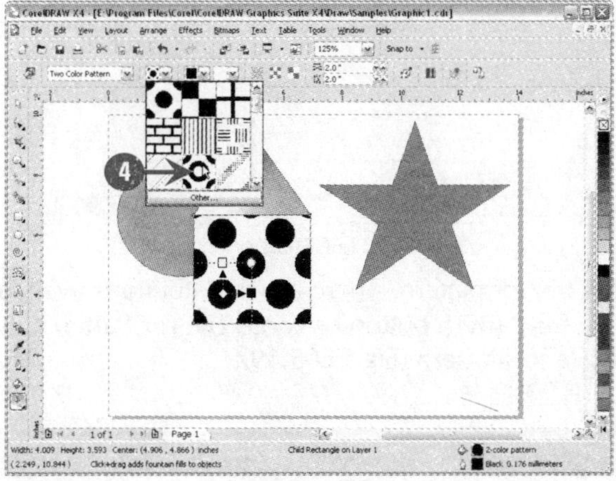

Fig.CD-5.16

5. *Open* the **Front Color** color picker and *select* a color from the Color palette to select the front color for the fill (Fig.CD-5.17).

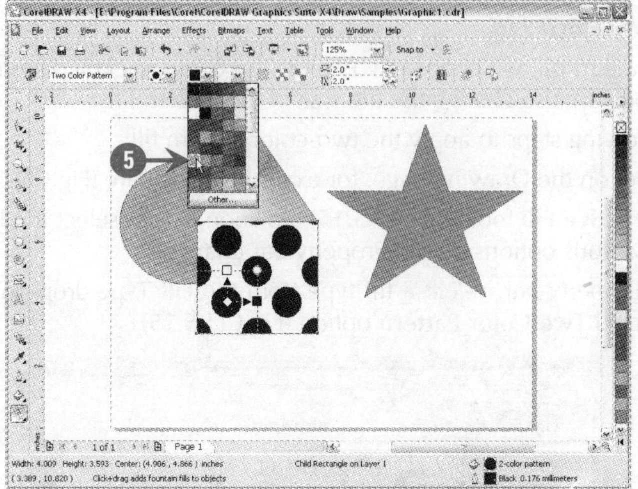

Fig.CD-5.17

6. Next, *open* the **Back Color** color picker and *select* a color to apply the background for the pattern fill, as shown in Fig.CD-5.18.

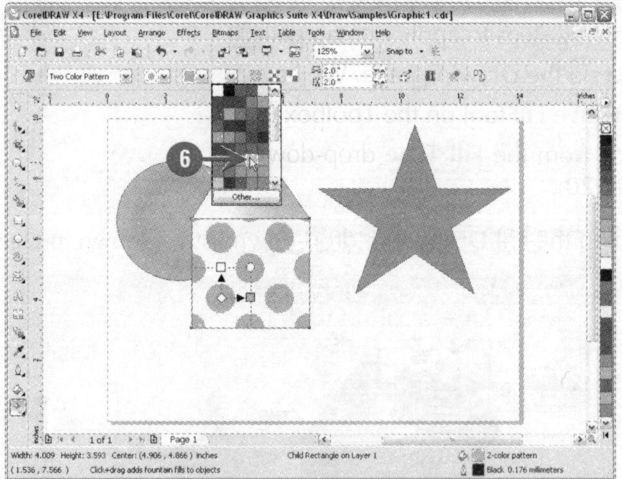

Fig.CD-5.18

7. You can change the tile for pattern. There are three buttons available **Small Tile for Pattern** button, **Medium Tile for Pattern** button or **Large Tile for Patten** button. In our case, we have selected the **Small Tile for Pattern** (Fig.CD-5.19).

Note

You can also change the tile pattern from the Edit Tiling for Pattern spin box by typing the values as per need for filling the drawing.

The result of applying the two-color pattern fill to the object is shown in Fig.CD-5.19.

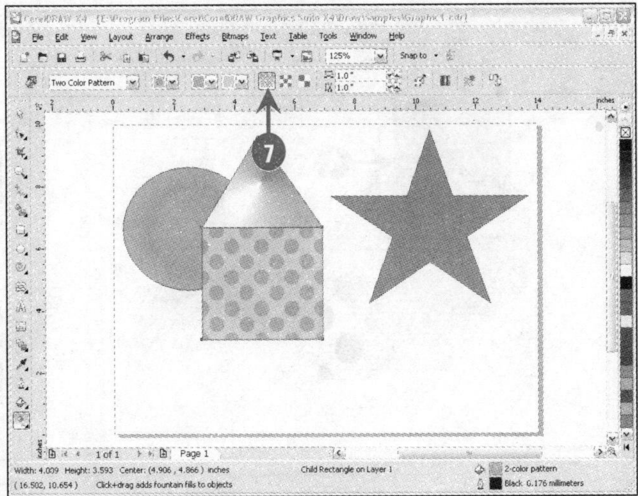

Fig.CD-5.19

Using Bitmap Pattern Fill

The bitmap pattern fill is a bitmap image. After selecting a bitmap image for the bitmap pattern fill, you can specify the tile size of the pattern fills.

Undertake the following steps to apply bitmap pattern fill:

1. *Select* an object on the Drawing page. We have selected the star, as shown in Fig.CD-5.20.
2. *Click* the **Interactive Fill** tool on the Toolbox (FigCD-5.20).
3. *Select* a fill type from the **Fill Type** drop-down list, we have selected **Bitmap Color Pattern** option (FigCD-5.20).

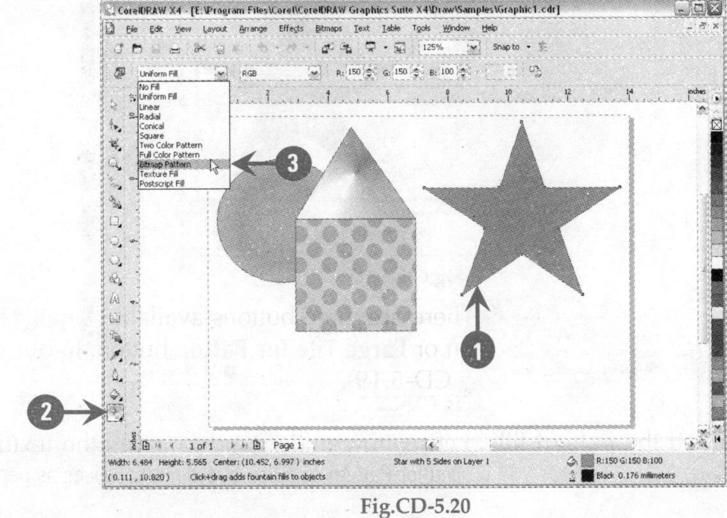

Fig.CD-5.20

4. *Open* the **Fill Dropdown** picker and *select* a pattern, as shown in (FigCD-5.21).

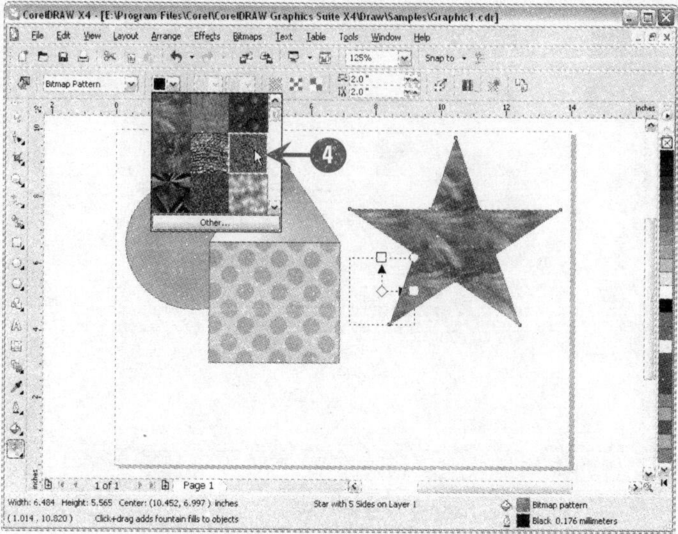

Fig.CD-5.21

5. To change the tile for the pattern. There are three buttons available **Small Tile for Pattern**, **Medium Tile for Pattern** or **Large Tile for Patten**. In our case, we have selected the **Small Tile for Pattern** (FigCD-5.22).

The selected bitmap pattern fill is applied to the star, as shown in FigCD-5.22.

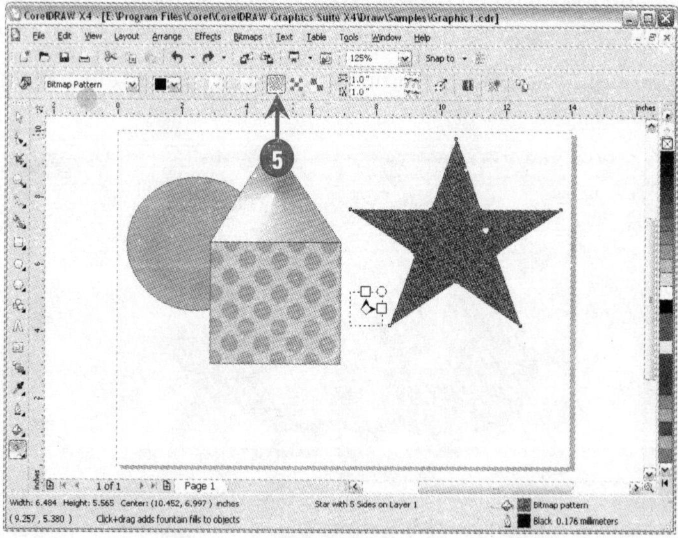

Fig.CD-5.22

Now, you have learned the pattern fills. Let us now understand to apply the texture fills to an object.

Using Texture Fills

A texture fill is used to fill an object with a texture and enhance its look. CorelDRAW provide libraries of textures which you can use to fill an object. At the time of choosing a texture, you can edit colors of texture, set its resolution rate, preview, and save the modified texture fill. However, you cannot overwrite a texture fill present in a texture. You have to save the texture fill with a unique name. The only limitation with texture fill is that it only supports RGB color model. However other color models can be used as reference to edit or create a color of your choice.

Undertake the following steps to apply the texture fills to the object:

1. *Select* an object on the Drawing page. In our case, it is an arrow (Fig.CD-5.23).
2. *Click* the arrow on the lower-right corner of the **Fill** tool and then *click* the **Texture Fill** tool on the flyout (Fig.CD-5.23). A **Texture Fill** dialog box appears (Fig.CD-5.24).

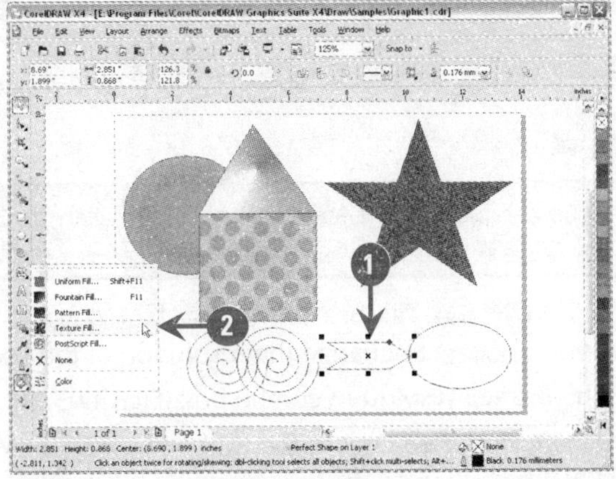

Fig.CD-5.23

3. *Select* a texture library from the **Texture Library** combo box. We have selected **Sample 6** option (Fig.CD-5.24).

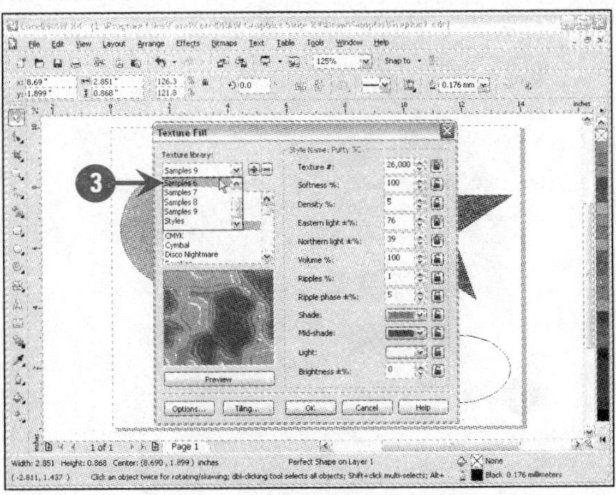

Fig.CD-5.24

4. Next, *select* a texture from the **Texture list** list box. In our case it is **Brake light** option (Fig.CD-5.25).

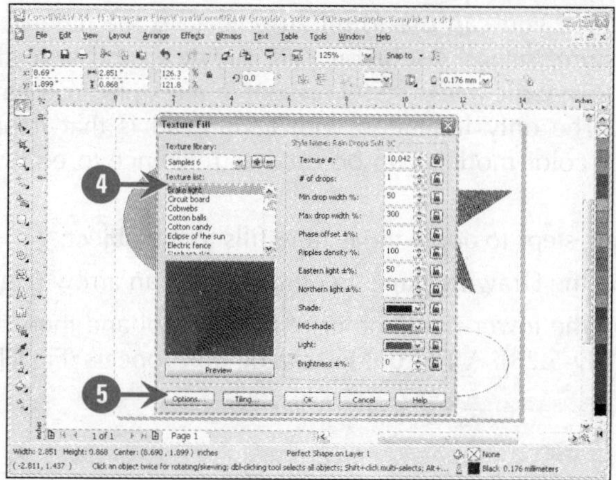

Fig.CD-5.25

Note

To create the custom texture fill, you can change the various setting options under the Style Name group. Under Style Name group, you can specify the option like brightness, shading and so on.

5. *Click* the **Options** button in the **Texture Fill** dialog box (Fig.CD-5.26), a new dialog box named **Texture Options**, appears to change the resolution of the texture fill (Fig.CD-5.26).
6. Set the resolution in the **Bitmap resolution** combo box (Fig.CD-5.26). In our case it is **350** dpi.
7. You can also specify the texture size limit in the list box beside the **Maximum tile width** option under **Texture size limit** group. In our case, the maximum tile width is 2049 pixels (Fig.CD-5.26).
8. *Click* the **OK** button in the **Texture Options** dialog box (Fig.CD-5.26), your setting is saved and the dialog box disappears.

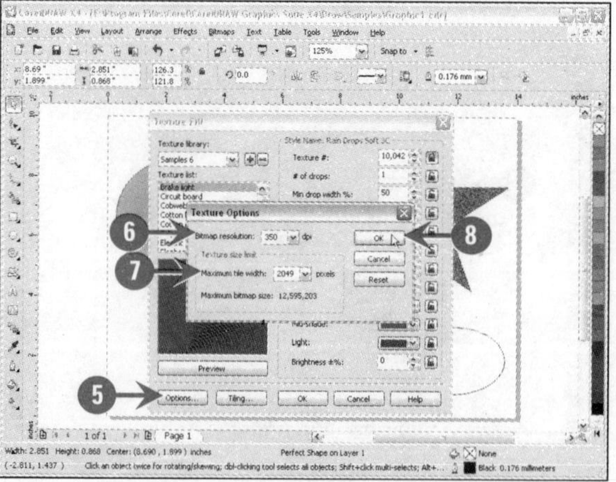

Fig.CD-5.26

9. *Click* the **Tiling** button in the **Texture Fill** dialog box. A **Tiling** dialog box appears (Fig.CD-5.27).
10. *Set* values in the **X** and **Y** spin boxes under the **Origin** group to change the origin of the texture fill, (Fig.CD-5.27).
11. *Set* the width and height of the texture tiles in the **Width** and **Height** spin boxes under the **Size** group to change the size of the texture tiles, (Fig.CD-5.27). In our case, width is **2.851″**and height is **0.868″**.
12. *Set* a skew value in the **Skew** spin box to skew the texture fill. In our case, it is **0** (Fig.CD-5.27).
13. *Set* a rotation value in the **Rotate** spin box to rotate a texture fill. In our case, it is **10** (Fig.CD-5.27).
14. To offset the tile origin of the texture fill, *select* the **Row** or **Column** radio button. In our case, it is **Column** option (Fig.CD-5.27).
15. *Set* an amount of offset in the **% of tile size** spin box under **Row or column offset** group . In our case, % of the tile size is **0** (Fig.CD-5.27).
16. *Click* the **OK** button in the **Tiling** dialog box (Fig.CD-5.27). The Tiling dialog box disappears and the setting will be saved.
17. *Click* the **OK** button in the **Texture Fill** dialog box (Fig.CD-5.27).

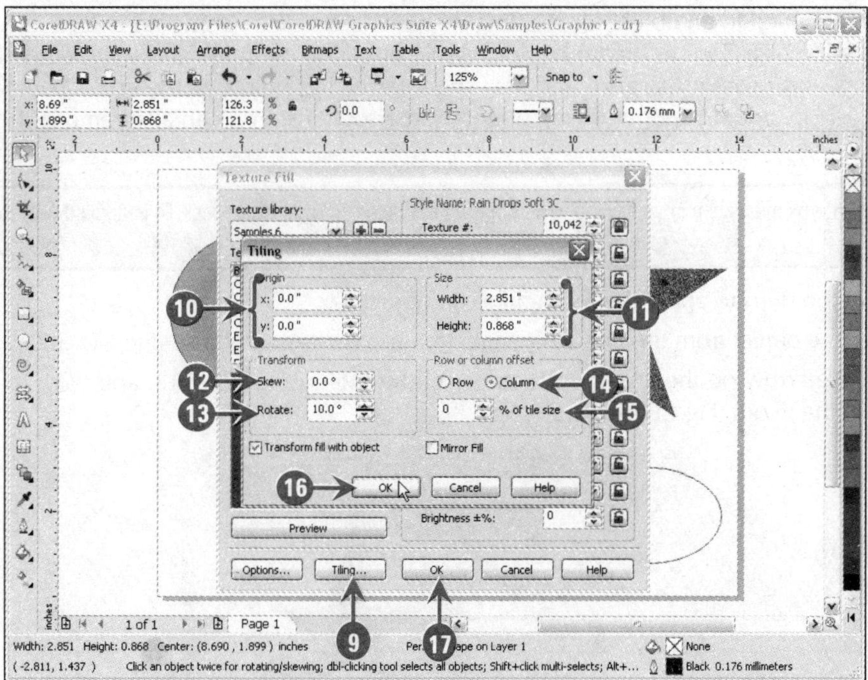

Fig.CD-5.27

The texture fill is applied to the arrow, as shown in Fig.CD-5.28.

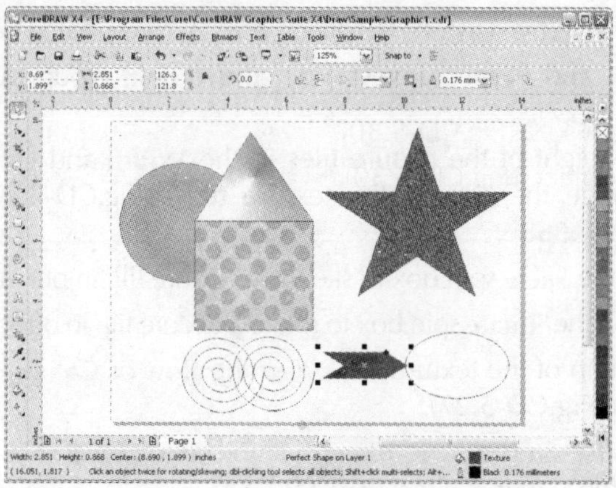

Fig.CD-5.28

After learning the texture fills, let us now learn applying mesh fills to an object.

Using Mesh Fills

Mesh fill is applied to an object for creating unique effects such as smooth color transition in any direction without having to create blends. While applying the mesh fill, we specify the number of columns and rows in the grid, and also the intersecting points of the grid., You can edit the mesh fill grid by adding and removing nodes or intersections. You can also remove the mesh.

Note

One thing that you must keep in your mind while applying the mesh fill is that the mesh fill is applied only to the closed objects.

Undertake the steps to apply the mesh fill to an object:

1. *Select* the object from the Drawing page. In our case it is an ellipse (Fig.CD-5.29).
2. *Click* the arrow on the lower-right corner of the **Interactive Fill** tool, and *click* the **Mesh Fill** tool in the flyout (Fig.CD-5.29).

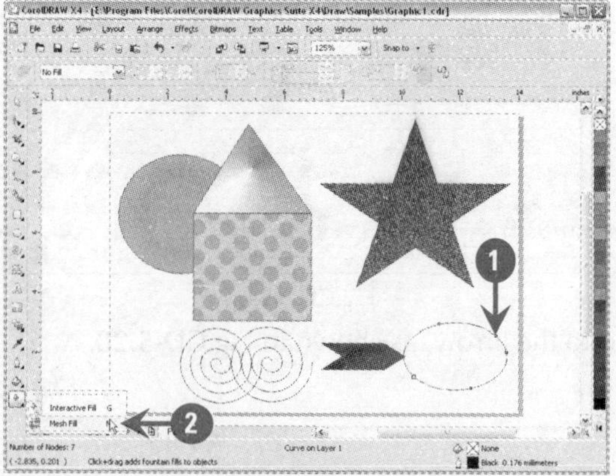

Fig.CD-5.29

3. *Type* a value in the top portion of the **Grid Size** spin box on the Property bar to set the number of columns. And to set the number of rows, *type* a value in the lower portion of the **Grid Size** spin box on the Property box. In our case, the number of columns are **2** and number of rows are also **2** (Fig.CD-5.30).
4. *Click* a grid on the object (Fig.CD-5.30).

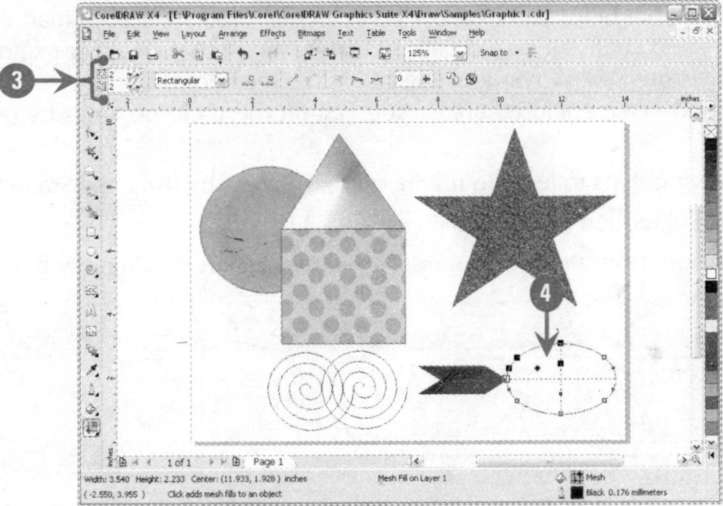

Fig.CD-5.30

5. *Click* a color swatch in the Color palette to fill the color in a grid of the object (Fig.CD-5.31). It applies the color in the selected grid of the object. In our case the selected grid is upper left grid in the object and the selected color is Yellow.

Repeat the step 4th and 5th to apply the mesh fill to the other grids in the object. Fig.CD-5.31 shows the mesh fill applied to the object.

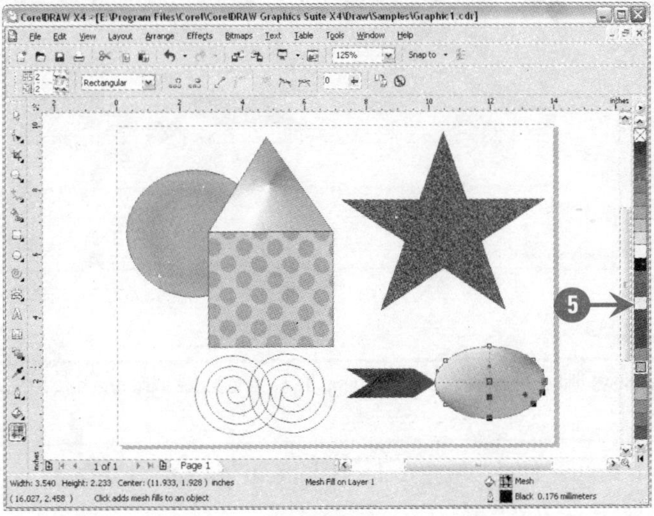

Fig.CD-5.31

Let us now learn to fill an enclosed area by using the Smart fill tool.

Using Fills to Areas

The fill tools that we used till now are useful to apply fills only to the larger areas of an object but the enclosed areas (the area where one object overlaps the other one and make a loop) were left out. The Smart Fill tool helps you to apply fill to an enclosed area. The Smart Fill tool detects the edges of an area and creates a closed path so that it can fill that area. For example, see in the Drawing page of the CorelDRAW window (Fig.CD-5.32), the two spirals intersects each others at number of points, and make enclosed areas. You can fill these closed areas by using the Smart Fill tool.

Undertake the following steps to learn to fill the enclosed areas by using the Smart Fill tool:

1. *Click* the **Smart Fill** tool on the Toolbox (Fig.CD-5.32).
2. *Select* a fill property from the **Fill Options** drop-down list on the Property bar. In our case, it is **Specify** (Fig.CD-5.32).

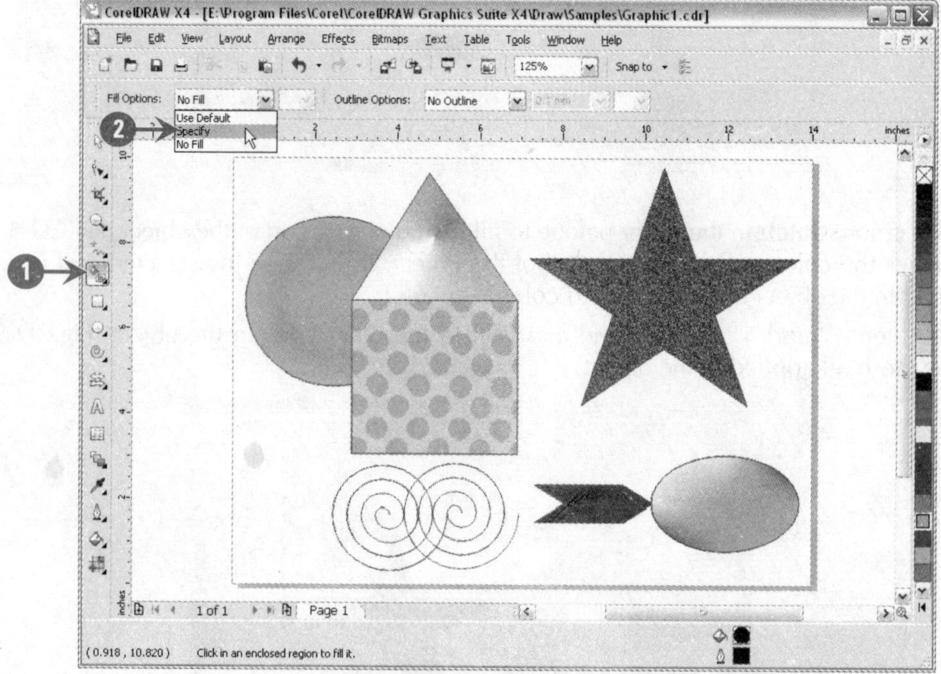

Fig.CD-5.32

Note

> The Use Default option allows filling area with default setting. If you select the third one that is No Fill, applies no fill to the area.

3. *Select* a color from the **Fill Colour** Color palette, (Fig.CD-5.33).

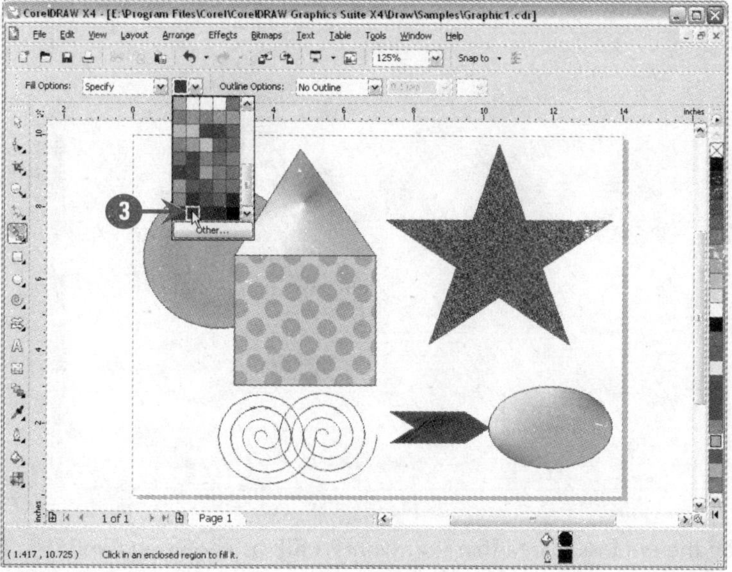

Fig.CD-5.33

4. *Select* an outline property from the **Outline Options** drop-down list to set the outline width. In our case it is **Specify** option (Fig.CD-5.34) that allows you to specify the outline width of the enclosed area.

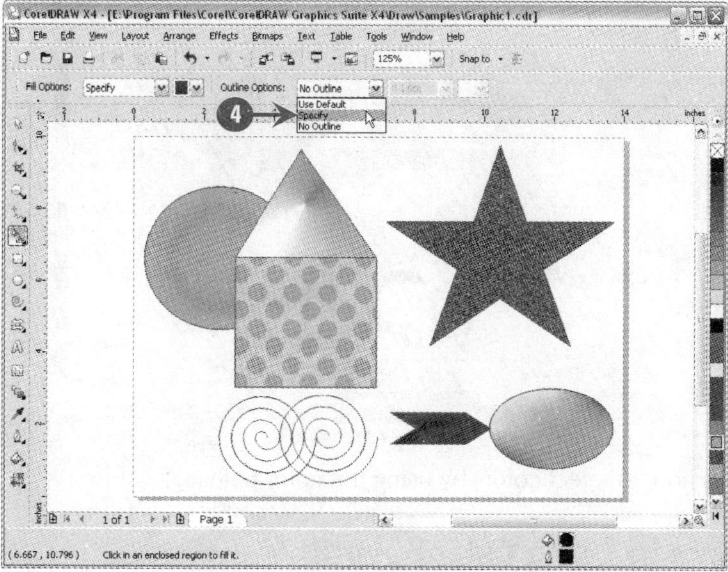

Fig.CD-5.34

5. *Select* the outline width from the **Outline Width** combo box Fig.CD-5.35.
6. *Select* the outline color from the **Outline Colour** combo box (Fig.CD-5.35).

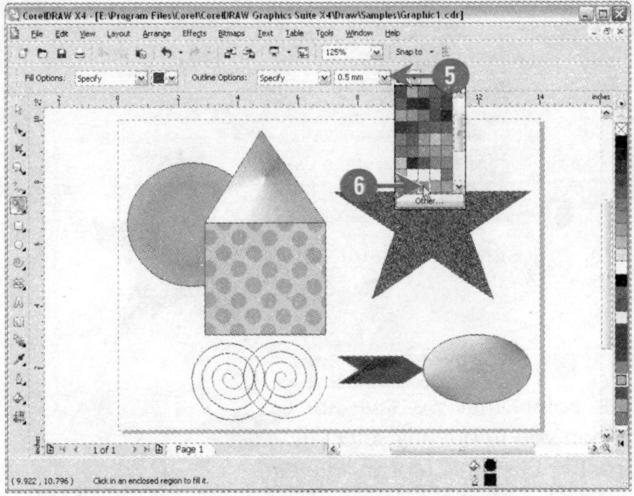

Fig.CD-5.35

7. *Click* inside the enclosed area that you want to fill, as shown in Fig.CD-5.36. The mesh fill is applied to the enclosed area (Fig.CD-5.36).
8. You can save the drawing by *clicking* the **Save** button on the Toolbar (Fig.CD-5.36).

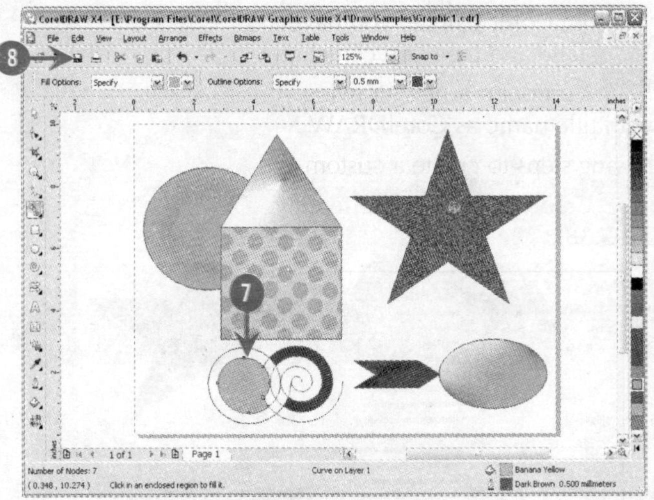

Fig.CD-5.36

Let us now learn how to select colors by using the color palette.

Selecting Colors by Using Color Palette

A Color palette is a collection of the solid colors from which you can select colors for fills and outlines or for highlighting the text. For selecting the fill and outline colors, you can use the fixed or custom color palette. The default Color palette is the Color palette that is pre-defined and comes with the CorelDRAW software that contains 99 colors from the CMYK (cyan, magenta, yellow, and black) model. The custom color palette is the Color palette in which colors are defined by the user.

Note

> To fill an object with color of a Color palette, simply select the object with Selection tool and then click on desired color swatch in the Color palette located on the right side of the Drawing page. To know details about fill and out fill colors refer to 'Select Color for an Object' section of Chapter: 3 Working with Objects.

After selecting a color by using the default color palette, let us now learn to create a custom color palette.

Creating Custom Color Palette

Collection of various colors that we save are called the custom Color palette. Custom color palettes are useful when you frequently select the same colors, or when you want to work with a specific set of colors. The custom Color palette can be created by selecting each color manually or by using the colors in an object or from a document. Let us understand each of the methods and learn how to create the custom Color palette.

Creating a Custom Color Palette by Selecting Colors Manually

You can create the custom Color palette by choosing each color manually.To add the colors manually on your custom Color palette, you have to choose a color model such as RGB, CMYK and so on or a Color palette and then you can change the color composition..

From the Fig.CD-5.36, you open a new drawing. The CorelDRAW window appears with a new drawing window with title name as CorelDRAW X4- [Graphics-2].

Undertake the following steps to create a custom Color palette:

1. *Select* **Windows→Color-Palettes→Palette Editor** (Fig.CD-5.37). A **Palette Editor** dialog box appears (Fig.CD-5.38).

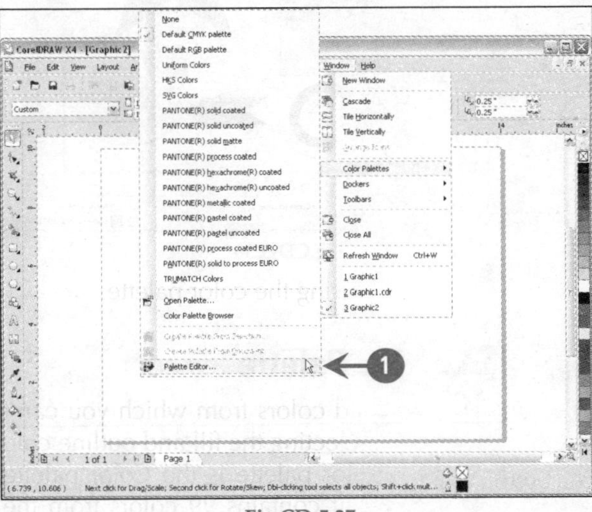

Fig.CD-5.37

2. *Click* the **New Palette** button, a **New Palette** dialog box appears (Fig.CD-5.38).

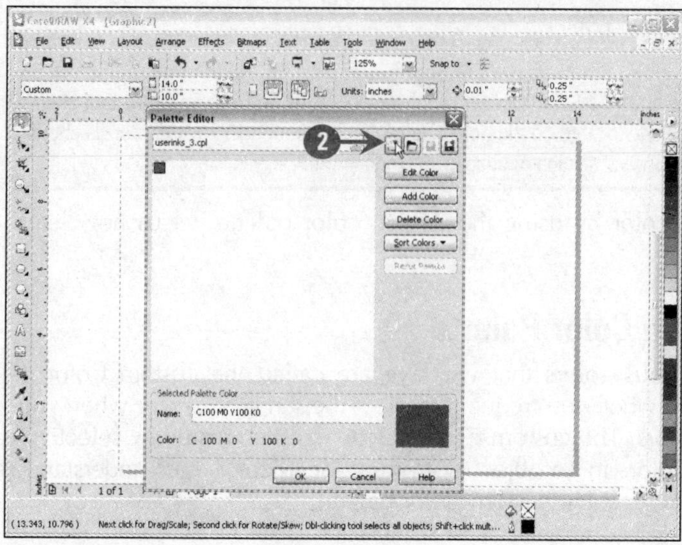

Fig.CD-5.38

3. *Type* the file name in the **File name** text box (Fig.CD-5.39).
4. *Click* the **Save in** combo box and choose a desired location from the drop-down list to save the color palette. In our case we are using the default location, that is **Palettes** folder, offered by CorelDRAW to save the color palette (Fig.CD-5.39).
5. *Click* the **Save** button (Fig.CD-5.39).

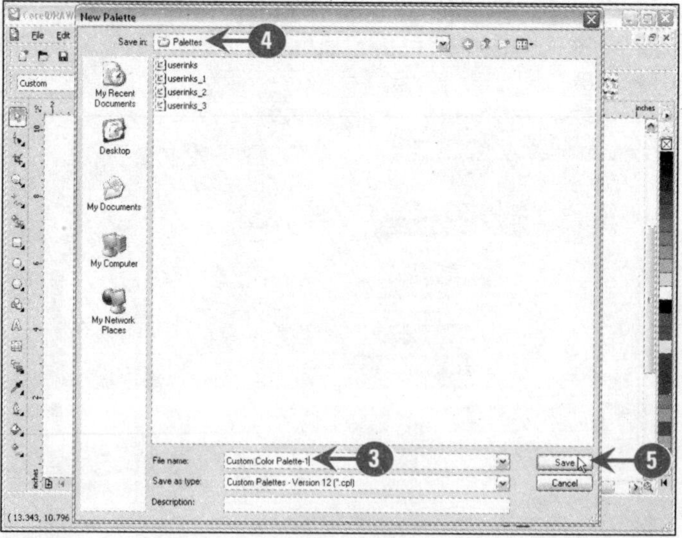

Fig.CD-5.39

6. *Click* the **Add Color** button (Fig.CD-5.40), a **Select Color** dialog box appears (Fig.CD-5.41).

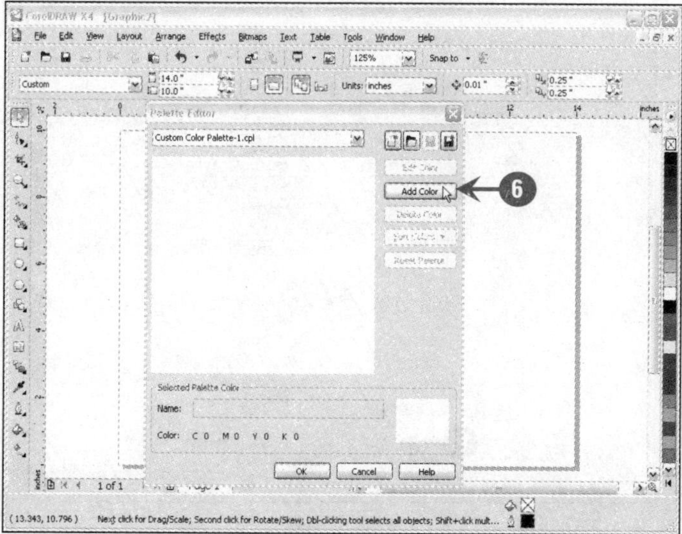

Fig.CD-5.40

7. From the **Select Color** dialog box, you have to select the color. To do this opens a tab among the **Model, Mixers or Palettes**. In our case, the **Models** tab is opened. Under this tab, *select* a mode from the **Model** combo box (Fig.CD-5.41).
8. *Set* the various components for the colors under the **Components** group (Fig.CD-5.41).
9. *Click* the **Add to Palette** button, and then *click* the **Close** button in the dialog box (Fig.CD-5.41).

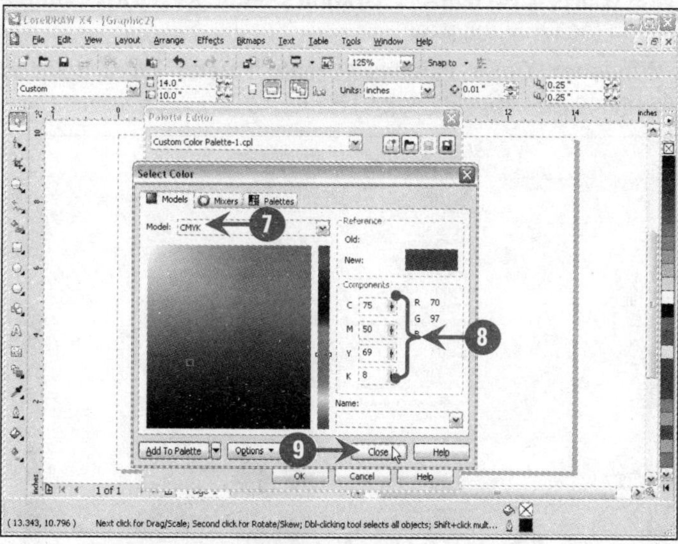

Fig.CD-5.41

10. *Click* the **OK** button in the **Palette Editor** dialog box. The created Color palette will be stored in the selected location (default location) (Fig.CD-5.42).

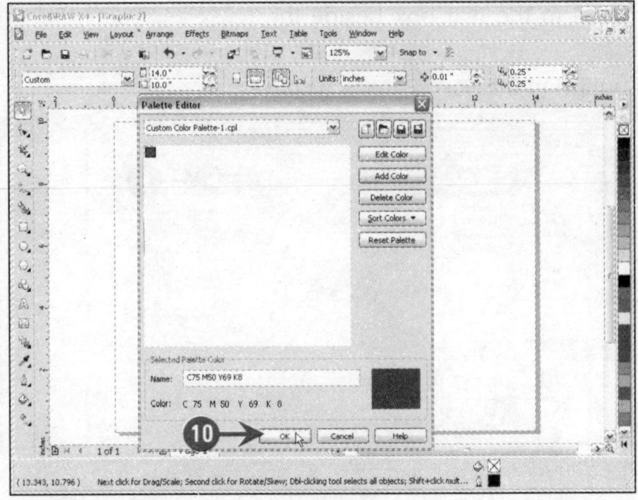

Fig.CD-5.42

Creating a Color Palette from an Object

You can create a color palette by using the colors in an object. This Color palette is helpful when you frequently choose the same colors that an object contains. After creating this custom Color palette, you can use the colors while filling the object.

1. *Open* the **Graphics1.cdr** drawing that is an existing drawing. The path of the file is **E:\Program Files\Corel\CorelDRAW Graphics Suite X4\Draw\Sample\Graphic1.cdr** and *select* an object on the Drawing page.
2. Next, *select* **Windows→Color Palettes→Create Palette From Selection** (Fig.CD-5.43). A Save Palette As dialog box appears (Fig.CD-5.44).

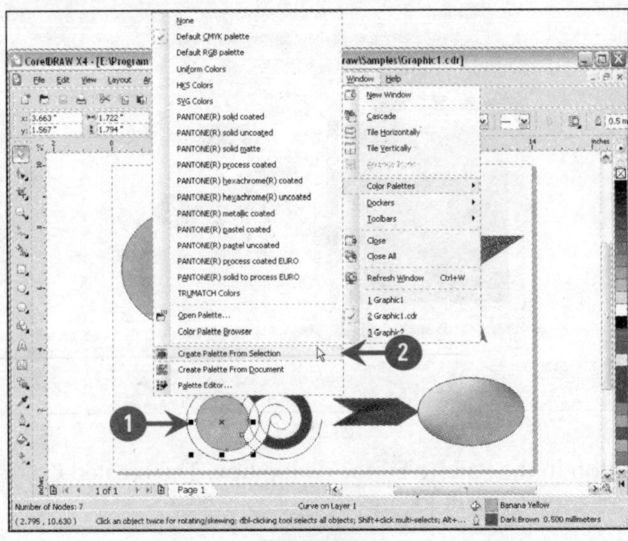

Fig.CD-5.43

3. *Type* the file name in the text box beside the **File name** option. In our case, it is **Custom Color Palette-2**.
4. *Click* the **Save** button in the **Save Palette As** dialog box, as shown in (Fig.CD-5.44). .

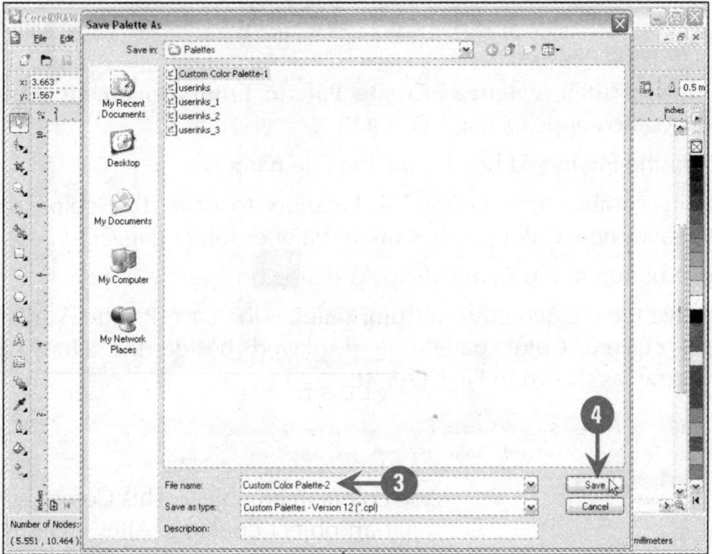

Fig.CD-5.44

As soon as you click the Save button in the Save Palette As dialog box, the custom Color palette is saved and is displayed beside the default Color palette on the right end of the CorelDRAW window, as shown in Fig.CD-5.45.

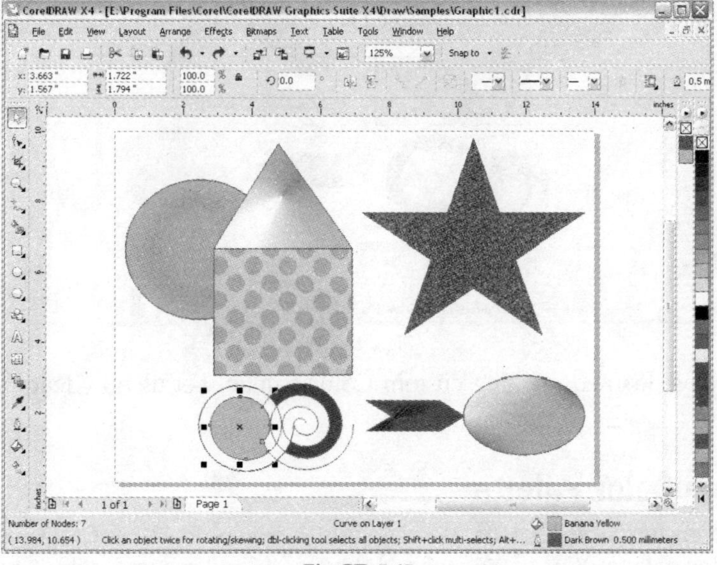

Fig.CD-5.45

Creating a Color Palette from a Document

You can create the custom Color palette by using colors in an entire area of your Drawing page. The created Color palette will show the swatches that are being used in document.

Undertake the following steps to create a custom Color palette by using the colors that are present in your Drawing page:

1. *Select* **Windows→Color Palettes→Create Palette From Document** (Fig.CD-5.43). A Save Palette As dialog box appears (Fig.CD-5.44).
2. *Type* name for the file in text box beside the File name.
3. From **Save** in combo box, *choose* a location to save the color palette. By default, CorelDRAW saves new Color palettes under Palettes folder (Fig.CD-5. 46).
4. *Click* the **Save** button in the Save Palette As dialog box.

As soon as you save the created custom Color palette, the Save Palette As dialog box disappears and the created custom Color palette is displayed beside the Drawing window of the CorelDRAW window, as shown in Fig.CD-5.46.

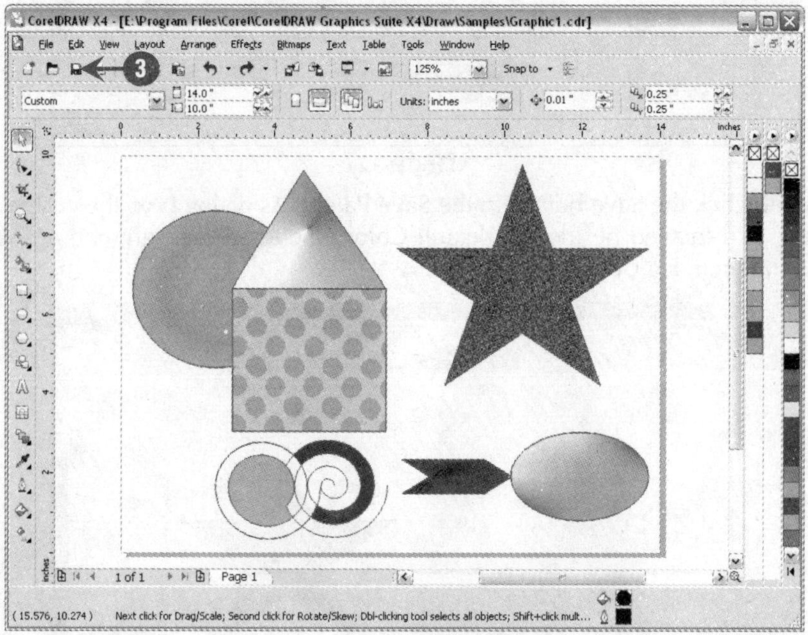

Fig.CD-5.46

Till now, you have learned creating custom Color palette. Let us now learn to edit the custom Color palette.

Editing Custom Color Palette

After creating a custom Color palette, you can add more colors in the Color palette at the time of editing the Color palette. You can change, delete, sort, and rename colors. Let us learn how to edit a Color palette.

Undertake the following steps to learn to edit a Color palette:

1. *Open* a new drawing and *select* **Windows→Color Palettes→Palette Editor** (Fig.CD-5.43). A **Palette Editor** dialog box appears (Fig.CD-5.47).
2. *Click* the combo box at the top of **Palette Editor** dialog box and choose the name of Color palette under the User Palettes folder. In our case, the dialog box is showing the Custom Color Palette – 1 (Fig.CD-5.47).
3. *Click* the **Edit Color** button (Fig.CD-5.47). A **Select Color** dialog box appears (Fig.CD-5.48).

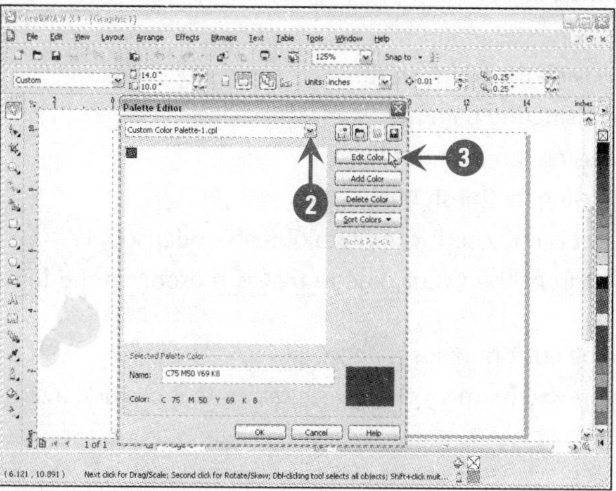

Fig.CD-5. 47

4. *Select* a color value for the CMYK color model from the dialog box by setting the color composition under the **Components** group. In our case, the color values for each of the component of CMYK color model are 75, 51, 53, and 5 (Fig.CD-5.48).
5. *Click* the **OK** button (Fig.CD-5.48). The Select Color dialog box disappears and the **Palette Editor** dialog box re-appears.

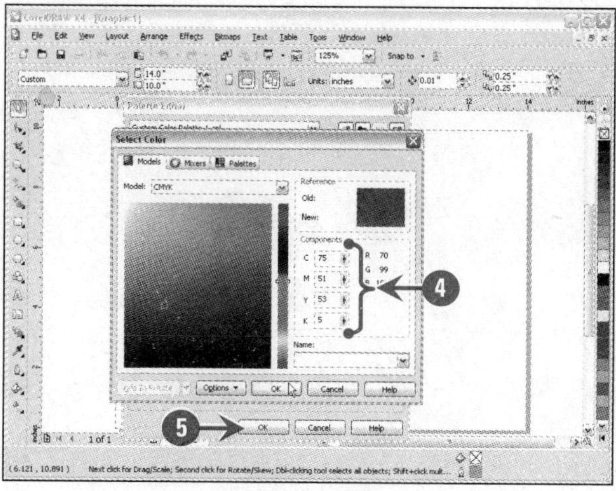

Fig.CD-5. 48

6. *Click* the **OK** button in the **Palette Editor** dialog box.

It will save the settings made by you while editing the custom color palette.

With this we come to the end of the chapter. Before proceeding ahead towards the next chapter, let us refresh the learning by summarizing the main points.

Summary

In this chapter we learned about:

- Filling objects by using the uniform fills
- Filling objects by using the fountain fills
- Filling objects by using the pattern fills
- Filling objects by using the texture fills
- Filling objects by using the mesh fills
- Filling the area that is enclosed when two objects collapsed
- Selecting the color from the Color palette that is present on the left end of the CorelDRAW window
- Creating and editing custom color palette

In the next chapter, you will learn working with tables that provide a structured layout to present text and graphics.

Chapter 6

Introduction to Tables

In this Section

- Adding a Table
- Selecting and Moving Table Components
- Inserting and Deleting Table Rows and Columns
- Formatting Tables and Cells
- Merging and Splitting Table Cells

A table provides a structured layout to present text and graphics. CorelDRAW X4 provides a new, interactive tool named as Table tool. By using this tool, user can create a table. You can also create a table by importing content from Microsoft Excel spreadsheets or by importing tables created in a word-processing application, such as Microsoft Word. In this chapter, you will learn about adding a table to your Drawing page, selecting and moving the table components, inserting and deleting table rows and table columns, formatting tables and table cells, and merging or splitting table cells.

Adding a Table

You can create a table using the Table tool for creating a structured layout in your Drawing page. At the time of creation of the table, you can define the number of columns and rows in a table. Let's first learn how to draw a table using the Table tool.

Undertake the following steps to add a table to your drawing:

1. *Click* the **Table** tool on the Toolbox of the CorelDRAW X4 window (Fig.CD-6.1).
2. In the Property bar, *type* values in the **Number of Rows and Columns in Tables** spin boxes to specify the number of rows and columns in a table (Fig.CD-6.1).
3. *Click* and drag the mouse-pointer diagonally to draw the table as shown in Fig.CD.6.1.

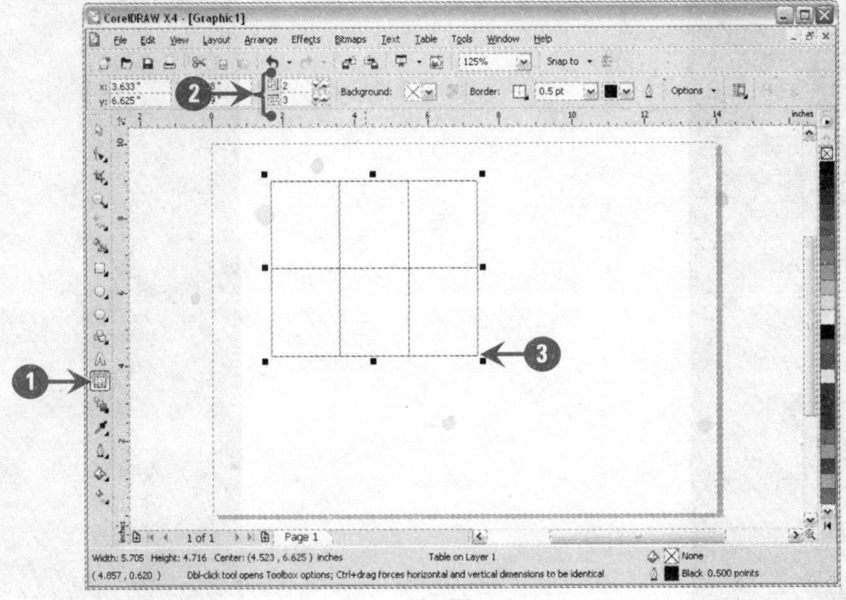

Fig.CD-6. 1

Note

You can re-size the table by dragging the handles to the desired size. After adding a table, you can modify the table border, its background, and thickness.

You can also create a table by converting the text to a table.

After adding a table, let's now learn to select the table components such as table rows and columns and move the table components.

Selecting and Moving Table Components

Before inserting rows or columns, changing the table border or adding a background fill color, you need to select a table, its rows, columns or cells. You can move the selected rows and columns to a different location in the table. You can also move a table column or a table row from one table to another. Let's discuss all these in detail.

Selecting a Table, Row, Column or Cell

You can select the whole table, a table row, table column or a particular table cell as per your requirements. CorelDRAW X4 provides you a very simple method to perform these actions. Undertake the following steps to select a table, row or column:

1. *Select* the **Table** tool from the Toolbox and *click* the table drawn in the Drawing page (Fig.CD-6.2).

Note

> Selecting the table without choosing the Table tool will not help you in performing any actions on the table such as , selecting rows, columns, entire table, inserting rows and columns and so on. Without the Table tool, CorelDRAW will treat the table as an object.

2. *Select* **Table→Select→Table** (Fig.CD-6.2).

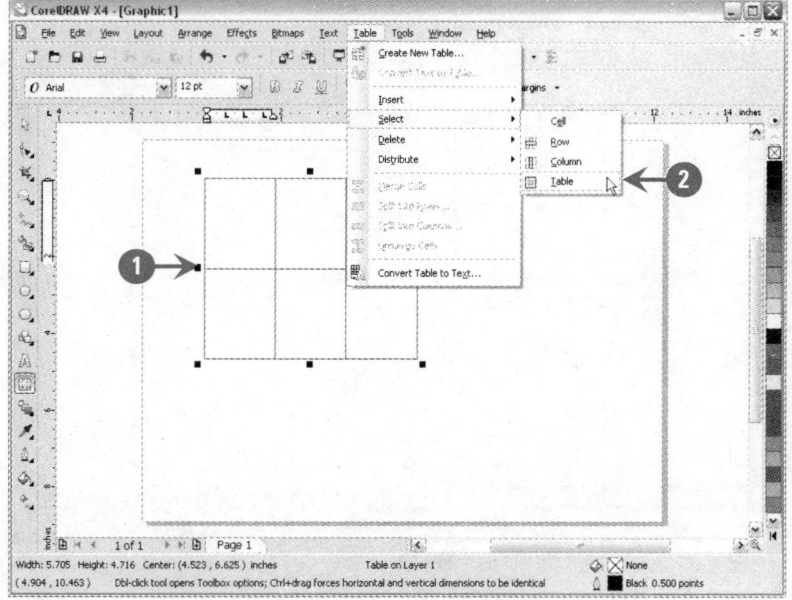

Fig.CD-6.2

The table gets selected as shown in Fig.CD-6.3.

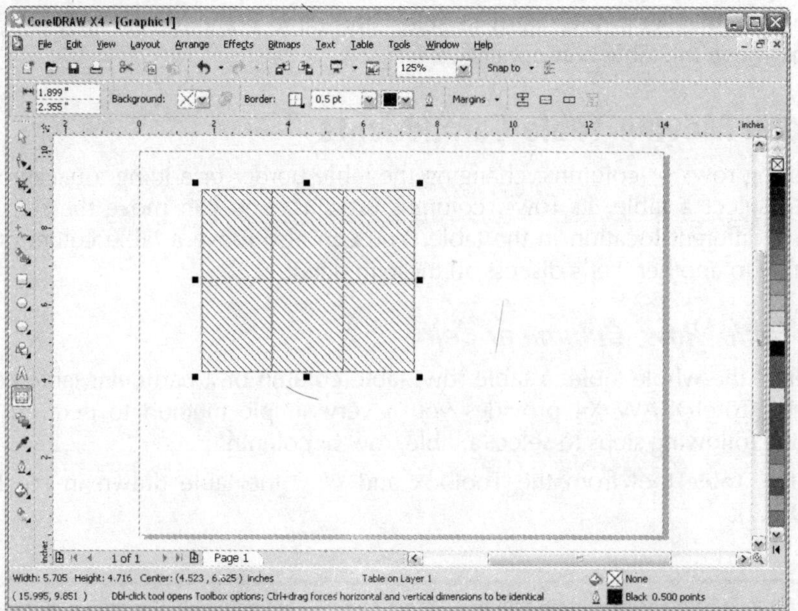

Fig.CD-6.3

3. To *select* a row, *click* a cell in that row and *select* **Table→Select→Row** (Fig.CD-6.4).

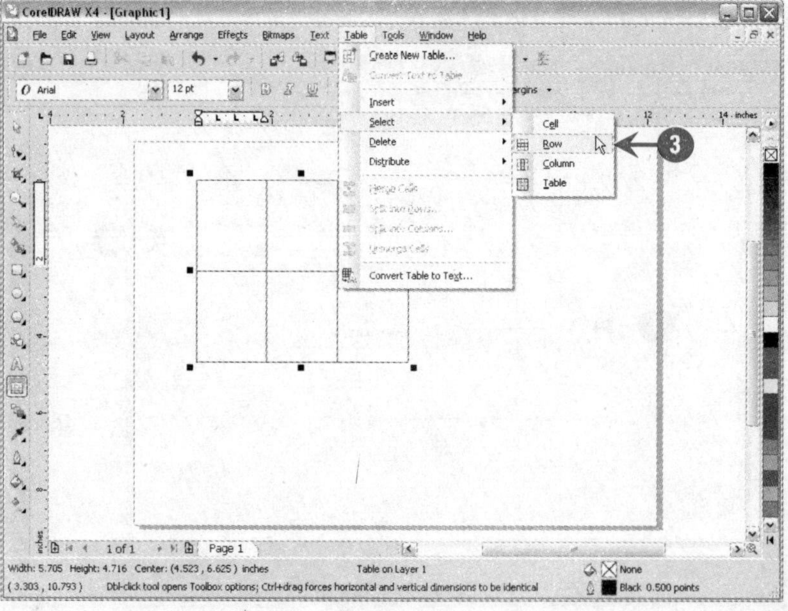

Fig.CD-6.4

The row gets selected as shown in Fig.CD-6.5.

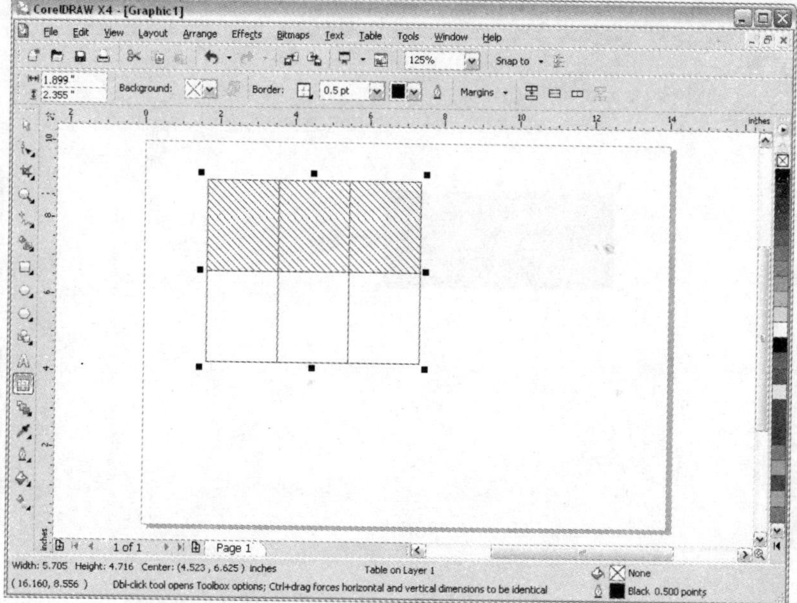

Fig.CD-6.5

Note

Similarly, to select a column or cell, first click a column or cell in the table and then select Table→Select→<Column or Cell> (Fig.CD-6.4). The column or cell gets selected.

Now, let's learn to move a row or a column in a table.

Moving a Table Row or Column

You can move the table row or column to another location in a table as per your requirement. We move the table row or column to another row or column within a table to transfer the data. This helps avoid reinsertion of data into the row or column.

Let us now undertake the following steps to move the table row or column:

1. *Select* the table row or column that you want to move. In this case, we have selected the first row of the table as shown in Fig.CD-6.6.
2. In the color palette, *click* on the desired color swatch to fill the row you are about to move. In our case, the selected color is **Purple.** This will help you in tracing the movement of row in the table. The color of the selected row changes, as shown in Fig.CD-6.6.

Note

Since, by default, rows and columns of a table are not filled with any color. So, it becomes difficult for a user to trace the movement and the final location of the moved row or column expect for the moving outline. So, to track the changes, the row has been colored purple.

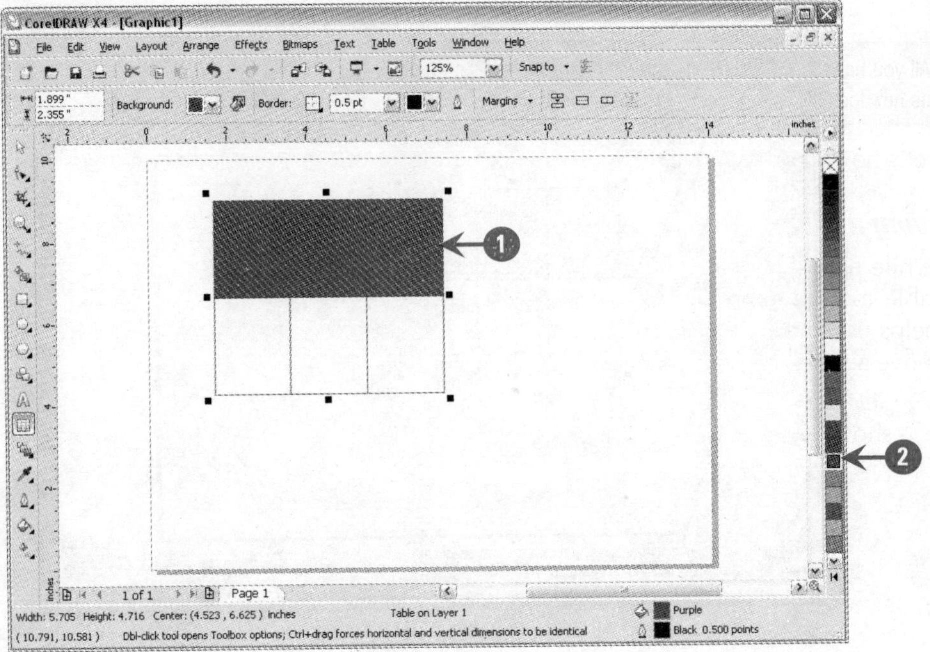

Fig.CD-6.6

3. *Drag* the selected row to the second row in the table as shown in Fig.CD-6.7. The selected row has been moved to the second row in the table.

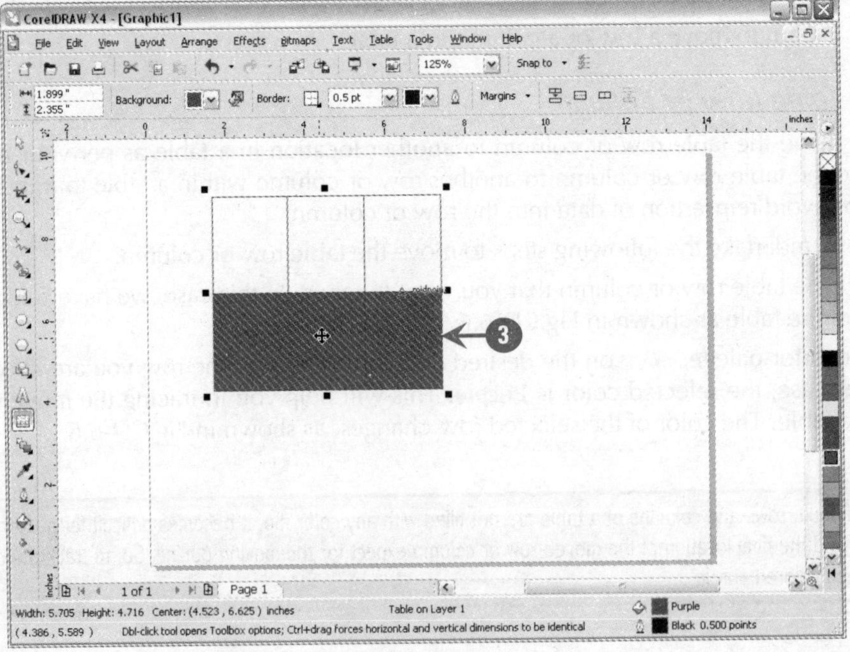

Fig.CD-6.7

Note

All you have to do is to select the desired row or column with the help of Table tool and then drag the row or column to its new location.

Let's now learn to move the table row or column of a table to another table.

Moving a Table Row or Table Column to Another Table

While providing a structured layout, sometimes you may need to move a row or a column in a table to another table. We move the table row or column to another table with its data. This helps users to avoid the recreation of data into the new table. Undertake the following steps to move a table row or column to another table:

1. *Select* a table row or column that you want to move. In this case, we have selected a row as shown in Fig.CD-6.8.

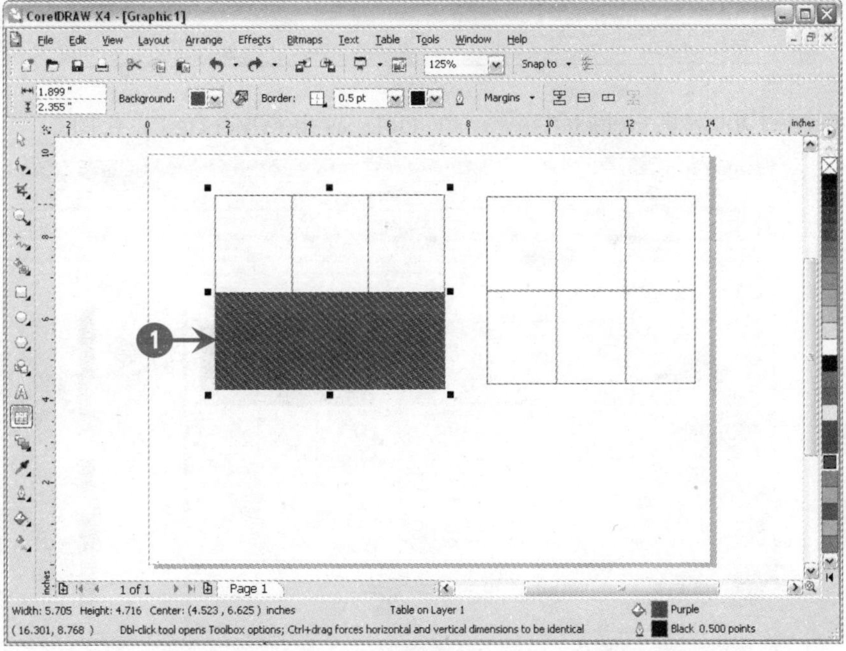

Fig.CD-6.8

2. *Select* **Edit→Cut**. CorelDRAW now stores the selected row in a temporary location known as the Clipboard.
3. *Select* a row in another table (Fig.CD-6.9).
4. *Select* **Edit→Paste**. A **Paste Rows** dialog box appears as shown in Fig.CD-6.9.
5. From the dialog box, *select* the option of where you want to paste the row. We have selected the **Insert above Selected Row** option as shown in Fig.CD-6.9.
6. *Click* the **OK** button (Fig.CD-6.9).

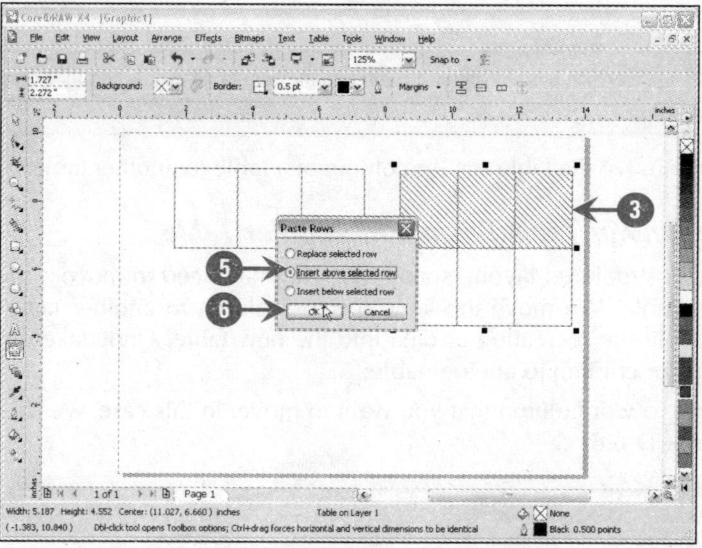

Fig.CD-6.9

A row is inserted above the selected row in the table, as shown in Fig.CD-6.10.

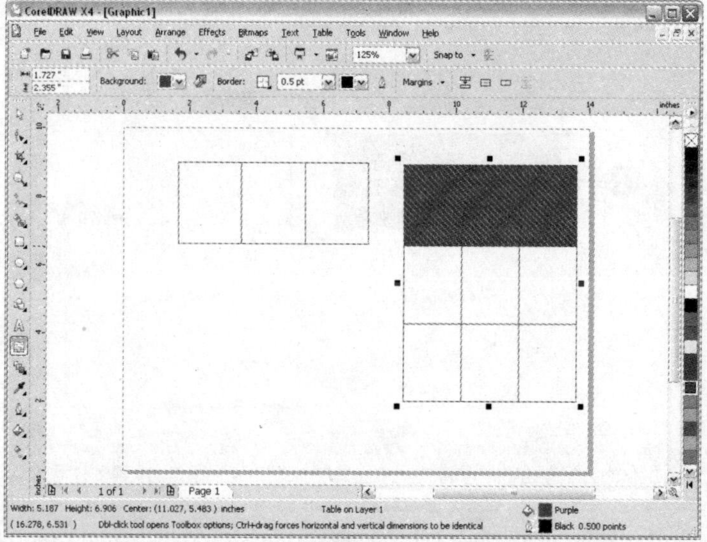

Fig.CD-6.10

Note

You can move a table row or column to another table by cutting a row or column from one table and pasting it in another table.

After moving the table row to another table, let's now learn to insert and delete rows or columns in a table.

Inserting and Deleting Table Rows and Columns

You can either insert a row or multiple rows in a table. The table rows or table columns can be inserted above or below the selected row, as per the requirement. If there are extra table rows or columns, they can be deleted. Let's first discuss about inserting the table rows or columns in a table.

Inserting Table Rows or Columns

While working with table, sometimes you may need some more rows or columns. For example, suppose we have a table with only one row and three columns and we need to insert two more rows for adding extra information such as text or graphics; the newly inserted rows help us add this information to the table.

Undertake the following steps to insert the table rows or columns:

1. *Select* the row or column in a table in which you want to insert rows. We have selected a row (Fig.CD-6.11).

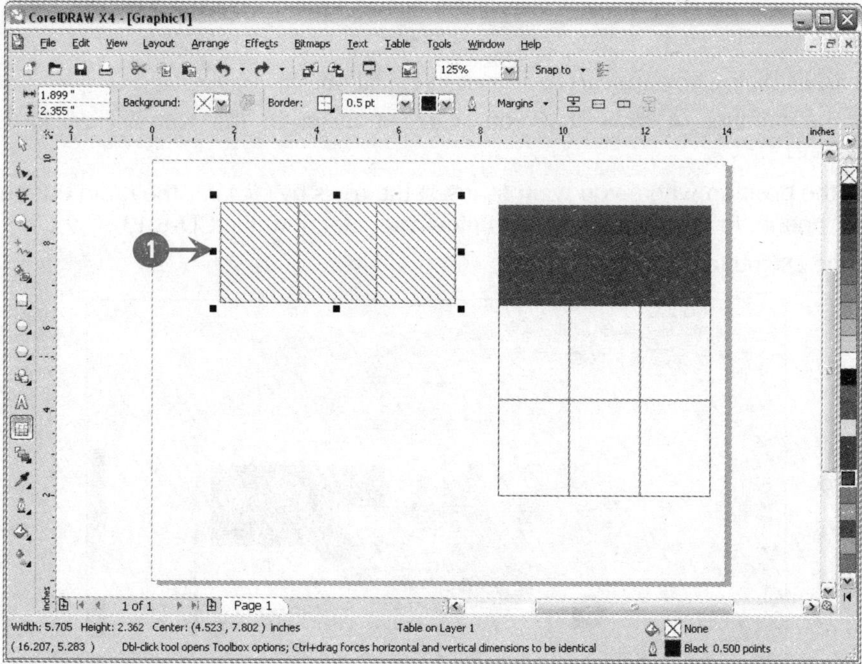

Fig.CD-6.11

2. *Select* **Table→Insert→Insert Rows** (Fig.CD-6.12). The same procedure can be followed for inserting columns.

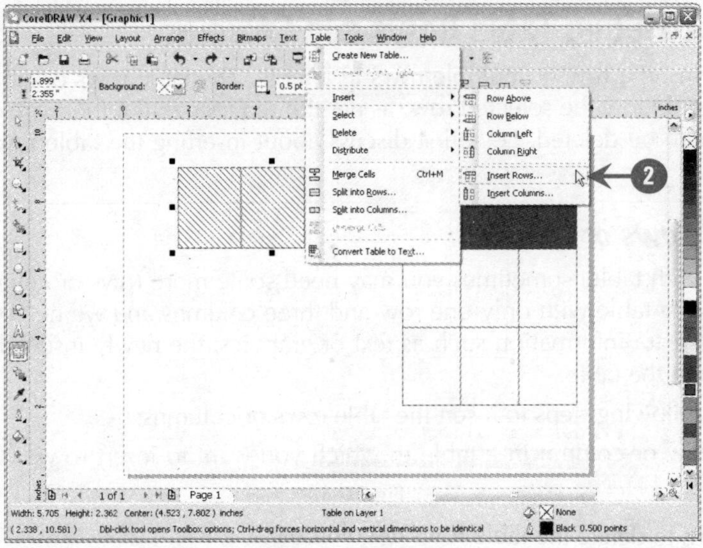

Fig.CD-6.12

An **Insert Rows** dialog box appears as shown in Fig.CD-6.13.

3. *Type* the number of rows that you want to insert in the **Number of Rows** text box (Fig.CD-6.13).
4. *Select* the position where you want to insert the rows by *clicking* the radio button beside the **Where** option. In this case, we *select* **Below the selection** (Fig.CD-6.13).
5. *Click* the **OK** button (Fig.CD-6.13).

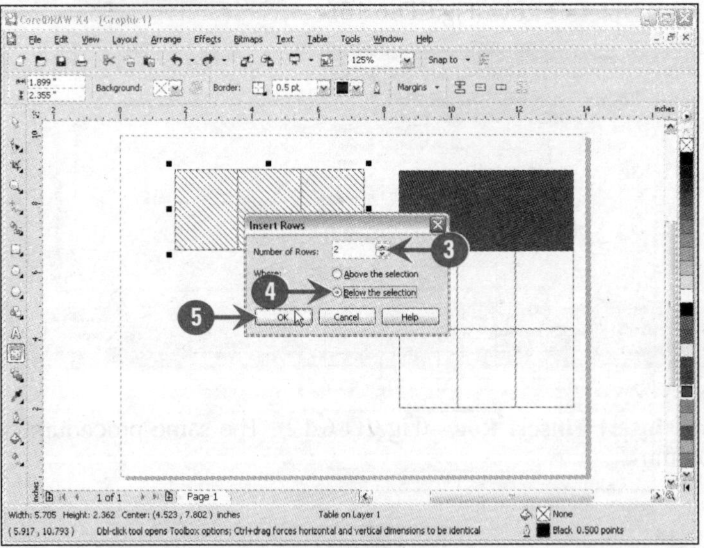

Fig.CD-6.13

The rows are inserted in the table, as shown in Fig.CD-6.14.

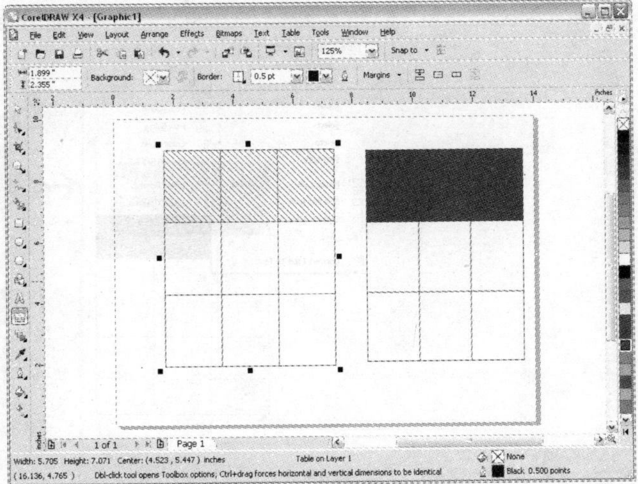

Fig.CD-6.14

Now, let us learn to delete the table rows or columns.

Deleting Table Rows and Columns

While creating the table, you define the number of rows and columns in a table. But, it sometime happens that some rows or columns are extra in the table. These extra rows or columns can be deleted .

Undertake the following steps to delete a table row:

1. *Select* a row or column that you want to delete (Fig.CD-6.15).
2. *Select*→**Table**→**Delete**→**Row** (Fig.CD-6.15).

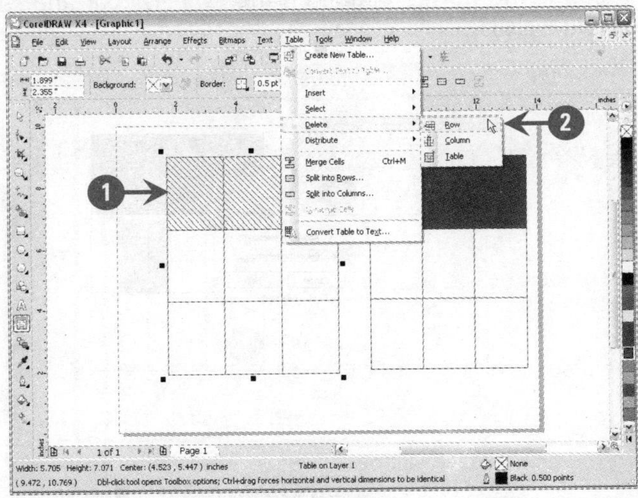

Fig.CD-6.15

The selected row will be deleted as shown in Fig.CD-6.16.

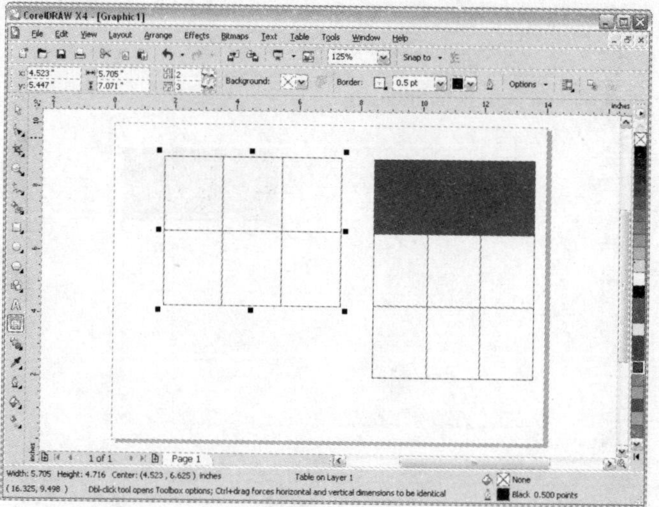

Fig.CD-6.16

After learning how to insert and delete the table rows or columns, let's now learn the formatting of tables and cells.

Formatting Tables and Cells

The basic purpose of formatting tables and cells is to change the appearance of tables and cells. It can be done by modifying the border, border thickness, background color of the tables or cells. Undertake the following steps to format the table:

1. *Select* the table that you want to format (Fig.CD-6.17).
2. *Click* the button beside the **Border** option on the **Property** bar and *select* a border style of the table as shown in Fig.CD.6.17.

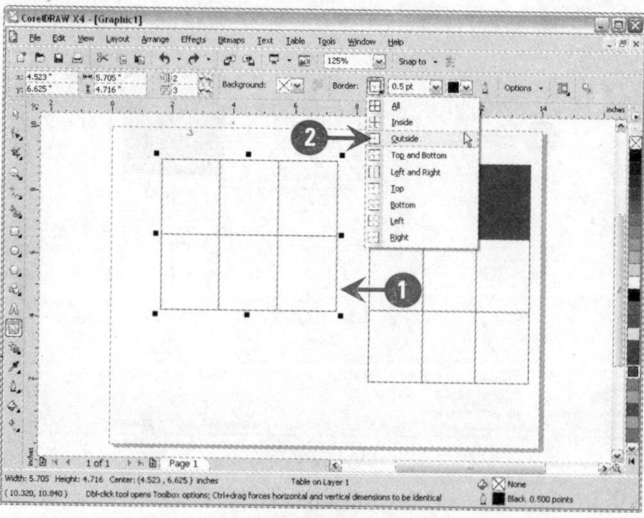

Fig.CD-6.17

3. To change the border thickness of the table, *select* a thickness option from the list box as shown in Fig.CD-6.18.

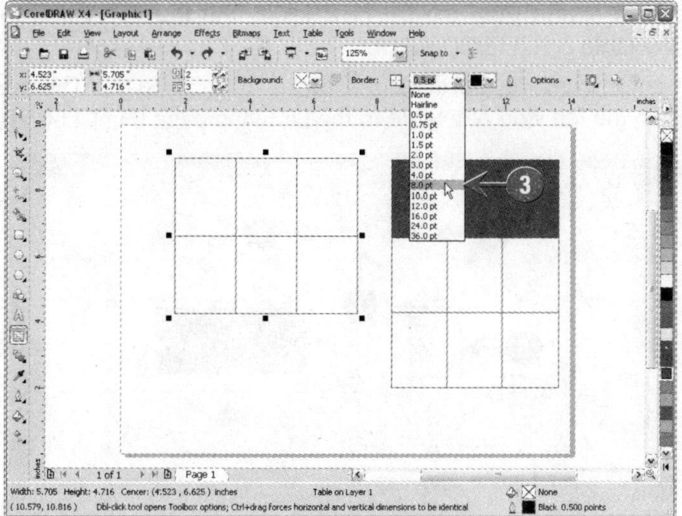

Fig.CD-6.18

4. To *select* a border color, *click* the color picker in the **Property** bar and *select* a color from the **Color** palette as shown in Fig.CD-6.19.

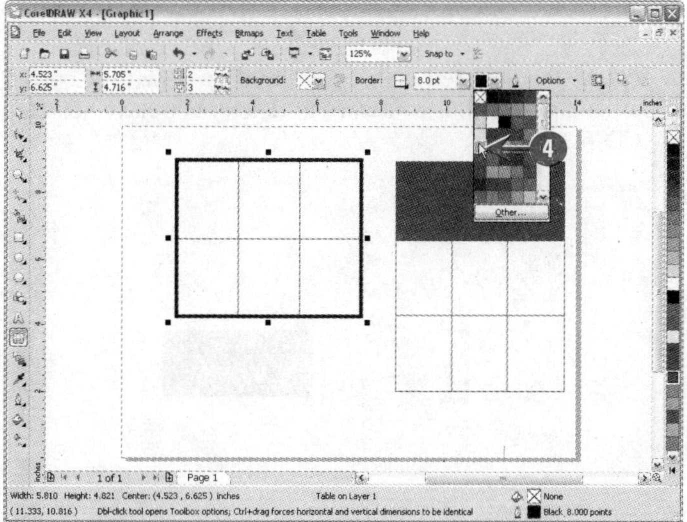

Fig.CD-6.19

The way, we presently modified a table, the same way, you can modify a cell of the table by applying the border style, thickness, color, on the selected cell.

5. *Select* the cell that you want to format. In our case, it is the second cell of the first row (Fig.CD-6.20)

6. *Click* the button beside the **Border** option on the **Property** bar and *select* a border style for the table cell. In our case, the border style is **Outside** (Fig.CD-6.20).
7. *Select* a thickness option from the list box beside the **Border** option to change the border thickness of the table cell (Fig.CD-6.20).
8. *Select* a cell color from the **Border** color picker (Fig.CD-6.20). The applied change in the cell is shown on the left side of a table in the Drawing page (Fig.CD-6.20).

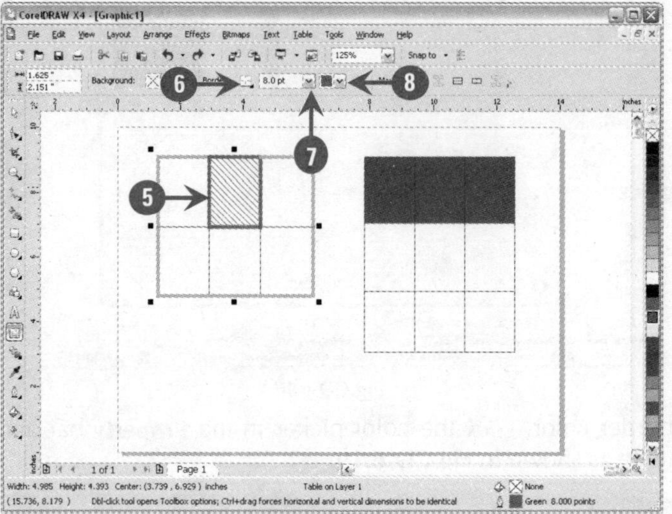

Fig.CD-6.20

9. To remove an edge of the selected cell, *open* the drop-down list beside the **Border** option, and *select* the particular edge that you want to delete. We have selected the **Bottom** option as shown in Fig.CD-6.21.

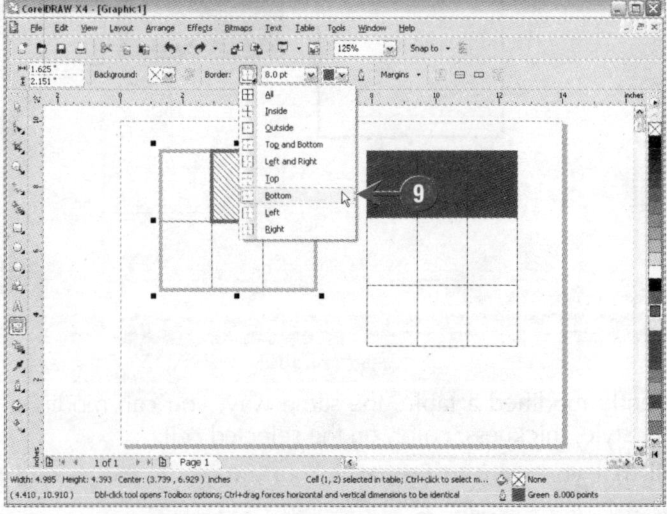

Fig.CD-6.21

10. *Click* the **Border** color picker and *select* the no color option from the Color palette as shown in Fig.CD-6.22.

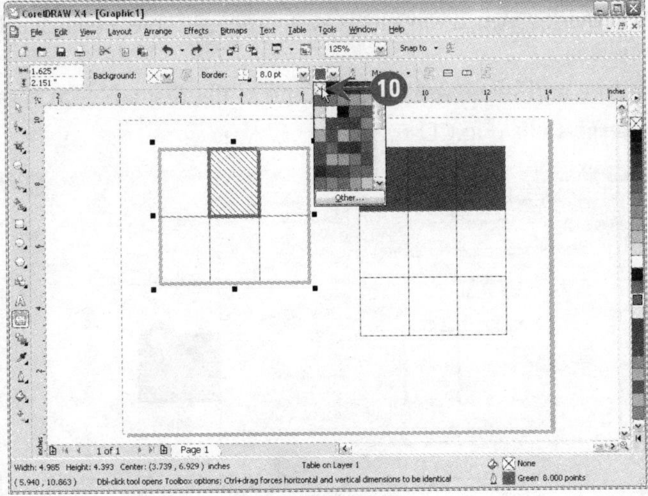

Fig.CD-6.22

You can see in Fig.CD-6.23 that there is no color at the bottom edge of the selected cell.

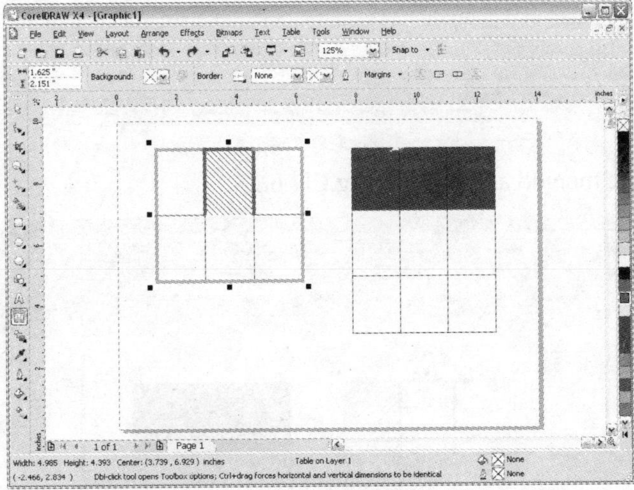

Fig.CD-6.23

Let's now learn to merge and split table cells.

Merging and Splitting Table Cells

You can merge adjacent table rows, columns or cells. You can also split a table cell, row or a column into any number of cells, horizontally or vertically. Splitting allows you to create new table cells, rows or columns without changing the size table. The merged table rows or columns can also be unmerged. Let's now first learn about merging table cells.

Merging Table Cells

Merging e adjacent table rows, columns or table cells, allows you to change the appearance of a table. CorelDRAW provides you a simple way to merge table cells. Undertake the following steps to merge the cells:

1. *Select* the **Table** tool and *select* the third column of the first table, as shown in Fig.CD-6.24.
2. *Select* **Table→Merge Cells** (Fig.CD-6.24).

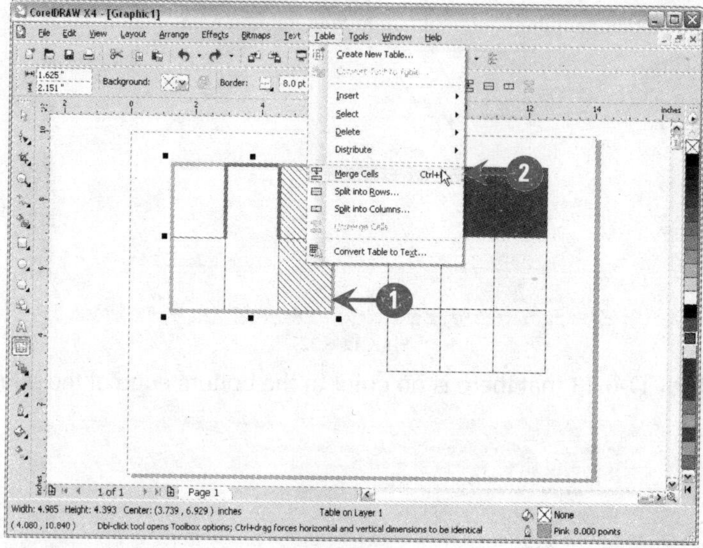

Fig.CD-6.24

The selected cells are merged as shown in Fig.CD-6.25.

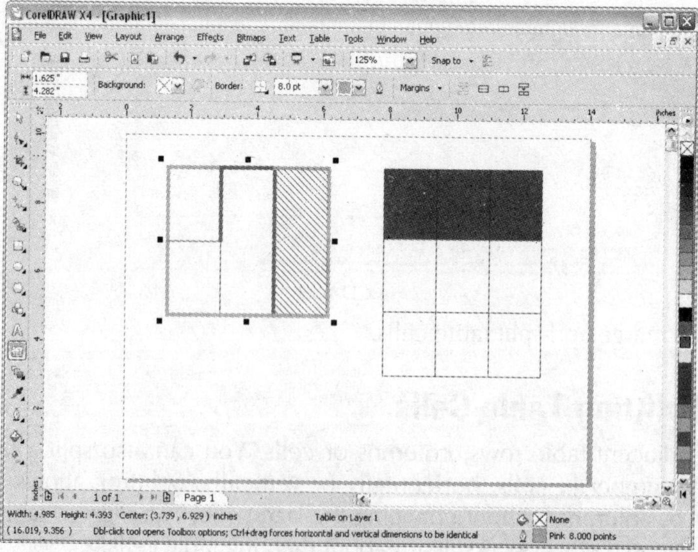

Fig.CD-6.25

Note

> The cells can be unmerged by selecting Table→Unmerge Cells.

Splitting Table Cells

You can split a single cell into a specified number of cells horizontally or vertically. There are two buttons on the Property bar for splitting the cell:

- The **Split the selected cell into a specified number of cells horizontally** (▤) button splits a single cell into a number of cells horizontally.
- The **Split the selected cell into a specified number of cells vertically** (▤) button is used to split a cell into a number of cells vertically.

Undertake the following steps to split a cell:

1. *Select* the cells that you want to split (Fig.CD-6.26).
2. *Click* the **Split the selected cell into a specified number of cells horizontally** button (▤) on the **Property** bar to split the cell into number of cells, horizontally. A **Split Cells** dialog box appears as shown in Fig.CD-6.26.
3. *Type* the number of cells you want to divide the selected cell into in the spin box beside the **Number of rows**. *Click* the **OK** button (Fig.CD-6.26).

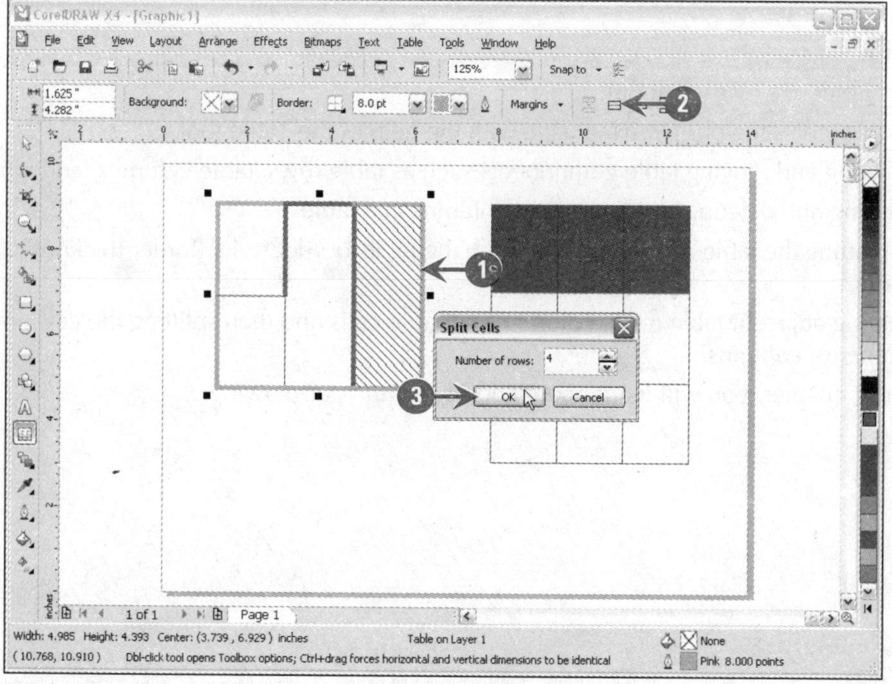

Fig.CD-6.26

The selected cell is split into the desired number of cells as shown in Fig.CD.6.27.

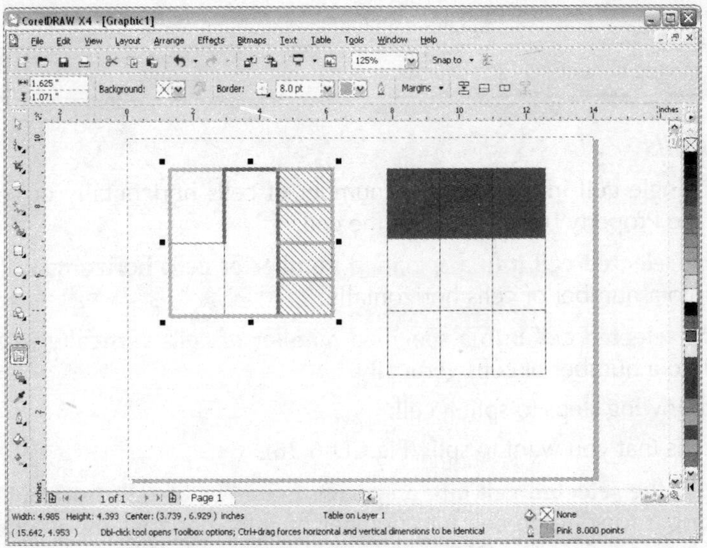

Fig.CD-6.27

With this, we come to the end of the chapter. Before proceeding ahead towards the next chapter, let's summarize the main points of this chapter.

Summary

In this chapter, we learned about:

- Adding tables to your Drawing page with the help of the Table tool.
- Selecting and moving table components such as table rows, table columns, and table cells.
- Inserting and deleting table rows and columns in a table.
- Formatting the table and table cells by changing its border style, border thickness and border color.
- Merging adjacent table rows, columns and table cells and then splitting the cells into desired number of columns.

In the next chapter, you will learn about adding text in your drawing.

Chapter 7

Working with Text

In this Section

- Types of Text
- Converting Text from One Type to Another
- Changing the Appearances of Text
- Find and Replace
- Applying Effects to the Text
- Wrapping Paragraph Text around Objects
- Fitting Text to an Object's Path
- Moving Text between Frames or Text Objects
- Converting Text to Object using Curve Command
- Working with Text in Tables

In graphic and layout designing applications, text plays an important role in displaying information, characters or symbols in different languages such as English and Devnagri. For displaying information, almost every graphic and designing layout application provides built-in support for text. The built-in support across different applications is known as Text tool ; In CorelDRAW, you can add text by using this tool. Once you have added text to the document, you can apply various formatting options such as font type, font size, font style, or aligning and spacing of text, and so on. In CorelDRAW you can apply effects such as fitting text to a path, wrapping text around an object and using drop cap.

In this chapter, you will learn to change the appearance of text by applying different formatting methods such as font size, face, and alignment; edit text by finding and replacing instances of word/phrase in the document; search the document for spelling and grammar mistakes; apply effects on text; converting text into curved object.

Types of Text

In CorelDRAW, you can create two types of text–Artistic and Paragraph text for your drawing. In both types of text, you have to select the Text tool. When you create Artistic text, you simply type text in the Drawing page, when you create Paragraph text, you have to first create a text frame then type text within that frame. Let us discuss briefly about them.

- **Artistic Text:** Artistic text is a type of text in CorelDRAW that is used to create short lines of text such as titles or to apply graphics effects such as fitting text to a path. This is because Artistic text is artistically versatile and easy to work with and therefore allows you to add a variety of special effects to the text and transform it in a number of ways. You just have to click at the point where you want to insert the text and start typing. Artistic text is more often used for typing single lines of text for example, titles, headings, and so on. It is also used to add special effects such as drop caps.
- **Paragraph Text:** Paragraph text is used in case of text-intensive projects. For example, certain ads, brochures and so on that require large blocks of text to be added. In such cases, the Paragraph text is more appropriate than the Artistic text. In the Paragraph text, the text is created in frames and you can use various paragraph formatting features like bulleted lists, tabs and indents, drop caps and so on.

Note

You can also perform the following actions on both types of text:

1. Changing the typeface and type size.
2. Changing the font style (bold, italics and so on).
3. Changing the text spacing.
4. Carrying out a spell check or a grammar check.
5. Formatting individual character within words.

Preparing a Layout for Using the Text

A page layout defines the geometry of a page such as how many regions will appear and how will the regions be organized on the page. Before creating text in your drawing, let us prepare a layout for the book cover. For this, we will draw four rectangles in the Drawing page of CorelDRAW window and fill them with colors.

Let us now start creating the book cover. For this, first open the CorelDRAW and then, undertake the following steps:

1. *Open* a new CorelDRAW document page *by clicking* the **New** button in the Toolbar (Fig.CD-7.1).
2. *Draw a* rectangle and *fill* it with a color say **Powder Blue** swatch from the Colors palette (Fig.CD-7.1).
3. *Draw* the second rectangle beside the first rectangle and *fill* it with a color say **Pale Yellow** (Fig.CD-7.1).

Note

> To fill an object, please refer under 'Setting Color for an Object' section in the chapter: 3 Working with Objects.

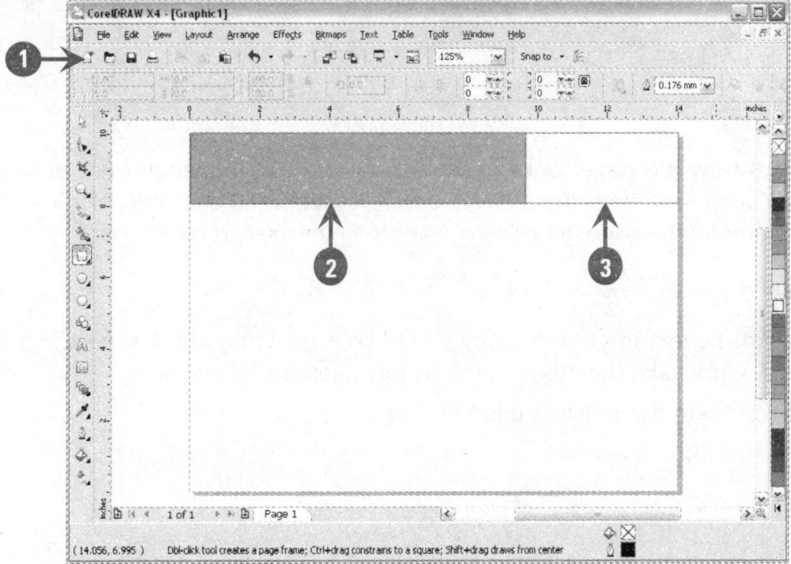

Fig.CD-7.1

4. *Click* the **Pick** tool in the Toolbox (Fig.CD-7.2).
5. *Select* the first rectangle. Now *press* **CTRL+D** to create a duplicate of the selected rectangle. *Place* the duplicate rectangle below first rectangle and resize and position it as shown in Fig.CD-7.2.

Note

> If you are duplicating the object for the first time, a Duplicate offset dialog box appears. Specify a value in the Horizontal offset and Vertical offset spin boxes to specify the distance between duplicate and original object along the X and Y axes.
>
> Please refer for duplicating objects under "Copying, Duplicating, and Deleting Objects" and positioning objects under "Positioning Objects" in Chapter: 3 Working with Objects.

6. *Select* the second rectangle. *Press* **CTRL+D** to create a duplicate of second rectangle. *Place* it below the second rectangle and resize it as shown in Fig.CD-7.2).

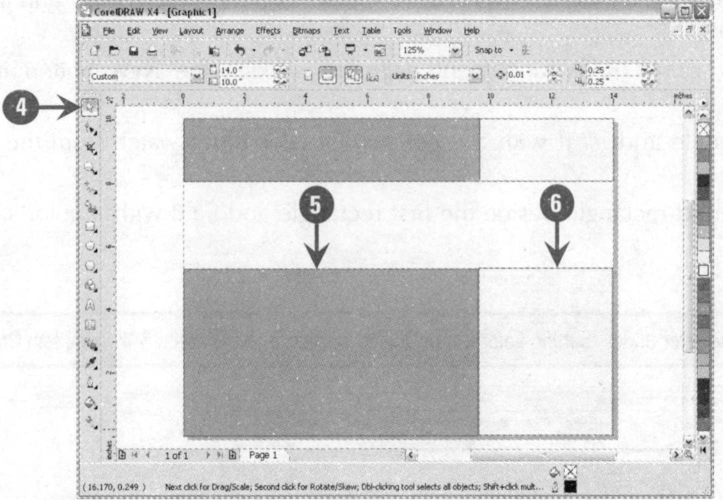

Fig CD-7.2

Fig.CD-7.2 shows how the page looks like when all the four rectangles are drawn in it. After creating the rectangles, filling them with colors, resizing them and placing them at the appropriate location on the page, let us now learn to enter the text on the page.

Creating Artistic Text

You can create Artistic text in your drawing where you need to add titles, headings or any other short lines of text. Undertake the following steps to create the Artistic text:

1. *Click* the **Text** tool in the Toolbox (Fig.CD-7.3).

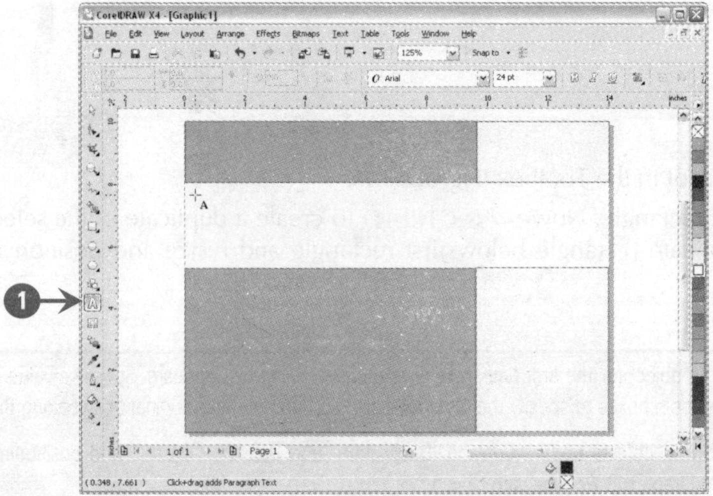

Fig.CD-7.3

2. *Click* the just below the first rectangle, and *type* the text **Road Construction** (Fig.CD-7.4). *Press* the **Enter** key to move the cursor to the next line.
3. *Type* **Highway Development From Nation Building** (Fig.CD-7.4).

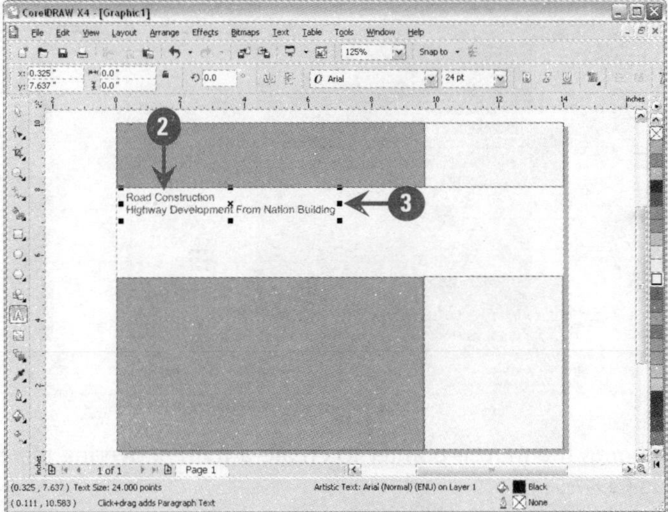

Fig.CD-7.4

4. *Click* in the middle of the fourth rectangle and type **4** (Fig.CD-7.5).

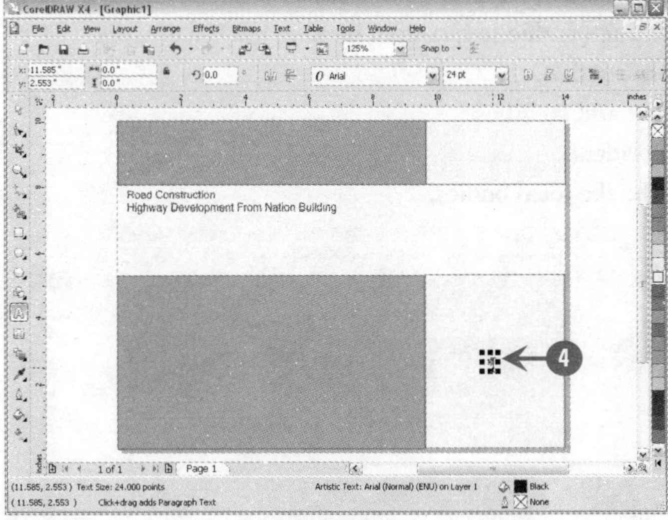

Fig.CD-7.5

Creating Paragraph Text

You can create Paragraph text whenever you need large block of text in your drawing. To create Paragraph text, first create a Paragraph text frame and then type the text within the text frame. undertake the following to enter Paragraph text:

1. *Click* the **Text** tool in the Toolbox (Fig.CD-7.6).

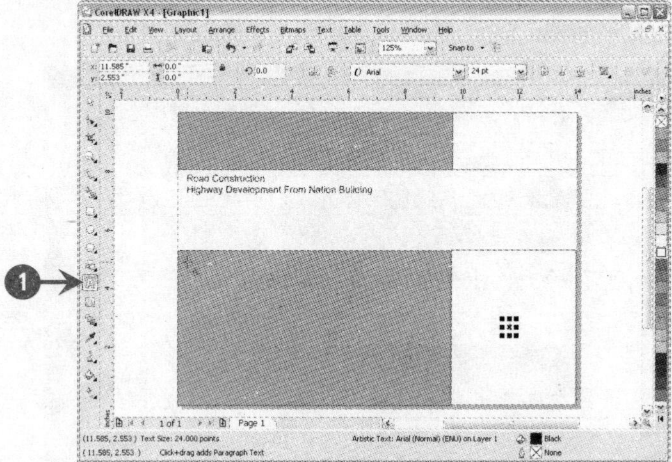

Fig.CD-7.6

2. Now, *click* and *drag* the mouse-pointer to create a frame covering the entire third rectangle as shown in Fig.CD-7.7.
3. Now, *type* the following text inside the frame (Fig.CD-7.7).

This book will help you to understand:

Shortage of Experienced and Trained Consultants.

Problems with Contractors due to quantum jump in quality of work.

Poor quality of construction.

Lack of management and facilities.

Large number of accidents.

Investments made by the local bodies.

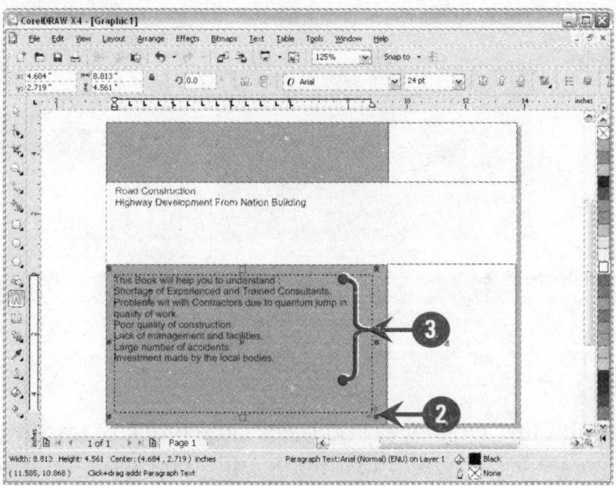

Fig.CD-7.7

Note

> If you have added more text that can be fitted within the text frame you have created, then a small black filled down-arrow appears below the frame indicating that the frame contains more text. You can however resize the text frame to make all the text visible by dragging this small down-arrow or dragging one of the surrounding handles to increase the size of the frame.

4. Now, *click* and *drag* the mouse-pointer to create a frame in the fourth rectangle as shown in Fig.CD-7.8.
5. *Type* **Edition** within the frame in the fourth rectangle as shown in Fig.CD-7.8.

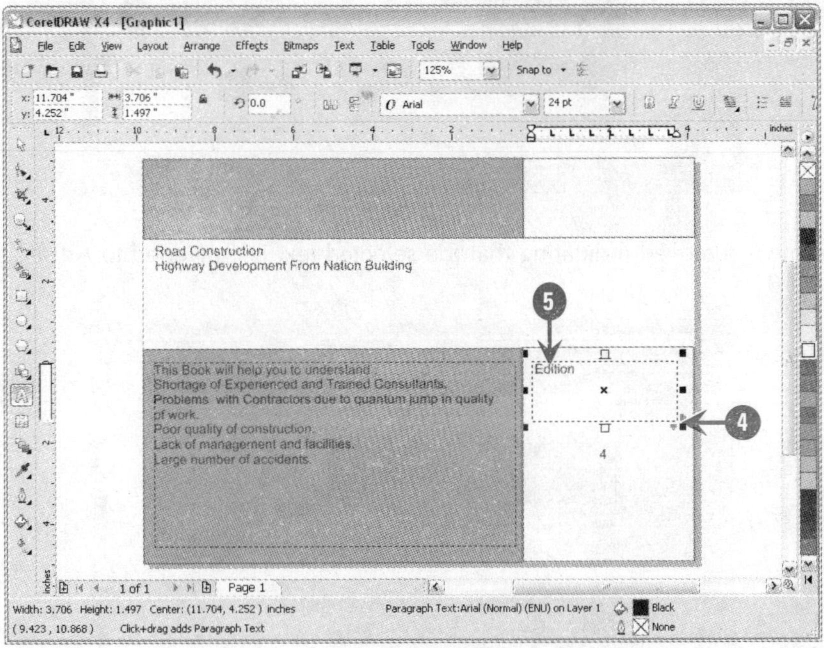

Fig.CD-7.8

You have learned to create Artistic as well as Paragraph text, let us now learn to convert one text to another.

Converting Text from One Type to Another

If you have typed the text in the Artistic mode and want to change it to the Paragraph mode or vice-versa, you can easily do so. This saves us the trouble of typing the entire text in the other mode again.

Undertake the following steps to convert the Paragraph text to Artistic text:

1. *Select* the **Pick** tool in the Toolbox (Fig.CD-7.9).
2. *Click* anywhere on the frame that contains text **Edition** in the fourth rectangle. The frame of the paragraph text is selected (Fig.CD-7.9).
3. Next, *select* **Text→Convert To Artistic Text** (Fig.CD-7.9).

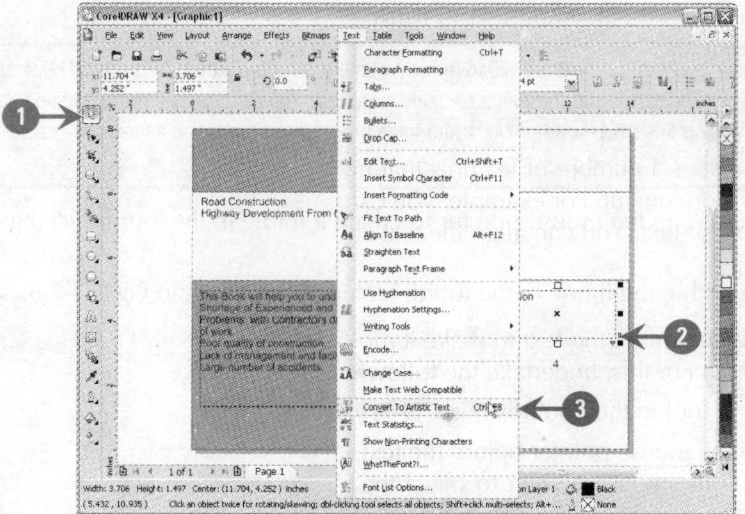

Fig.CD-7.9

The text frame is removed indicating that the selected text is converted to Artistic text as shown in Fig.CD-7.10.

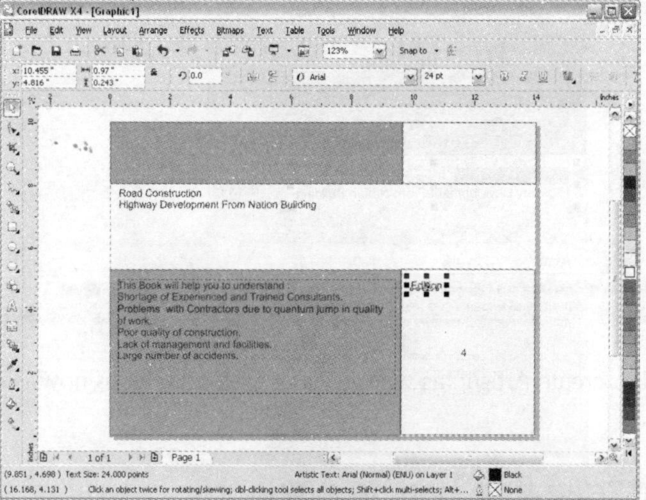

Fig.CD-7.10

Note

Similarly, for converting the Artistic text to the Paragraph text, select the Pick tool from the Toolbox and then select the Paragraph text that you want to convert and then

Select Text→Convert To Paragraph text. The selected Paragraph text would be converted into the Artistic text.

You can save your drawing in a location on your computer. As soon as you save your drawing, it will change the title bar. The existing drawing can be further used whenever required.

After learning to convert Paragraph text to Artistic text or vice-versa, let us now learn to change the appearances of text.

Changing the Appearances of Text

CorelDRAW provides a number of features that helps to change the appearances of the text you have entered in a document. For example, you can change the font of the text, as well as the font size and color of the text. You can align the text and change the text spacing.

Changing a Font

You can change the font of the text to make it more appealing. Let us change the font of the text, Road Construction. For this, undertake the following steps:

1. *Click* the **Text** tool in the Toolbox (Fig.CD-7.11).
2. Now, *place* the **mouse** pointer before the text **Road Construction**. Keeping the mouse button *pressed*, *drag* the mouse-pointer to *select* the text. The text appears highlighted as shown in Fig.CD-7.11.

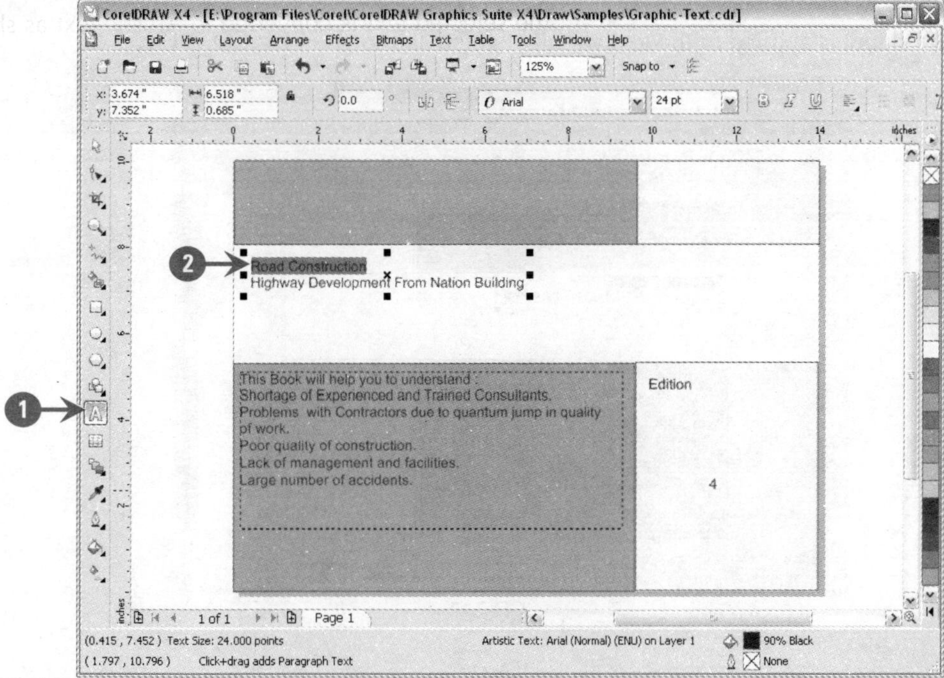

Fig.CD-7.11

3. From the **Property bar**, *select* a font from the **Font List** drop-down list. A Font list displays the names of all the fonts installed on your computer. As you move the mouse-pointer over different font names in the Font list, the Live Preview effect of CorelDRAW changes the appearance of selected text. In our case, we have selected the **Arial Black** font (Fig.CD-7.12).

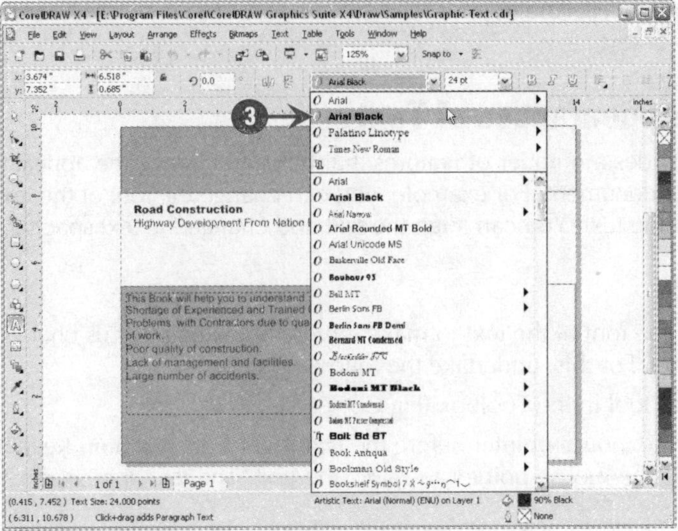

Fig.CD-7.12

The selected font is applied to the text we highlighted as shown in Fig.CD-7.13.

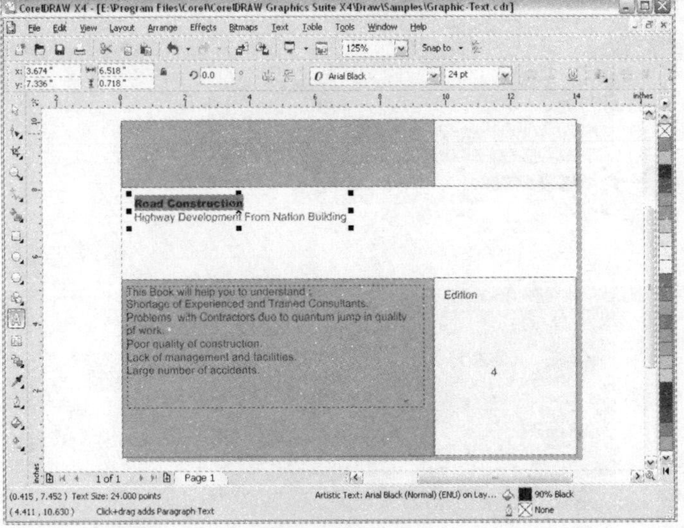

Fig.CD-7.13

Changing the Font Size and Color of the Text

You can change the font size as well as the color of the text to make your text presentable. Undertake the following steps to change the font size and color of the text:

1. *Click* the **Text** tool in the Toolbox if it is not selected (Fig.CD-7.14).
2. Now, *select* text **Road Construction** (Fig.CD-7.14).

3. *Select* a font size from the **Font Size drop-down list** (Fig.CD-7.14). For example in our case it is **36pt** (Fig.CD-7.14).

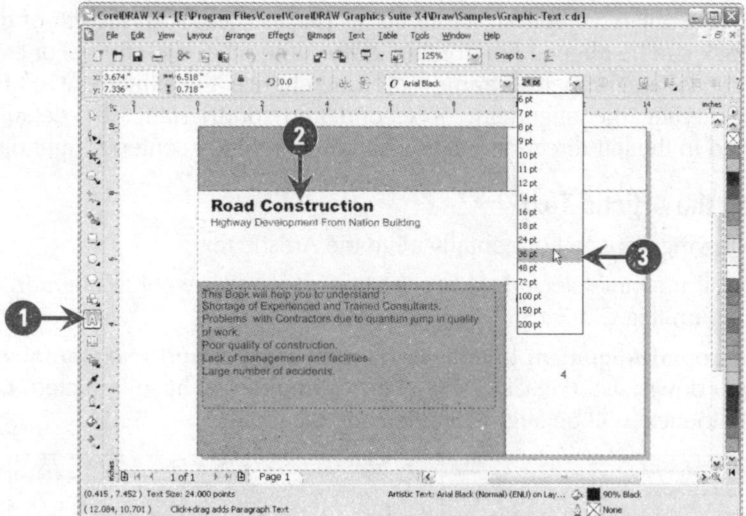

Fig.CD-7.14

4. *Change* the font size of **4** in the fourth rectangle in the same way as we have described in the previous steps. We have set the font size for it is **200 pt**. the result will be seen in the Fig.CD-7.15.
5. To change the color of the text, *select* the text and *click* a color swatch on the Color palette as shown in Fig.CD-7.15. The color of the selected Artistic text changes to **Purple**.

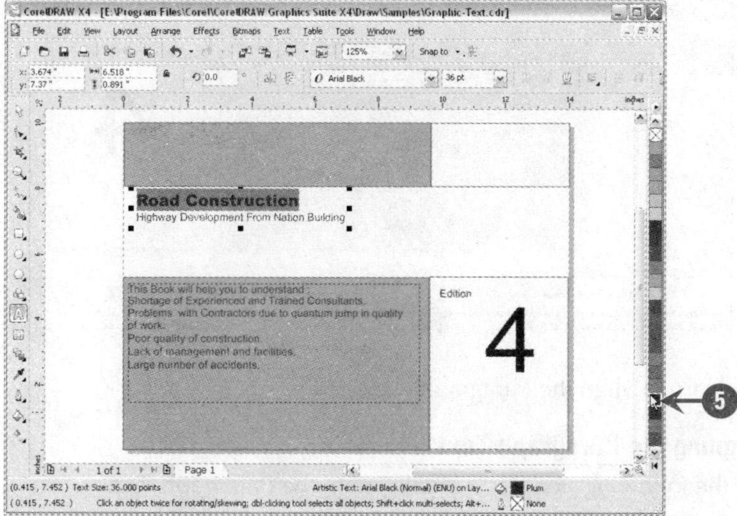

Fig.CD-7.15

You have learned to change the font size and color of the text. Let's now discuss changing the alignment of the text.

Changing the Alignment

You can align both Artistic as well as Paragraph text. In context to Paragraph text, you have the choice to align it vertically top, bottom, or center as per the height and width of the text frame. The paragraph block can be aligned horizontally or to some other direction.. For example, out of four paragraphs in a Paragraph text frame you can change the alignment of first and third paragraph while keeping the alignment of second and fourth static. By default, the text is horizontally aligned in the left direction but you can align it to the center or right direction.

Horizontally Aligning the Artistic Text

Undertake the following steps to horizontally align the Artistic text:

1. *Click* **Text** tool if it is not selected. *Select* the text which you want to align. In our case it is, **Road Construction** (Fig.CD-7.15).
2. *Click* the **Horizontal Alignment** button on the Property bar and *select* an alignment option from the drop-down list (Fig.CD-7.16). For example we have selected **Center** option (Fig.CD-7.16), the text will be aligned in the center.

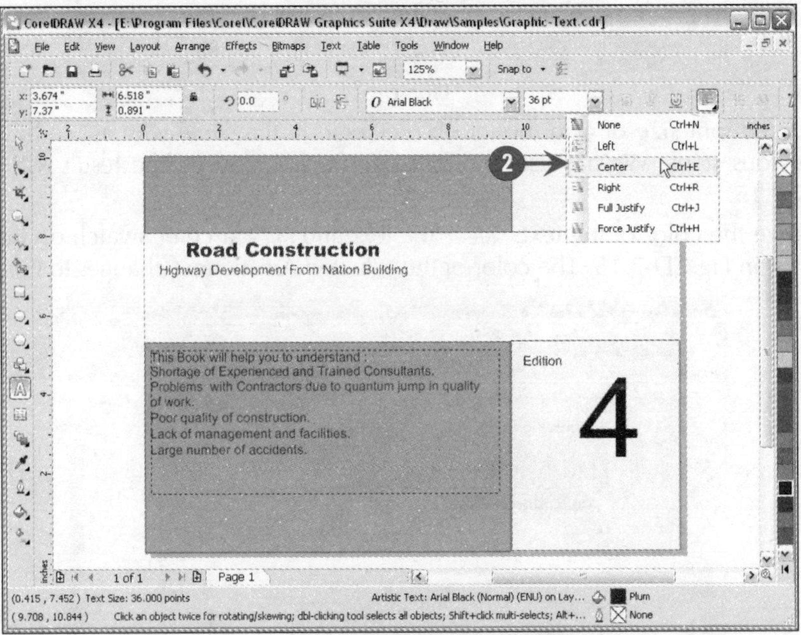

Fig.CD-7.16

Let us now learn to align the Paragraph text.

Vertically Aligning the Paragraph Text

Undertake the following steps to vertically align the Paragraph text:

1. *Select* the Paragraph text frame in the third rectangle (Fig.CD-7.17).
2. *Select* **Text→Paragraph Formatting** (Fig.CD-7.17). A **Paragraph Formatting** docker appears, as shown in the Fig.CD-7.18.

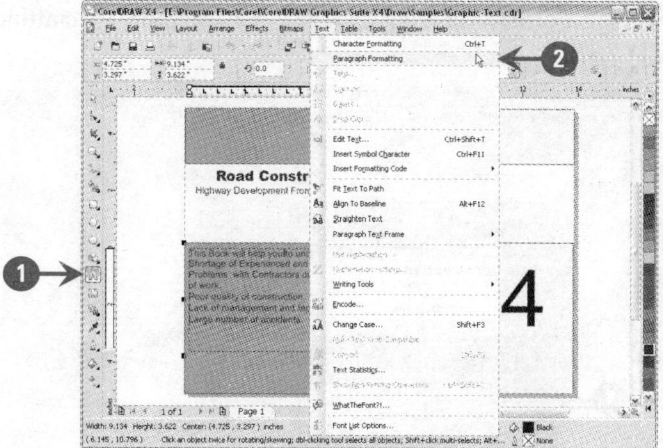

Fig.CD-7.17

3. In the **Paragraph Formatting** docker under the **Alignment** group, *open* the **Vertical** drop down list and *select* an alignment option. For example, in our case it is **Center** (Fig.CD-7.18). Paragraph text will be vertically aligned in the center with respect to the text frame (Fig.CD-7.18).

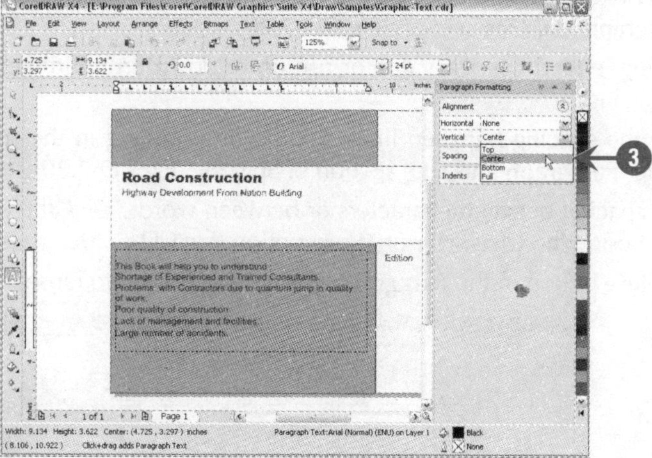

Fig.CD-7.18

Changing the Text Spacing

You can change the space between two characters or between two words in your document. In CorelDRAW you can also change the spacing between two lines in selected paragraphs, in an entire Paragraph text frame or in artistic text. In case of Paragraph text, change spacing between lines of text applies only to lines of text within the same paragraph. You can also change the spacing between the Paragraphs in a Paragraph text.

Undertake the following steps to apply text spacing in a Paragraph text:

1. *Select* a Paragraph text frame (Fig.CD-7.19).

2. *Select* **Text→Paragraph Formatting** (Fig.CD-7.17). A **Paragraph Formatting** docker appears as shown in Fig.CD-7.19.

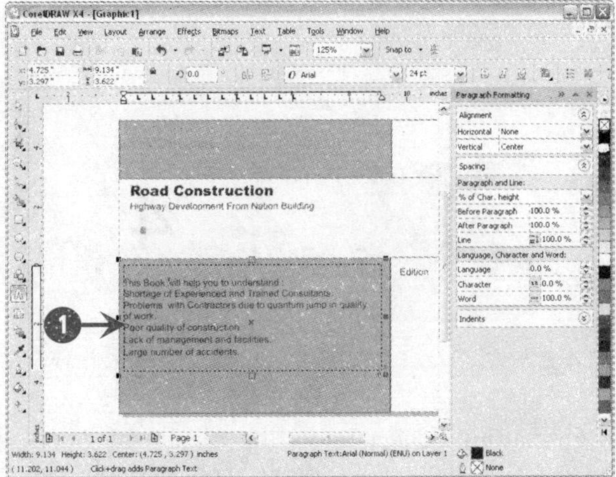

Fig.CD-7.19

3. *Expand* the **Spacing** group. Under **Spacing** group *set* the spacing before or after a paragraph in the spin boxes beside the appropriate option such as **Before Paragraph**, **After Paragraph** under **Paragraph and Line** section (Fig.CD-7.20).

To adjust spacing, either type the value or use up or down arrow in the spin box to increase or decrease the spacing.

4. To change the spacing between lines, set the line spacing in the spin box beside the **Line** option under **Paragraph and Line** section of Spacing (Fig.CD-7.20).
5. To change spacing between characters or between words, *click* the up or down arrow in the spin boxes beside the **Character** or **Word** option (Fig.CD-7.20).
6. *Click* the **Close** button in the **Paragraph Formatting** docker to close it (Fig.CD-7.20).

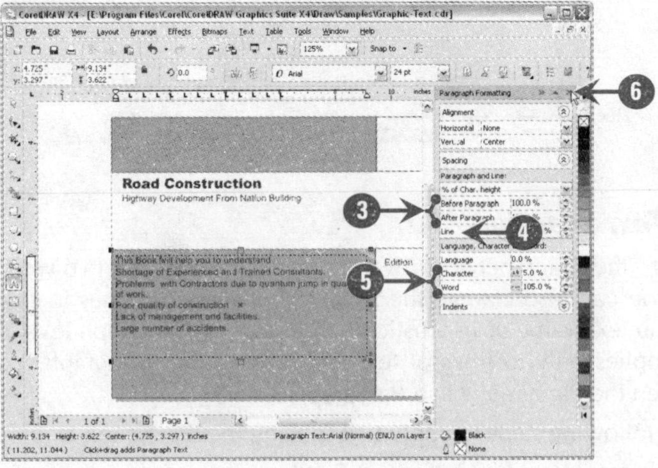

Fig.CD-7.20

Let us now learn to find a specific text in an open document and replacing it with some other text.

Find and Replace

CorelDRAW also provides another interesting feature called as Find and Replace feature that enables us to search for specific text within the currently active document. This feature helps saving time as compared to manual searching that is otherwise time consuming. After finding a specific text, you can replace it with some other text immediately.

Finding the Text

Sometimes you need to find a word or a phrase in the document in which you are working and it becomes difficult if you have to search it manually. CorelDRAW provides a feature of finding text so that you can easily search the specific text in your document. Using this feature you can begin searching for the specific text from the current cursor position. Click at the position from where you want to start your search.

Undertake the following steps to find a text:

1. *Click* the **Text** tool on the Toolbox and then *select* the text that you want to find in the document. In our case, we have selected the Paragraph text in the third rectangle as shown in Fig.CD-7.21.
2. *Select* **Text→Edit Text** (Fig.CD-7.21). An **Edit Text** dialog box appears (Fig.CD-7.22).

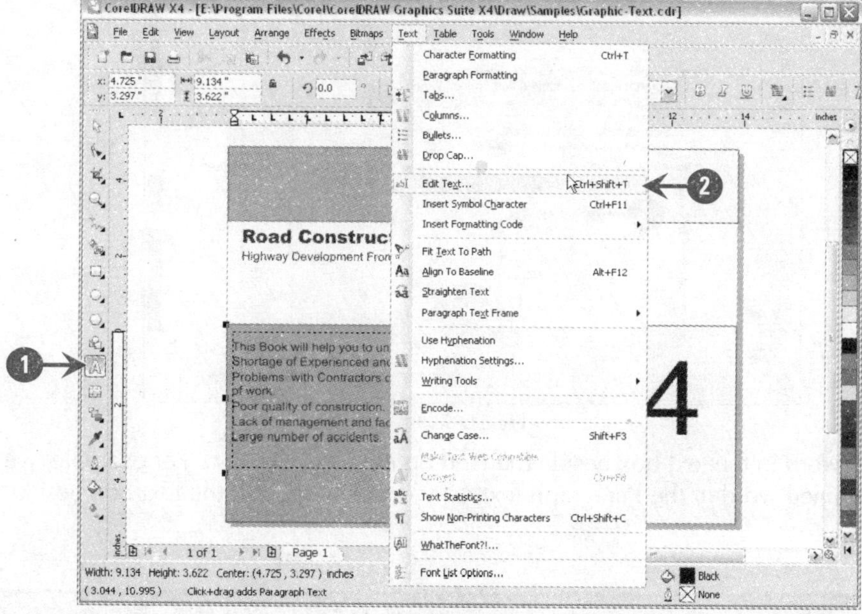

Fig.CD-7.21

3. *Click* the **Options** button as shown in Fig.CD-7.22. A drop-down list appears (Fig.CD-7.23).

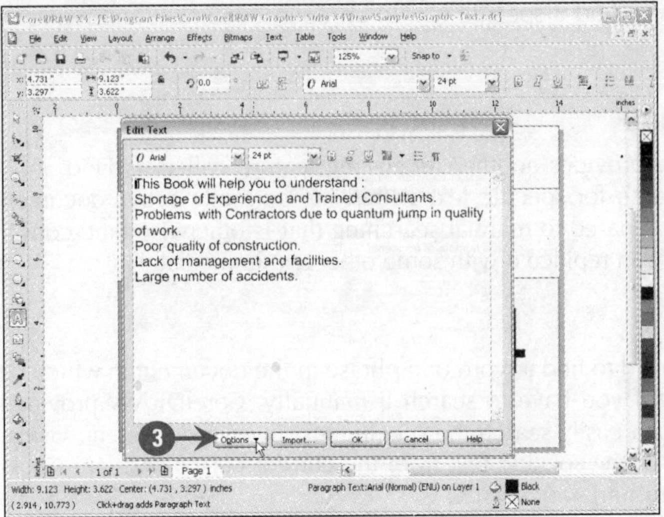

Fig.CD-7.22

4. *Click* the **Find Text** option (Fig.CD-7.23). A **Find Text** dialog box appears (Fig.CD-7.24).

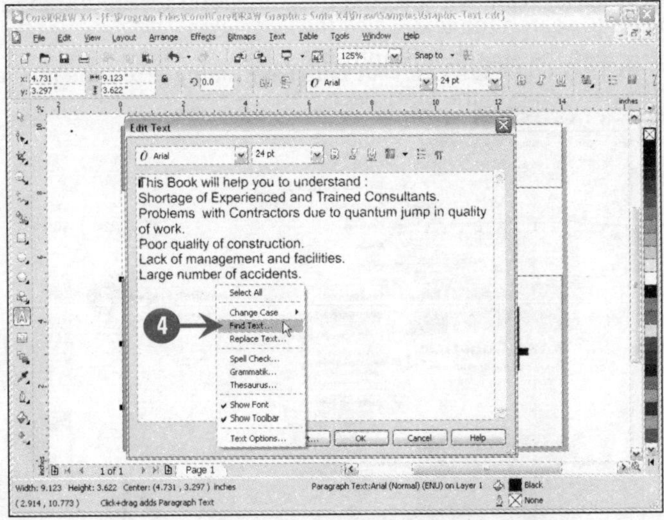

Fig.CD-7.23

5. *Type* the word in the text box beside the **Find** option (Fig.CD-7.24). For example, we want to search **trained** word in the Paragraph text, so we type trained in the text box beside the **Find** option.

Note

> To make your search case-specific, select the Match case checkbox in the Find Text dialog box.

6. *Click* the **Find Next** button in the dialog box as shown in Fig.CD-7.24. CorelDRAW finds the first occurrence of the word trained, it will appear highlighted in the text (Fig.CD-7.24).

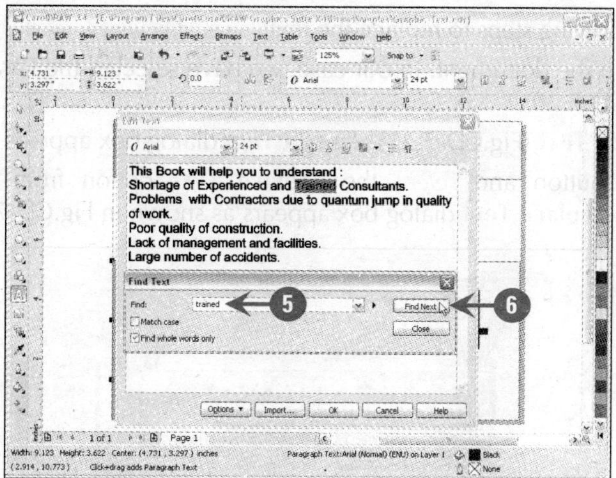

Fig.CD-7.24

7. To find the next occurrence of the text in the document, *click* the **Find Next** button in the dialog box (Fig.CD-7.25).
8. When the entire text is searched, a **Find and Replace** message box appears asking you whether you want to search the text. *Click* the **No** button in the **Find and Replace** dialog box (Fig.CD-7.25) to close the search, instantly the message box disappears.
9. Next, *click* the **Close** button in the **Find Text** dialog box to close the dialog box (Fig.CD-7.25).

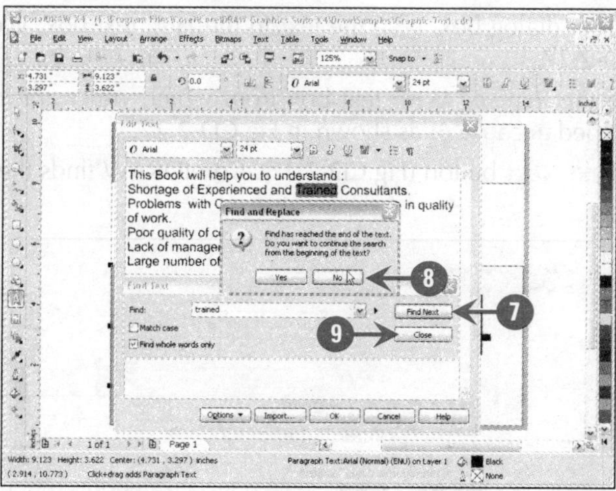

Fig.CD-7.25

Replacing the Text

After searching the desired text if you wish to replace it with other text, you can do so by using (plz insert the name of the feature here).

Undertaking the following steps to replace the text:

1. *Select* the text in the document. In our case, we have selected the Paragraph text in the third rectangle (Fig.CD-7.20).
2. *Select* **Text→Edit Text** (Fig.CD-7.21). An **Edit Text** dialog box appears (Fig.CD-7.26).
3. *Click* **Options** button and *select* the **Replace Text** option from the list as shown in Fig.CD-7.26. A **Replace Text** dialog box appears as shown in Fig.CD-7.27.

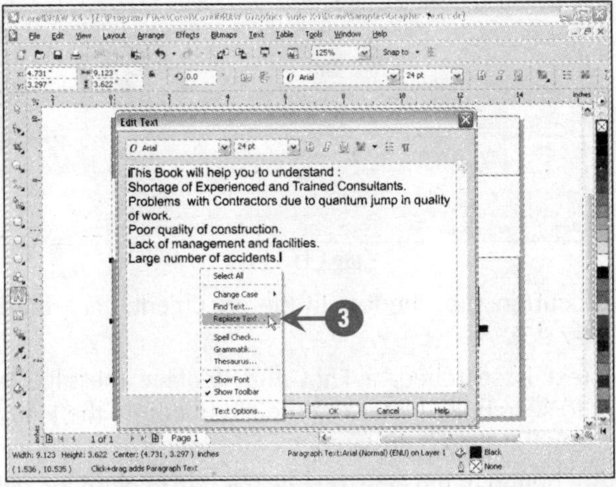

Fig.CD-7.26

4. In the **Replace Text** dialog box, *type* the text in the **Find** text box. We have typed **due to** as shown in Fig.CD-7.27.
5. *Type* the text in the **Replace With** text box from which you want to replace the searched text. We have typed **because of** as shown in Fig.CD-7.27.
6. Next, *click* the **Find Next** button (Fig.CD-7.27). CorelDRAW finds the first occurrence of the specified text.

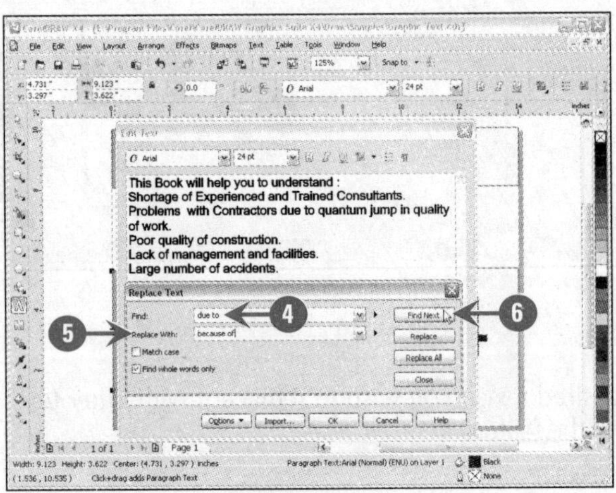

Fig.CD-7.27

7. Next, *click* the **Replace** button (Fig.CD-7.28). CorelDRAW replaces that occurrence of text with the text typed in the **Replace With** text box.

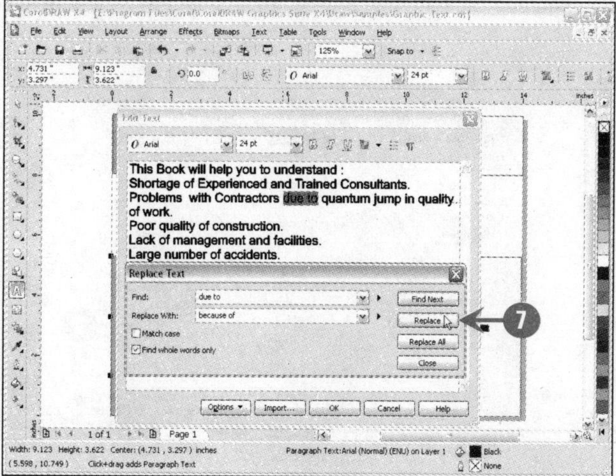

Fig.CD-7.28

Note

By clicking the Replace All button in the Replace Text dialog box (Fig.CD-7.28), you can replace every occurrence of the text typed in the Find text box with the text typed in the Replace With text box.

8. When all the similar occurrence of the word is replaced by the new word, a **Find and Replace** dialog box appears asking whether you want to search the document again. *Click* the **No** button in the dialog box (Fig.CD-7.29).

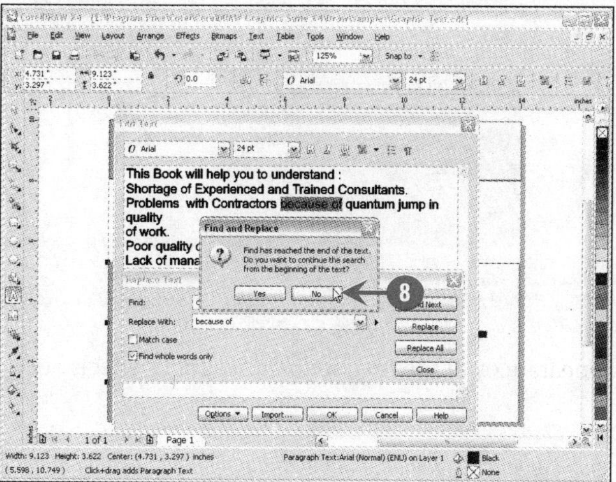

Fig.CD-7.29

9. *Click* the **Close** button in the **Replace Text** dialog box to close it (Fig.CD-7.30).
10. *Click* the **OK** button in the **Edit Text** dialog box (Fig.CD-7.30).

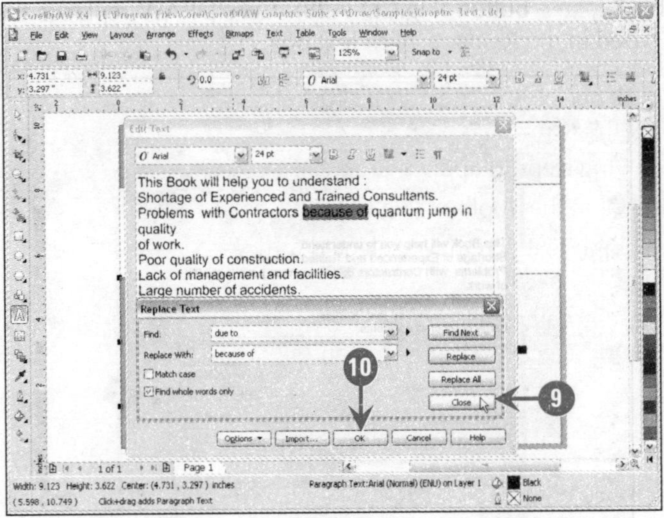

Fig.CD-7.30

As soon as you click the OK button in the dialog box, the dialog box closes and then you will see the replacement in the third rectangle of the Drawing page (Fig.CD-7.31).

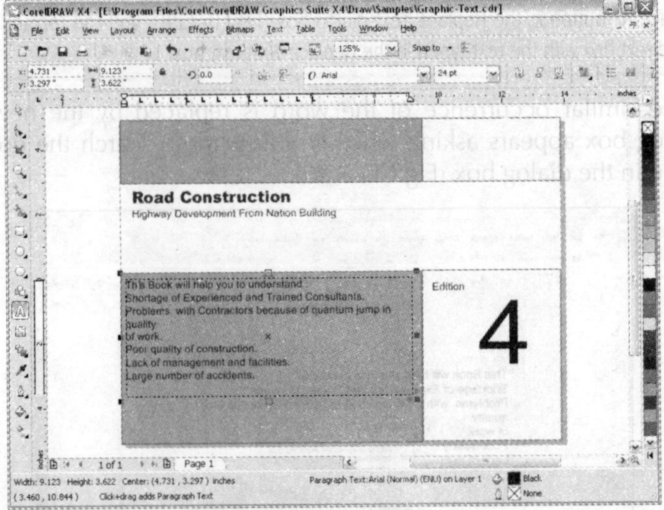

Fig.CD-7.31

After changing the appearances of the text, let us now apply effects such as drop cap and bullets to text.

Applying Effects to the Text

You can apply various special effects such as drop cap and bulleted list for the Paragraph text. When you apply the drop caps to the Paragraphs, the initial letter of the paragraph is enlarged.

Applying a Drop Cap

While applying the drop cap to the Paragraph text, you can customize the drop cap settings such as specifying the number of lines next to a drop cap and specify the distance between the drop cap and the body of the text.

Undertake the following steps to apply a drop cap to the Paragraph text:

1. *Click* the **Text** tool in the Toolbox (Fig.CD-7.32).
2. *Select* the Paragraph text. We have selected the Paragraph text present in the third rectangle as shown in Fig.CD-7.32.
3. *Click* the mouse-pointer before the initial letter of a paragraph in a Paragraph text (Fig.CD-7.32) and *Select* **Text→Drop Cap** (Fig.CD-7.32). A **Drop Cap** dialog box appears (Fig.CD-7.33).

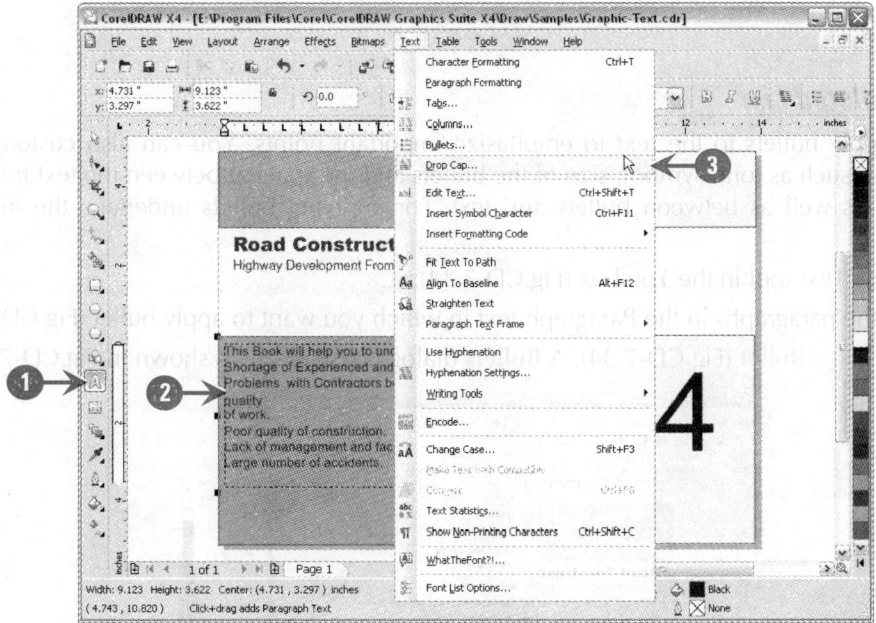

Fig.CD-7.32

4. *Select* check box beside the **Use drop cap** option (Fig.CD-7.33).
5. *Select* the check box beside the **Preview** option to view the drop cap at the time it is applied to the text (Fig.CD-7.33).
6. *Type* a value in the spin box beside the option **Number of lines dropped**. In our case it is **2** (Fig.CD-7.33).
7. *Type* a value in the spin box beside the option **Space after drop cap**. In our case it is **0.2** (Fig.CD-7.33). You can also select the check box beside the **Use hanging indent style for drop cap** option to offset the drop cap from the body of text.
8. *Click* the **OK** button in the dialog box (Fig.CD-7.33). The drop cap will be applied to the Paragraph text.

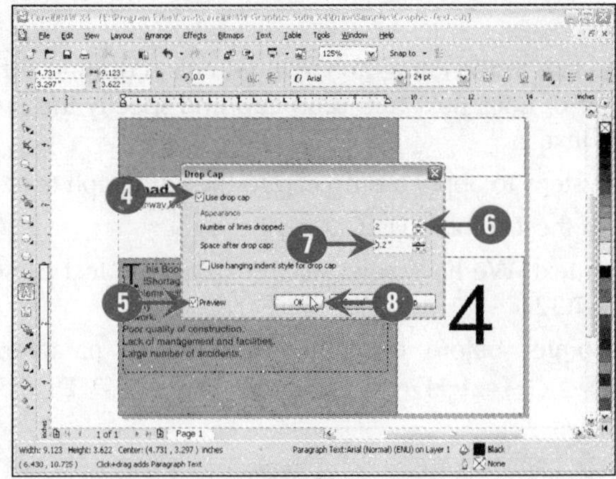

Fig.CD-7.33

Applying Bulleted List

You can apply bullets to the text to emphasize important points. You can also customize the appearances such as font, symbol, size of the bullets and the spacing between the text frame and the bullets as well as between bullets and text. For applying bullets undertake the following steps:

1. *Click* the **Text** tool in the Toolbox (Fig.CD-7.34).
2. *Select* the paragraphs in the Paragraph text in which you want to apply bullet (Fig.CD-7.34).
3. *Select* **Text→Bullet** (Fig.CD-7.34). A **Bullets** dialog box appears as shown in Fig.CD-7.35.

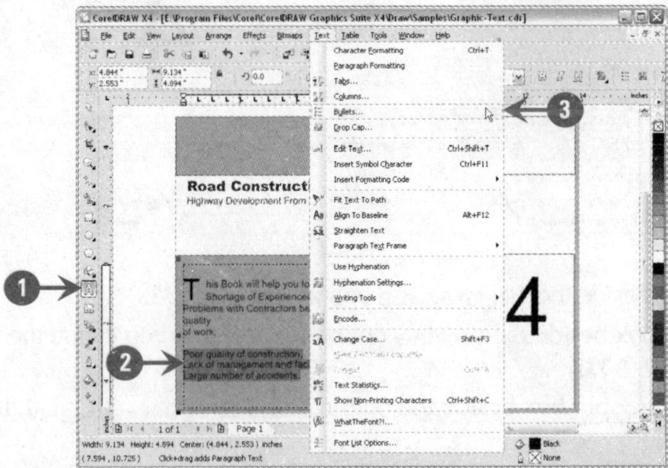

Fig.CD-7.34

4. *Select* the check box beside the **Use Bullets** (Fig.CD-7.35).

You can set the appearances such as Font, symbol, size and Spacing between the bullet and text frame as well as between bullet and text.

5. In the **Appearances** group, *select* a font from the **Font** combo box (Fig.CD-7.35).

6. *Select* a symbol, **Symbol** combo box list as shown in Fig.CD-7.35.

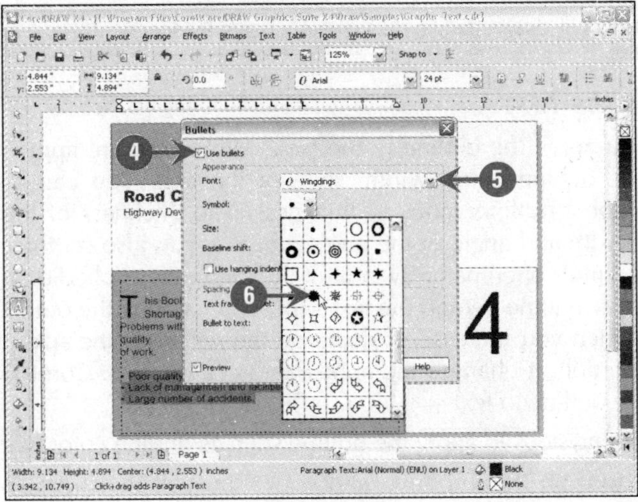

Fig.CD-7.35

7. For specifying the size of the bullet, *type* values in the **Size** spin box (Fig.CD-7.36). In our case it is **17.34 pt.**
8. For specifying the distance the bullet is shifted from the base line, *type* values in the spin box beside the **Balance shift** option (Fig.CD-7.36). In our case it is **0.0 pt.**
9. Under the **Spacing** area, type a value in the spin box beside the **Text from to bullet** option to specify the distance between text frames to bullet (Fig.CD-7.36).
10. *Type* a value in the spin box beside the **Bullet to text** option to specify the distance between the bullets to the text (Fig.CD-7.36).
11. *Click* the **OK** button (Fig.CD-7.36).

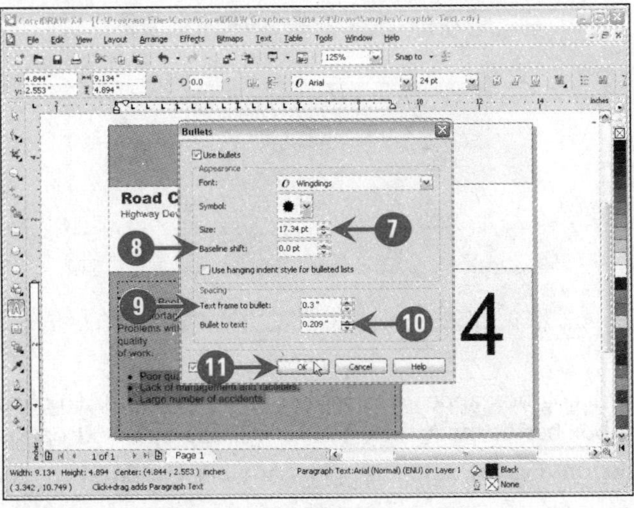

Fig.CD-7.36

Note

You can directly apply bullets by clicking the Show/Hide Bullet button in the Property bar.

Applying Outline to the Text

CorelDRAW lets you apply the outline to the text. While you are applying outline to the text, you can specify the outline color, width, style of the text. You can also create calligraphy outline. The calligraphic outline varies in thickness. The thickness of the calligraphic outlines depends upon the width and angle of the pen's nib. You can also set the corners of outline and end points of the outline's open path. By default the outline is applied on the top of the text's fill but you can also apply outline behind the text's fill. You can link the outline thickness to the size of the text so that when you increase or decrease the text size, the size of the outline changes with the same proportion. It changes the appearances of the text. CorelDRAW provide Outline Pen tool to apply the outline to text.

Undertake the following steps to apply the outline such as outline color, width, style to the text:

1. *Click* the **Text** tool on the Toolbox, and *select* the text in which you want to apply the outline fill to text. In our case the selected text is Artistic text below the first rectangle as shown in Fig.CD-7.37.
2. Next, *click* the **Outline** tool on the toolbox, and *select* the **Outline Pen** tool in the flyout as shown in Fig.CD-7.37.

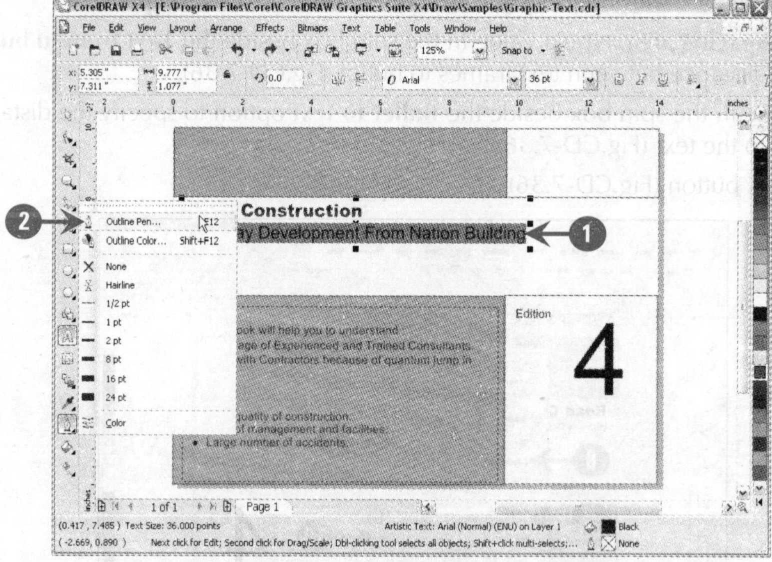

Fig.CD-7.37

3. An **Outline Pen** dialog box appears as shown in Fig.CD-7.38. To change the setting of text, *select* the check box beside the **Artistic Text** and **Paragraph Text** options (Fig.CD-7.38).
4. *Click* the **OK** button (Fig.CD-7.38). It opens another **Outline Pen** dialog box as shown in Fig.CD-7.39.

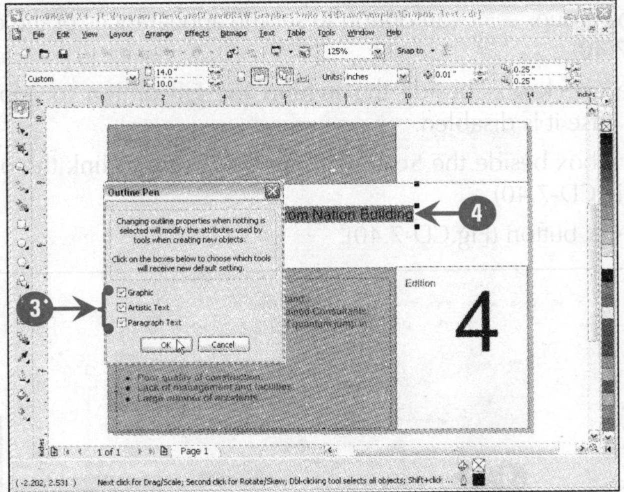

Fig.CD-7.38

All the options in the dialog box are disabled except the Width list box. The list box below the Width option contains None width. When you choose a width for the outline, the options present in the dialog box are enabled and you are able to set these options.

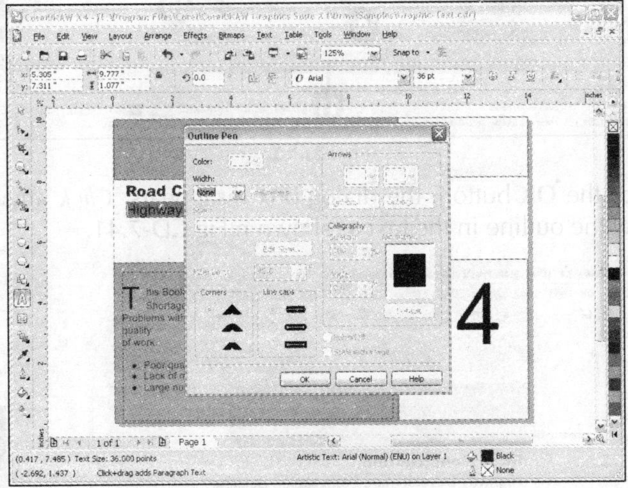

Fig.CD-7.39

5. *Select* a width and width unit from the **Width** drop-down lists. In our case the width is .5 mm and unit is millimeter as shown in Fig.CD-7.40.
6. *Select* an outline style from the **Style** drop-down list (Fig.CD-7.40).
7. In the Calligraphy area, you can change the width and angle of pen's nib. *Set* value in the spin box below the **Stretch** option to change the width and *set* value in the **Angle** box to change the angle of the pen's nib. In our case width is **15** % and angle is **0** degree (Fig.CD-7.40).
8. In the **Corners** group, *select* a corner type for the outline (Fig.CD-7.40).

9. In the **Line Caps** group, *select* an option to set the appearances of the end points in the open paths (Fig.CD-7.40).

You can select the check box beside the **Behind the Fill** option to apply outline behind the object's fill. In our case it is disabled.

10. *Select* the check box beside the **Scale with image option** to link the outline thickness to the object's size (Fig.CD-7.40).
11. Next, *click* the **OK** button (Fig.CD-7.40).

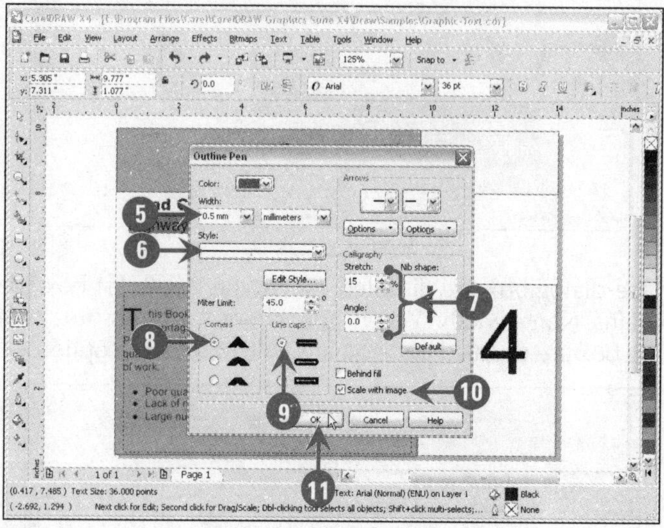

Fig.CD-7.40

12. When you click the **OK** button, the dialog box disappears. *Click* anywhere in the Drawing window to view the outline in the text as shown n Fig.CD-7.41.

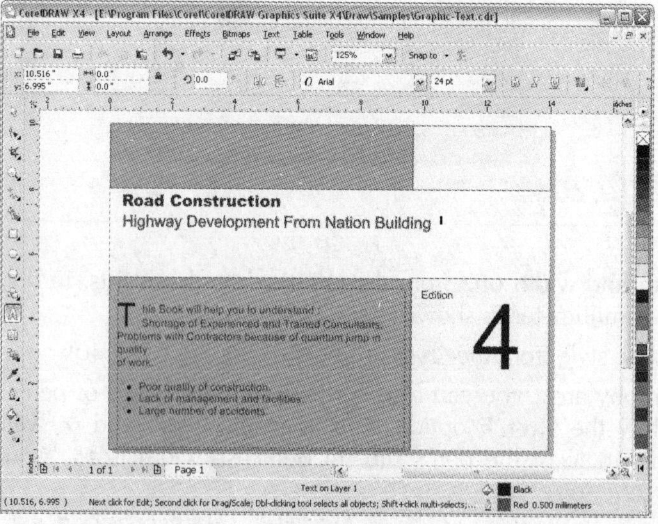

Fig.CD-7.41

After applying effects such as drop cap and bullets, let us now learn wrapping Paragraph text around objects.

Wrapping Paragraph Text around Objects

To change the shape of text, you can wrap Paragraph text around an object, Artistic text, or a Paragraph text frame. There are two categories of wrapping Paragraph text, one category is contour wrapping style and another is square wrapping style. The contour wrapping style follows the curve of object while the square wrapping style follows the boundary box of the object. The space between the object or text and the wrapping paragraph text can also be adjusted.

Undertake the following steps to wrap Paragraph text around an object or text:

1. *Click* the **Pick** tool and *select* the object. Here we have selected the object in the first rectangle (Fig.CD-7.42).

Note

> To create an object that is shown in the first rectangle (Fig.CD-7.42), draw a small rectangle within the first rectangle and create it's duplicate. Fill these rectangles as shown in Fig.CD-7.42 and group them. You have learned how to group the object under 'Grouping Objects' in the Chapter: 3 Working with Objects.

2. Next, *click* the **Wrap Paragraph Text** button in the Property bar. The Wrapping Style docker appears, as shown in Fig.CD-7.42.
3. *Select* a wrapping style. We have selected **Text Flows Right** option under Square wrapping style as shown in Fig.CD-7.42.
4. To increase or decrease the space between wrapping text and object, use up or down arrow in the spin box below the **Text wrap offset** option (Fig.CD-7.42).
5. *Close* the docker by *clicking* the **Close** button on the title of the docker (Fig.CD-7.42).

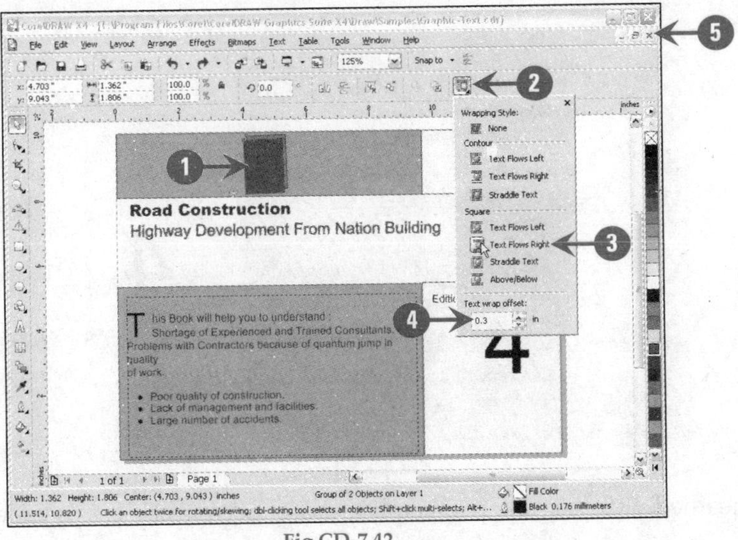

Fig.CD-7.42

6. Next, drag the selected object from the first rectangle to the third rectangle within the Paragraph text (Fig.CD-7.43).

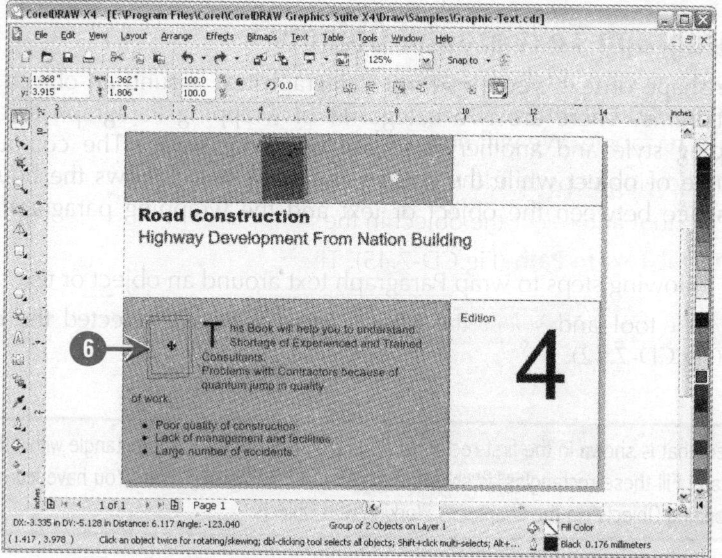

Fig.CD-7.43

As soon as you drag the object from the first rectangle to third rectangle and place the object in the left of the Paragraph text, the text will be moved to the right of the object as shown in Fig.CD-7.44.

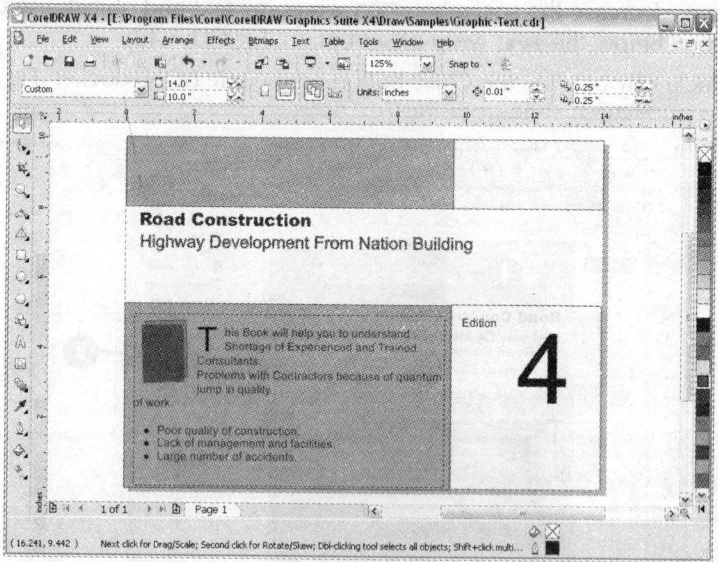

Fig.CD-7.44

You have learned wrapping the paragraph text around objects. Let us now add text along the path.

Fitting Text to an Object's Path

You can add text along an object's path. The path of an object can be opened or closed. Open path is the path whose starting point and ending point are not connected and close path is the path whose starting point and ending point is connected. You can fit the Artistic text to an open or close path but you can add the Paragraph text to an open path only. After fitting text to a path, you can set the position of the text relative to that path. Suppose, we draw a closed path say an ellipse in the first rectangle. We will now add the text along the path.

Undertake the following steps to add text along the path:

1. *Click* the **Pick** tool and *select* the object in the Fig.CD-7.45. In our case the object is ellipse.
2. *Select* **Text→Fit Text to Path** (Fig.CD-7.45). The text cursor is appears on the path.

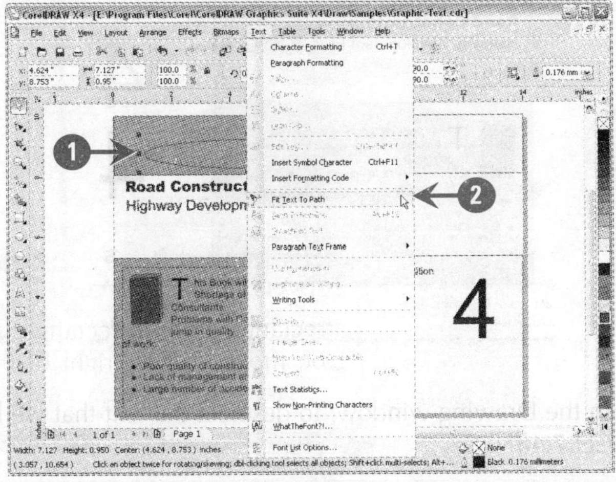

Fig.CD-7.45

3. *Select* a text orientation style from the **Text Orientation** drop-down list on the Property bar (Fig.CD-7.46).

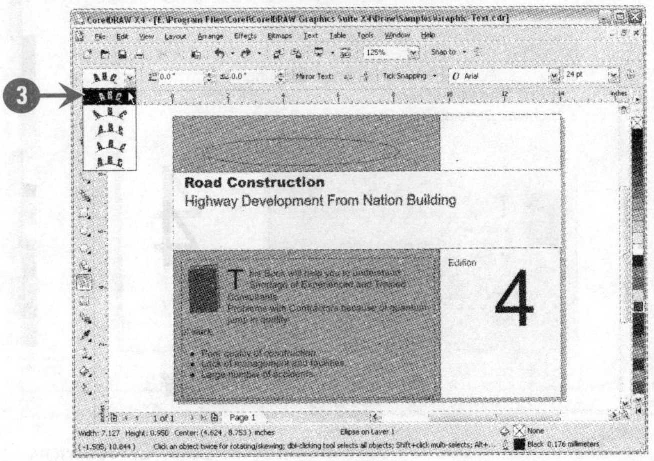

Fig.CD-7.46

4. You can set the distance between the text and object's path from the **Distance from Path spin** box in the Property bar by using the up or down arrow in the spin box (Fig.CD-7.47).
5. In the Property bar, set the horizontal position of the text along the path by clicking the up or down arrow button in the **Horizontal Offset** spin box (Fig.CD-7.47).
6. Now, *type* the text along the path as shown in Fig.CD-7.47.

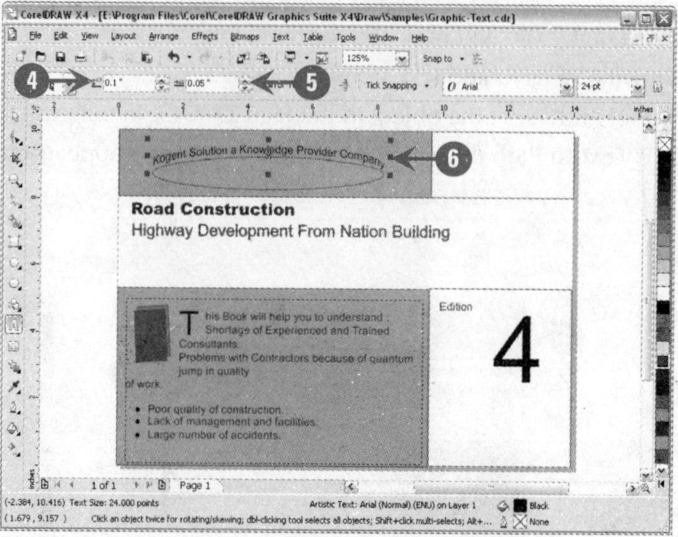

Fig.CD-7.47

7. *Click* anywhere in the Drawing window, to deselect the text that we have typed on the path as shown in Fig.CD.7.48.

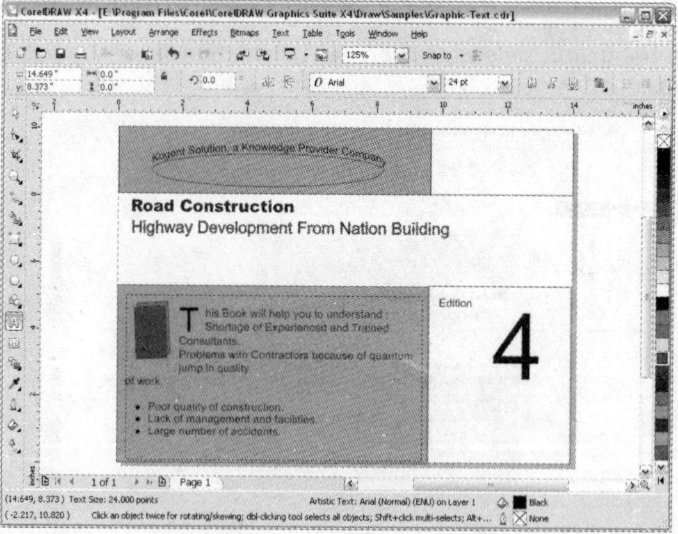

Fig.CD-7.48

After adding text to a path, let us now learn to move the text between two frames.

Moving Text between Frames or Text Objects

In CorelDRAW, you can move Paragraph text between the two Paragraph text frames. Artistic text can also be moved between two Artistic text objects. The movement of Paragraph text to an Artistic text object or Artistic text to a Paragraph text frame can also possible. Moving text between frames or text objects helps you to escape re-writing text. For example, if a Paragraph text frame contains some text that you want to add in the other Paragraph text frame then instead of rewriting the entire text again you can just move the text between frames to save your time.

In the Fig.CD-7.49, there are two Paragraph text frame in the Drawing page, here we move the text from the left side Paragraph text frame to right side Paragraph text.

Undertake the following steps to learn to move the text between two text frames:

1. *Click* the **Text** tool in the Toolbox, and *select* the text in that you want to move (Fig.CD-7.49).
2. Next, drag the text to the right side Paragraph text frame as shown in Fig.CD-7.49.

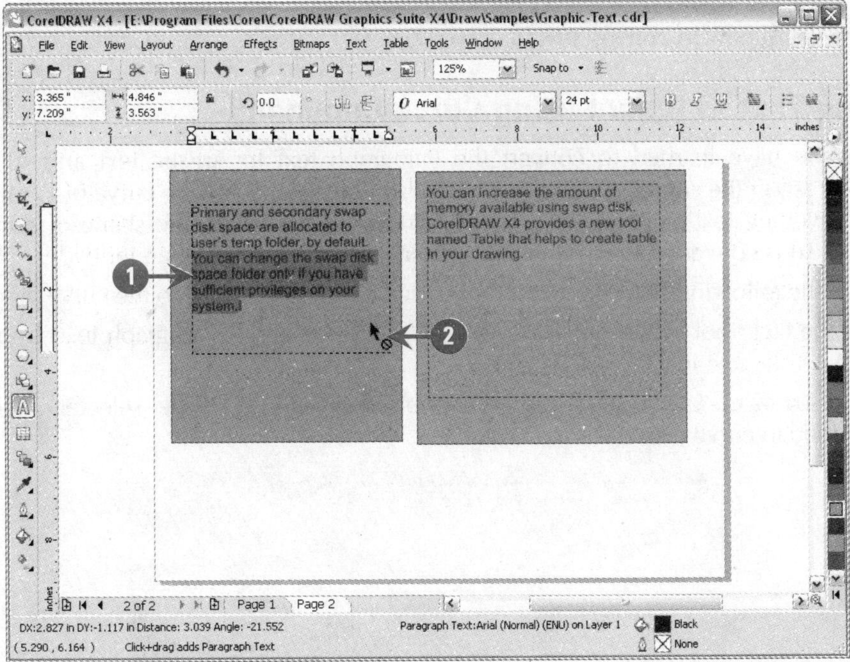

Fig.CD-7.49

You can see from the Fig.CD-7.50 the movement of the text from the left side Paragraph text frame to right side Paragraph text frame.

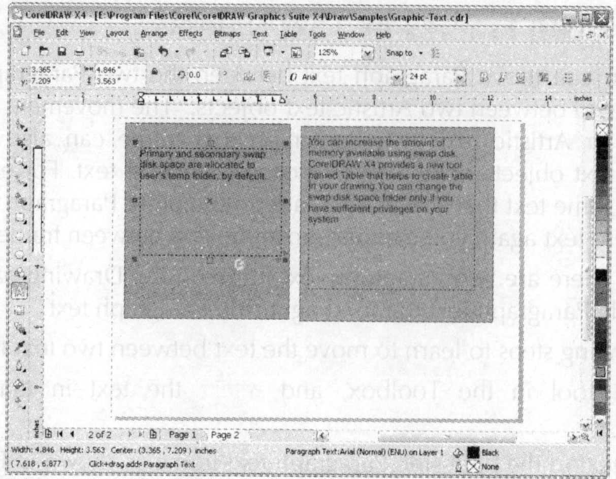

Fig.CD-7.50

Let us now learn how to convert text to curve object.

Converting Text to Object using Curve Command

Till now you have learned to convert the Paragraph text to Artistic text and Artistic text to Paragraph text, in the similar manner you can also convert the Artistic curve or Paragraph text to curve. Converting text to curve object, you can easily customize the shape of a curve object. When the text is converted to curve object, you can edit the shape of an individual character.

Undertake the following steps to covert the Artistic or Paragraph text to the curve object:

1. *Click* the **Pick** tool in the Toolbox, and *select* the Artistic or Paragraph text. In our case, we select Artistic text in the Fig.CD-7.51.
2. *Select* **Arrange→Convert to Curves** option (Fig.CD-7.51). The selected Artistic text is converted to curve object .

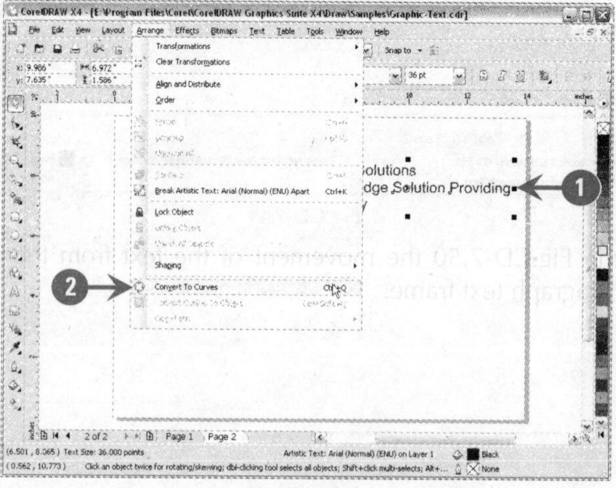

Fig.CD-7.51

Breaking Apart Text

When you convert text to curve object, you can provide the desired shape to whole object. But if you want to edit a particular character, then you have to break the text apart. Breaking text apart means each character of the text behaves like a separate object. You can now edit characters individually.

Undertake the following steps to break the curve object apart:

1. *Click* the **Pick** tool and *select* the object.
2. *Select* **Arrange→Break Curve Apart** (Fig.CD-7.52). Now, you can select a single character or a group of character and change the shape of the selected character or group of character.

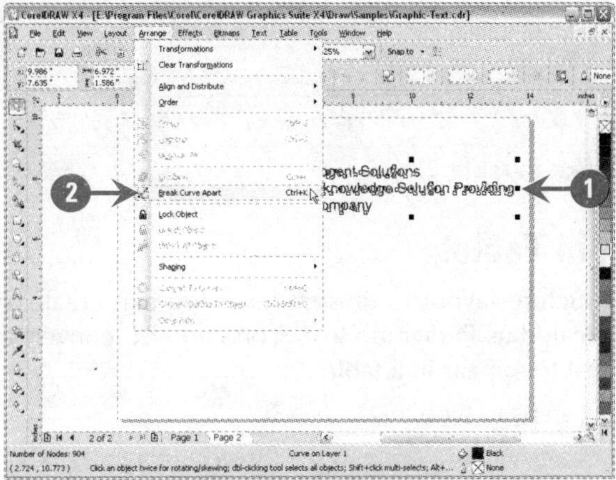

Fig.CD-7.52

3. Next, *select* a character which you want to edit and drag the handles to resize it as shown in Fig.CD-7.53.

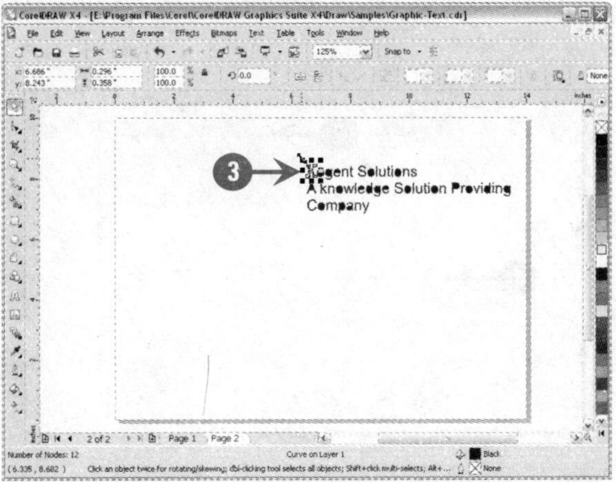

Fig.CD-7.53

Further you can use the Shape tool to provide the desired shape by dragging nodes like shown in Fig.CD-7.54.

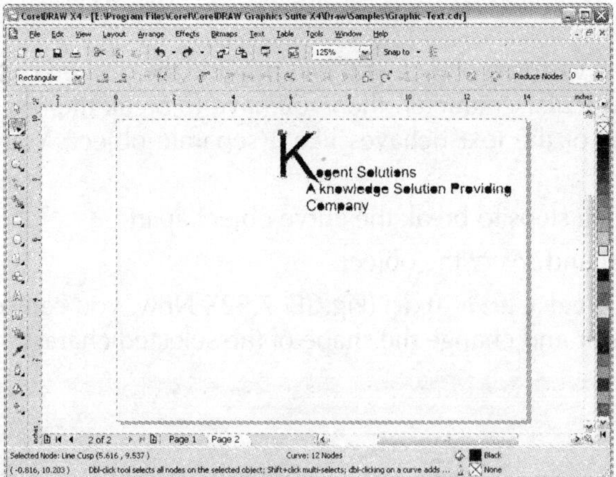

Fig.CD-7.54

Lets us now work with text in table.

Working with Text in Tables

A table provides the structure layout to present text. You can create text in the table cells. The text in a table cells is treated as Paragraph text. You can also convert the table to text, if you no longer want the table text to appear in a table.

Undertake the following steps to type text in a cell:

1. *Select* the **Table** tool and *draw* a table in the Drawing page (Fig.CD-7.55).
2. *Click* the **Options** button in the Property bar, a docker window appears as shown in Fig.CD-7.55. *Select* the check box beside the **Automatically resize cells when typing** option.

When this option is selected, the cell size will be automatically increased at the time the cell is full with text and still needed more space for further adding text in the cell.

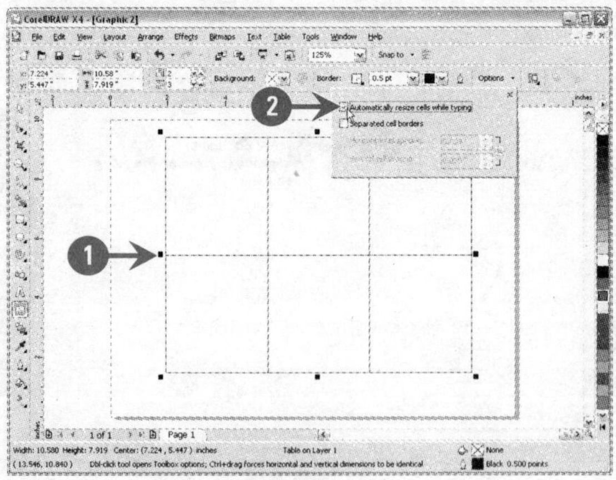

Fig.CD-7. 55

3. Next, *click* in the cell and *type* the text in the cell (Fig.CD-7.56).

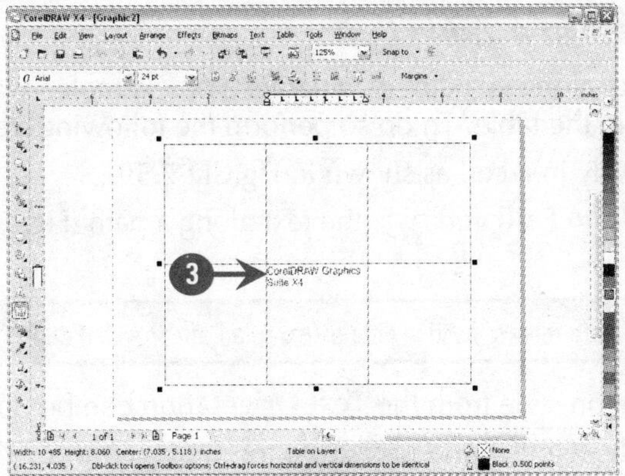

Fig.CD-7.56

4. *Click* the **Changes the vertical alignment of text** button on the Property bar and *select* an alignment option from the drop-down list as shown in Fig.CD-7.57. For example, we *select* the **Central Vertical alignment** option as shown in Fig.CD-7.57.

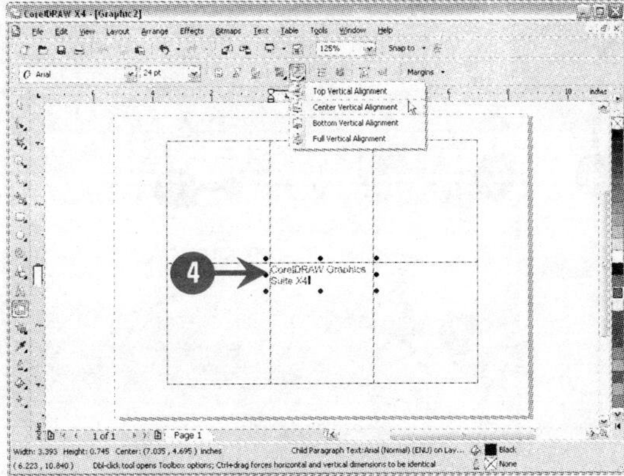

Fig.CD-7.57

The selected text is aligned in the central in the cell as shown in Fig.CD-7.58.

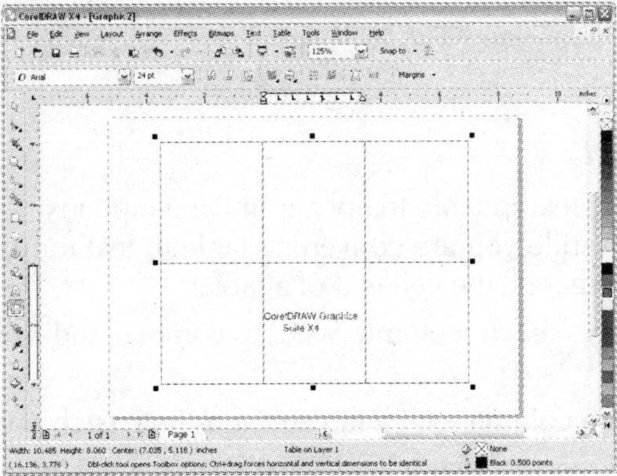

Fig.CD-7.58

Fitting Text along a Path in a Table Cell

You can also type text along a path in a table. For example, we want the text to appear diagonally along a cell in the table. To do so perform the following steps:

1. *Draw* a line diagonally in a cell as shown in Fig.CD-7.59.
2. *Select* **Text→Fit Text to Path** and *type* the text along a path (Fig.CD-7.59).

Note

> To know more about text and path refer to section Fitting Text to a Path provided earlier in the chapter

3. *Select* a text orientation style from the **Text Orientation** combo box (Fig.CD-7.59).
4. *Set* the distance between text and path from the **Distance from Path** spin box. In our case it is **0.15** (Fig.CD-7.59).
5. *Set* the horizontal position of the text along the path by *clicking* the up or down arrow button in the **Horizontal Offset** spin box (Fig.CD-7.59). Horizontal Offset value decides relative horizontal position of text on the path.

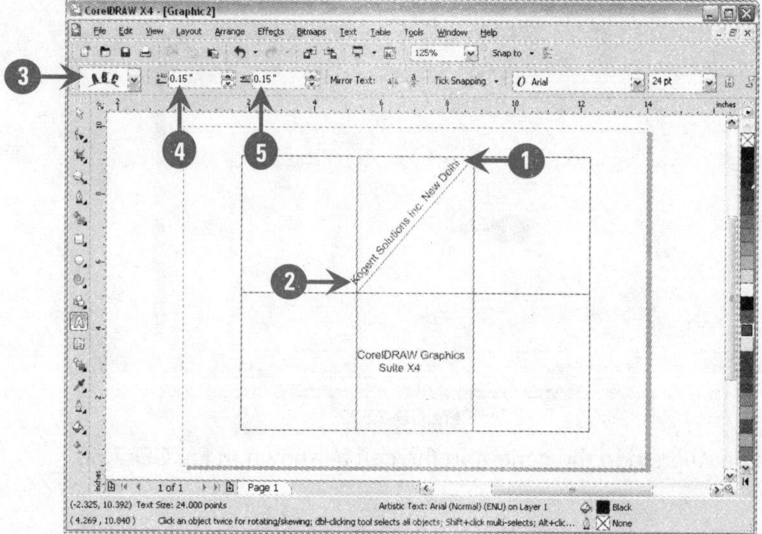

Fig.CD-7.59

Converting Table to Text

Whenever you require the text in table to appear in Paragraph text format then you can do so by converting table to text. While you are converting table to text form, you need to choose one of the following options to separate the cell text of a table:

- **Commas:** It substitutes each column with a comma and substitutes each row with a paragraph marker.
- **Tabs:** It substitute each column with a tab and substitute each row with a paragraph marker.
- **Paragraphs:** It replaces each column in a separate paragraph marker.

- **User defined**: It substitutes each column with a specified character and substitute each row with a paragraph marker.

Undertake the following steps to convert a table to text:

1. *Click* the **Table** tool and *select* a table (Fig.CD-7.60).
2. *Select* **Table→Convert Table to Text** (Fig.CD-7.60). A **Convert Table to Text** dialog box appears (Fig.CD-7.61).

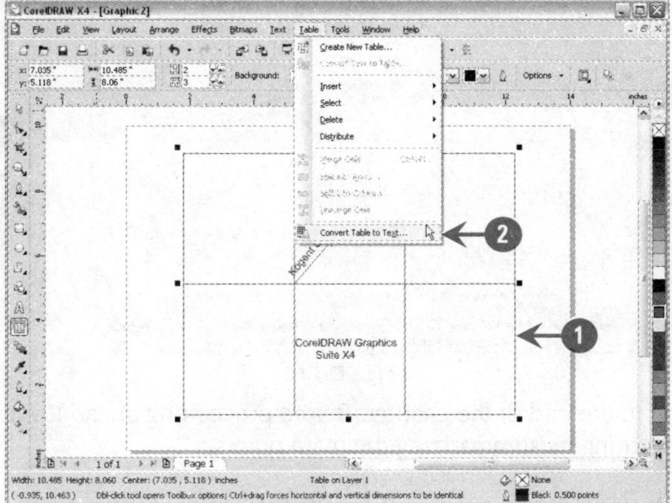

Fig.CD-7.60

3. *Select* the radio button beside the **Paragraphs** option to replace each column in a separate paragraph marker (Fig.CD-7.61).
4. *Click* the **OK** button (Fig.CD-7.61).

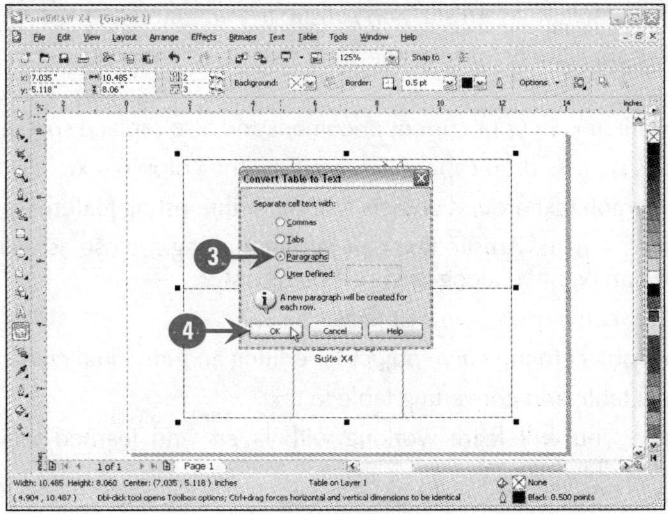

Fig.CD-7.61

The table is converted to text as shown in Fig.CD-7.62.

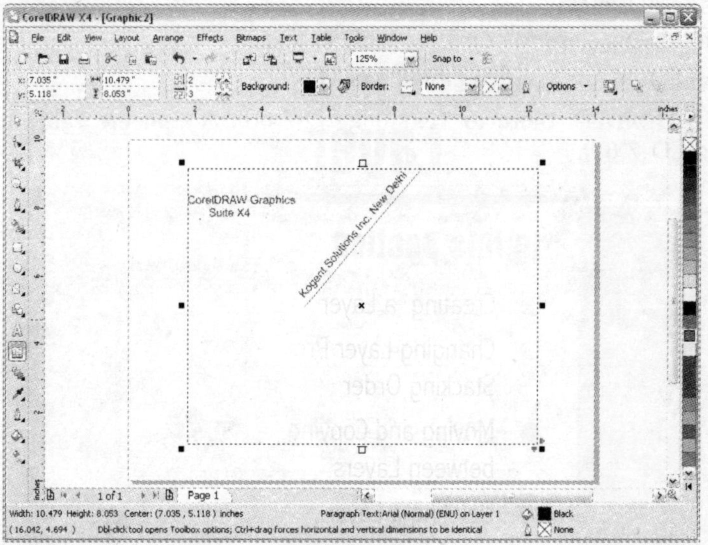

Fig.CD-7.62

With this we come to the end of the chapter. Before proceeding ahead towards the next chapter, let us refresh the learning by summarizing the main points.

Summary

In this chapter, you learned about:

- Types of text in CorelDRAW, which are Artistic and Paragraph text.
- Creating Artistic and Paragraph text in your drawing.
- Converting the Paragraph to Artistic and Artistic to Paragraph text.
- Changing the appearances of text, the font, font size, color of text, aligning text and text spacing.
- Finding a specific text in your current document and also replace specific text.
- Applying effects such as drop cap, bullets, and outline color to text.
- Wrapping Paragraph text around objects is another interesting feature.
- Fitting text along a path. Artistic text can be fitted along a close as well as open paths but Paragraph text can be fitted along the open paths only.
- Moving text between frames or text objects.
- Concerting text object to the curve object for editing an individual character.
- Adding text in a table and converting table to text.

In the next chapter, you will learn working with layers and learned their importance while creating the complex drawings.

Chapter 8

Working with Layers

In this Section

- Creating a Layer
- Changing Layer Properties and Stacking Order
- Moving and Copying Objects between Layers
- Deleting a Layer

In CorelDRAW, layers are an important concept. These are an integral part of CorelDRAW. Generally, all CorelDRAW drawings consist of stacked objects and this stacking of objects, contributes to the appearance of the drawing. Layers are an effective way of organizing the objects on these layers. Using layers you can change the attributes of an individual object or group of objects of each layer by selecting different options which include Show or Hide and Lock or Unlock options.

Layers are invisible planes occupied by various objects in the CorelDRAW window. Using layers, you can easily edit and organize complex drawings. You can perform this task by dividing the drawing into multiple layers and each layer containing a portion of the complete drawing. There are two types of layers in CorelDRAW:

- Local layers
- Master layers

The Local layer consists of contents that are specific to a particular page. The Master layer consists of the contents that are applied on all pages of the documents. Local layer, that is, Layer 1 is known as the default layer and all the components of a drawing are placed on this layer until a different layer is not selected. A selected layer always appears in bold Red font.

Creating a Layer

In CorelDRAW, you can create one or more layers to organize the contents of your drawing. Creating new layers helps you to work with larger documents. You can create a layer using the Object manager option from the Tools menu. The newly created layer of the Drawing page of the CorelDRAW window will be visible only in the Object manager docker. Whenever you create a new layer, decide whether you need a Master layer or a Local layer.

If you want the layer to repeat on every page then you can create and use the Master layer or else you should create and use a Local layer. If you don't create a new layer then all the contents of your drawing will be placed on the default layer represented by Layer 1. To use a layer in the drawing, you must first make the layer active by clicking the layer name in the Object manager docker.

Undertake the following steps to create a layer:

1. *Select* **Tools→Object Manager** (Fig.CD-8.1).

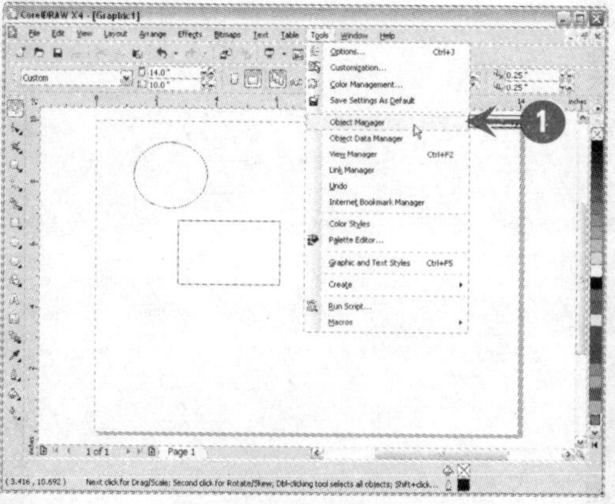

Fig.CD-8.1

An **Object manager** docker appears, as shown in Fig.CD-8.2.

2. *Click* the **Object Manager Options** button on the top right corner of the **Object manager** docker and *select* the **New layer** option to create a local layer, as shown in Fig.CD-8.2.

Note

> To create a Master layer, select New master Layer option from the Object manager options flyout.

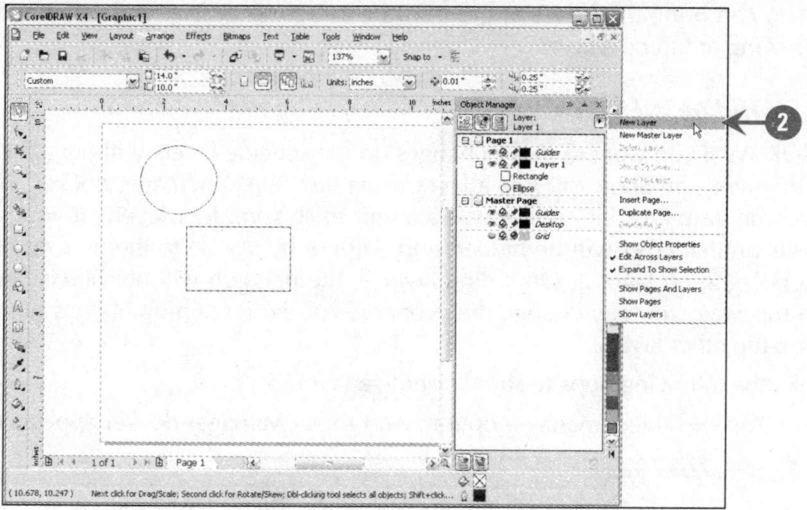

Fig.CD-8.2

3. A new layer appears in the **Object Manager** docker. It is represented in **Red** bold font because it is an **Active** layer and anything you draw appears on this layer, as shown in Fig.CD-8.3.

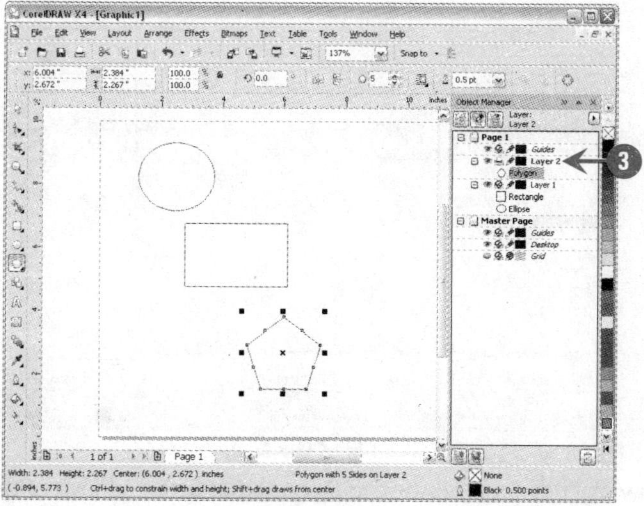

Fig.CD-8.3

Let's now learn how to change the layer properties and the stacking order.

Changing Layer Properties and Stacking Order

In CorelDRAW, you can make changes in the properties of the layer such as name, visibility, printability, editability and whether the layer is a Master layer or not. Thus, it's not necessary that you should work with the default properties only; you can also customize them. While working with the objects, if you want to change the stacking order of the objects, the changes apply within the layer on which it is located. Similarly, you can also change the stacking order of layers. You can bring the layers at the front or back, top or bottom positions. Let's discuss first about showing or hiding a layer.

Showing or Hiding a Layer

In CorelDRAW if you want to make changes on the specific layers without affecting other layer's objects then you can Show or Hide a layer using the Object manager docker. The objects on the layer become visible or invisible if you attempt to show/hide a layer. If you hide, a layer then the objects on that layer will be hidden and will not be visible to the user. In our case, we have drawn a polygon on layer 2. On hiding layer 2, the polygon will not be visible on the Drawing page. In this way, you can change the properties of the remaining objects without affecting the objects on the other layers.

Undertake the following steps to show or hide a layer:

1. *Select* **Tools→Object manager** option. An **Object Manager** docker appears (Fig.CD-8.4).

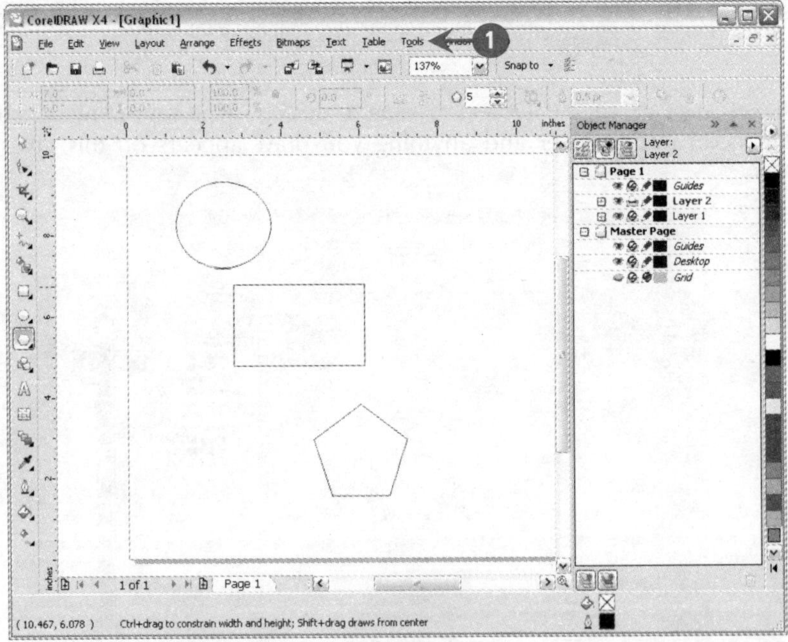

Fig.CD-8.4

2. *Click* the **Show or Hide** icon beside the layer name. Selected layer along with the objects on it become visible or invisible. In our case, the selected layer is Layer 2 (Fig.CD-8.5).

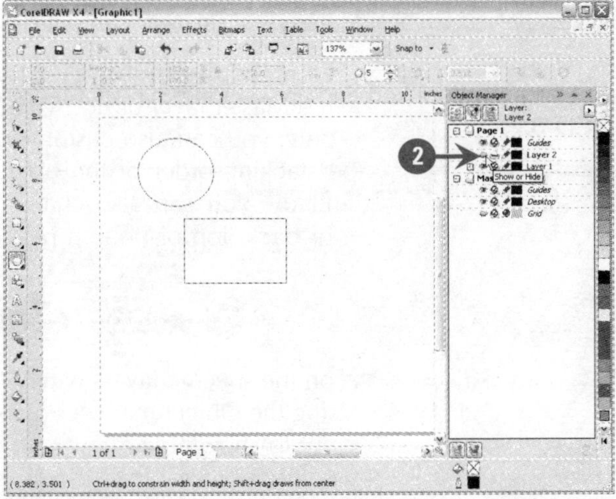

Fig.CD-8.5

After showing or hiding a layer, let's now learn how to set the editing properties of a layer.

Setting Editing Properties of a Layer

CorelDRAW allows you to set the editing properties of a layer. You can lock or unlock a layer; but you can't perform any work on the locked layer and the objects on it.

Undertake the following steps to set the editing properties of a layer:

1. *Select* **Tools→Object manager** option. An **Object manager** docker appears, as shown in Fig.CD-8.6.

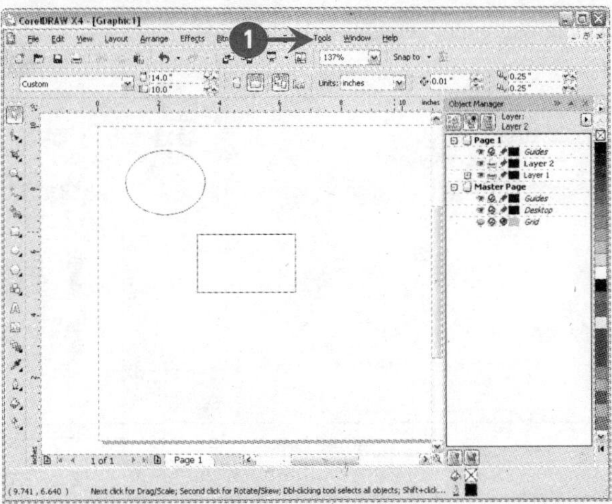

Fig.CD-8.6

2. *Click* the name of the layer you want to edit in the **Object manager** docker. The selected layer's name appears in **Red** bold font. In this case, we have selected Layer 1, as shown in Fig.CD-8.7.

3. *Click* the **Lock or Unlock** icon beside **Layer 1.** In our case, we have locked the object (Fig.CD- 8.7).

The Objects placed on Layer 1 are locked and are no longer available for editing on the Drawing page, as shown in Fig.CD-8.7.

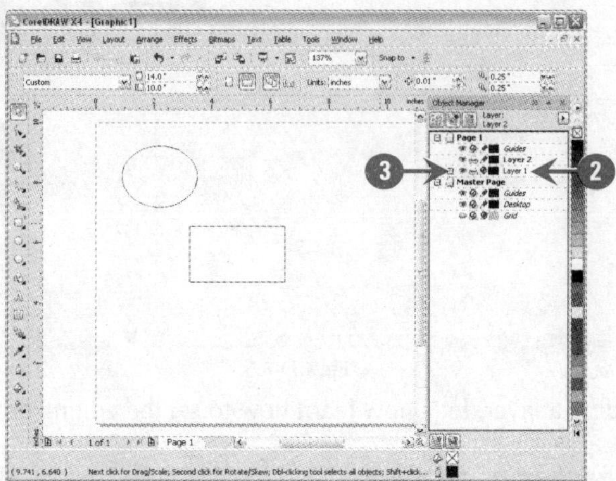

Fig.CD-8.7

4. *Click* the **Object Manager** Options button and *clear* the **Edit Across Layers** option to perform editing on the active layer only; but if you want to perform editing on all layers, then don't disable it, as shown in Fig.CD-8.8.

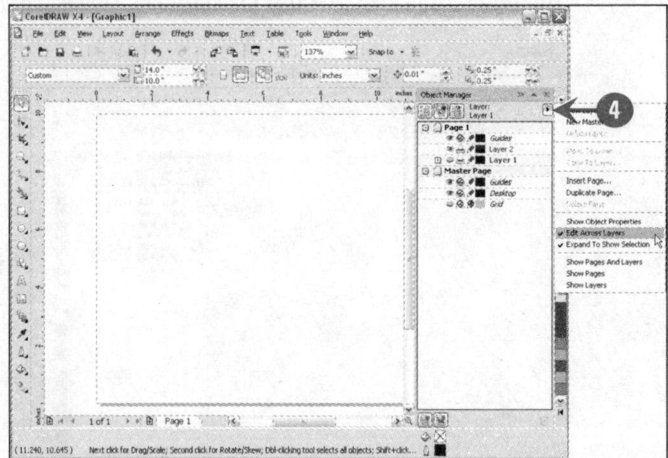

Fig.CD-8.8

Note

By default, the Edit Across Layers option in Object manager docker is enabled.

After setting the editing properties in a layer, let's now learn how to alter the position of a layer in the stacking order.

Altering the Position of a Layer in the Stacking Order

CorelDRAW allows you to move the layers. If you move a layer on a single page or between pages, it results in changed stacking order of the layers. By changing the stacking order, you can change the appearance of the objects on a layer. If you draw a circle on one layer and later you draw a rectangle on another layer, then by default, circle will be hidden behind the rectangle. But, if you want to show the circle above the rectangle then you need to alter the position of layers.

Undertake the following steps to alter the position of a layer in the stacking order:

1. *Select* **Tools→Object manager**. An **Object manager** docker appears as shown in Fig.CD-8.9.

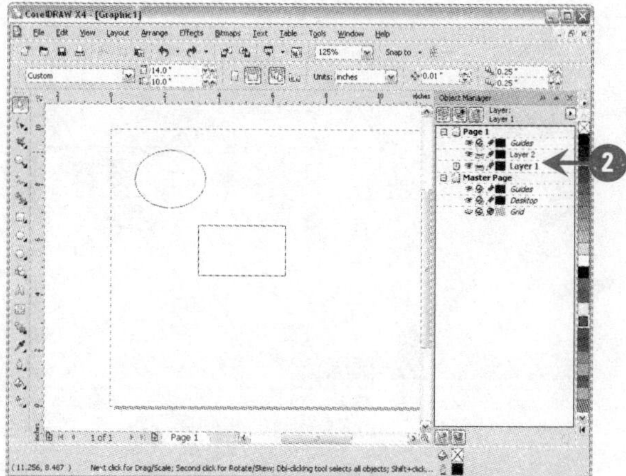

Fig.CD-8.9

2. *Select* the layer name to alter the position and drag the layer name to a new position (Fig.CD-8.9). The position of the layer changes in the stacking order as shown in Fig.CD-8.10.

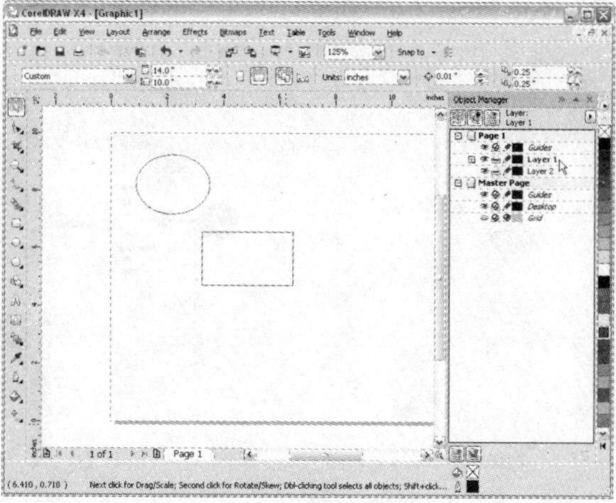

Fig.CD-8.10

This is how the position of the layer is altered in the stacking order. Now, let's learn how to move and copy objects between layers.

Moving and Copying Objects between Layers

As you know, you can move or copy objects in CorelDRAW. You can also move or copy the selected objects to different layers. In CorelDRAW, the Object manager docker allows you to move or copy an object to a layer.

Undertake the following steps to move and copy objects between layers:

1. *Select* **Tools→Object manager**. An **Object manager** docker appears, as shown in Fig.CD-8.11.

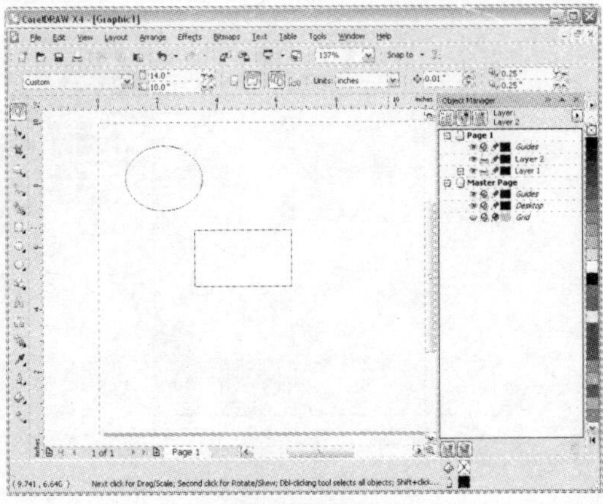

Fig.CD-8.11

2. *Select* an object in the **Object Manager** docker to move or copy (Fig.CD-8.12).
3. *Click* the **Object Manager Options** button and *select* an option from the list of the available options, as shown in Fig.CD-8.12. In our case, we have selected **Move to Layer** option which causes the object to move from one layer to another layer.

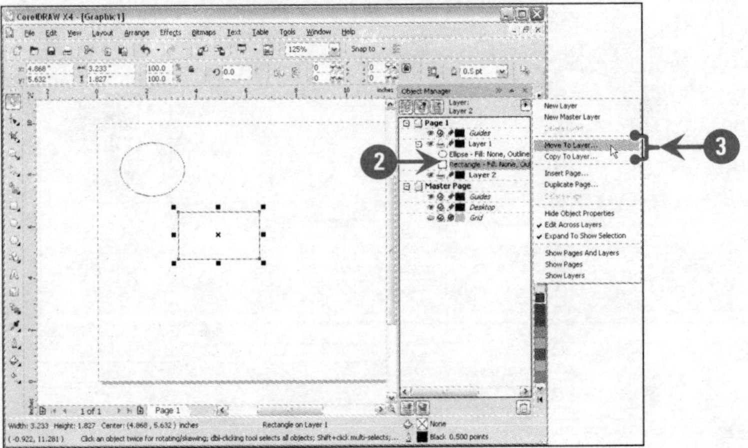

Fig.CD-8.12

4. *Select* the layer on which you want to perform the operation. Selected object moves to layer 2. In our case, the selected object is a rectangle which is moved from layer 1 to layer 2, as shown in Fig.CD-8.13.

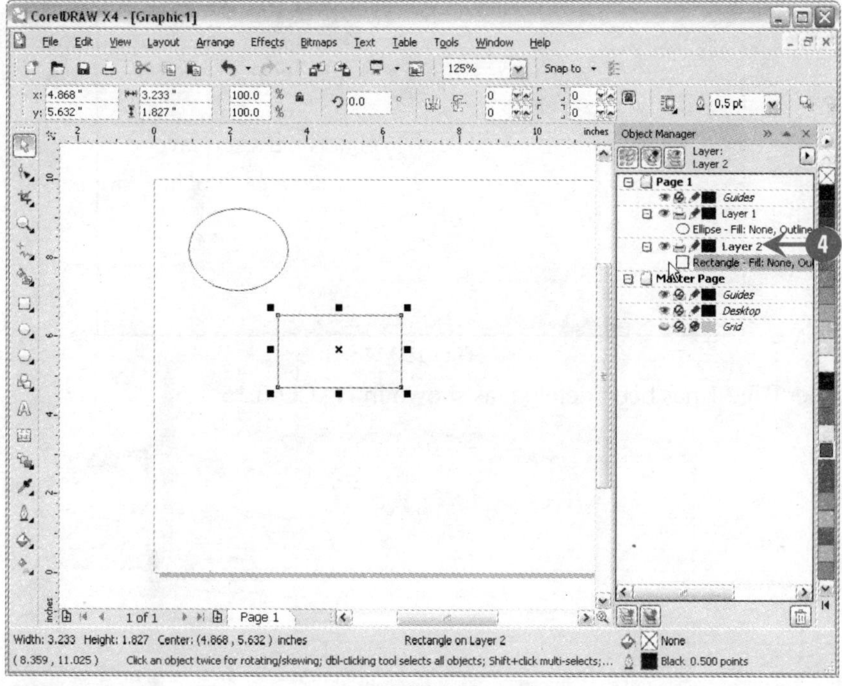

Fig.CD-8.13

After moving and copying objects between the layers, now you will learn how to delete a layer in the next section.

Deleting a Layer

If you don't need a layer in your document, then you can delete that particular layer using the Object manager docker. In CorelDRAW, when you delete a layer, all the objects on that layer are also deleted. In order to preserve those objects, move them to a different layer before deleting the current layer.

Undertake the following steps to delete a layer:

1. *Select* **Tools→Object Manager**. An Object manager docker appears.
2. *Click* the name of the layer which needs to be deleted. In our case, it is **Layer 1** (Fig.CD-8.14).
3. *Click* the **Object Manager** options button and *select* the **Delete layer** option to delete a layer as shown in Fig.CD-8.14.

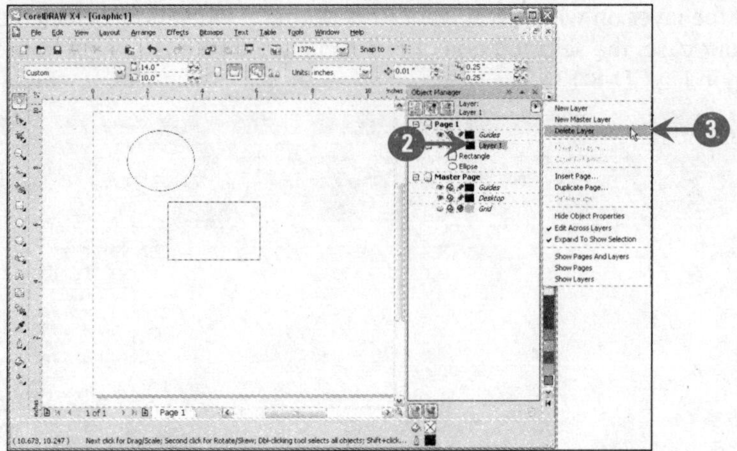

Fig.CD-8.14

Layer 1 under Page 1 has been deleted, as shown in Fig.CD-8.15.

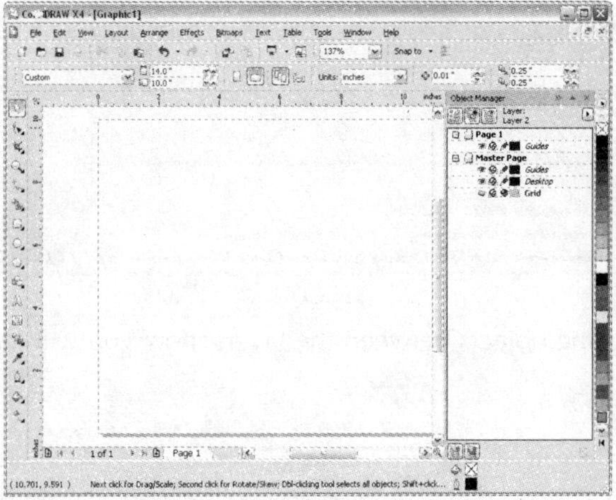

Fig.CD-8.15

With this, we come to the end of this chapter. Before proceeding ahead towards the next chapter, let's summarize the main points of this chapter.

Summary

In this chapter, you learned about:

- Creation of a layer.
- Change the different properties of a layer.
- Modify the stacking order of layers.
- Move and copy objects between layers.
- Deletion of a layer

In the next chapter, you will learn to work with Bitmaps.

Chapter 9

Working with Bitmaps

In this Section

- About Vector and Bitmap Images
- Changing Vector Images into Bitmap Images
- Importing a Bitmap into a Drawing
- Cropping, Resampling, and Resizing a Bitmap
- Using Special Effects to Bitmaps
- Setting Color and Tone Quickly using the Image Adjustment Lab Command
- Tracing Bitmaps

Till now, we have worked with the vector images. As we know that all the images saved in CorelDRAW are of .CDR format and this format belongs to the vector image family. This chapter discusses about working with the bitmap images. In certain cases, you may require the bitmap images that let you apply special effects to the objects within CorelDRAW.

In this chapter, you will learn the difference between vector images and bitmap images, changing the vector images to bitmap images, importing a bitmap, cropping, resampling, and resizing a bitmap, applying special effects, setting color and tone in the image adjustment lab, tracing bitmaps.

About Vector and Bitmap Images

Before working with images in CorelDRAW, you must have knowledge of two major types of graphics, bitmap images and vector images. Let us have a look on these images in detail.

Bitmap Images

Bitmap images consist of dots (or pixels) arranged to form graphics. Bitmap images are resolution dependent. Resolution means the number of pixels in an image. CorelDRAW provides us the facility to import a variety of bitmap formats into CorelDRAW documents. Once the bitmap image is imported into CorelDRAW document, you can modify it in different ways. For example, you can trace bitmap, apply some effect on it, and make adjustments to its color mode, brightness, contrast, and so on. Some commonly used bitmap formats which are frequently imported in CorelDRAW documents are **BMP**, **GIF**, **JPEG**, **PNG**, **TIFF** and so on.

Vector Images

Vector images are written in or defined by algebraic equations. Vector images are resolution independent. Therefore, they can be rescaled without losing any information, without affecting the quality of the image and without any changes in the definition because they are not as complex as bitmap. The example of common vector formats is CDR (CorelDRAW), AI (Adobe Illustrator).

Changing Vector Images into Bitmap Images

CorelDRAW provides the facility of converting vector images into bitmap images. Usually, vector images are considered to convert into bitmap because a number of CorelDRAW features such as, special effects like 3D Effects can be applied to bitmaps only. The process of converting a vector image into bitmap image is called rasterizing. Let us now learn first about converting the vector image into bitmap image.

Converting Vector Images into Bitmap Images

You can convert vector image into bitmap image in CorelDRAW. While converting the vector image, you can select the color mode of the bitmap. The color mode helps in determining the type of colors that constitute the bitmap. The file size may increase or decrease depending upon the selected color mode. For example, a simple Bitmap file created in MS Paint might have smaller file size with RGB color mode, on the other hand, a Bitmap file created in Photoshop with CMYK color mode might have larger file size.

Undertake the following steps to convert vector image into bitmap:

1. *Open* a vector image in your Drawing window. *Select* the object.
2. *Select* **Bitmaps→Convert to Bitmap** (Fig.CD-9.1). A **Convert to Bitmap** dialog box appears, as shown in Fig.CD-9.2.

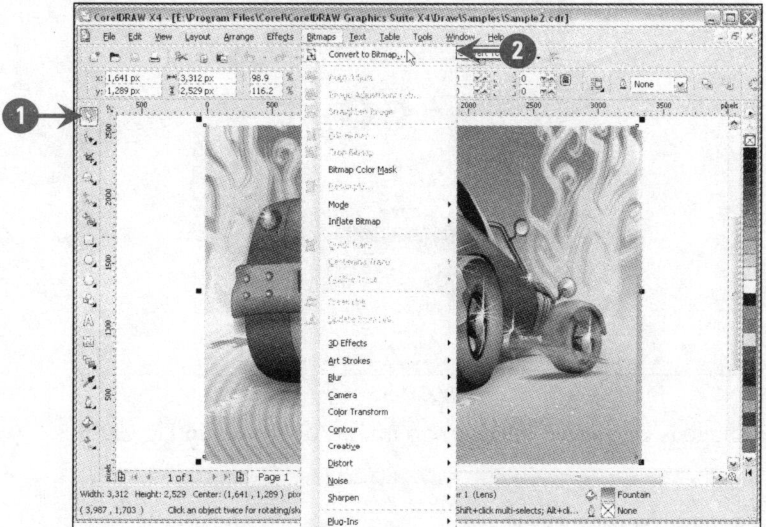

Fig.CD-9.1

3. *Click* the down arrow button in the list box beside the **Resolution** option. A drop down list appears. *Select* a resolution option. In our case, the resolution is **300 dpi** (Fig.CD-9.2).
4. Under the **Color** group, you can choose the color mode in the list box beside the **Color mode** option. In our case, it is **CMYK Color 32-bit** (Fig.CD-9.2).

Selecting the Dithering check box under the Color box lets you simulate a greater number of colors than those available in the image. However, if you select Color mode with 24 bit or more than 24 bit (for RGB as well as for CMYK color schemes) then Dithering cannot be applied on the image. Since, we have selected CMYK Color 32-bit color mode, the Dithering option is appearing disabled inFig.CD-9.2.

5. You can select the check box beside the **Apply ICC Profile** option under the **Color** group to apply the International Color Consortium profiles to standardize colors across devices and color spaces (Fig.CD-9.2).
6. You can select the check box beside the **Always overprint black** option to overprint black when black is the top color (Fig.CD-9.2). In our case, the check box is clear.
7. *Select* the check box beside the **Anti-aliasing** option to smooth the edges of the bitmap (Fig.CD-9.2).
8. *Select* the check box beside the **Transparent Background** option to make the background of bitmap transparent (Fig.CD-9.2).
9. *Click* the **OK** button in the dialog box (Fig.CD-9.2).

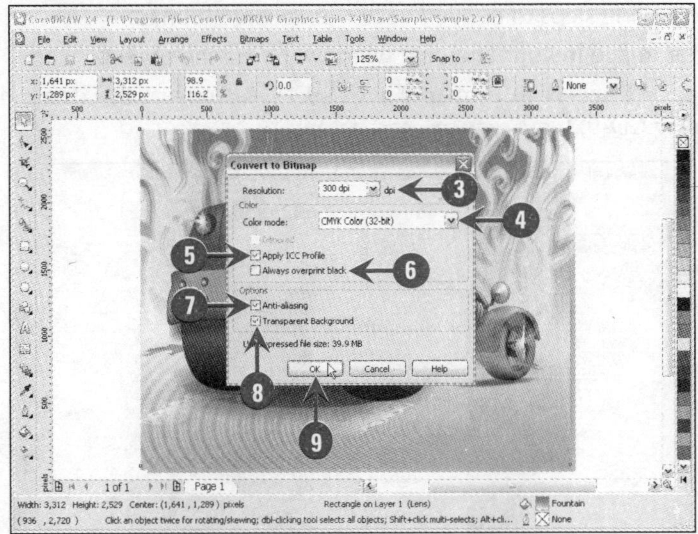

Fig.CD-9.2

Now, the vector image is converted into bitmap image, as shown in Fig.CD-9.3.

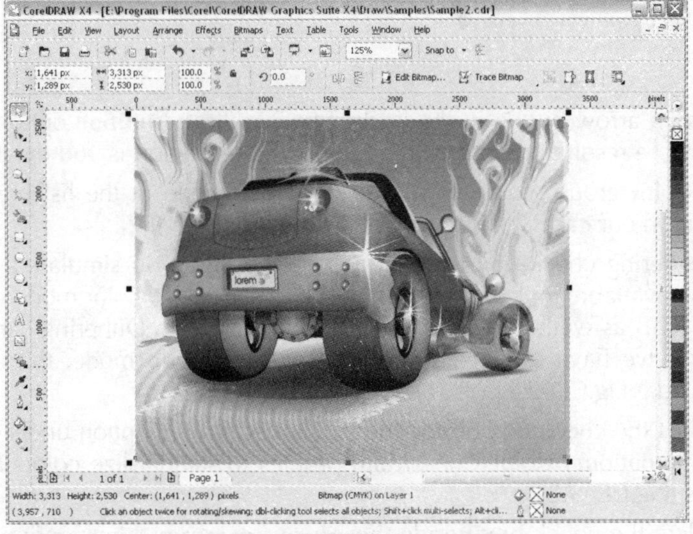

Fig.CD-9.3

Converting Vector Images into a Bitmap when Exporting

You can convert a vector image into a bitmap at the time when you are exporting it. Undertake the following steps to convert vector image to a bitmap:

1. *Open* a vector image in the Drawing window. *Select* **File→Export** (Fig.CD-9.4). The **Export** dialog box appears (Fig.CD-9.5).

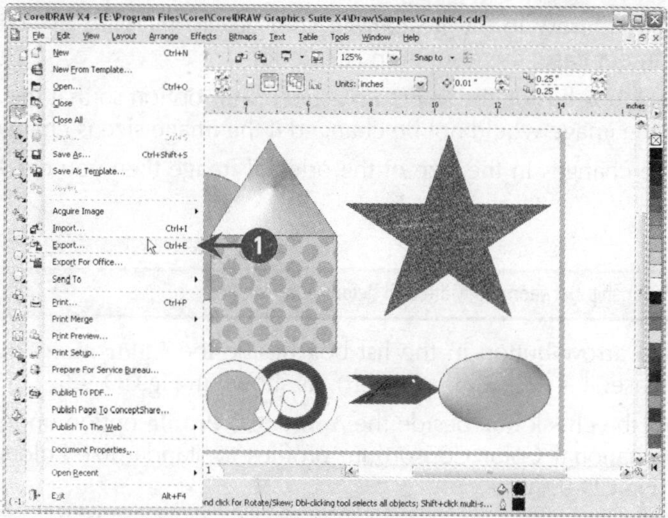

Fig.CD-9.4

2. Navigate the location where you want to save the file. In our case, the selected location is **Desktop** (Fig.CD-9.5).
3. *Type* the file name in the text box beside the **File name** option (Fig.CD-9.5).
4. *Select* a bitmap format from the **Save as type** drop-down list. In our case, it is **BMP-Windows Bitmap** (Fig.CD-9.5).
5. *Click* the **Export** button in the dialog box (Fig.CD-9.5). As soon as, you *click* the **Export** button, a **Convert to Bitmap** dialog box appears (Fig.CD-9.6).

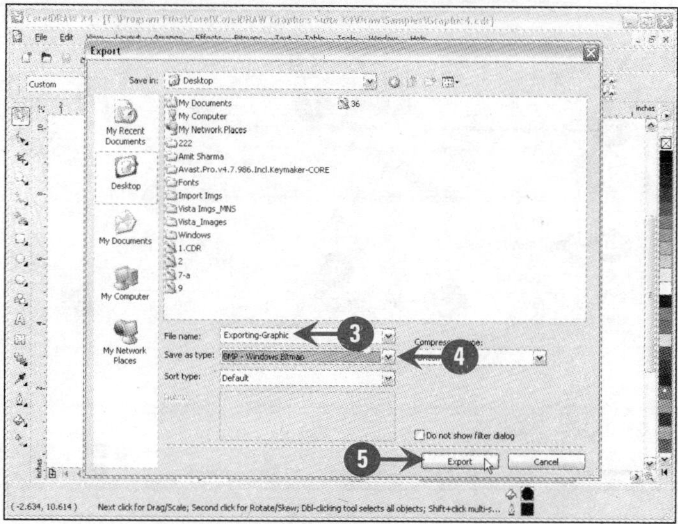

Fig.CD-9.5

6. In the **Image Size** group, *click* up or down arrows in the **Width** and **Height** spin boxes to specify the image dimension (Fig.CD-9.6).

7. *Click* up or down arrow in the **Resolution** spin box to increase or decrease the resolution (Fig.CD-9.6). In our case, the resolution is **350** dpi.
8. *Select* the check box beside the **Maintain aspect ratio** option so that the ratio between width and height of the image would not be changed if the image size is changed (Fig.CD-9.6).

If you do not make changes in the size of the original image then you can enable the Maintain original size option.

Note

> Aspect ratio is the relationship between the width and height of an image.

9. *Click* the down arrow button in the list box beside the **Color mode** option. *Select* a color mode. In our case, it is **RGB Color (24-bit)**, as shown in Fig.CD-9.6.
10. You can select the check box beside the **Apply ICC Profile** option under the **Color** group to apply the International Color Consortium profiles to standardize colors across devices and color spaces (Fig.CD-9.6).
11. In the **Options** group, *select* the check box beside the **Anti-aliasing** option to smooth the edges of the bitmap (Fig.CD-9.6).
12. *Click* the **OK** button (Fig.CD-9.6).

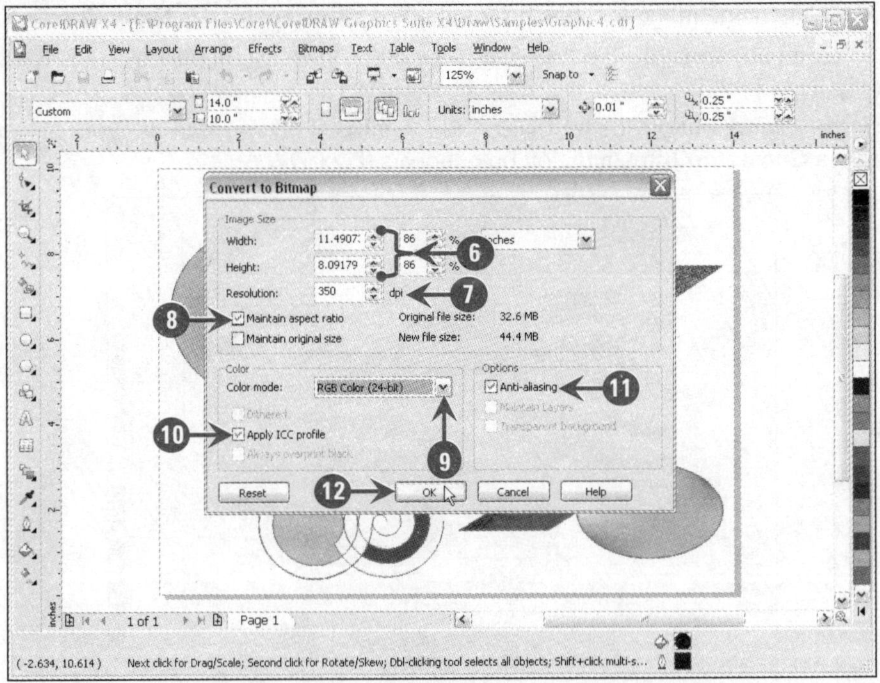

Fig.CD-9.6

Now, the image will be converted to bitmap format, as shown in Fig.CD-9.7.

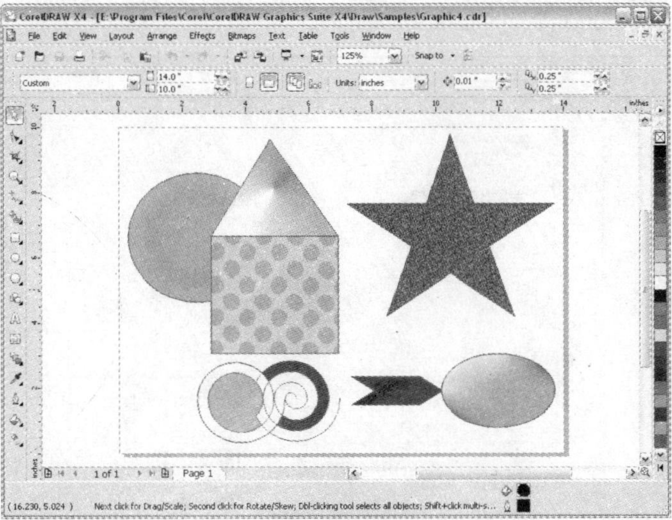

Fig.CD-9.7

Importing a Bitmap into a Drawing

You can import a bitmap created in other application such as Photoshop or Paint to CorelDRAW. The following operations can be performed on the imported image.

Undertake the following steps to import a bitmap:

1. *Select* **File→Import** (Fig.CD-CD-9.8). Instantly, the **Import** dialog box appears, as shown in Fig.CD-9.9.

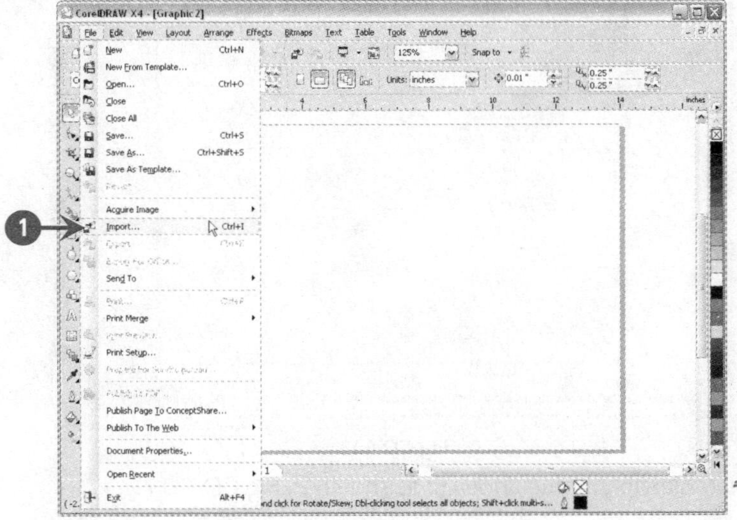

Fig.CD-9.8

2. Navigate the location where the bitmap file is stored. *Select* the bitmap file. In our case, the selected file is **Img23** in the **Local Disk (E:)**, as shown in Fig.CD-9.9.

3. *Click* the **Import** button (Fig.CD-9.9).

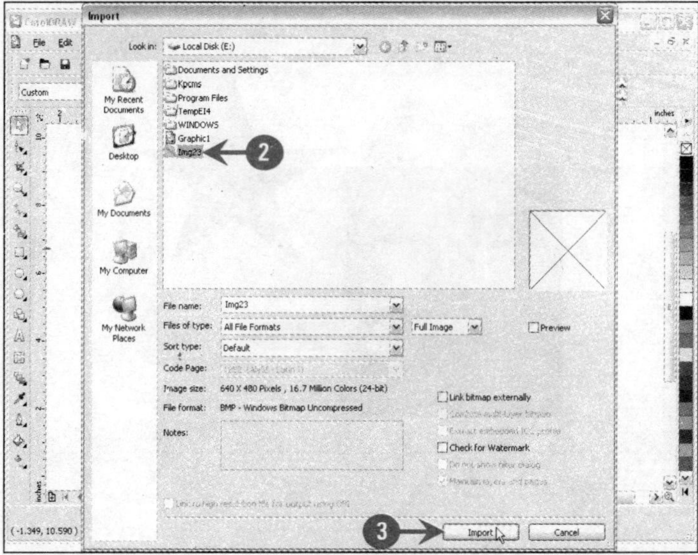

Fig.CD-9.9

4. *Place* the mouse-pointer in the Drawing page where you want to place the imported graphic and *click* in the Drawing page, as shown in Fig.CD-9.10.

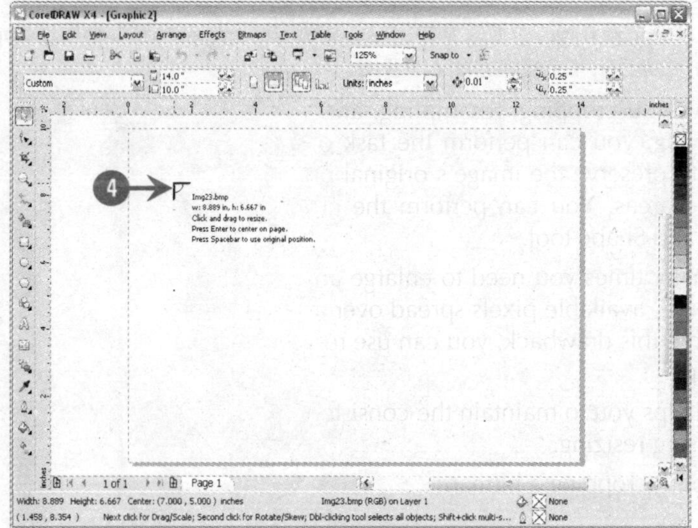

Fig.CD-9.10

Now, the imported bitmap graphic appears, as shown in Fig.CD-9.11.

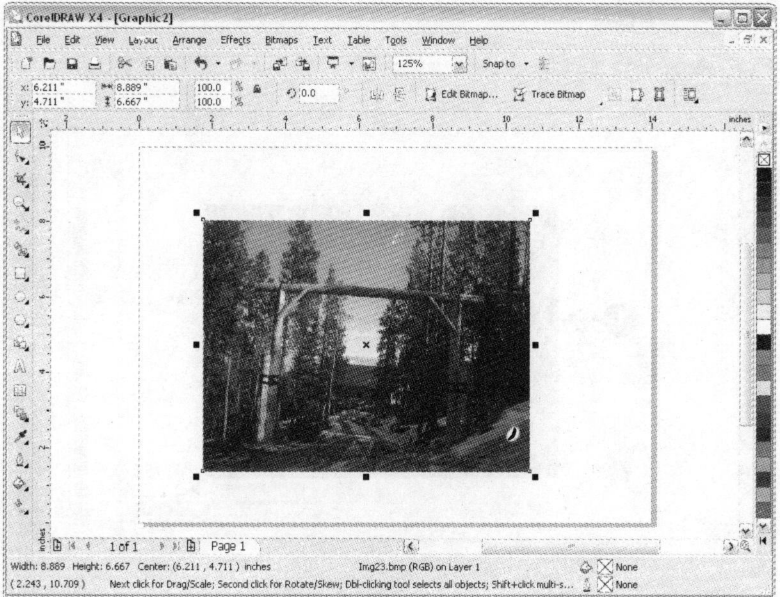

Fig.CD-9.11

After importing the bitmap image, you will learn to cropping, re-sampling, and resizing the bitmap, and can also apply the different special effects such as 3D Effects, Art Strokes, Blur, and Contour.

Cropping, Resampling, and Resizing a Bitmap

CorelDRAW allows you cropping, resampling, and resizing a bitmap image. Once you add an image to the drawing, you can perform the task of cropping, resampling, and resizing. These features help you to preserve the image's original properties. Cropping helps you to remove the unnecessary image areas. You can perform the cropping of an image with the help of Crop Bitmap command and Shape tool.

In CorelDRAW, many times you need to enlarge an image without changing the resolution and during this procedure, available pixels spread over a larger area. This results in the loss of image details. To overcome this drawback, you can use resampling to add pixels to preserve the details of the original image.

CorelDRAW also helps you to maintain the consistent number of pixels in the image in a smaller or larger area by using resizing.

Let us learn first about cropping a bitmap.

Cropping a Bitmap

Cropping refers to the trimming of the image to a certain size. It helps in removing the irrelevant areas from the image.

Undertake the following steps to perform the cropping of a bitmap image:

1. *Click* **Pick** tool and *select* a bitmap image to perform cropping action (Fig.CD-9.12).

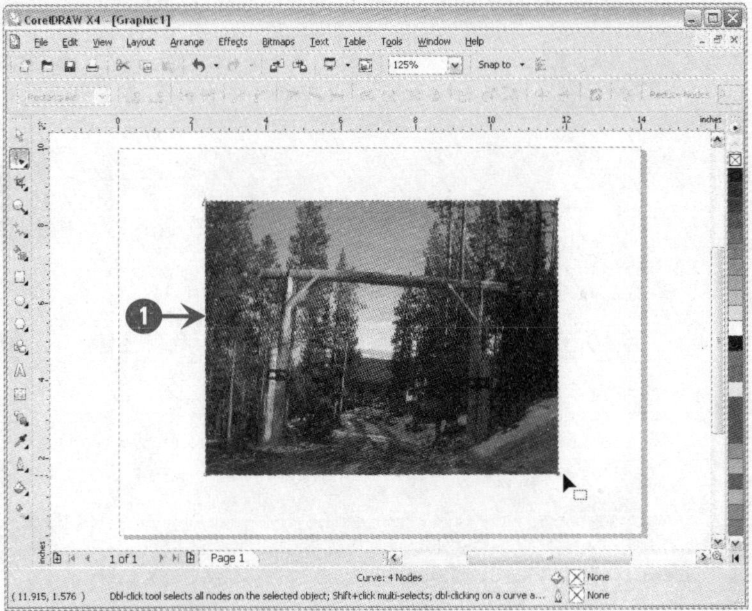

Fig.CD-9.12

2. *Drag* the corner nodes of the image to reshape the image and *double-click* the node boundary using the **Shape** tool where you want to add a node (Fig.CD-9.13).

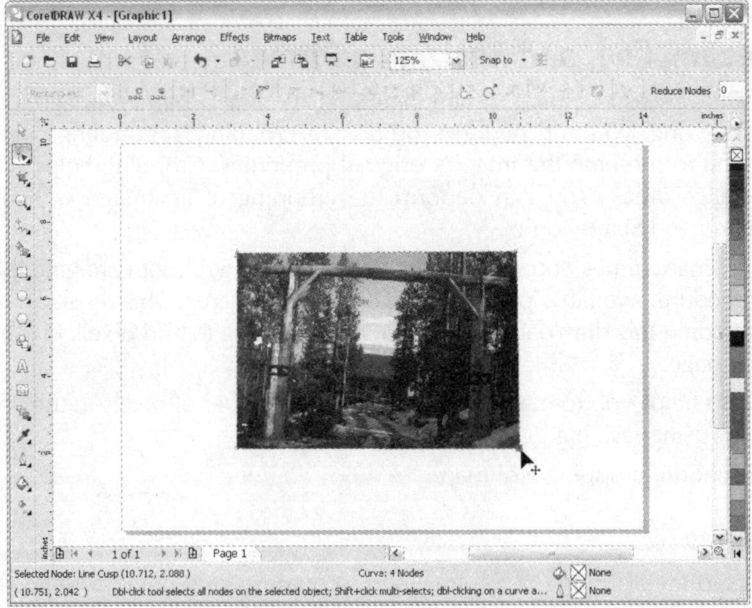

Fig.CD-9.13

3. *Select* **Bitmaps→Crop Bitmap** (Fig.CD-9.14).

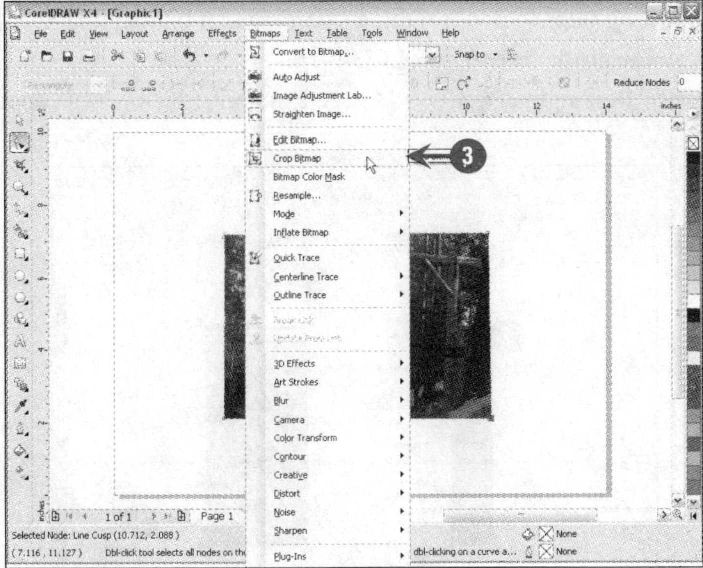

Fig.CD-9.14

Shape of the image changes, as shown in Fig.CD-9.15.

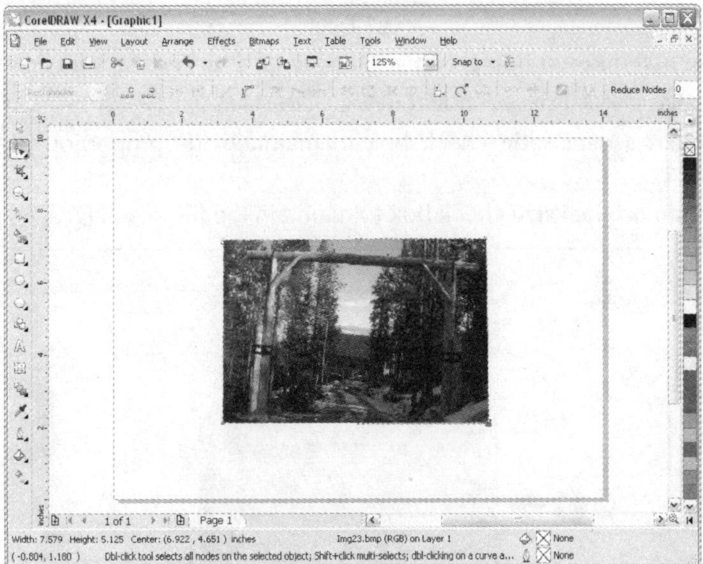

Fig.CD-9.15

After cropping a bitmap, let us now learn how to resample a bitmap.

Resampling a Bitmap

CorelDRAW lets you perform the resampling of the bitmap image by changing the image or resolution or both. This can be performed by the addition or removal of the pixels.

Undertake the following steps to perform the resampling of a bitmap image:

1. *Select* a bitmap image, as shown in Fig.CD-9.16.
2. *Select* **Bitmaps→Resample** (Fig.CD-9.16). A **Resample** dialog box appears, as shown in Fig.CD-9.17.

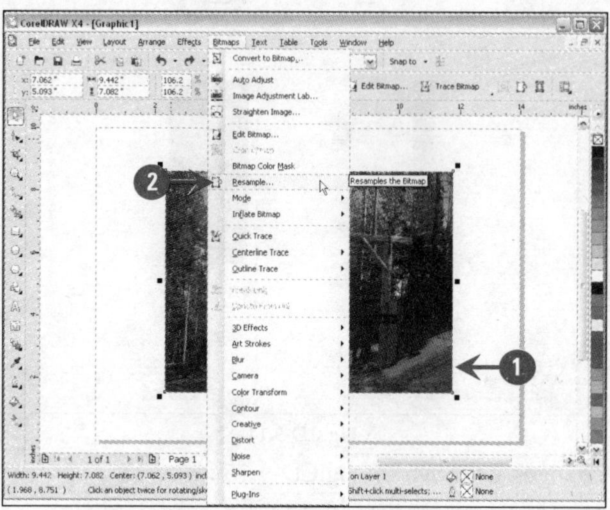

Fig.CD-9.16

3. *Type* a value in the **Resolution group** in **Horizontal** and **Vertical** spin boxes (Fig.CD-9.17).
4. *Select* **Anti-alias** check box, as shown in Fig.CD-9.17.
5. *Select* **Maintain aspect ratio** check box to maintain the proportion of the bitmap image (Fig.CD-9.17).
6. *Select* **Maintain original size** check box to maintain the file size (Fig.CD-9.17).

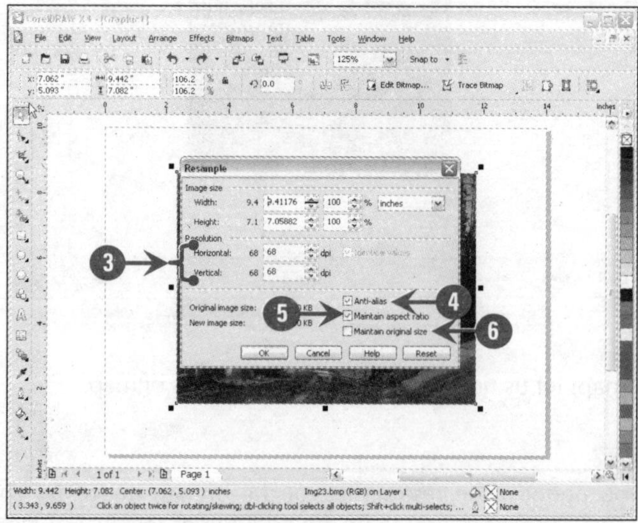

Fig.CD-9.17

Image after entering the values is shown here in the Fig.CD-9.18

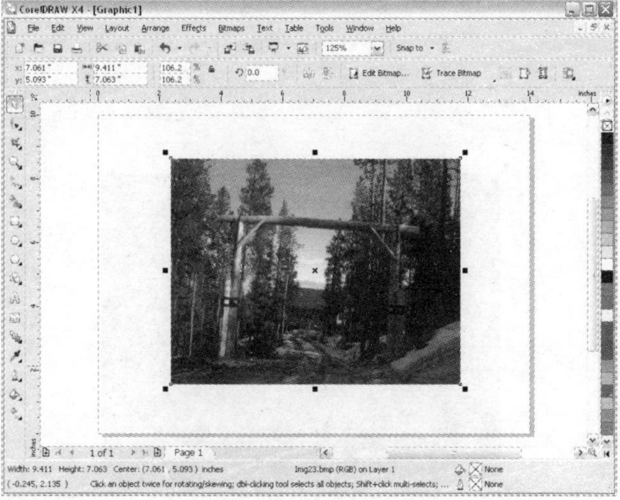

Fig.CD-9.18

After resampling a bitmap, let us now learn how to resize a bitmap.

Resizing a Bitmap

CorelDRAW allows you to resize a bitmap image. This feature helps in maintaining the pixels in a smaller or larger image area.

Undertake the following steps to resize a bitmap image:

1. *Select* a bitmap image, as shown in Fig.CD-9.19.
2. *Select* **Bitmaps→Resample** (Fig.CD-9.16). A **Resample** dialog box appears, as shown in Fig.CD-9.19.

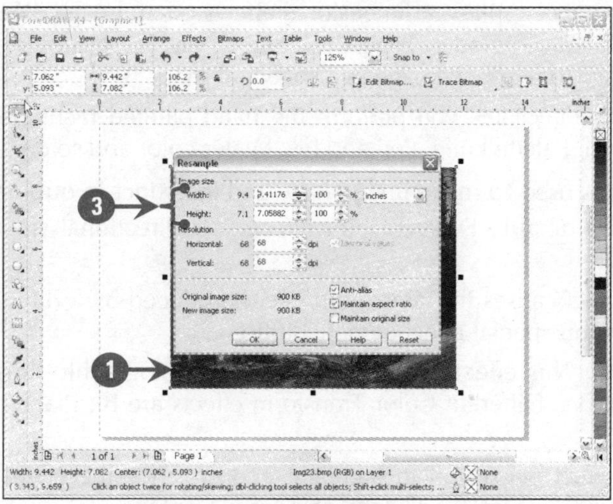

Fig.CD-9.19

3. *Type* a value in the **Image size** group in the **Width** and **Height** spin boxes (Fig.CD-9.19). Size of the image changes, as shown in Fig.CD-9.20.

Fig.CD-9.20

After resizing a bitmap, let us now learn how to use special effects to bitmap in the following section.

Using Special Effects to Bitmaps

In CorelDRAW, you can implement various special effects to modify the original image. These special effects bring changes in various fields such as image orientation and color features. Various special effects available in CorelDRAW are as follows:

- **3D Effects:** This effect applies 3 dimensional effects on an image. Some commonly used 3D effects are 3D Rotate, Cylinder, Page Curl, and so on. For example, you can apply Sphere effect on an image to produce image in a spherical shape.
- **Art Strokes:** This effect lets you perform the hand painted technique. Different Art stroke effects are Crayon, Palette knife, Pen and Ink, Water color and so on.
- **Blur:** This effect is used **to make image hazy and indistinct in outline or shape and also to make image dim or dull.** Different blur effects are Directional smooth, Low pass, Soften, zoom and so on.
- **Camera:** This effect causes the simulation effect produced by a diffusion lens. There is only one effect under this special effect namely diffuse.
- **Color Transform:** This effect helps you to create photographic illusions by reducing and replacing the colors. Different Color Transform effects are Bit Plane, Halftone, Psychedelic, and Solarize.
- **Contour:** This effect helps you to highlight and enhance the edges of an image and this effect includes Edge Detect, Find Edges, and Trace Contour.

- **Creative:** This effect helps you to apply various texture and shape to an image. Various Creative effects are Frames, Particles, Scatter, Smoked glass, Weather and so on.
- **Distort:** This effect helps you to distort the surface of the image. Various Distort effects are Block, Displace, Offset, Ripple, and Tile.
- **Noise:** This effect helps you to modify the coarseness of the image and different Noise effects are Add noise, Maximum, Median, Minimum, and Remove Noise.
- **Sharpen:** This effect helps you to focus and enhance the edges of an image by adding Sharpening effect. Different Sharpen effects are Adaptive Unsharp, Directional Sharpen, High Pass, Sharpen, and Unsharp Mask.
- **Plug-ins:** This helps you to use a third party filter to apply effects to bitmaps.

Let us now learn to apply some commonly used effects on bitmaps such as 3D effect, color transform effect and sharpen effect.

Applying 3D Effects to a Bitmap

CorelDRAW lets you provide with the feature of 3D Effects. This effect helps you to create the illusion of depth in the drawing. 3D Effect comprises of some other effects. These effects are as follows: 3D Rotate, Cylinder, Emboss, Page Curl, Perspective, Pinch/Punch, and Sphere.

Undertake the following steps to apply 3D Effects to a bitmap image:

1. *Select* a bitmap image, as shown in Fig.CD-9.21.
2. *Select* **Bitmaps→3D Effects→3D Rotate** (Fig.CD-9.21). A **3D Rotate** dialog box appears, as shown in Fig.CD-9.22.

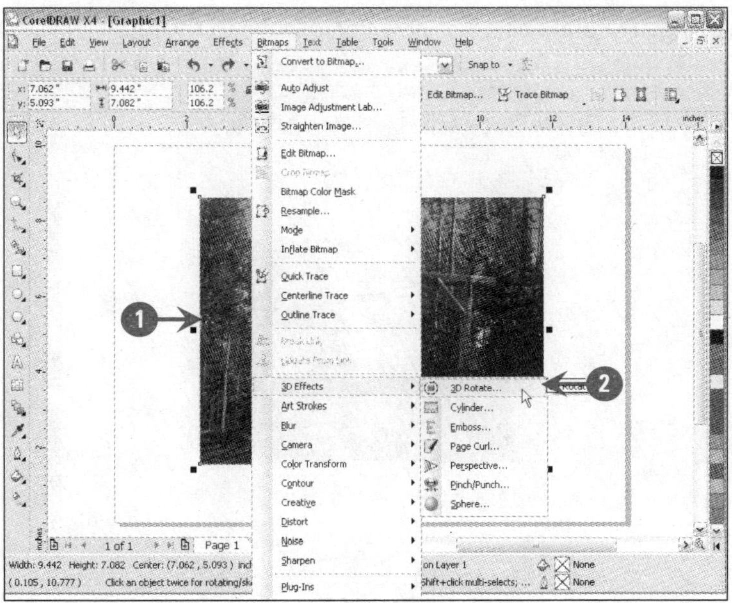

Fig.CD-9.21

3. *Type* a value in the **Vertical** and **Horizontal** spin boxes (Fig.CD-9.22).

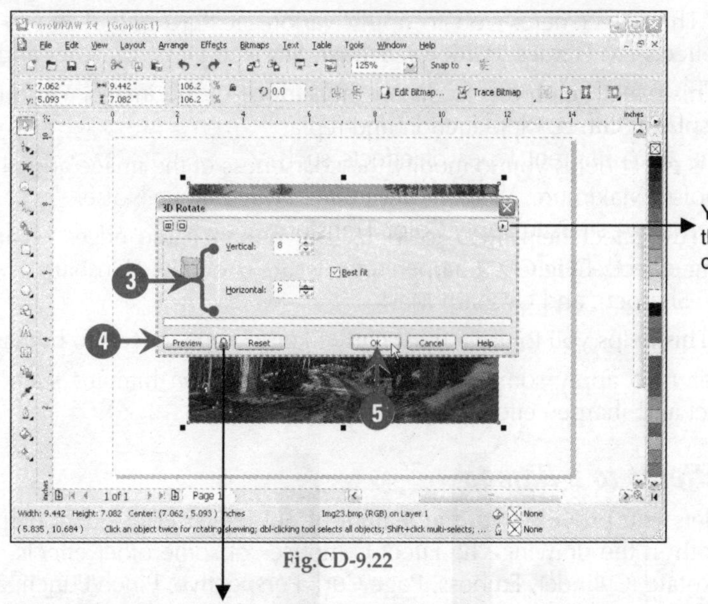

You can also access the special effects by clicking the Arrow button.

Fig.CD-9.22

Click Lock button to disable Preview button. This results in the live preview of the applied effects.

4. *Click* **Preview** button to see the preview of the image after applying the **3D Rotate** effect (Fig.CD-9.22).
5. *Click* **OK** button to apply the effect (Fig.CD-9.22).

Image after applying **3D Rotate** effect is shown here in Fig.CD-9.23.

Fig.CD-9.23

After applying 3D Effects to bitmaps, let us now learn how to apply color transform effect to a bitmap.

Applying Color Transform Effect to a Bitmap

CorelDRAW allows you to apply various color transform effects which results in creating pictorial illusions using the color reduction and replacements. Color Transform Effect allows you to work with the four different types of effects such as Bit Plane, Halftone, Psychedelic, and Solarize.

Undertake the following steps to apply Color Transform Effect to a bitmap image:

1. *Select* a bitmap image (Fig.CD-9.24).

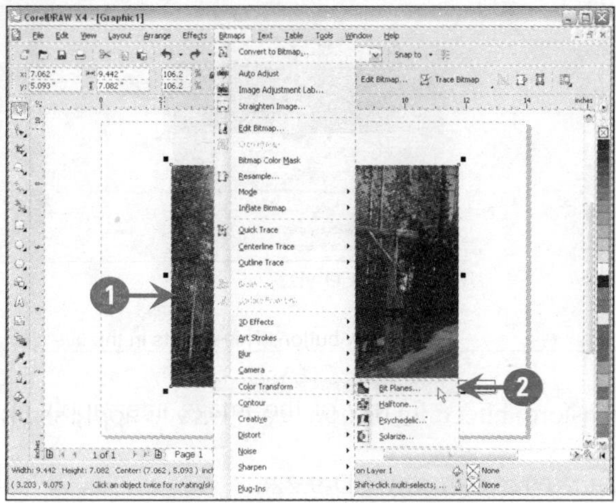

Fig.CD-9.24

2. *Select* **Bitmaps→Color Transform→Bit Planes** (Fig.CD-9.24). A **Bit Planes** dialog box appears, as shown in Fig.CD-9.25.
3. *Type* a value in any one of the three options: **Red**, **Green**, and **Blue** (Fig.CD-9.25).Value of the other two options automatically changes. You can also change the value by moving the slider.

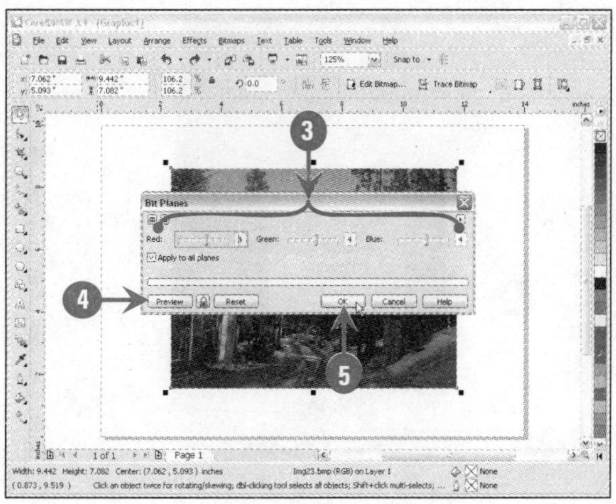

Fig.CD-9.25

4. *Click* **Preview** button to see the preview of the image after applying the **Bit Planes** effect (Fig.CD-9.25).
5. *Click* **OK** button to apply the effect (Fig.CD-9.25).

You can see the image after applying Bit Planes effect, as shown in the Fig.CD-9.26.

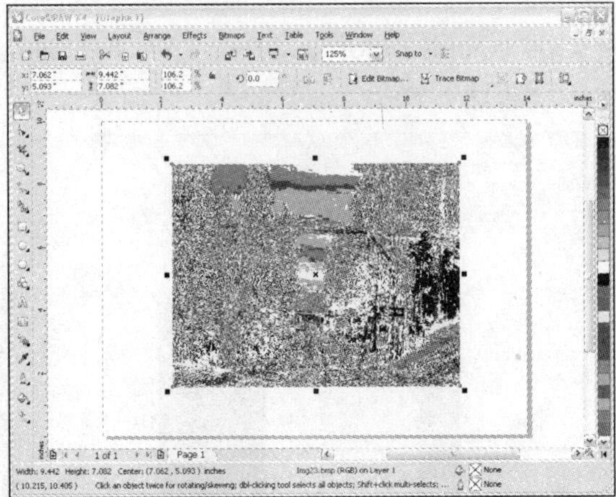

Fig.CD-9.26

After applying color transform effect, let us now learn how to apply sharpen effect.

Applying Sharpen Effect to a Bitmap

In CorelDRAW, if you want to focus and enhance the edges of a bitmap image you can apply Sharpen Effect. It is a simple illusion that makes the edges of an image more prominent. This helps in hiding the minor focusing errors. Sharpen effect includes Adaptive Unsharp, Directional Sharpen, High Pass, Sharpen, and Unsharp Mask.

Undertake the following steps to apply Sharpen effect to a bitmap:

1. *Select* a bitmap image (Fig.CD-9.27).

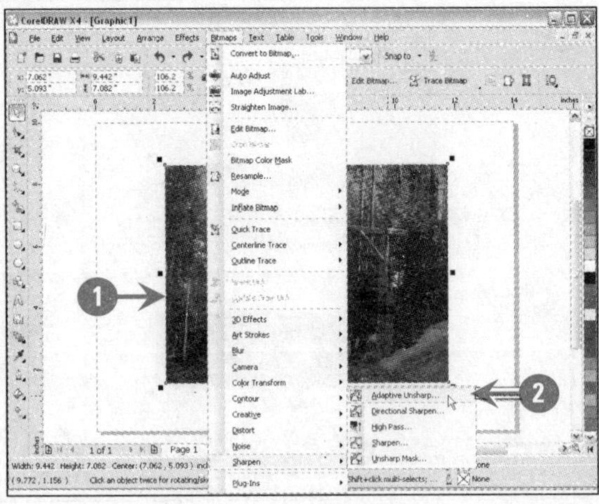

Fig.CD-9.27

2. *Select* **Bitmaps→Sharpen→Adaptive Unsharp** (Fig.CD-9.27). An **Adaptive Unsharp** dialog box appears, as shown in Fig.CD-9.28.
3. *Move* the slider beside **Percentage** option to change the value. You can also type a value for the percentage in the text box adjacent to the Percentage slider (Fig.CD-9.28).

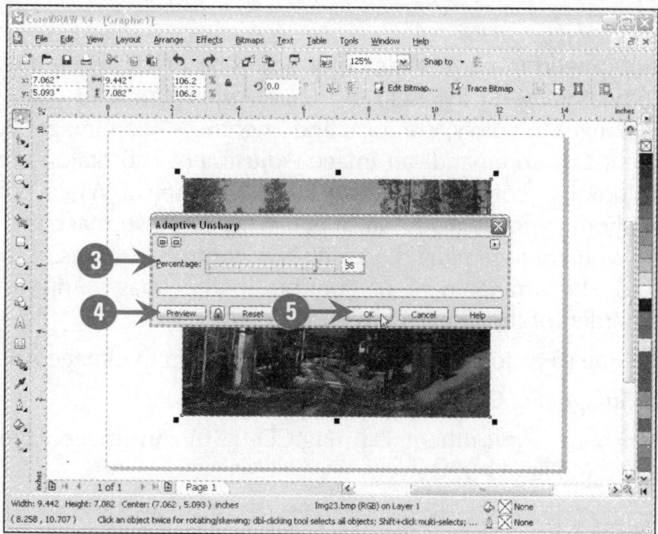

Fig.CD-9.28

4. *Click* **Preview** button to see the preview of the image after applying the **Adaptive Unsharp** effect (Fig.CD-9.28).
5. *Click* **OK** button to apply the effect (Fig.CD-9.28).

You can see image after applying **Adaptive Unsharp**, as shown in Fig.CD-9.29.

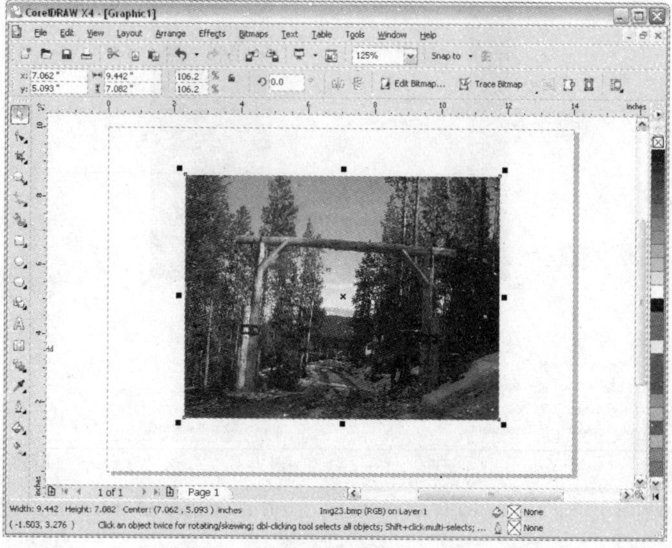

Fig.CD-9.29

After applying sharpen effect to a bitmap, let us now learn how to set color and tone in the Image Adjustment Lab in the next section.

Setting Color and Tone Quickly using the Image Adjustment Lab Command

In CorelDRAW, if you need to correct the color and tone of an image then you can use Image Adjustment Lab command. With the help of Image Adjustment Lab command, you can easily and quickly make changes to colors, contrast, and brightness of an image. Whenever you choose the Image Adjustment Lab command, an Image Adjustment Lab dialog box will appear on the screen. This dialog box has controls such as Auto adjust, Select White Point, and Select Black Point to automatically make changes to an image. You can also make changes manually to an image according to your requirements by using the controls such as Temperature, Brightness, Contrast and so on. The arrangement of controls in the Image Adjustment Lab dialog box appears in a logical order for the image correction.

Undertake the following steps to set color and tone quickly in the Image Adjustment Lab:

1. *Select* a bitmap image (Fig.CD-9.30).
2. *Select* **Bitmaps→Image Adjustment Lab** (Fig.CD-9.30). An **Image Adjustment Lab** window appears, as shown in Fig.CD-9.31.

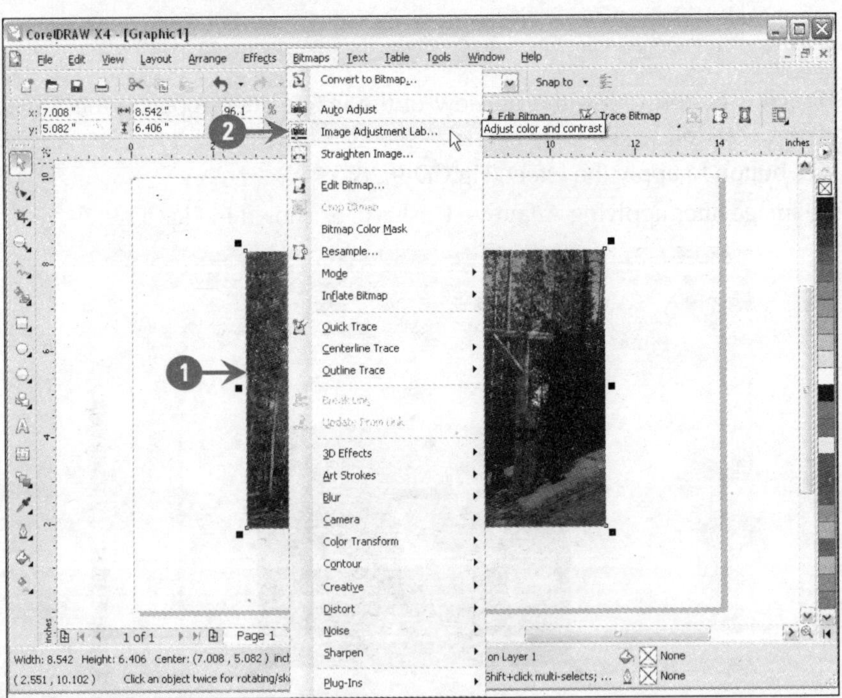

Fig.CD-9.30

3. *Move* the **Temperature** slider to warm and cool the colors of the image (Fig.CD-9.31).

Fig.CD-9.31

4. Now move the **Tint** slider to correct color casts by adjusting the green or magenta color in the image (Fig.CD-9.32).

Note

In the same way, you can move other slider options to adjust the color and tone of the image. Various slider options available in the Image Adjustment Lab are: Saturation, Brightness, Contrast, Highlights, Shadows, and Midtones (Fig.CD-9.32).

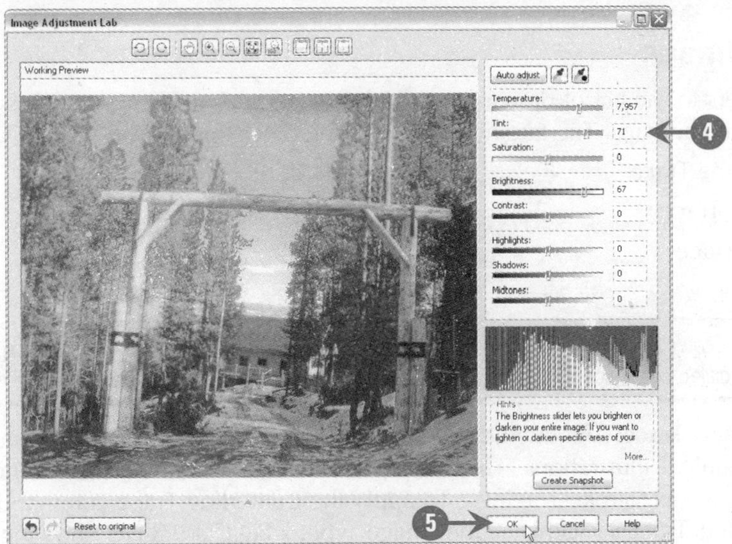

Fig.CD-9.32

5. *Click* **OK** button to close the **Image Adjustment Lab** window and the color and tone of the image changes (Fig.CD-9.33).

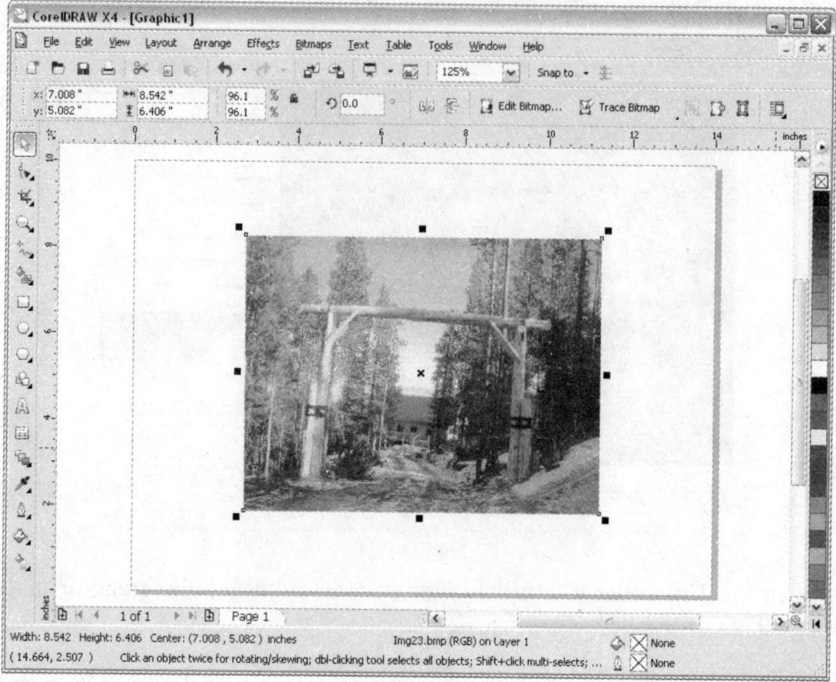

Fig.CD-9.33

After setting color and tone in the Image Adjustment Lab, let us now learn how to trace bitmaps and edit the traced outcomes in the next section.

Tracing Bitmaps

Tracing refers to the act of drawing a diagram or outline. CorelDRAW offers you three methods for tracing the bitmaps. The tracing methods offered by CorelDRAW are:

- Centerline Trace
- Outline Trace
- Quick Trace

Note

If you choose Centerline or Outline tracing command then Power TRACE dialog box will always appear. You can use the Power TRACE dialog box to specify tracing values and see the preview of traced bitmap within the dialog box itself.

- **Centerline Trace:** This method is mainly used for tracing maps, signatures, line drawings, and technical illustrations. This tracing method uses unfilled closed and open curves. It is also known as "Stroke Tracing". To apply the Centerline Trace command, choose Bitmap → Centerline Trace→<name of the image type>. Fig.CD-9.34 is showing the Power TRACE dialog box after selecting Technical Illustration image type under Centerline Trace type.

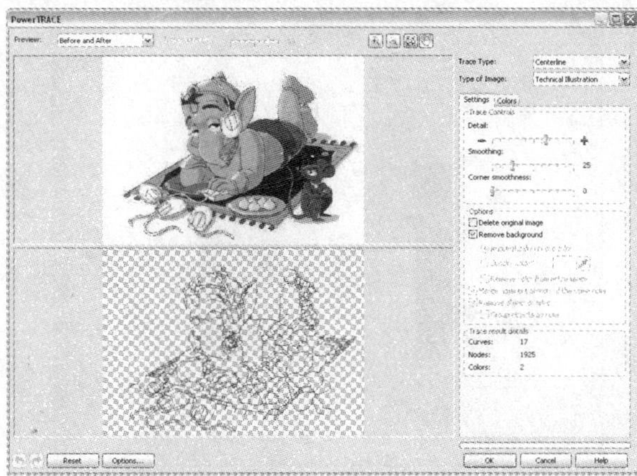

Fig.CD-9.34

- **Outline Trace:** This method is used for tracing the line art, logo, detailed logo, clip art, low quality image, and high quality image. This method uses curve objects with no outlines and is also known as "Fill" or "Contour tracing". To apply the Outline Trace command, choose Bitmap→ Outline Trace→<name of the image type>. Fig.CD-9.35 is showing the Power TRACE dialog box after selecting Logo tracing under the Outline Trace type.

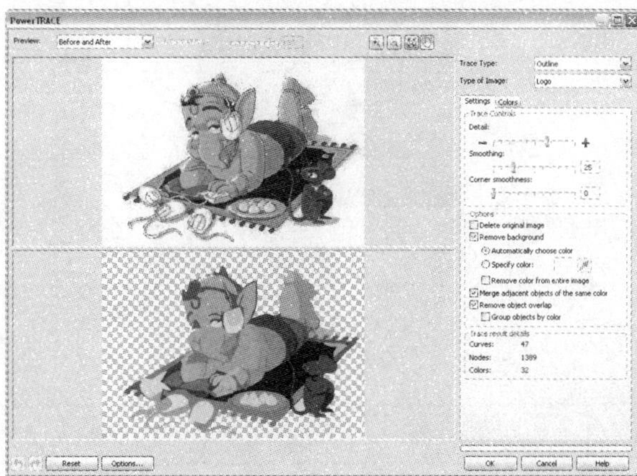

Fig.CD-9.35

- **Quick Trace:** If you are not keen in specifying detailed values to trace a bitmap then CorelDRAW offers the Quick Trace command. By using this command, you can trace the bitmap without displaying any dialog box and specifying values.

The Quick Trace Command in CorelDRAW

Apart from the earlier mentioned two methods, this method is user friendly, commonly used and easy to use. You can trace a bitmap in only one step by using Quick Trace command.

Undertake the following steps to trace a bitmap in one step:

1. *Select* a bitmap image (Fig.CD-9.36).
2. *Select* **Bitmaps→Quick Trace** (Fig.CD-9.36).

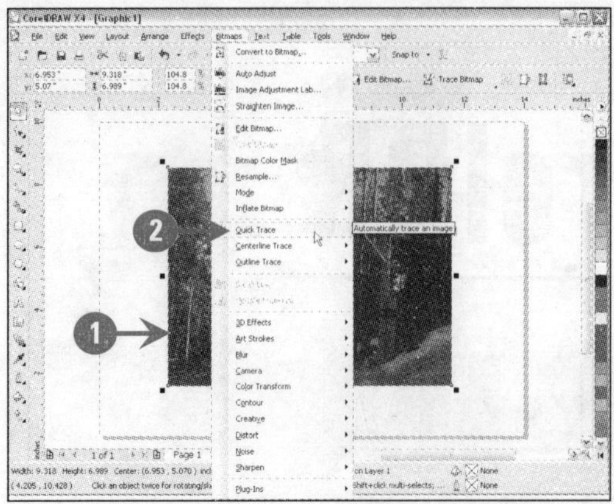

Fig.CD-9.36

Now, Traced image is shown in the Fig.CD-9.37.

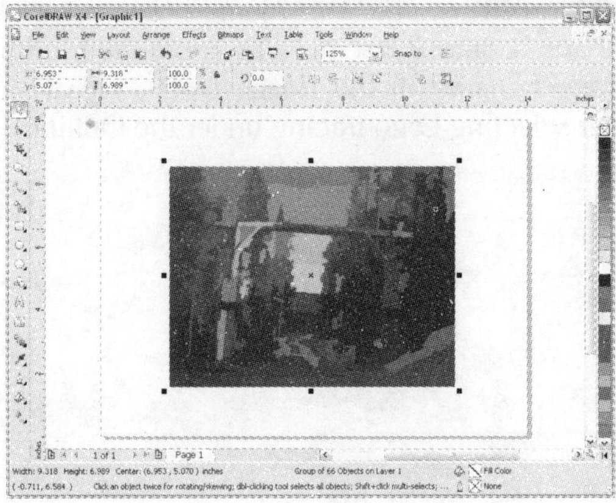

Fig.CD-9.37

Note

You can also trace the selected bitmap by using the Quick Trace button (Trace Bitmap) on the Property bar.

With this, we come to the end of the chapter. Before proceeding ahead towards the next chapter, let's summarize the main points of this chapter.

Summary

In this chapter, you learned about:

- Bitmap images consist of pixels while the vector images are defined by algebraic equations.
- Conversion of vector images to bitmap images.
- After importing a bitmap image into your drawing in the CorelDRAW window, you can crop, resample, and resize the image.
- You can apply special effects to bitmap and set the color and tone through image adjustment lab.
- In the last, you have learned to trace a bitmap image.